CompTIA Security+ Certification Guide

Master IT security essentials and exam topics for CompTIA
Security+ SY0-501 certification

Ian Neil

BIRMINGHAM - MUMBAI

CompTIA Security+ Certification Guide

Commissioning Editor: Gebin George
Acquisition Editor: Rahul Nair
Content Development Editor: Arjun Joshi
Technical Editor: Varsha Shivhare
Copy Editor: Safis Editing
Project Coordinator: Kinjal Bari
Proofreader: Safis Editing
Indexer: Tejal Daruwale Soni
Graphics: Jisha Chirayil
Production Coordinator: Shraddha Falebhai

First published: September 2018

Production reference: 4100619

Published by Packt Publishing Ltd.
Livery Place
35 Livery Street
Birmingham
B3 2PB, UK.

ISBN 978-1-78934-801-9

www.packtpub.com

Subscribe to our online digital library for full access to over 7,000 books and videos, as well as industry leading tools to help you plan your personal development and advance your career. For more information, please visit our website.

Why subscribe?

- Spend less time learning and more time coding with practical eBooks and Videos from over 4,000 industry professionals

- Improve your learning with Skill Plans built especially for you

- Get a free eBook or video every month

- Fully searchable for easy access to vital information

- Copy and paste, print, and bookmark content

Did you know that Packt offers eBook versions of every book published, with PDF and ePub files available? You can upgrade to the eBook version at www.packt.com and as a print book customer, you are entitled to a discount on the eBook copy. Get in touch with us at customercare@packtpub.com for more details.

At www.packt.com, you can also read a collection of free technical articles, sign up for a range of free newsletters, and receive exclusive discounts and offers on Packt books and eBooks.

Contributor

About the author

Ian Neil is one of the world's top trainers of Security+ 501, who has the ability to break down information into manageable chunks helping no background knowledge. Ian was a finalist of the Learning and Performance Institute Trainer of the Year Awards. He has worked for the US Army in Europe and designed a Security+ course that catered to people from all backgrounds and not just the IT professional, with an extremely successful pass rate.

He was instrumental in helping Microsoft get their office in Bucharest off the ground, where he won a recognition award for being one of their top trainers. Ian is an MCT, MCSE, A+, Network+, Security+, CASP, and RESILIA practitioner who over the past 20 years has worked with high-end training providers.

Packt is searching for authors like you

If you're interested in becoming an author for Packt, please visit `authors.packtpub.com` and apply today. We have worked with thousands of developers and tech professionals, just like you, to help them share their insight with the global tech community. You can make a general application, apply for a specific hot topic that we are recruiting an author for, or submit your own idea.

Table of Contents

Preface

This book will help you to understand security fundamentals, ranging from the CIA triad right through to identity and access management. This book describes network infrastructure and how it is evolving with the implementation of virtualization, and different cloud models and their storage. You will learn how to secure devices and applications that are used by a company.

 Refer to www.ianneil501.com for additional exam resources.

Who this book is for

This book is designed for anyone who is seeking to pass the CompTIA Security+ SY0-501 exam. It is a stepping stone for anyone who wants to become a security professional or move into cyber security.

What this book covers

Chapter 1, *Understanding Security Fundamentals*, covers some security fundamentals that will be expanded upon in later chapters.

Chapter 2, *Conducting Risk Analysis*, looks at the types of threats and vulnerabilities, and at the roles that different threat actors play.

Chapter 3, *Implementing Security Policies and Procedures*, looks at reference architectures, different guides, and how best to dispose of data.

Chapter 4, *Delving into Identity and Access Management*, looks at different types of authentication and how to dispose of data. We will first look at the concepts of identity and access management.

Chapter 5, *Understanding Network Components*, examines networking components and how they could affect the security of your network. We will look at firewalls, switches, and routers.

Chapter 6, *Understanding Cloud Models and Virtualization*, teaches about virtualization, deployment, and security issues. We will get acquainted with various cloud models, looking at their deployment and storage environments.

Chapter 7, *Managing Hosts and Application Deployment*, looks at different mobile devices and their characteristics, as well as the applications that run on these devices.

Chapter 8, *Protecting Against Attacks and Vulnerabilities*, explores attacks and vulnerabilities, taking each type of attack in turn and examining its unique characteristics. This module is probably the most heavily tested module in the Security+ exam.

Chapter 9, *Implementing Public Key Infrastructure*, gets into the different encryption types and how certificates are issued and used.

Chapter 10, *Responding to Security Incidents*, deals with incident response, focusing on the collection of volatile evidence for forensic analysis.

Chapter 11, *Managing Business Continuity*, turns its attention toward our business environment to consider the provision of system availability, looking at selecting the most appropriate method for recovery following a disaster.

Chapter 12, *Mock Exam 1*, includes mock questions, along with explanations, which will help in assessing whether you're ready for the test.

Chapter 13, *Mock Exam 2*, includes more mock questions, along with explanations, which will help in assessing whether you're ready for the test.

Appendix A, *Preparing for the CompTIA Security+ 501 Exam*, is included to help students pass the Security+ exam first time.

Appendix B, *Acronyms*, contains full forms of the abbreviations used in all the chapters.

To get the most out of this book

This certification guide assumes no prior knowledge of the product.

Download the color images

We also provide a PDF file that has color images of the screenshots/diagrams used in this book. You can download it here: http://www.packtpub.com/sites/default/files/downloads/9781789348019_ColorImages.pdf.

Conventions used

There are a number of text conventions used throughout this book.

`CodeInText`: Indicates code words in text, database table names, folder names, filenames, file extensions, pathnames, dummy URLs, user input, and Twitter handles. Here is an example: "For example, if we take the word `pass` in plaintext, it may then be converted to UDVV; this way it is difficult to understand."

Bold: Indicates a new term, an important word, or words that you see onscreen. For example, words in menus or dialog boxes appear in the text like this. Here is an example: "The most common **asymmetric algorithms** include the Diffie Hellman, which creates a secure session so that symmetric data can flow securely."

 Warnings or important notes appear like this.

 Tips and tricks appear like this.

Get in touch

Feedback from our readers is always welcome.

General feedback: If you have questions about any aspect of this book, mention the book title in the subject of your message and email us at `customercare@packtpub.com`.

Errata: Although we have taken every care to ensure the accuracy of our content, mistakes do happen. If you have found a mistake in this book, we would be grateful if you would report this to us. Please visit `www.packt.com/submit-errata`, selecting your book, clicking on the Errata Submission Form link, and entering the details.

Piracy: If you come across any illegal copies of our works in any form on the Internet, we would be grateful if you would provide us with the location address or website name. Please contact us at `copyright@packt.com` with a link to the material.

If you are interested in becoming an author: If there is a topic that you have expertise in and you are interested in either writing or contributing to a book, please visit `authors.packtpub.com`.

Reviews

Please leave a review. Once you have read and used this book, why not leave a review on the site that you purchased it from? Potential readers can then see and use your unbiased opinion to make purchase decisions, we at Packt can understand what you think about our products, and our authors can see your feedback on their book. Thank you!

For more information about Packt, please visit `packt.com`.

1
Understanding Security Fundamentals

In this chapter, we will look at a number of security fundamentals; some of these will be expanded upon in later chapters. For the exam, you will need to know all of the information in this book as the exam is fairly tricky.

We will cover the following exam objectives in this chapter:

- **Explaining the importance of physical security controls**: Lighting—signs—fencing/gate/cage—security guards—alarms—safe—secure cabinets/enclosures—protected distribution/protected cabling—Air gap—Mantrap—Faraday cage—lock types—biometrics—barricades/bollards—tokens/cards—environmental controls—HVAC—hot and cold aisles—fire suppression—cable locks—screen filters—cameras—motion detection—logs—infrared detection—key management

- **Given a scenario, implement identity and access management controls**: Access control models—MAC—DAC—ABAC—role-based access control—rule-based access control—physical access control—proximity cards—smart cards

- **Comparing and contrasting various types of controls**: Deterrent—preventive—detective—corrective—compensating—technical—administrative—physical

- **Explaining cryptography algorithms and their basic characteristics:** Hashing algorithms—MD5—SHA—HMAC—RIPEMD

CIA Triad Concept

Most security books start with the basics of security by featuring the CIA triad—this is a model designed to guide policies for information security within an organization. It is a widely used security model and it stands for confidentiality, integrity, and availability, the three key principles that should be used to guarantee having a secure system:

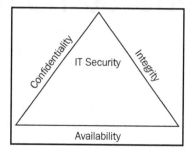

Figure 1: CIA triad

We'll discuss these principles in more depth here:

- **Confidentiality**: Prevents the disclosure of data to unauthorized people so that only authorized people have access to data, this is known as the need to know basis. Only those who should know the contents should be given access. An example would be that your medical history is only available to your doctor and nobody else.

  We also tend to encrypt data to keep it confidential. There are two types of encryption known as symmetric and asymmetric. Symmetric encryption uses one key known as the private key or shared key. Asymmetric encryption uses two keys known as private key and the public key.

- **Integrity**: This means that you know that data has not been altered or tampered with. We use a technique called hashing that takes the data and converts it into a numerical value. If you run the hash when you suspect changes have taken place, and if the numerical value has changed, then the data has been tampered with. Common hashing algorithms in the exam are **Secure Hash Algorithm version 1 (SHA1)** and **Message Digest version 5 (MD5)**.

- **Availability**: Availability could be using **Redundant Array of Independent Disks (RAID)** disks or maybe fail-over clustering. Availability ensures that data is always available; an example would be if you wanted to purchase an airplane ticket and the system came back with an error and you could not purchase it, this could be frustrating.

Identifying Security Controls

There are a wide variety of different security controls that are used to mitigate the risk of being attacked; the three main security controls are technical, administrator, and physical. In this section, we are going to look at these in more detail; you need to be familiar with each of these controls and when each of them should be applied. Let's start by looking at the three main controls.

Administrative Controls

Administrative controls are mainly written by managers to create organizational policies to reduce the risk within companies. An example could be an internet use policy so that the employees realize that the internet can only be used for company business and not used for social media during the working day. Another administrative control would be completing a holiday request form; the form would be available from the internal forms library.

 Administrative controls could be writing a policy, completing a form, and getting your ID badge re-keyed annually.

Some of the administrative measures are as follows:

- **Annual Security Awareness Training**: This is an annual event where you are reminded about what you should be doing on a daily basis to keep the company safe. An example would be when you are finished for the day that you clear your desk and lock all documents away; another would remind you that your identity badge should be worn at all times and you should challenge anyone not wearing a badge. Another example is that companies now need their employees to complete cyber security training as the risk is getting greater each day.
- **Annual Risk Assessment**: A company will have a risk register where the financial director will look at all of the risks associated with money and the IT manager will look at all of the risks posed by the IT infrastructure. As technology changes and the hackers get more sophisticated, the risks can become greater.

- **Penetration Testing/Vulnerability Scanning**: A vulnerability scan is not intrusive as it merely checks for vulnerabilities, whereas a penetration test is more intrusive and can exploit vulnerabilities. These will be explained further into this book.

- **Change Management**: This is a process that a company adopts so that changes don't cause any security risks to the company. A change to one department could impact another department. The **Change Advisory Board (CAB)** assists with the prioritization and priority of changes; they also look at the financial benefits of the change and they may accept or reject the changes proposed for the benefit of the company. **Information technology** (IT) evolves rapidly and our processes will need to change to cope with potential security risks associated with newer technology.

Technical Controls

Technical controls are those implemented by the IT team to reduce the risk to the business. These could include the following:

- **Firewall Rules**: Firewalls prevent unauthorized access to the network by IP address, application, or protocol. These are covered in depth later in this book.

- **Antivirus/Antimalware**: This is the most common threat to the business and we must ensure that all servers and desktops are protected and up to date.

- **Screen Savers**: These log computers off when they are idle, preventing access.

- **Screen Filters**: These prevent people walking past from reading the data on your screen.

- **Intrusion Prevention Systems (IPS)/Intrusion Detection Systems (IDS)**: The intrusion detection system monitors the network for any changes and the intrusion prevention system stops the attacks.

 Technical controls could be installing a screensaver or configuring firewall rules. These controls mitigate risk.

Physical Controls

Physical controls are controls that you can touch, for example:

- **Cable Locks**: These are attached to laptops to secure them so that nobody can steal them.
- **Laptop Safe**: Laptops and tablets are expensive, but the data they hold could be priceless, therefore there are safes for the storage of laptops and tablets.
- **Biometric Locks**: Biometrics are unique to each person; examples would be using their fingerprint, retina, palm, voice, an iris scanner, or facial recognition.
- **Fences/Gates**: The first line of defense should be a perimeter fence as the openness of many sites renders them highly vulnerable to intruders. Access to the site can be controlled by using a gate either manned by a security guard or with a proximity reader. A timber fence does not provide as much protection as a high steel fence.
- **Burglar Alarms**: These are set when the premises is not occupied, so when someone tries to break into your premises, it will trigger the alarm and notify the monitoring company or local police.
- **Fire Alarms/Smoke Detectors**: In a company, there will be fire alarms or smoke detectors in every room so that when a fire breaks out, and the alarms go off, the people inside the premises are given the opportunity to escape.
- **Lighting**: Lighting is installed for two main reasons: the first reason is so that anyone trying to enter your site at night can be seen and the second reason is for safety.
- **Security Guards**: They check the identity cards of people entering the building to stop unauthorized access. This also helps deter people trying to enter a building illegally.
- **Mantraps**: These are turnstile devices that only allow one person in at a time. They maintain a safe and secure environment mainly for a data center. A data center hosts many servers for different companies.
- **Perimeter Protection**: Fences, gates, and lights could protect the perimeter of your company. We could place bollards in front of a building to stop a car driving through the entrance. These normally protect ATM cash machines from being hit by a vehicle.
- **Internal Protection**: We could have safes and secure enclosures; the first example would be a toughened glass container or a sturdy mesh, both with locks to reduce access. We could also have protected distribution for cabling; this looks like metal poles that would have network cables inside. Screen filters used on a desktop could prevent someone from reading the screen.

- **Faraday Cage**: This is a metal structure, like a metal mesh used to house chickens. The cage prevents wireless or cellular phones from working inside the company. This could be built into the structure of a room used as a secure area. They would also prevent emissions escaping from your company.
- **Key Management**: This is where departmental keys are signed out and signed back in daily to prevent someone taking the keys away and cutting copies of them.
- **Proximity card**: These are contactless devices where a smart card is put near the proximity card device to gain access to a door or building.
- **Tokens**: Tokens are small physical devices where you touch the proximity card to enter a restricted area of a building. Some tokens allow you to open and lock doors by pressing the middle of the token itself; others display a code for a number of seconds before it expires.
- **Environmental Controls**: Heating, Ventilation, and Air-Conditioning (HVAC), and fire suppression systems, are also security controls. In a data center or a server room, the temperature needs to be kept cool or the servers inside will overheat and fail. They use a technique called hot and cold aisles.

HVAC systems help provide availability to servers in the data center, ensuring they don't overheat.

- **Air Gap**: This is where a device has been taken off your network to isolate it. For example, you may want to isolate a computer that can complete a BACS transfer from the other computers in the finance department.
- **Motion Detection/Cameras**: These could be deemed physical controls, but the exam is focused on these being deterrent controls, they could also be detective controls providing non-repudiation.
- **Barricades**: Barricades can be erected across roads to stop traffic entering your site, but will not stop someone getting out of a car and jumping over them. You will need to use them in conjunction with security guards to fully protect your site.
- **Bollards**: Bollards are becoming very common as they control access by cars and stop them ramming through a front door. They stop ram raiders from stealing a cash machine or crashing into a jeweler's shop. They can be made from steel or concrete and are placed about four feet apart. In some countries, they are installed to prevent car bombers driving their vehicle into a group of people, maybe inside a shopping mall.

Preventative Controls

Preventative Controls are in place to deter any attack; this could be having a security guard with a large dog walking around the perimeter of your company. This would make someone trying to break in think twice. Some of the preventive measures that are taken are as follows:

- **Disable User Accounts**: When someone leaves a company, the first thing that happens is that their account is disabled, as we don't want to lose information that they have access to, and then we change the password so that they cannot access it. We may disable an account while people are on secondment or maternity leave.
- **Operating System Hardening**: This makes a computer's operating system more secure. It often requires numerous actions such as configuring system and network components properly, turning off features and services that it does not use, and applying the latest software and antivirus updates. There will be no vulnerabilities.

Deterrent Controls

Deterrent Controls could be CCTV and motions sensors. When someone is walking past a building and the motion sensors detect them, it turns lights on to deter them.

A building with a sign saying that it is being filmed with CCTV prevents someone from breaking into your premises, as they think they are being filmed, even though there may not be a camera inside—but they don't know that.

 CCTV and motion sensors as deterrents. CCTV is a form of detective control following an incident, where you review the footage to see how the incident happened.

Detective Controls

Detective controls are used to investigate an incident that has happened and needs to be investigated; these could include the following:

- **CCTV** records events as they happen and from that you can see who has entered a particular room or has climbed through a window at the rear of a building.

- **Log Files** are text files that record events and the times that they occurred; they can log trends and patterns over a period of time. For example, servers, desktops, and firewalls are all events. Once you know the time and date of an event, you can gather information from various log files. These can be stored in **Write-Once Read-Many** (**WORM**) drives so that they can be read but not tampered with.

Corrective Controls

Corrective Controls are the actions you take to recover from an incident. You may lose a hard drive that contained data; in that case, you would replace the data from a backup you had previously taken.

Fire-Suppression Systems are another form of corrective control. You may have had a fire in your data center that has destroyed many servers, therefore when you purchase a replacement, you may install an oxygen suppressant system. This method uses argon/nitrogen and sometimes a small element of $CO2$ to displace the oxygen in the server room. The basis of this method is to reduce the oxygen level to below 15% because it will suppress a fire.

Compensating Controls

Compensating Controls can be called **Alternative Controls**; this is a mechanism that is put in place to satisfy the requirements of a security measure that is deemed too difficult or impractical to implement at the present time. It is similar to when you go shopping and you have $100 in cash - once you have spent your cash, you will have to use a credit card as a compensating control.

An example of this is where a new person has just been employed by the company, and the normal way to log in is to use a **smart card** and PIN. This resembles a bank card with a chip where you insert it into your laptop or keyboard and then insert a PIN to log in. Maybe it takes 3-5 days to get a new smart card, so during the waiting period, they may log in using a username and password:

Access Controls

The three main parts of access controls are identifying an individual, authenticating them when they insert a password or PIN, and then authorization, where an individual has different forms of access to different data. For example, someone working in finance will need a higher level of security clearance and have to access different data than a person who dispatched an order in finished goods:

- **Identification**: This is similar to everyone who has their own bank account; the account is identified by the account details on the bank card. Identification in a security environment may involve having a user account, a smart card, or maybe a fingerprint reader—this is unique to that individual.
- **Authentication:** Once the individual inserts their method of identification, they next to be authenticated, for example, by inserting a password or a PIN.
- **Authorization**: This is the level of access you have to selective data. You are normally a member of certain groups, for example, a sales manager could access data from the sales group and then access data from the managers group. You will only be given the minimum amount of access required to perform your job; this is known as least privilege.

Discretionary Access Control

Discretionary access control involves **New Technology File System (NTFS)** file permissions, which are used in Microsoft operating systems. The user is only given the access that he/she needs to perform their job.

The permissions are as follows:

- **Full Control**: Full access
- **Modify**: Change data, read, and read and execute
- **Read and Execute**: Read the file and run a program if one is inside it
- **List Folder Contents**: Expand a folder to see the subfolders inside it
- **Read**: Read the contents
- **Write**: Allows you to write to the file
- **Special Permissions**: Allows granular access; for example, it breaks each of the previous permissions down to a more granular level

- **Data Creator/Owner**: The person that creates the unclassified data is called the owner and they are responsible for checking who has access to that data:

Permissions for 501 example.txt   ✕

Security

Object name: C:\Users\Administrator\Desktop\501\501 example

Group or user names:

    👤 Neil (DESKTOP-QR6R2DA\Ian)

                      [Add...]   [Remove]

Permissions for Neil   Allow   Deny

	Allow	Deny
Full control	☐	☐
Modify	☐	☐
Read & execute	☑	☐
Read	☑	☐
Write	☐	☐

      [OK]   [Cancel]   [Apply]

Least Privilege

Least Privilege is where you give someone only the most limited access required so that they can perform their job role; this is known as "need to know" basis. The company will write a least privilege policy so that the administrators know how to manage it.

Mandatory Access Control

Mandatory Access Control (**MAC**) is based on the classification level of the data. MAC looks at how much damage they could cause to the interest of the nation. These are as follows:

- **Top Secret**: Highest level, exceptionally grave damage
- **Secret**: Causes serious damage
- **Confidential**: Causes damage
- **Restricted**: Undesirable effects

Examples of **Mandatory Access Control** (**MAC**) are as follows:

Data types	Classification
Nuclear energy project	Top Secret
Research and development	Secret
Ongoing legal issues	Confidential
Government payroll	Restricted

These are the roles:

- **Custodian**: The custodian is the person who stores and manages classified data.
- **Security Administrator**: The security administrator is the person who gives access to classified data once clearance has been approved.
- **Owner**: This is the person who writes and data and they are the only people that can determine the classification. For example if they are writing a secret document they will pitch it at that level, no higher.

Linux Permissions (not SELinux)

File Permissions: Linux permissions come in a numerical format; the first number represents the owner, the second number represents the group, and the third number represents all other users:

- **Permissions**:
    - **Owner**: First number
    - **Group**: Second number
    - **All other users**: Third number

- **Numerical values**:
    - **4**: Read (r)
    - **2**: Write (w)
    - **1**: Execute (x)

Unlike a Windows permission that will execute an application, the execute function in Linux allows you to view or search.

A permission of 6 would be read and write. A value of 2 would be write, and a value of 7 would be read, write, and execute. Some examples are as follows:

- **Example 1**: If I have 764 access to File A, this could be broken down as:
    - **Owner**: Read, write, and execute
    - **Group**: Read, write
    - **All other users**: Read
- **Example 2**: Determine which of the following permissions to File B is the highest and which is the lowest:
    - 776 File B, also shown as `rwx rwx -rw`
    - 677 File B
    - 777 File B

The highest would therefore be the third example

Another way it is shown in the exam is by using three sets of three dashes, for example:

- Owner full control would be shown as `rwx --- ---`
- Group full control `--- rwx ---`
- User full control `--- --- rwx`

 The higher the number, the higher the permissions; the lowest number is the one with the least permissions.

You can also change permissions in Linux: If permissions to File C is 654 and we wish to change these permissions, we will run the `chmod 777 File C` command, which changes the permissions to File C.

Role-Based Access Control

This is a subset of duties within a department. An example would be two people with the finance department who only handle the petty cash. In IT terms, it could be that only two of the IT team administer the email server.

Rule-Based Access Control

In **Rule-Based Access Control** (**RBAC**), a rule is applied to all of the people within a department, for example, contractors will only have access between 8 a.m. and 5 p.m., and the help desk people will only be able to access Building 1, where their place of work is. It can be time-based or have some sort of restriction, but it applies to the whole department.

Attribute-Based Access Control

In **Attribute-Based Access Control** (**ABAC**), access is restricted based on an attribute in the account. John could be an executive and some data could be restricted to only those with the executive attribute. This is a user attribute from the directory services such as a department or a location. You may wish to give different level of control to different departments.

Group-Based Access

To control access to data, people may be put into groups to simplify access. An example would be if there were two people who worked in **Information Technology** (**IT**) who needed access to older IT data. These people are called Bill and Ben:

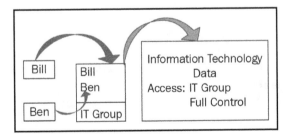

Everyone in the sales team may have full control of the sales data by using group-based access, but you may need two new starters to have only read access. In this case, you would create a group called new starters and give those people inside that group only read permission to the data.

If access to data is done via group-based access, then any solution in the exam will be a group-based answer.

Hashing and Data Integrity

- **Hashing**: It is where the data inside a document is hashed using an algorithm such as **Secure Hash Algorithm version 1 (SHA1)** and **Message Digest version 5 (MD5)**. This turns the data inside the file into a long text string known as a hash value; this is also known as a message digest.
- **Hashing the Same Data**: If you copy a file and therefore have two files containing the same data, and if you hash them with the same hashing algorithm, it will always produce the same hash value. Even if from two different vendors.
- **Verifying Integrity**: During forensic analysis, the scientist takes a copy of the data prior to investigation. To ensure that he/she has not tampered with it during investigation, he/she will hash the data before starting and then compare the hash to the data when he/she has finished. If the hash matches, then we know that the integrity of the data is intact.
- **One-way function**: For the purpose of the exam, hashing is a one-way function and cannot be reversed.
- **HMAC authentication**: In cryptography, an **HMAC** (sometimes known as either keyed-hash message authentication code or hash-based message authentication code) is a specific type of **Message Authentication Code (MAC)** involving a cryptographic hash function and a secret cryptographic key. We can have HMAC-MD5 or HMAC-SHA1; the exam provides both data integrity and data authentication.
- **Digital signature**: This is used to verify the integrity of an email so that you know it has not been tampered with in transit. The private certificate used to sign the email that creates a one-way hash function and when it arrives at its destination the recipient has already been given a public key to verify that it has not been tampered with in transit. This will be covered in more depth later in this book.

Can you read data that has been hashed? Hashing does not hide the data as a digitally signed email could still be read—it only verifies integrity. If you wish to stop someone reading the email in transit, you need to encrypt it.

- **RACE Integrity Primitives Evaluation Message Digest (RIPEMD):** This is a 128-bit hashing function. RIPEMD (https://en.wikipedia.org/wiki/RIPEMD) has been replaced by RIPEMD-160, RIPEMD-256, and RIPEMD-320. For the purpose of the exam, you need to know that it can be used to hash data.

Hash Practical

The reason that we hash a file is to verify its integrity so that we know if someone has tampered with it.

Hash Exercise

In this exercise, we have a file called `data.txt`. First of all, I use a free MD5 hashing tool and browse to the `data.txt` file, which generates a hash value. I have also created a folder called `Move` data to here:

1. Get the original hash:

2. Copy the hash from the current hash value to the original hash value.

3. Copy the `data.txt` file to the `Move data to here` folder, then go to the MD5 hash software and browse to the `data.txt` file in the new location, and press verify. The values should be the same as shown here:

The values are the same, therefore we know the integrity of the data is intact and it has not been tampered with when moving the `readme.txt` file.

4. Next, we go into the `data.txt` file and change a single character, add an extra dot at the end of a sentence, or even enter a space that cannot be seen. We then take another hash of the data and we will then see that the hash value is different and does not match; this means that the data has been tampered with:

Defense in Depth Model

Defense in Depth is the concept of protecting a company's data with a series of defensive layers so that if one layer fails, another layer will already be in place to thwart an attack. We start with our data, then we encrypt it to protect it:

- The data is stored on a server
- The data has file permissions
- The data is encrypted
- The data is in a secure area of the building
- There is a security guard at the building entrance checking identification
- There is CCTV on the perimeter
- There is a high fence on the perimeter

Therefore, before someone can steal the data, they have seven layers of security that they must pass through. The concept of defense in depth is that if one layer fails, then the next layer protects:

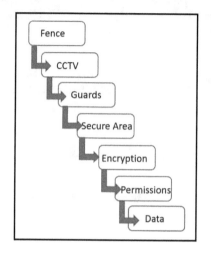

Review Questions

1. What are the three components of the CIA triad?
2. Why might a CCTV camera be sited outside a building without any film inside?
3. What does confidentiality mean?
4. How can we protect a data center from people entering it?
5. What is the purpose of an air gap?
6. Name three administrative controls.
7. Name three physical controls.
8. Following an incident, what type of control will be used when researching how the incident happened?
9. How do I know if the integrity of my data is intact?

10. What is a corrective control?
11. What is the purpose of hashing?
12. If I hash the same data with different SHA1 applications, what will the output be?
13. What two things does HMAC provide?
14. What type of control is it when I change the firewall rules?
15. What is used to log in to a system that works in conjunction with a PIN?
16. What is the name of the person who looks after classified data and who is the person that gives people access to the classified data?
17. When you use a DAC model for access, who determines who gains access to the data?
18. What is least privilege?
19. What access control method does SELinux utilize?
20. What is the Linux permission of 777? What access does it give you?
21. What does the Linux permission execute allow me to do?
22. The sales team are allowed to log in to the company between 9 a.m. and 10 p.m. What type of access control is being used?
23. Two people from the finance team are only allowed to authorize the payment of checks; what type of access control are they using?
24. What is the purpose of the defense in depth model?
25. When someone leaves the company what is the first thing we should do with their user account?

Answers and Explanations

1. Confidentiality means only allowing those authorized to access data. Integrity means that data has not been tampered with. Availability means that data is available when you need it, for example when purchasing an airline ticket.

2. We could place a CCTV camera in a prominent location as a deterrent; people walking past cannot tell if it has film or not, so we are using it as a deterrent.

3. Confidentiality means that we are limiting access to data to only those who should have access.

4. To stop people entering a data center, we would install a mantrap, a turnstile device, so that we can control who accesses the data center, one at a time.

5. An air gap is what it says on the tin, it is a gap between your network and a machine you would use an air gap maybe between Research and Development Machine and the corporate network. You basically isolated a system.

6. Administrative controls could be writing a new policy to make the company run smoothly; we may have just implemented change management. You could implement a new form to ensure that all of the data required for an application is supplied. We could run an annual security awareness training day, complete a risk assessment, or perform penetration testing.

7. Physical control is huge. Remember that these can be physically touched. You can choose three from: cable locks, laptop safe, biometric locks, fences, gates, burglar alarms, fire alarms, lights, security guards, bollards, barricades, a Faraday cage, key management, proximity cards, tokens, HVAC, an air gap, motion sensors, and cameras and biometric devices such as an iris scanner.

8. If we investigate an incident, we need to collect all of the facts about the incident; this is a detective control. Think of a detective such as Sherlock Holmes who is always investigating mysteries.

9. If we hash the data before and after, and the hash value remains the same, then the integrity of the data is intact. If the second hash is different, the data has been tampered with.

10. A corrective control is a one-way function where an incident has happened and we want to redeem the situation. For example, if the hard drive on my laptop fails, then I will purchase a new hard drive, put it into my laptop, install the operating system and application, then obtain a copy of my data from a backup.

11. Hashing is a technique that lets you know if data has been tampered with, but it does not hide the data.

12. If the same data is hashed with two different applications that can hash data with SHA1, then the hash value will be the same.

13. HMAC provides data integrity and data authentication. You can use HMAC-SHA1 or HMAC-MD5.

14. If I change firewall rules, I am doing this to reduce risk; it is carried out by administrators, therefore it is a technical control.

15. A smart card is a credit card-type device that has a chip built in; once inserted into the keyboard or USB card reader, you will then be asked to enter a PIN.

16. The person who stores and manages classified data is called the custodian. The person who gives access to the classified data is the security administrator. Prior to getting access to the data, the person may well be vetted.

17. In the DAC model, the data is unclassified and the data creator, who is also called the owner, will decide who gains access to the data and its classification.

18. Least privilege is a technique that says that people should only get the most limited access to data that they need to perform their job.

19. SELinux uses the MAC model to access data. This is the secure version of Linux.

20. In Linux 777, give the owner who is the first digit, the group that is the sent digit and all users who are the third group read, write, and execute. It could also be a rwx.

21. The Linux permission for execute (x) allows you to search for or view data.

22. An access control method that applies either a time restriction or location restriction is called rule-based access.

23. A subset of a department with access to a subset of duties is called role-based access.

24. The defense in depth model has many different layers; the idea behind this is if one layer is broken through, the next layer will provide protection.

25. When someone leaves the company, we should disable their account so that the keys associated with it are still available. The next stage is to change the password so nobody can access it, especially the person who has just left.

2
Conducting Risk Analysis

As a security professional, you will need to understand that identifying and managing risks can help to keep your company's environment safe from various types of attacks. In this chapter, we will look at types of threats and vulnerabilities and the roles that different threat actors play.

We will cover the following exam objectives in this chapter:

- **Explain threat actor types and attributes**: Types of actors: script kiddies—hacktivists—organized crime—nation states/APT—insiders—competitors. Attributes of actors: internal/external—level of sophistication—resources/funding—intent/motivation. Use of open source intelligence

- **Explain the importance of policies, plans, and procedures related to organizational security**: Standard operating procedure—agreement types—BPA—SLA—ISA—MOU/MOA. Personnel management: mandatory vacations—job rotation—separation of duties—clean desk—background checks—exit interviews—role-based awareness training—continuing education—acceptable use policy/rules of behavior—adverse actions. General security policies: social media networks/applications—personal email.

- **Summarize business impact analysis concepts**: RTO/RPO—MTBF—MTTR—mission-essential functions—identification of critical systems—impact—life—property—safety—finance—reputation. Privacy impact assessment—privacy threshold assessment.

- **Explain risk management processes and concepts**: Threat assessment: environmental—manmade—internal versus external. Risk assessment: SLE—ALE—ARO—asset value—risk register—likelihood of occurrence—supply chain assessment—impact—quantitative—qualitative. Testing: penetration testing authorization—vulnerability testing —authorization. Risk response techniques: accept—transfer—avoid—mitigate.

Risk Management

Risk management is the process of identifying risks within a company and making decisions about how to reduce the risks so that an incident does not cause harm to the company and its assets. You may not be able to eliminate the risk completely, but you may be able to put procedures in place to reduce it or keep it an acceptable level.

The first step in risk management is to identify the asset. Is it a top secret document? If that was the case you'd limit access to the document. The top secret document would be stored in a secure area at all times; nobody would be able to take copies or photographs of it.

For example, if you had 1 kg of trash and you placed it outside your front door at night, you would be certain that in the morning it would still be there; however, if the asset was 1 kg of 24-carat gold and you left it outside your house at night, it would probably not be there in the morning.

The first step in risk management is identifying the asset, because how we classify the asset will determine how the asset is handled, stored, protected, and who has access to it.

Importance of Policy, Plans, and Procedures

Creating policies, plans, and procedures is a part of risk management and helps to reduce the attack surface and prevent incidents from happening. Let's look at the different type of policies that can be used.

Standard Operating Procedures

Standard Operating Procedures (SOP) give us step-by-step instructions about how an activity is to be carried out. An example would be how to back up data. The SOP will state which data needs to be backed up daily, weekly, or monthly. Critical data would be backed up every two hours, whereas archive data may be backed up monthly. The SOP would also state the medium to be used for the backup; it may be backed up to a NetApp or network share rather than to tape so that quicker recovery can be carried out.

Stage one in risk assessment is the classification of the asset; this then determines how it is accessed, stored, and handled.

Agreement Types

Contracts between companies that want to purchase or sell services are very common as they protect both partners participating in the contract. We will now look at different agreement types that may be used in those contracts:

- **Business Partnership Agreement (BPA)**: A BPA is used between two companies who want to participate in a business venture to make a profit. It sets out how much each partner should contribute, their rights and responsibilities, the rules for the day-to-day running of the business, who makes the decisions, and how the profits are agreed and shared. It also has rules for the partnership ending either over time or if one of the partners dies.
- **Service Level Agreement (SLA)**: A SLA is a contract between a service provider and a company receiving the service that defines the level of service expected from the service provider; it is based on metrics within a specific time frame. The agreement can be either a fix or a response over a certain period of time.

SLA is measure in metrics, as to what percentage has been achieved.

For example, your company has an SLA with a service provider that will fix your printer within 4 hours. If the printer breaks down then the service provider needs to repair the printer within four hours or face a penalty. An SLA only relates to one product or service at one time. A company may have several SLAs in place that cover all of their equipment.

- **Interconnection Security Agreement (ISA)**: An ISA states how connections should be made between two business partners. If one of the business partners is a government agency and the connection agreement is not enforced, it could pose a security risk to their network. The connection agreement could specify which type of VPN and tunnel should be used or it could state that a dedicated T3 line is used to make the connection between them.
- **Memorandum of Understanding (MOU)**: An MOU is a formal agreement between two or more parties. MOUs are stronger than a gentlemen's agreement and both parties must be willing to make a serious commitment to each other, but they are not legally binding.
- **Memorandum of Agreement (MOA)**: An MOA is similar to an MOU but serves as a legal document and describes the terms and details of the agreement.
- **Non-Disclosure Agreement (NDA)**: An NDA is a legally binding contract made between an employee or a business partner where they promise not to disclose trade secrets to others without proper authorization. The reason for this is to stop trade secrets or proprietary information being sold on to competitors.

Personnel Management - Policies and Procedures

Employing personnel is a key function in a successful business; however, employing people is high risk as we need to employ the right type of person, who must be bright enough to identify cyber-crime attacks. To help reduce the risk that employees face or to prevent human resources from employing the wrong person and prevent fraud on an ongoing basis, the following policies can be adopted.

- **Job Rotation**: Job rotation is used for two main reasons - the first is so that all staff can be trained in all aspects of the jobs in the company. Employees may change departments every six months; this way, they get fully trained. The second reason is that by rotating jobs, any theft or fraudulent activities can be discovered by the new person coming in.

- **Mandatory Vacations**: Mandatory vacation helps detect whether an employee has been involved in fraudulent activities by forcing them to take holidays of a week or more. When people are involved in fraudulent activities they tend not to take many holidays so that the fraud cannot be discovered. This is especially rife in jobs in which people have fiscal trust, such as someone working in finance or someone who can authorize credit card payments.
- **Separation of Duties**: Separation of duties is having more than one person participate in completing a task; this is internal control to prevent fraud or error. An example would be where a person who worked in the finance department collected all money being paid in and then authorized all payment being paid out. A charity in the United Kingdom was defrauded out of £1.3 million over a period of six years. If they had two distinct finance jobs, where one person received the money and another authorized payments, the embezzlement would have been prevented. This is the aim of separation of duties: no one person does the whole task.

Example 1. All members of the IT team can make any changes to the network firewall; this creates a huge risk to the network. An auditor could recommend that each time a firewall rule is changed it is authorized by the Change Advisory Board and two people should be responsible for checking the changes to the firewall. With two people being responsible for making the changes, any errors should be eliminated. This is an example of separation of duties.

Example 2. When I first got married, we opened a joint bank account that only my wages were paid into. My wife spent money from this account even though she had her own account. I paid in, my wife withdrew - a true separation of duties. Nowadays I have my own account!

Separation of duties is where one person does not complete all configuration or transactions by themselves.

Other policies adopted by the company to help reduce risk are as follows:

- **Clean Desk Policy**: A clean desk policy (sometimes known as clear desk policy) is a company policy that specifies that employees should clear their desks of all papers at the end of the day. This prevents the cleaning staff or anyone else from breaking into the building and reading those papers.

- **Background Checks**: Completing background checks on new employees may involve looking into criminal records, employment and education history, driving license and credit checks. This is to ensure that what the person has stated on their CV (resume) is correct. More stringent background checks are needed for those working with children or handling finance.

- **Exit Interview**: The purpose of an exit interview is to find out the reason behind why the employee has decided to leave; this can be used to improve employment retention.

- **Acceptable User Policy** (**AUP**): The purpose of the AUP is to let the employee or contractor know what they can/cannot do with company computers and **Bring Your Own Device** (**BYOD**) devices. It lays out the practices relating to how you can access the company network and the internet. It will also lay down practices that are forbidden, such as using blogs and social media sites such as Facebook or Twitter while at work.

- **Rules of Behavior**: Rules of behavior lay down the rules of how employees should conduct themselves when at work. There should be no bullying, discrimination, or sexual harassment. Employees should work together for good and for the benefit of the company, even if they are not from the same background. People should respect and tolerate other employee's religious beliefs even though they may not be their own beliefs and they may not agree with them.

- **Adverse Action**: Adverse action is action that when taken is unlawful .The Fair Work Act defines a number of actions as adverse actions. An example could be threatening an employee, injuring them during their employment, or discriminating against them.

- **Policy Violations**: When employees or contractors do not follow the policies or procedures that they have agreed to, this may result in either disciplinary procedures or, if serious, instant dismissal. This is normally behavioral based.

Role-Based Awareness Training

Role-based awareness training is mandatory training that an employee carries out on an annual basis; an example of this would be security awareness training that is used by companies to reduce their security risks. During the training, employees will learn about social engineering attacks where the employee is targeted, for example, a phishing email. There will be more information about attacks in `Chapter 8`, *Protecting Against Attacks and Vulnerabilities*.

 Policy violation is where SOP and policies have been ignored. Transferring data from outside the company without using a VPN, this is policy violation because the data is not secure.

General Security Policies

General security policies affecting an employee using the internet are as follows:

- **Social Media Networks/Applications**: Many people have social media accounts, such as Twitter, Facebook, Reddit, or Instagram. These sites store personal details about everyone who has an account, and employees need to be careful with the information that they post on these sites. For example, you could put your date of birth, where you live, your personal preferences, and your email address. This information is a security risk and it could lead to a phishing attack or identify theft.

- **Cognitive hacking** is where a computer or information system attack relies on changing human users' perceptions and corresponding behaviors in order to be successful. This is a social engineering attack and the information required could be found on your various social media websites or applications.

- You may also put comments on social media websites that could discredit your employer or one of their customers, and this could lead to dismissal. These comments may also prevent you from gaining future employment as employers normally complete a background check and also look at your social media accounts.

- If you have different social media sites, don't use the same password for each of them, especially if it is the same as your online banking account. One account hacked means that all accounts are hacked.

- **Personal email**: Your company mailbox must not be used for personal email. For example, if you decide to sell your car and then email all of the staff in the company - you will violate the Acceptable Use Policy.

Business Impact Analysis Concepts

Business impact analysis (BIA) looks at the financial loss relating to an incident and does not look at how the threat or how an event occurred. It measures the additional cost due to various factors.

Financial loss factors include the following:

- Loss of sales
- Regulatory fines and contract penalties
- Purchase of new equipment to return to an operational state
- Additional labor required until returning to an operational state
- Do we need to seek a new property to operate in?

Impact factors include the following:

- Loss of company brand or reputation
- Loss of life
- Were safety procedures in place?

BIA looks at the financial loss but does not look at the threat.

Privacy Threshold Assessment/Privacy Impact Assessment

Personal data use, storage, and access are regulated, and a company will be fined if they do not handle data properly. There are two policies that we need to look at, and these are the privacy threshold assessment and the privacy impact assessment. Let's now look at these:

- **Privacy Threshold Assessment**: This assessment is to help identify personal information, described as either **Personally Identifiable Information (PII)**, **Sensitive Personal Information (SPI)**, or **Public Health Information (PHI)**, as used in information security and privacy laws.

- **Privacy Impact Assessment (PIA)**: A PIA is an analysis of how personally identifiable information is collected, used, shared, and maintained. Should you have a project that requires access to the PII, SPI, or PHI information, you may need to fill in a PIA screening form justifying the need for its use.

Mission Essential Functions/Identification of Critical Systems

When we look at BIA as a whole, we have to see what the company's mission essential functions are; for example, an airline depends heavily on its website to sell airline tickets. If this was to fail it would result in loss of revenue. Critical systems for the airline would be the server that the website was placed on, as well as its ability to contact a back-end database server, such as SQL, that holds ticketing information, processes the credit card transactions, and contains the order history for each of their customers.

Example 1

What would be the mission-essential functions of a newspaper, and what would be its critical systems?

Newspapers generate revenue not only via sales but more importantly by selling advertisement space in the paper. The mission-essential function would be the program that creates the advertisements, and the critical systems would be the server that the program resides upon, the database for processing payments, and the systems used to print the newspapers.

Supply Chain Risk Assessment

Your supply chain is the companies that you totally rely upon to provide the materials for you to carry out a business function or make a product for sale. Let's say that you are a laptop manufacturer and Company A provides the batteries and Company B provides the power supplies. If either of these runs short of either batteries or power supplies it stops you from manufacturing and selling your laptops.

Example 2

Company C provides your broadband internet access and you are totally reliant upon them for the internet - you may mitigate the risk of the internet failing by adopting vendor diversity, where you purchase broadband from Company D so that if either of your suppliers fails you still have internet access, which is now crucial to any modern business.

Business Impact Analysis Concepts

The following concepts are used to carry out the business impact analysis:

- **Recovery Point Object (RPO)**: RPO is how much time a company can last without its data before it affects operations. This is also known as acceptable downtime; if a company agrees that it can be without data for three hours, then the RPO is three hours. If the IT systems in a company suffer a loss of service at 13:00 hours, then the RPO would be 16:00 hours. Any repair beyond that time would have an adverse impact on the business.
- **Recovery Time Object (RTO)**: RTO is the time that the company has been returned to an operational state. In the RPO scenario, we would like the RTO to be before 16:00 hours. If the RTO is beyond 16:00 hours, then once again it has an adverse impact on the business.
- **Mean Time to Repair (MTTR)**: MTTR is the average amount of time it takes to repair a system. If my car broke down at 14:00 hours and it was repaired at 16:00 hours the MTTR would be two hours.
- **Mean Time Between Failures (MTBF)**: MTBF shows the reliability of a system. If I purchase a new car for $50,000 on January 1 then it breaks down on January 2, 4, 6, and 8, I would take it back to the garage as the MTBF would be pretty high. For $50,000, I want a car that is more reliable.
- **Mean Time to Failure (MTTF)**: MTTF is the predicted lifespan of a system. Normally, an IT system is expected to last about five years, therefore its MTTF is five years. If I bought a car in 1960 and I had to scrap it in 1992, the MTTF of the car would be 32 years.

RPO is the acceptable downtime, whereas RTO is the return to an operational state.

Calculating Loss

The following concepts can be used to calculate the actual loss of equipment throughout the year and may be used to determine whether we need to take out additional insurance against the loss of the equipment:

- **Single Loss Expectancy (SLE):** The SLE is the loss of one item. For example, if my laptop is worth $1,000 and I lose it while travelling, then my SLE would be $1,000.
- **Annual Rate of Occurrence (ARO):** The ARO is the number of times that an item has been lost in a year. If an IT team loses six laptops in a year, the ARO would be six.
- **Annual Loss Expectancy (ALE):** The ALE is calculated by multiplying the SLE by the ARO - in the previous examples we have *$1,000 x 6 = $6,000*. The ALE is the total loss in a year.

Example 3

A multinational corporation loses 300 laptops annually and these laptops are valued at $850; would they take out an insurance policy to cover the costs of replacement if the insurance premiums were $21,250 monthly?

The answer is no, because the cost of replacing them is the same as the cost of the insurance. They would take a risk on not losing 300 laptops next year.

The calculations are as follows:

- **ALE:** SLE x ARO
- **ALE:** $850 x 300 = $225,000
- **Monthly cost:** $225,000/12 = $21,250

Annual loss expectancy = Single loss expectancy X Annual rate of occurrence.

Risk Procedures and Concepts

Risk is the probability that an event will happen - it could bring profit to you. For example, if you place a bet in roulette at a casino then you could win money. It is, however, more likely that a risk will result in financial loss or loss of service. Companies will adopt a risk management strategy to reduce the risk they are exposed to, but may not be able to eliminate the loss completely. In IT, new technology comes out every day and poses new risks to businesses, and therefore risk management is ever evolving.

The main components are assets, risks, threats, and vulnerabilities:

- **Asset**: The first stage in risk management is the identification and classification of the asset. If the asset is a top secret document, you will handle and store it differently than an asset that is unclassified and available for free on the internet.
- **Risk**: Risk is the probability that an event could occur, resulting in financial loss or loss of service.
- **Threat**: A threat is someone or something that wants to inflict loss on a company by exploiting vulnerabilities. It could be a hacker that wants to steal a company's data.
- **Vulnerability**: This is the weakness that helps an attacker exploit a system. It could be a weakness in a software package or a misconfiguration of a firewall.

A threat is something that will pose a danger by exploiting vulnerability. Vulnerability is a weakness that may be exploited, and risk is the probability that an event will happen.

Threat Assessment

A threat assessment helps a company classify its assets and then looks at the vulnerabilities of that asset. It will look at all of the threats the company may face, the probably of the threat happening, and the potential loss should the threat be successful:

- **Environmental Threat**: This threat is based on environmental factors, for example, the likelihood of a flood, hurricane, or tornado. If you live in Florida there is a peak season for hurricanes from mid-August to October, whereas if you live in Scotland, the last time they had a minor hurricane was in 1968. Florida has a high risk of having a hurricane, whereas Scotland would be an extremely low risk.
- **Man-Made Threat**: This is a human threat - it could be a malicious insider attack where an employee deliberately deletes data, or could just be an accidental deletion by an incompetent member of staff.

- **Internal Threat**: This could be a disgruntled employee, sometimes called the malicious insider threat - they could deliberately sabotage data and IT systems. This malicious insider threat is the hardest to discover as they can hide their tracks or use someone else's credentials.
- **External Threat**: This could be a hacker or could be a threat such as a flood, hurricane, or tornado.

Threat Actors

A threat actor is another name for a hacker or attacker who is likely to attack your company; they all have different attributes. They will investigate your company from the outside, looking for details on social media and search engines. Security companies provide an open source intelligence test and inform you of your vulnerabilities in terms of threat actors. Let's now look at threat actor types:

- Hacktivist: A hacktivist is an external threat who defaces your website or breaks into your computer or network. They are politically motivated.
- **Competitor**: A competitor is another company in the same industry as your company who tries to gain information from you on new products in the hope that they can build it faster and get it to market before you.

 A competitor is a threat actor who will try and steal a company's trade secrets to gain a market edge.

- **Script Kiddie**: A script kiddie is a person who does not have high technical knowledge and uses script and code that he finds to make an attack against your company. His motivation is that he wants to be seen as a famous hacker.
- **Nation State**: A nation state is another country that poses a threat to your country; their motivation is that they want to undermine your nation.
- **Advanced Persistent Threat (APT)**: An advanced persistent threat is an external threat that tries to steal data from your network, but they are there for an extremely long period of time. They are very sophisticated and could be funded by a foreign government.
- **Organized Crime**: Organized crime refers to criminals who target companies mainly to steal data and to sell it to competitors or the highest bidder to make a profit. They have people working for them that have a high level of sophistication and their motivation is financial wealth.

- **Insider Threat**: An insider threat is a disgruntled employee who might have been overlooked for promotion and their relationship with their company has gone sour. They are also known as malicious insider threats and are the most difficult to protect yourself from.

Risk Treatment

In a risk treatment, the risk owner, who is the best person to classify the asset, looks at each individual risk; they will then decide what action is best to reduce the risk to the company. The risk will then be included in the company's risk register so that it can be monitored. New risks should be recorded in the risk register immediately and the risk register should be reviewed every six months, because risks change frequently as technology changes:

 Residual risk is the amount of risk remaining after you mitigate the risk. Remember you cannot eliminate a risk totally.

- **Risk Acceptance** is evaluating the risk and then deciding not to take any action as you believe the probability of it happening is very low or the impact is low. For example, I have company premises in Scotland and I was quoted $1,000 a year to insure the building against earthquakes. I would not take the insurance and accepted the risk. This is because earthquakes rarely happen in Scotland and if they do, then their magnitude is very small and the cost of any damage is likely to be less than $1,000 even if it happens.
- **Risk Transference** is where you decide that the risk is great and you want to offload the responsibility to a third party. For example, I purchase a car and decide that there is a high risk of someone crashing into the car, so I take out car insurance to transfer the risk to the insurance company. The car is insured, but I am still the owner. Another example is an IT company installing an Exchange 2016 email server, but nobody in the company knows how to support it, therefore the risk of something going wrong is high so they take out an SLA with an outsourcing company to manage the mail server.

- **Risk Avoidance** is where the risk is too high so you decide to not carry out the task. For example, you are standing at the edge of the Grand Canyon looking down and you can see the drop is about 1,200 feet. You are thinking of jumping down to the bottom without a parachute but common-sense kicks in and tells that you are likely to die, therefore you decide to adopt risk avoidance and not jump, as the risk is too high.

- **Risk Mitigation** is where you are evaluating the risk and decide whether the risk as it stands will result in financial loss, loss of service, or being vulnerable to attack. For example you leave your home in the morning to go to work - if you leave the door open, someone will enter your property and take some of your personal possessions. You then adopt risk mitigation by closing and locking the door. Another example is this: you purchase 50 new laptops for your company, with software installed, but there is no anti-virus software. There is a high risk that you could encounter a virus, therefore you decide to mitigate the risk by installing anti-virus software on all of the laptops. Risk mitigation is technical control.

Risk Register

When we look at the overall risk for the company we will use a risk register. This is a list of all of the risks a company could face. The risk to the finance department with be assessed by the financial director and IT-related risk would be looked at by the IT manager. Each department can identify the assets, classify them, and decide on the risk treatment. The financial director and IT manager are known as risk owners - they are responsible for them:

Ser	Date	Owner	Description	Probability	Impact	Severity	Treatment	Contingency	Action taken
1	01/05/18	IT Manager	Loss of Switch	Low	High	High	Transfer. 2-hour fix SLA	Purchase spare switch	02/05/2018

Qualitative/Quantitative Risk Analysis

There are two different approaches to risk management and they are qualitative and quantitative risk assessments. Let's look at both of them:

- **Qualitative Risk Analysis**: Qualitative risk analysis is when the risk is evaluated as a high, medium, or low risk.
- **Quantitative Risk Analysis**: Quantitative risk analysis is where you look at the high qualitative risks and give them a number value so that you can associate them with a cost for the risk.

In this example, we are going to grade a risk and its probability from 1 - 9, with 1 being low and 9 being high. If we look at the impact of losing a mail server, the qualitative risk analysis would say that it is high, but the probability of losing it would be low:

Qualitative	Probability	Quantitative risk
9	3	9*3=27

Review Questions

1. What is the purpose of standard operating procedures?
2. What is the purpose of BPA?
3. What is the difference between an MOU and an MOA?
4. What is the purpose of an ISA?
5. What is the benefit of introducing separation of duties into the finance department?
6. What is the purpose of a risk register?
7. What is the purpose of job rotation?
8. What is the purpose of mandatory vacations?
9. What is the first stage in risk assessment?
10. Why would a company introduce a clean desk policy?
11. If someone brought their own laptop to be used at work, apart from an on-boarding policy, what other policy should be introduced?
12. What is the purpose of an exit interview?
13. When would you adopt risk avoidance?

14. What is the purpose of risk transference?
15. What are rules of behavior?
16. Why would a company run an annual security awareness training program?
17. What is cognitive hacking and what should we avoid to mitigate it?
18. What would happen if I tried to sell my car and sent an email to everyone who worked in my company using my Gmail account?
19. Why would I make a risk assessment from one of my main suppliers?
20. What is the driving force of Business Impact Analysis?
21. What is the relationship between RPO and RTO?
22. What information can be established from MTTR?
23. What is the purpose of MTBF?
24. What is the purpose of SLE and how is it calculated?
25. How can we calculate the **Annual Loss Expectancy (ALE)**?

Answers and Explanations

1. Standard operating procedures are step-by-step instructions about how a task should be carried out so that employees know exactly what to do.

2. A BPA is used by companies in a joint venture and it lays out each party's contribution, their rights and responsibilities, how decisions are made, and who makes them.

3. A memorandum of understanding is a formal agreement between two parties but it is not legally binding, whereas the memorandum of agreement is similar but is legally binding.

4. An **Interconnection Security Agreement** (**ISA**) states how connections should be made between two business partners. They decide on what type of connection and how to secure it; for example, they may use a VPN to communicate.

5. If we adopted separation of duties in the finance department, we would ensure that nobody in the department did both parts of a transaction. For example, we would have one person collecting revenue and another person authorizing payments.

6. A risk register lays out all of the risks that a company faces; each risk will have a risk owner who specializes in that area and decides on the risk treatment.

7. Job rotation ensures that employees work in all departments so that if someone leaves at short notice or is ill, cover can be provided. It also ensures that any fraud or theft can be detected.

8. Mandatory vacations ensure that an employee takes at least five days of holiday and someone provides cover for them; this also ensures that fraud or theft can be detected.

9. The first stage in risk assessment is identifying and classifying an asset. How the asset is treated, accessed, or scored is based on the classification.

10. A clean desk policy is to ensure that no document containing company data is left unattended overnight.

11. Someone bringing their own laptop is called BYOD and this is governed by two policies, the on-boarding policy and the **Acceptable Use Policy** (**AUP**). The AUP lays out how the laptop can be used, and accessing social media sites such as Facebook or Twitter are forbidden while using the device at work.

12. An exit interview is to find out the reason why the employee has decided to leave; it may be the management style or other factors in the company. The information from an exit interview may help the employer improve terms and conditions and therefore have a higher retention rate.

13. When a risk is deemed too dangerous or high risk and could end in loss of life or financial loss, we would treat the risk with risk avoidance and avoid the activity.

14. Risk transference is where the risk is medium to high and you wish to offload the risk to a third party, for example, insuring your car.

15. Rules of behavior are how people should conduct themselves at work to prevent discrimination or bullying.

16. Annual security awareness training advises employees of the risk of using email, the internet, and posting information on social media websites. It also informs employees of any new risk posed since the last training.

17. Cognitive hacking is where a computer or information system attack relies on changing human users' perceptions and corresponding behaviors in order to be successful. This is a social engineering attack, and we could reduce the risk by being careful about what we post on social media websites.

18. Sending an email to everyone who works in your company using your Gmail account is a violation of the AUP and could lead to disciplinary action.

19. A manufacturing company would carry out supply chain risk assessment because they need a reputable supplier of raw materials so that they can manufacture goods.

20. Business impact analysis is just money; it looks at the financial impact following an event. The loss of earning, the cost of purchasing new equipment, and regulatory fines are calculated.

21. The **Recovery Point Object (RPO)** is the acceptable downtime that a company can suffer without causing damage to the company, whereas the **Recovery Time Object (RTO)** is the time that the company is returned to an operational state - this should be within the RPO.

22. **Mean Time to Repair (MTTR)** is the average time it takes to repair a system, but in the exam, it could be seen as the time to repair a system and not the average time.

23. **Mean Time Between Failure (MTBF)** is the measurement of the reliability of a system.

24. **Single Loss Expectancy (SLE)** is the cost of the loss of one item; if I lose a tablet worth $1,000, then the SLE is $1,000.

25. The **Annual Loss Expectancy (ALE)** is calculated by multiplying the SLE by the ARO (the number of losses per year). If I lose six laptops a year worth $1,000 each, the ALE would be $6,000.

3
Implementing Security Policies and Procedures

In this chapter, we will look at different frameworks and guides and how to best dispose of data. We will start off by looking at frameworks, reference architecture, and guides.

We will cover the following exam objectives in this chapter:

- **Explain use cases and purpose for frameworks, best practices, and secure configuration guides**: Industry-standard frameworks and reference architectures: regulatory—non-regulatory—national versus international—industry-specific frameworks. Benchmarks/secure configuration guides: platform/vendor-specific guides—web server—operating system—application server—network infrastructure devices. General purpose guides: vendor diversity—control diversity—administrative—technical—user training.

- **Given a scenario, carry out data security and privacy practices**: Data destruction and media sanitization: burning—shredding—pulping—pulverizing—degaussing—purging – wiping. Data sensitivity labeling and handling: confidential—private—public—proprietary—PII—PHI. Data roles: owner—steward/custodian—privacy officer. Data retention: legal and compliance.

Industry-Standard Frameworks and Reference Architecture

Industry-Standard Frameworks are a set of criteria within an industry relating to carrying out operations known as *best practices*; this is the best way that the operations should be set up and carried out. Best practices produce better results than a standard way of setting up the operations.

These industry standard frameworks are carried out by all members of that industry. In networking, the **International Standard Organization (ISO)** is responsible for the industry framework within communications and the IT industry. The ISO is a body comprising international standards bodies that mainly look at communication.

A **Reference Architecture** is a document or a set of documents to which a project manager or other interested party can refer for best practices; this will include documents relating to hardware, software, processes, specifications, and configurations, as well as logical components and interrelationships.

ISO/IEC 17789:2014 specifies the **cloud computing reference architecture (CCRA)**. The reference architecture includes the cloud computing roles, cloud computing activities, and the cloud computing functional components and their relationships.

OSI Reference Model

ISO developed the **Open Systems Interconnection model (OSI model)**. It is a conceptual model that standardizes the communication functions of a telecommunications or computing system, without regard to its internal structure and technology.

The purpose of the OSI reference model is to provide guidance to vendors and developers so that products they develop can communicate with one another.

The OSI reference model is a seven-layer model, and each layer provides specific services. The CompTIA Security+ exam focuses mainly on layers 2, 3, and 7:

Layer	Description	Purpose	Packet structure	Devices
7	Application	The applications are windows sockets, such as HTTP for web browsers or SMTP for email.		WAF
6	Presentation	Formats data into a character format that can be understood. It can also encrypt data.		
5	Session	Responsible for logging in and out.		
4	Transport	TCP - connection orientated; UDP - connectionless	Datagrams	
3	Network	Responsible for **Internet Protocol (IP)** addressing and packet delivery	Packets	Layer 3 switch router
2	Data link	Works with **Media Access Control (MAC)** addresses. Checks for transmission errors from incoming data and regulates the flow of data	Frames	Switch VLAN IPSec ARP
1	Physical	Transmits data in raw format bits over a physical medium (cables)	Bits	Hub repeater

Exam tip: Although Security+ is not a networking exam, you must ensure that you are familiar with devices that operate at layers 2, 3, and 7. These will be covered fully in `Chapter 5`, *Understanding Network Components*.

TCP/IP Model

The TCP/IP protocol is the protocol or language used in modern communications; it is the only protocol used by the internet. The TCP/IP model is derived from the OSI reference model, and it is a four-layer model:

Layers	TCP/IP model layers	Corresponding OSI layers
4	Application	Application, presentation, and session
3	Transport	Transport
2	Internet	Network
1	Network	Data link and physical

Types of Frameworks

There are different types of frameworks covered in the Security+ exam, and they are listed here:

- **Regulatory**: Regulatory frameworks are based on statute law and governmental regulations that companies must abide by at all times. Failure to do so will result in a regulatory fine:
  - **Example 1**: The **General Data Protection Regulation** (**GDPR**) (EU) 2016/679 is a regulation in EU law on data protection and privacy for all individuals within the European Union. It addresses the export of personal data outside the EU. Companies within the European Union can be fined 4% of their annual turnover, up to €20 million.
  - **Example 2**: The **Health Insurance Portability and Accountability Act** of 1996 (**HIPAA**) is United States' legislation that provides data privacy and security regulations for safeguarding medical information. Regulatory fines ranging from $100 – $1.5 million can be awarded for each violation.

- **Non-Regulatory**: This is not enforceable by law and is optional, but provides a framework that organizations can follow as a best practice.
  - **Example 3**: Information Technology Infrastructure Library (ITIL) is a set of detailed practices for IT Service Management through a service lifecycle. The ITIL five distinct life cycle stages:
    - Service Strategy.
    - Service Design.
    - Service Transition.
    - Service Operation.
    - Continual Service Improvement.
  - **Example 4**: COBIT 5 is similar to ITIL in that provides to provide management with an information technology (IT) governance model that helps in delivering value from IT and managing the risks associated with IT. The five COBIT 5 principles are:
    - Meeting stakeholder needs.
    - Covering the enterprise end to end.
    - Applying a single integrated framework.
    - Enabling a holistic approach.
    - Separating governance from management.

- **National versus International**: National frameworks could be the Data Protection Act 2018, which is a United Kingdom regulation on data protection and how data can be used; it was given Royal Assent from the Queen of England on May 23, 2018. An international frameworks example is the **IS0/IEC 27002**, which provides a framework for IT security and is used by the international community.
- **Industry-Specific Frameworks - Finance**: The **International Financial Reporting Standards Foundation (IFRS)** is a non-profit accounting organization. The purpose of the IFRS is to standardize financial reporting internationally. It only deals with the finance industry.

Benchmarks/Secure Configuration Guides

Every company faces the challenge of protecting its servers and computers from an ever-increasing cyber security threat. There are many different types of servers: web servers, email servers, and database servers, and each of these has different configurations and services, so the baselines are different for each type of server. Vendors and manufacturers will provide platform/vendor guides so that their product can be configured as per their own best practices so that they perform as best they can.

 Exam tip: Policies are written so that the security administrator knows what to configure, and end users know what part they play in keeping the company secure.

Policies and User Guides

The management team will create policies that need to be adhered to by all employees, and these policies are created to help reduce the risk to the business and are mandatory; failure to carry out these policies is called **policy violation** and may lead to disciplinary action:

- **Policies**: IT is immense, so if the management team says to the security administrators to go and set up IT security, the administrators would not know what to do, or where to start. Do they want firewall rules to be set up, or permissions set on files?

If a policy was created so that Data Loss Prevention (DLP) templates were created to prevent Personally Identified Information (PII) or sensitive data being emailed out of the company, then the Security Administrators would know exactly what to do.

The purpose of policies is to ensure that the security administrator knows what tasks they need to perform and also that end users know what their responsibilities are within each policy. Policies are an administrative control to help reduce risk.

- **Least Privilege Policy**: This policy states that access to data should be restricted and that employees should be given the minimum access required so that they can perform their job. In the military, it is known as the need-to-know principle, where if you don't need to know it, then you have no access.

- **On-Boarding Policy**: Companies allow employees to bring their own devices - **Bring Your Own Device (BYOD)** - to work, and part of the process is carrying out **on-boarding** and **off-boarding**. The on-boarding policy states that the device must be checked for viruses, and any application that could cause damage to the company's network should be removed before the device can be used to access the network. If someone brings their own device to work and fails to carry out the on-boarding properly, then the company could be infected by a virus.

- **Off-Boarding Policy**: When someone leaves your company, then the business data used on BYOD devices needs to be removed before departure. If off-boarding is not carried out properly, an ex-employee could leave with company data on their device.

- **Acceptable Use Policy (AUP)**: The purpose of the AUP is to let the company employee or contractor know what they can do with company computers and BYOD devices. It lays out the practices on how you can access the company network and the internet. It will also state which practices are forbidden, such as using blogs and social media sites such as Facebook or Twitter while at work.

- **Remote Access Policy**: A remote access policy may state that when a remote user is connecting to the company's network, they must use a secure VPN such as L2TP/IPSec. Policy violation would be trying to connect by another method and lead to data being compromised.

- **Auditing**: The company employs an internal auditor to ensure that the employees carry out the policies and procedures written by the management team. The auditor does not have the authority to stop any processes, but they will report back to management. The outcome following an audit will result in **change management** or a policy being re-written.

> Exam tip: The auditor is a snitch; they won't ever stop a process, but they always inform the management of non-compliance to company policies. The outcome following an audit will result in either change management or a new policy being written.

- **Data-Retention Policy**: For legal and compliance reasons, you may need to keep certain data for different periods of time; for example, some financial data needs to be retained for six years, whereas medical data may need to be kept for 20–30 years, depending on the type. A data-retention policy ensures that legal and compliance issues are addressed.
- **Change Management**: Policies, procedures, and processes are in place so that the company is running efficiently and the risk is being managed properly; however, when newer technology is introduced, some of the procedures and processes may change. It could be that an auditor has identified a process that needs to change, so they report that to the manager, who will then adopt change management.

Change management requests are sent to a **Change Management Board** (**CMB**). The board looks at the change request, what the financial implications are, and how changing one process affects other processes. If the change is major, then a new policy could be written rather than just change management.

For example, new laptops are being purchased and configured for use within the company. The auditor is reviewing the process and finds that there is no anti-virus software being installed on these laptops; therefore, they report this to management. Management then looks at the processes that are laid down for configuring new laptops and then uses change management to change the processes so that, in future, anti-virus software is installed before rolling them out to the rest of the company.

Security Configuration Guides – Web Servers

There are two main web servers used by commercial companies. Microsoft has a web server called the **Internet Information Server**, and its rival is Apache. Web servers provide web pages for the public to view and, because they are in the public domain, they are prime targets for hackers. To help reduce the risk, both Microsoft and Apache provide security guides to help security teams reduce their footprint, making them more secure:

- Microsoft has created a user guide called *Basic Security Practices for Web Applications*. This helps security administrators protect web applications running on a web server, and this can be seen at `https://msdn.microsoft.com/en-gb/library/zdh19h94.aspx`.

- Apache has created and article called security tips that can be seen at `https://httpd.apache.org/docs/2.4/misc/security_tips.html`.

Web server security guides rely upon the latest updates being in place, services that are not required being turned off, and the operating systems to be hardened, to make them as secure as possible and reduce the risk of attack.

Network Infrastructure Device User Guides

CISCO produce the best high-end network devices and, because the networking world is ever evolving, CISCO has produced an infrastructure upgrade guide so that companies can use it as a best practice when upgrading their network device. It can be seen at `https://www.cisco.com/c/m/en_us/solutions/enterprise-networks/infrastructure-upgrade-guide.html`.

General Purpose Guides

Security is critical for providing a safe working environment, and we now need to look at guidelines for vendor diversity, control diversity, technical controls, administrative controls, and the benefits of user training:

- **Vendor Diversity**: Companies need to be running 24/7, and therefore need to put in place vendor diversity. This may mean that they will get internet access from two different companies so that when one fails, the other can keep the company up and running. Vendor diversity provides both reliability and resiliency.

  Example: Firewalls are a mission-critical network device that prevent unauthorized access to your network. In the Security+ exam, they tend to be used in a back-to-back configuration.

  If we purchase the two firewalls from Vendor A, we may also have two firewalls from Vendor B with the same configuration kept in a secure area within your company. Should there be a failure with one of the firewalls or a vulnerability with the Vendor A firewall, then we can then quickly swap those with the firewalls from Vendor B. This ensures that the network remains secure at all times.

- **Control Diversity**: Control diversity goes back to the Depth in Defense Model, where many different controls are in place so that if one control fails, then the other control stops the attack.

  Example: A firewall protects our network against attacks and has been very successful in preventing attacks, but if a hacker manages to get through the firewall, then the control diversity installs a network **Intrusion Detection System (IDS)** that will alert the networks and security administrators about attacks inside the network.

- **Administrative Controls**: Administrative controls provide security to the company. An example of this would be to have an outside agency carry out a penetration test or a vulnerability scan. Rules for the penetration test would have to be established before the test, as you may want the penetration tester to exploit the vulnerability totally and see how far an attacker would have got, or maybe just inform you of the vulnerability. Another administrator control would be to carry out an internal audit.

- **User Training**: Most cyber security attacks happen because of mistakes being made by people, so an important step in keeping your company safe is to provide user training so that employees are not vulnerable to malicious telephone calls and phishing emails, and annual training reminds them of their responsibilities.

Implementing Data Security and Privacy Practices

One of the most critical areas in data security is storing, accessing, and destroying data when it is no longer required. In this section, we will look at the types, control, and destruction of data.

Destroying Data and Sanitizing Media

Data is controlled, handled, and stored based on its classification and privacy markings. Once this data has outlived its use, it needs to be destroyed so that it cannot be read by a third party. Data can be stored electronically on a computer's hard drive or kept as a hard copy by being printed. Most companies employ a third-party organization that specializes in data destruction and can provide a destruction certificate. Let's look at the different methods of destruction:

- **Burning**: A company will have many **burn bags** that are normally paper-based and contain classified or sensitive information. These burns bags will be picked up periodically by a third party, who will place the data in the incinerator, where it will be burned. Burning is seen as more secure than shredding.
- **Shredding**: There are three main paper shredders. The first is a strip-cut shredder, which shreds the paper into strips, and they are pretty useless. The second type of shredder is a cross-cut shredder, where the paper is cut into small pieces. However, the best shredder is the micro-cut shredder, which turns the paper into confetti, and this is difficult to put back together. After paper has been shredded, it is not secure, as scanners can put it back together, so the next step is to pulp the shredded paper:

Destruction of hard drives can also be done by shredders that break the hard drive up into small chunks. Take a look at the preceding photo, which shows the results of hard-drive shredding. Some hard-drive shredders can shred hard drives into much smaller chunks or even powder.

- **Pulping**: After paper has been shredded into small pieces, the next step is to ensure that it cannot be reconstructed by pulping the data. You put the paper shreds into a container, and then pour water or sulfuric acid on them to turn it into a sludge of cellulose fibers, making it impossible to reconstruct them.
- **Pulverizing**: Pulverizing can be used for hard drives or optical media such as CD/DVD ROMs; they are either hit using a lump hammer or sledgehammer, turning them into small pieces.
- **Degaussing**: Degaussing is where a magnetic field is applied to a hard drive or tape drive in order to remove data.
- **Purging Data:** Purging is the process of removing unwanted data from a database server, such as SQL Server. Do not confuse it with deletion, which removes all of your data.
- **Wiping Data**: Wiping data is the process of removing data from a mobile device such as a smartphone. Most **Mobile Device Management** (**MDM**) systems can remote wipe data when it is stolen to prevent access.
- **Cluster Tip Wiping**: If you use an NTFS file system, data is stored in storage areas called clusters, and the default size of a cluster is 4 KB. If I have a file that is 11 KB in size, and the first two clusters are fully loaded with 8 KB of data, the last cluster (which is called the cluster tip) has 3 KB of data and an area of 1 KB that has no data. Cluster tip wiping ensures that no data remnants are left behind in the 1 KB space.

Data Sensitivity – Labeling and Handling

Securing and handling data is a critical part of security, as companies spend so much money on the **Research and Development** (**R&D**) of a product because they don't want their competitors to know about their new product until it goes on the market. It is very important that the data is labeled according to its classification. Military data in the UK army is classified as unclassified, restricted, confidential, secret, and top secret, whereas a civilian company may classify data as confidential, private, public, and proprietary.

The first stage of risk management is classification of the asset, which determines how we handle, access, store, and destroy the data:

- **Confidential Data**: Normally, R&D and legal data will be classified as confidential data; disclosure would cause damage to the company.
- **Private Data**: This data could be a list of products and the minimum sales price; we would not want customers to know this. It could also be sensitive data such as PII or **Protected Health Information** (PHI) data.
- **Public Data**: This is data that is available to anyone, such as yesterday's news, leaflets, or brochures that have been distributed everywhere. Anyone has access to this data.
- **Proprietary Data**: This is data generated by a company, such as its trade secrets, or work done by the R&D department.
- **Personally Identifiable Information (PII)**: This is information that can identify a person, such as their date of birth, biometric information, or their social security number.
- **Protected Health Information (PHI)**: This is information stored in a person's medical records.
- **Privacy**: Privacy law or data protection laws prohibit the disclosure or misuse of information about private individuals. In the United Kingdom, there is the Data Protection Act (1998), which protects the privacy of data.

Data Retention – Legal and Compliance

Data is retained either for legal reasons or to be compliant with statute law, which could be either the length of time the data should be retained or the national boundaries that data must be stored within. Multinational companies cannot just simply move data between national boundaries, compliance forbids it:

- **Legal Hold**: Legal hold is where either litigation is ongoing or the police are investigating an individual. Legal hold is normally done with mailboxes; the person has their mailbox placed on legal hold so that they can receive emails and reply, but they cannot delete any emails. This is to ensure that evidence is not destroyed.
- **Data Compliance**: There are different national laws about the retention, movement, storage, and disclosure of data to protect the individual. In the United Kingdom, most financial accounts data must be retained for at least six years; medical data can range from 20-30 years, depending on the type of data; and pension data must be retained indefinitely. Companies that are not data compliant within the country in which they operate could face a regulatory fine that goes into millions of pounds or dollars.

Data Roles

Everyone within a company will access data every day, but the company needs to control access to the data, and this is done by using data roles; we are now going to look at these roles:

- **Owner**: Someone within a company needs to have overall control of the data, and this is normally the **Chief Executive Officer** (**CEO**) or the Chairman. The owner can be known as the information owner or steward and is responsible for making decisions on its protection. The owner sets the data classification.
- **Custodian**: The data custodian is responsible for securing the data, backing it up, checking the data's integrity, and ensuring that the server holding the data has anti-virus software installed. They are responsible for ensuring that the data is made available, but they do not make critical decisions on the protection of the data, as that is made by the data owner.
- **Security Administrator**: The function of the security administrator is fulfilled by the IT team, and the team is responsible for ensuring that the least privilege policy is adhered to, as the team only gives access to the data to those who require it for their jobs.
- **Privacy Officer**: The data privacy officer is responsible for ensuring that access to the data is fulfilled according to the Legal and Compliance regulations.

Practical – Creating a Baseline

In this practical, we will download the **Microsoft Baseline Security Analyzer** (**MBSA**) tool, and then we will run the tool to see what missing patches and vulnerabilities it may have. The Windows 10 desktop that this demo will be run on has only recently had the latest update (two days ago):

1. Go to Google and insert the latest **MBSA** download (the current link is `https://www.microsoft.com/en-us/download/details.aspx?id=19892`; at the time of writing, this is MBSA 2.3):

Microsoft Baseline Security Analyzer 2.3 (for IT Professionals)

Important! Selecting a language below will dynamically change the complete page content to that language.

Select Language: English Download

The Microsoft Baseline Security Analyzer provides a streamlined method to identify missing security updates and common security misconfigurations. MBSA 2.3 release adds support for Windows 8.1, Windows 8, Windows Server 2012 R2, and Windows Server 2012. Windows 2000 will no longer be supported with this release.

⊕ Details

2. Select the language that you require, and then click on **Download**:

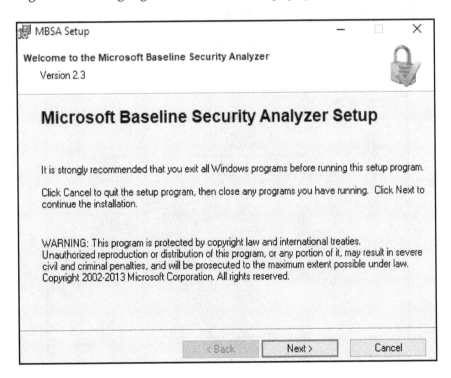

3. All Windows 10 and Windows 8 desktops use 64 bit; I have selected 64 bit with English as the language. Click **Next**. Allow popups, and then select **Run**:

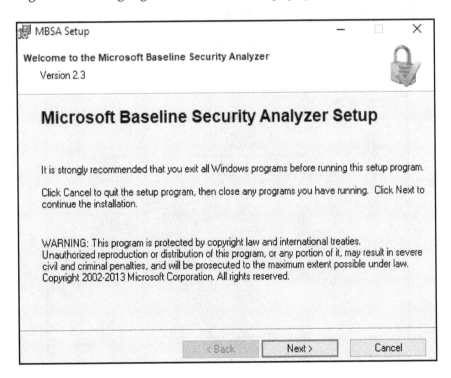

4. Press **Next**:

5. Select **I accept the license agreement**, and press **Next**:

6. In the wizard, you can select the destination folder; select **Next** in the screen that follows, and select **Install**. During the installation, the UAC prompt will appear. Select **Allow**, and then the installation will be complete:

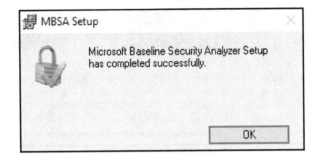

7. After the installation appears, there will be a shortcut on the desktop, as shown here:

8. Double-click the desktop icon; select **Allow** when the UAC prompt appears, and then the MBSA interface will appear:

9. From here, you can either scan a single computer or multiple computers; please select **Scan a computer**, and then press **Start scan**. At this stage, it downloads security update information from Microsoft, and this may take some time:

10. This then performs a scan, checking security update information from Microsoft.

The outcome of the scan will be similar to this:

The default scan result shows the vulnerabilities in red; blue is informational, and green is for the items that are compliant. Where there are vulnerabilities in red, the MBSA has hyperlinks so that these items can be resolved and so the desktop can be made as secure as possible.

Review Questions

1. What is an industry standard framework?
2. What is the OSI reference model, and how many layers does it have?
3. What is the TCP/IP protocol, and where is it used?
4. Which layer of the OSI reference model does a switch operate?
5. Which layer of the OSI reference model does a router operate?
6. What is a regulatory framework, and is it legally enforceable?
7. What type of frameworks are ITIL and Cobol 5, and are they legally enforceable?
8. What three policies are used in a BYOD environment, and what purpose does each of them serve?
9. What would happen if I were in an internet café at an airport and did not connect to the company network using a VPN and the data was intercepted?
10. The FBI were investigating John Smith; therefore, the IT team placed his account on Legal Hold. John Smith decided to leave the company on February 12, and the IT team decided to delete his account on April 12, as nobody from the FBI had requested any evidence. On April 13, the FBI contacted the company asking for evidence. What policy could have ensured that the evidence was available for the FBI?
11. What is the purpose of auditing, what power does the auditor have, and what is the likely outcome after the audit?
12. What is the purpose of change management?
13. Why do vendors produce security guides?
14. What is the purpose of vendor diversity?
15. What is the purpose of control diversity?
16. What type of control are penetration test or vulnerability scans?

17. How do companies normally dispose of classified printed material?
18. What is best way of disposing of a hard drive?
19. What is the purpose of pulping, and when would it normally be carried out?
20. What is the purpose of degaussing, and when will it be carried out?
21. What is cluster tip wiping?
22. If the company held information marked *Public* and *Private*, why would we then introduce classifications such as confidential and proprietary?
23. Who is responsible for the securing and backing up of data?
24. Who is responsible for allowing access to the data?
25. What is the purpose of a privacy officer?

Answers and Explanations

1. Industry standard frameworks are a set of criteria within an industry, relating to carrying out operations known as best practices. This is the best way that the operations should be set up and carried.

2. The **Open Systems Interconnection model** (**OSI model**) is a conceptual model that standardizes the communication functions of a telecommunications or computing system without regard to its internal structure and technology. It has seven layers—application, presentation, session, transport, network, data link, and physical; these are layers seven to one.

3. The TCP/IP protocol is the only protocol used in the internet, and most networks use it; each computer has an IP address to identify it.

4. A switch operates at layer 2: the data link layer. There is a multilayer switch that works at layer 3, but the exam focuses on a switch and VLAN operating at layer 2. A switch is an internal device.

5. A router whose function is to join networks together works at layer 3: the network layer. A router operates as an external device.

6. A regulatory framework is based on statute law and governmental regulations; is it legally enforceable?

7. ITIL and Cobol 5 are Non-Regulatory. These are not enforceable by law and are optional, but they provide a framework for companies to follow as a best practice for IT service management.

8. The three types of policies needed for a BYOD environment are on-boarding, off-boarding, and **Acceptable User Policy** (**AUP**). The on-boarding policy states what needs to be done before a device can be allowed access to the network, the AUP states how the device should be used and restricts access to games and social media. When the exam mentions a BYOD environment, think of on-boarding and AUPs. The off-boarding policies state how to decommission a device from your network.

9. Not using a VPN to connect to your network would be a policy violation against the remote access policy and would lead to disciplinary action being taken against the perpetrator.

10. A data retention policy stating that data should be kept for six months following a person leaving the company, or the data retention policy could state never delete data that has been placed on legal hold. Both of these would ensure that the FBI got its data.

11. The role of the auditor is to ensure that the company's policies and processes are being carried out, following an audit—either change management or the creation of a new policy are the likely outcomes.

12. Change management regulates changes within a company so that they are controlled and risk is managed effectively. This stop employees doing their own thing.

13. Vendors produce security guides so that their products can be set up by their best practices, making them as secure as possible.

14. Vendor diversity provides reliability and resiliency by having more than one solution in place; should one solution fail, then the company is still up and running. Business continuity is covered later in this book.

15. Should one control fail, then another is in place; an example of this is if an attacker gets over the perimeter fence, then a guard with a guard dog would stop them going any further.

16. Penetration tests and vulnerability scans are administrative controls; the vulnerability scan is less intrusive.

17. Classified printed documents are normally put in burn bags that are collected by a third-party agency, who then incinerates them and provides the company with a destruction certificate.

18. The best way to destroy a hard drive is to shred it. Pulverizing is an alternative, but it is not as effective.

19. Pulping can turn shredded paper into sludge by using water or sulfuric acid. Try and read it now!

20. Degaussing is where a magnetic field is applied to a hard drive, or a tape drive, to remove the data.

21. Cluster tip wiping is removing the last remnants of data stored in the last data cluster.

22. By having four classifications rather than two classifications, it can lead to better classifications of the data.

23. The custodian is responsible for securing and backing up data.

24. The security administrator is responsible for granting access to the data. Remember: this is not the owner.

25. The privacy officer is concerned with who is accessing the data and how is it shared; for example: are only doctors able to see a patient's medical history?

4
Delving into Identity and Access Management

In this chapter, we will look at different types of authentication and how to dispose of data. We will first look at identity and access management concepts.

We will cover the following exam objectives in this chapter:

- **Comparing and contrasting identity and access management concepts**:
    - Identification: authentication, authorization, and accounting (AAA)
    - Multifactor authentication: something you are—something you have—something you know—somewhere you are—something you do
    - Federation—single sign-on—transitive trust
- **Given a scenario, install and configure identity and access services**:
    - LDAP—Kerberos—TACACS+—CHAP—PAP—MSCHAP—RADIUS—SAML—OpenID Connect—OAuth —Shibboleth—Secure token—NTLM
- **Given a scenario, implement identity and access management controls**:
    - Biometric factors—fingerprint scanner—retinal scanner—iris scanner—voice recognition—facial recognition—false acceptance rate—false rejection rate—crossover error rate
    - Tokens—hardware—software—HOTP/TOTP
    - Certificate-based authentication—PIV/CAC/smart card—IEEE 802.1x

- **Given a scenario, differentiate common account management practices**:
  - Account types—user account—shared and generic accounts/credentials—guest accounts—service accounts—privileged accounts—permission auditing and review—usage auditing and review—time-of-day restrictions—re-certification—standard naming convention—account maintenance—group-based access control—location-based policies
  - Account policy enforcement—credential management—group policy—password complexity—expiration—recovery—disablement—lockout—password history—password reuse—password length

Understanding Identity and Access Management Concepts

One of the first areas in IT security is giving someone access to the company's network to use resources for their job. Each person needs some form of identification so that they can prove who they are; it could be anything ranging from a username to a smart card. It needs to be unique so that the person using that identity is accountable for its use. The second part after proving your identity is to provide authentication for that identity; this can be done in many ways for example inserting a password or if you have a smart card it would be a PIN. The final part is authorization that provides access to data.

Passwords

Passwords are one of the most common ways of authenticating a user; they are also the authentication factor that is most likely to be inserted incorrectly, maybe because they use uppercase and lowercase characters, numbers, and special characters not seen in programming. Some people may have the *Caps Lock* key reversed without knowing it. When a password is inserted, it is shown as a row of dots, therefore users cannot see their input; however, in the password box in Windows 10, you can press the eye icon to see the password that you have inserted. This reduces the risk of people being locked out.

Default/Administrator Password

An administrator should have two accounts, one for day-to-day work and the other for administrative tasks. If your company is using a device such as a wireless router, the default administrative username and password should be changed as they are normally posted on the internet and could be used for hacking your device/network.

Passwords – Group Policy

A group policy allows security administrators to create settings once and then push them out to all machines in their domain. This could cover maybe 5 - 10,000 machines. It reduces configuration errors and reduces the labor required to carry out the task. One portion of a group policy deals with passwords; please look at the screenshot:

Policy	Security Setting
Enforce password history	24 passwords remember
Maximum password age	42 days
Minimum password age	0 days
Minimum password length	0 characters
Password must meet complexity requirements	Disabled
Store passwords using reversible encryption	Disabled

Figure 1: Password policies

Let us look at each of these going from top to bottom:

- **Enforce Password History**: This prevents someone from just reusing the same password. The maximum number that can be remembered is 24 passwords as set in the screenshot. This would then mean that, when I set my first password, it would then need another 24 passwords before I could use it again.
- **Password Reuse**: Password reuse is a term used in the exam that means the same as password history. They both prevent someone from reusing the same password. Password history would be used for a Windows operating system and password reuse for any other products. An example of this could be a smartphone or an email application.
- **Maximum Password Age**: It is the maximum amount of days that a password can be used for before you are required to change it. The default is 42 days but, in a more secure environment, it could be lowered to maybe 21 days; this is really the maximum time that the password can be used. If it was set at 21 days, you could reset at any time before 21 days pass.

- **Minimum Password Age**: The minimum password age is to prevent someone from changing a password 25 times on the same day to enable them to come back to the original password. If you set the minimum password age to two days, then you could only change your password every two days. This is also known as the password expiry date. For example, if I set the password maximum age to 21 days, the password history to 24, and then the minimum password age to one day, this would prevent someone from reusing the same password. Each day, you could set your password but you could only use 21 passwords in the password cycle.

- **Password Must Meet Complexity Requirements**: Complex passwords (sometimes known as strong passwords) are formatted by choosing three groups from the following:
  - **Lowercase**: For example, a, b, and c
  - **Uppercase**: For example, A, B, and C
  - **Numbers**: For example, 1, 2, and 3
  - **Special characters not used in programming**: For example, $ and @

  If I choose the password P@$$w0rd, then it contains characters from all four groups but it would be cracked very quickly as most password crackers replace the letter o with a zero and replace an a with the @ sign.

- **Store Passwords using Reversible Encryption**: This is when a user needs to use their credentials to access a legacy (old) application; because it is storing them in reversible encryption, they could be stored in clear text—this is not good. Companies tend to have this option disabled at all times as it poses a security risk.

Account Lockout - Threshold: This determines the number of times that a user can try a password before the system locks you out; companies normally set this value to three or five attempts.

When purchasing devices, you should always change the default password that the manufacturer has set up to prevent someone hacking your device.

Once you are locked out, your account is disabled:

Policy	Security Setting
Account lockout duration	30 minutes
Account lockout threshold	3 invalid logon attempts
Reset account lockout counter after	30 minutes

Figure 2: Account lockout

Know the password options and types of password attacks thoroughly.

Account Lockout - Duration: Both the **Account Lockout Duration** and **Reset Account Lockout Counter After** should not be enabled. If these are disabled, the locked out person will have to contact the security administrator to have their password reset; this way the administrator knows who keeps forgetting their password and will monitoring them.

Password Recovery

People can be locked out from time to time by forgetting their password. They can reset their passwords by going to a portal and selecting forgotten my password, then filling in personal details and having the password reset option send a code to their phone via SMS or by email.

Some desktop operating systems allow you to create a password reset disk so that you can save to a SD card or a USB drive; this is not normally used in a corporate environment.

Authentication Factors

There are different authentication factors that range from something you know, for example a password, to something you are using, for example an iris scanner. The following are the different authentication factors:

- **Multi-Factor Authentication**: These factors are grouped into different types and the number of factors is the number of different groups being used. For example, if you have a smart card, this is something you have and the card's PIN is something you know; this means it is a dual factor, but the smart card and PIN is also known as multi-factor. So multi-factor could also be more than two different factors, it just means multiple factors.

- **Something you know**: This would be a username, password, PIN, or your date of birth; these are all something that you know.

- **Something you have**: This could be, for example, a secure token, key fob, or card. The hardware token is tamper proof and sends a different PIN every 60 seconds. The key fob is similar to some cards that are placed close to a proximity card; once you hear a beep then the door opens. A smart card that could be used with a PIN could also be something you have:

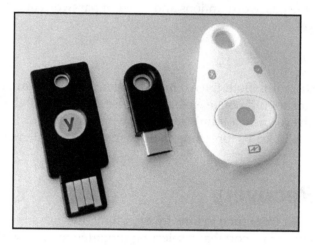

Figure 3: Hardware token and key fob used with proximity card

- **Something you are**: This is called biometric authentication; it is the trait of a person that is used for authentication, for example, using an iris or retina, palm or fingerprint reader, or your voice.

- **Something you do**: This would be swiping a card, inserting your signature, or maybe the way you walk (this is called your gait). It could also be the dwell time, for example, the speed that you type and how far in you press the keys.

- **Somewhere you are**: This would be a location that you are in. Are you in London or Disneyland, Florida? This is a location-based policy.

Number of Factor – Examples

Let us look at combining different factors to determine a single factor, dual factor, or multifactor. Here are different factor examples:

- **Single Factor**: If I have a username, password, and PIN then it is only single factor as they come from the same group.

The number of factors is determined by the different numbers of factor groups being mentioned.

- **Two Factor**: If you have a smart card and a PIN, this is two factor, also known as dual factor.
- **Multifactor**: This is where more than one factor can be used, for example, if you combine a hardware token with a PIN.

Transitive Trust

Transitive trust is where you have a parent domain and maybe one or more child domains; these would be called trees. Refer to the following diagram:

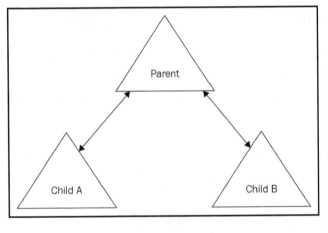

Figure 4: Transitive trust

Between the **Parent** domain and each child domain is two-way transitive trust, where resources can be shared two ways. Because the **Parent** domain trusts both child domains A and B, it can be said that **Child A** transitively trusts **Child B** as long as the administrator in **Child B** wishes to give someone from **Child A** access to resources and vice versa. Think of a domain as being people from the same company.

When the exam mentions third-party to third-party authentication, then that can only be federation services. Federation services needs cookies enabled.

Federation Services

Federation services are used when two different companies want to authenticate between each other when they participate in a joint venture. Think of two car manufacturers wanting to produce the best car engine in the world. Both companies have experts on engines but they want to work together to produce a super engine. The companies don't want to merge with each other; they want to retain their own identify and have their own management in place. These are known, to each other, as third parties.

Each of these companies will have their own directory database, for example, an active directory, that will only have users from their domain. Therefore, normal domain authentication will not work. Let us now look at the two different domains and their directory databases:

Company A	Company B
Mr. Red	Mr. Orange
Mr. Blue	Mr. Purple
Mr. Green	Mr. Yellow

Figure 5: Directory databases

Company A has three users in its active directory: Mr. Red, Mr. Blue, and Mr. Green. Company B also has three users: Mr. Orange, Mr. Purple, and Mr. Yellow. This means that they can only change passwords for the people in their own domain.

If Mr. Orange was to try and access the Company A domain he would need an account. Since he does not have an account, the security administrator from Company A has no way of providing authentication. He then needs to make an agreement with Company B to set up a federation trust where the people from the other domain would need to use alternative credentials instead of a username and password or a smart card and PIN. They use extended attributes.

User-Extended Attributes are extended attributes used by their directory services; they are, in addition to the basic attributes, comprised of the following:

- Employee ID
- Email address

They both have decided that the extended attributes that they will use will be the users email address. Because an email address is easy to find or guess, they will also need to use their domain password. This is known as a claim. When the exam talks about authentication using the phrase third party or extended attributes, think of federation services.

The two companies need to exchange the extended attribute information and need a special protocol to do that, so they use **Security Assertion Mark-up Language (SAML)** as it is XML-based authentication:

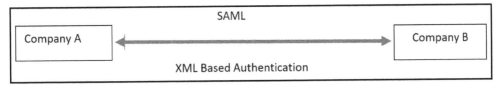

Figure 6: SAML

Federation Services - Authentication: In this scenario, Mr. Yellow is going to authenticate himself with Company A so that he can access limited resources. He contacts **Company A** through a web browser and it asks him for his email address and password:

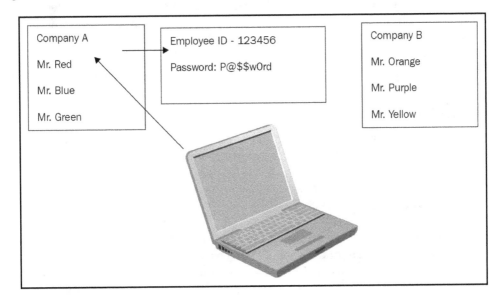

Figure 7

Federation Services - Exchange of Extended Attributes: Company A now uses SAML to send the authentication details of Mr. Yellow to Company B. Mr. Yellow's domain controller confirms that they are correct:

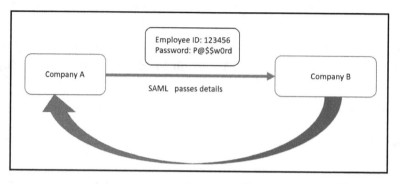

Figure 8: Extended attributes sent to Company A using SAML

Once Company B confirms that Mr. Yellow's extended attributes are valid, the Company A domain controller sends a certificate to Mr. Yellow's laptop; this certificate is used next time for authentication. They could alternatively use cookies.

 When the exam mentions authentication using extended attributes, they can only be federation services. Cookies used for authentication would also be federation services.

Shibboleth

Shibboleth is an open source federation service product that uses SAML authentication. It would be used in a small federation service environment.

Single Sign-On (SSO)

Single sign-on is used in a domain environment; this is where someone logs in to the domain and then can access several resources such as the file or email server without needing to input their credentials again. Think of it as an all-inclusive holiday where you book into your hotel and the receptionist gives you a wristband that you produce when you want to consume food and drink. Federation services and Kerberos (Microsoft authentication protocol) are both good examples of single sign-on. You log in once and access all of your resources without needing to insert your credentials again.

Installing and Configuring Identity and Access Services

Identity management in a corporate environment will use a directory database. We are going to look at Microsoft's Active Directory, where a protocol called the **Lightweight Directory Access Protocol** (**LDAP**) manages the users are groups. Let us look at how it works.

LDAP

Most companies have identity and access services through a directory that stores objects such as users and computer as X500 objects; these were developed by the **International Telecommunication Union** (**ITU**). These object form what is called a distinguished name and are organized and stored by the **Lightweight Directory Access Protocol** (**LDAP**).

There are only three values in X500 objects; these are DC (domain), **Organization Unit** (**OU**), and CN (anything else).

In this example, we have a domain called Domain A and an organizational unit called `Sales`; this is where all of the sales department users and computers would reside. We can see inside the `Sales` OU a computer called `Computer 1`:

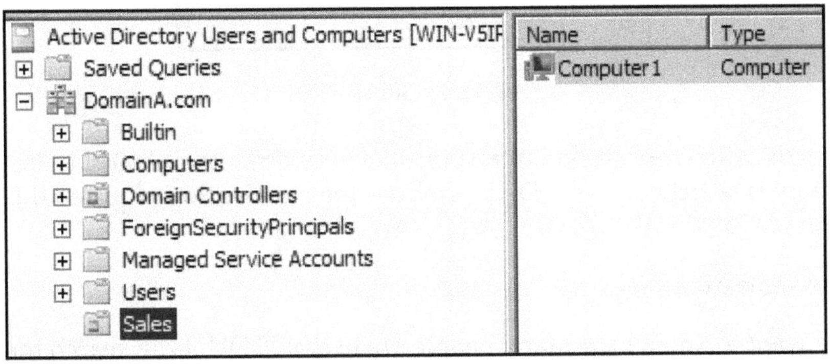

Active Directory Users and Computers [WIN-V5IF	Name	Type
⊞ Saved Queries	Computer1	Computer
⊟ DomainA.com		
⊞ Builtin		
⊞ Computers		
⊞ Domain Controllers		
⊞ ForeignSecurityPrincipals		
⊞ Managed Service Accounts		
⊞ Users		
Sales		

Figure 9: Active Directory

When creating the X500 object, we start off with the object itself, **Computer 1**, and then continue up through the structure. As **Computer 1** is neither an OU or domain, we give it a value of CN, then we move up the structure to **Sales**. As it is an OU, we give it that value. **Computer 1** is a CN, sales is a OU and the domain is into two portions, each having the value of DC. The distinguished name is here:

CN=Computer1, OU=Sales, DC=DomainA, DC=com

The way it is stored in the active directory can be viewed using a tool called **ADSI Edit**:

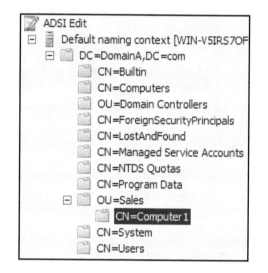

Figure 10: ADSI Edit

LDAP is the active directory storeman responsible for storing the X500 objects; when the Active Directory is searched, then LDAP provides the information required. LDAPS is the secure version of LDAP.

Following are some examples:

- If I want to know how many people are in the IT OU, I can search the Active Directory. LDAP provides the search and returns a reply saying that the IT department has 10 members.
- I am searching the Active Directory for a user called Fred. Once again LDAP finds the user. If you have 10,000 people in your domain, you will have them in different OUes to make it easier to find and manage them. However, if you need to find someone it will still be difficult; that is why we need LDAP to perform the search. It saves time.

Kerberos

Kerberos is the Microsoft authentication protocol that was introduced with the release of Windows Server 2000. It is the only authentication protocol that uses tickets, **Updated Sequence Numbers (USN)**, and is time stamped. The process of obtaining your service ticket is called a **Ticket Granting Ticket (TGT)** session. It is important that the time on all servers and computers are within five minutes of each other; time can be synchronized by using a time source such as the Atomic Time clock. The Security+ exam looks at Stratum time servers.

Stratum Time Servers: There are three types of Stratum time servers, Stratum 0, 1, and 2. Stratum 1 is internal and Stratum 0 is external and the reference time source. The way to remember this is that you can draw a clock face inside a zero making it the time source. The Stratum 1 time server is linked directly to Stratum 0, the time source. The Stratum 2 time server is linked to Stratum 1 through a network connection:

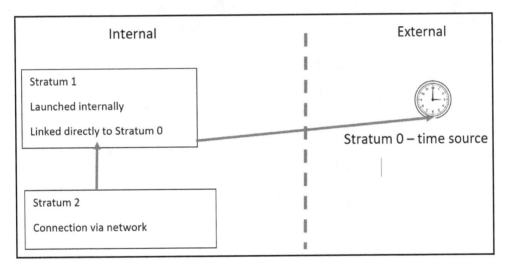

Figure 11: Stratum time servers

A TGT session is where a user sends their credentials (username and password, or it could be smart card and PIN) to a domain controller that starts the authentication process and, when it has been confirmed, will send back a **service ticket** that has a 10-hour lifespan. This service ticket is encrypted and cannot be altered:

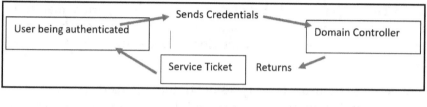

Figure 12: TGT session

Single Sign-On/Mutual Authentication: Kerberos provides single sign-on as the user needs to login in only once then uses their service ticket to prove who they are; this is exchanged for a **Session Ticket** with the server that they want to access resources on. In the example here, the user will use their service ticket for mutual authentication with an email server:

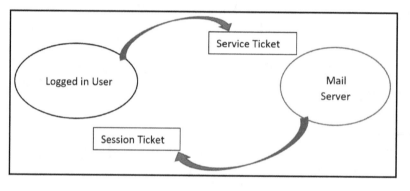

Figure 13: Mutual authentication

The preceding diagram shows the logged-in user exchanging their encrypted **Service Ticket** with the mail server which in return provides mutual authentication by returning a **Session Ticket**. The logged-in user checks the session ticket's timestamp is within five minutes of the domain controllers. This means that Kerberos can complete mutual authentication.

 You need to remember that Kerberos is the only authentication protocol that uses tickets. It will also prevent replay attacks as it uses USN numbers and timestamps. It can also prevent pass the hash attacks.

NT Lan Manager (NTLM): NTLM is a legacy authentication protocol that stores passwords using the MD4 hash that is very easy to crack. It was susceptible to the Pass the Hash attack; it was last used in a production environment in the 1990s. Kerberos prevents Pass the Hash attacks.

Internet-Based Open Source Authentication

More and more people are accessing web-based applications and need an account to log in, however, applications hosting companies do not want to be responsible for the creating and management of the account accessing the application. They use OAuth to help them facilitate this:

- **OAuth 2.0**: OAuth 2.0 provides authorization to enable third-party applications to obtain limited access to a web service. OAuth allows secure authorization in a simple and standard format for web, mobile, and desktop applications.
- **Open ID Connect**: Open ID Connect uses OAuth to allow users to log in to a web application without needing to manage the user's account. It allows users to authenticate by using their Google, Facebook, or Twitter account. For example, the Airbnb website that finds users accommodation allows you to sign up using your Google or Facebook account.

Authentication, Authorization, and Accounting (AAA) Servers

The main two AAA servers are Microsoft's Remote Authentication Dial-In User Service (RADIUS) and CISCO's Terminal Access Controller Access-Control System Plus (**TACACS+**). Both of these servers provide authentication, authorizing, and accounting:

- **RADIUS Server**: The RADIUS server is UDP-based and it authenticates servers such as Virtual Private Network (VPN) servers, Remote Access Services (RAS) servers, and the 802.1x authenticating switch. Each of these are known as RADIUS clients even though they are servers themselves. If I had a small company, I could outsource my remote access server but put in a RADIUS server, which would check any remote-access policies and verify that authentication was allowed by contacting a domain controller.

- **RADIUS Clients**: RADIUS clients are VPN servers, RAS server, and the 802.1x authentication switch. Every RADIUS client needs the secret key that is sometimes called the session key to join the RADIUS environment. RADIUS authentication communicates over the UDP port 1812. RADIUS accounting uses UDP Port 1813.

- **Diameter**: Diameter is the more modern version of RADIUS that works on TCP. For the exam, remember, Diameter is the AAA server that uses the EAP.
- **TACACS+**: This is a CISCO AAA server that used TCP so it is more secure than RADIUS and it uses TCP port 49 for authentication.

Authentication

A **Virtual Private Network** (**VPN**) allows someone working remotely either from a hotel room or home to connect securely through the internet to the corporate network. More information on how the VPN operates will be in `Chapter 5`, *Understanding Network Components*, of this book; we are going to look at VPN authentication methods later in this chapter:

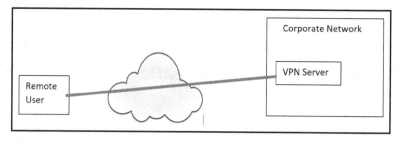

Figure 14: VPN

- **Remote Access Services (RAS)**: RAS is a legacy protocol that pre-dated the VPN; the RAS client used modems and a dial-up network using telephone lines. It was very restricted in speed.

- **Authentication for VPN/RAS**: There are numerous methods of authentication used by VPN or RAS. We will look at these here:

- **Password Authentication Protocol (PAP)**: PAP should be avoided at all costs as the passwords are transmitted as clear text and can be easily captured.

- **Challenge Handshake Authentication Protocol (CHAP)**: Challenge Handshake and Response (CHAP) was used to connect to an RAS server with a four-stage process:

Figure 15: Challenge Handshake authentication protocol

1. The client makes a connection request to the remote access server.
2. The RAS server replies with a challenge that is a random string.
3. The client uses their password as an encryption key to encrypt the challenge.
4. The RAS server encrypts the original challenge with the password stored for the user. If both values match, then the client is logged on.

- **MS CHAP/MSCHAP version 2**: MS CHAP/MSCHAP version 2 are Microsoft's version of MS CHAP. MS CHAP has been superseded by MS CHAP v2 and can be used by both VPN and RAS.

Learning About Identity and Access Management Controls

In this section, we are going to look at identity and management controls, starting with biometrics and moving on to security tokens and certificates. Let us first look at biometric controls followed by identity management using certificates.

Biometrics

Biometrics is a method of authentication using an individual's characteristics, for example, using a fingerprint as everyone's fingerprints are very different. In 1892, Inspector Eduardo Alvarez from Argentina made the first fingerprint identification in the case against Francisca Rojas, who had murdered her two sons and cut her own throat in an attempt to place blame on another, but the inspector proved that she was guilty.

We will now look at the types of biometrics:

- **Fingerprint Scanner**: Fingerprint scanners are now very common; for example, if you are going to the USA on holiday, when you go through customs, you are required to place all of your fingerprints in the scanner. Another use of a fingerprint scanner is when you are setting up your iPhone; you can set it up so that you press the home button to log in instead of using a password. Refer to the screenshot:

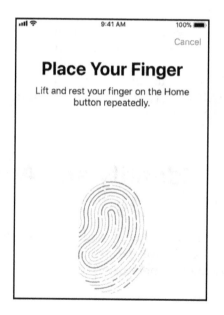

Figure 16: iPhone fingerprint scanner

  Retina and iris scanners both look at an individual's eye and the scanners themselves are physical devices.

- **Retina Scanner**: The retina is the light-sensitive layer of tissue that lines the inside of the eye and sends visual messages through the optic nerve to the brain. The blood vessels of the retina absorb light more readily than the surrounding tissue and are easily identified with appropriate lighting.
- **Iris Scanner**: The iris is the round, colored part of the eye. Iris recognition uses mathematical pattern-recognition techniques on video images of one or both of the irises of an individual's eyes—these patterns are very complex and unique. Most countries have issued biometric passports where the person inserts their passport into the reader and a camera about 1.5 meters away confirms the identity of the user by scanning their iris.
- **Voice Recognition**: Voice biometrics works by digitizing a profile of a person's speech to produce a stored model voice print; these prints are stored in databases similar to the storing of fingerprints or other biometric data.
- **Facial Recognition**: Facial recognition looks at the shape of the face and characteristics such as mouth, jaw, cheekbone, and nose. Light can be a factor when you use this software. There are much better versions of facial recognition, such as those that use infrared. You need to ensure that you are looking straight at the camera each time.

Microsoft has released a facial recognition program called Windows Hello, which was released with Windows 10; this uses a special USB infrared camera. It being infrared is much better than other facial recognition programs that can have problems with light.

- **False Acceptance Rate (FAR)**: FAR is what it says on the label: it accepts unauthorized users and allows them to gain access. It is known as a Type II error.
- **False Rejection Rate (FRR)**: FRR is where legitimate users who should gain access are rejected and cannot get in. It is known as a Type I error.
- **Crossover Error Rate (CER)**: This is where both the FAR and FRR are equal:

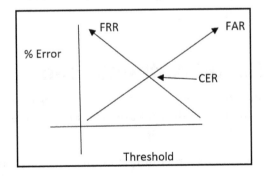

Figure 17: Crossover error rate

If the CER point is lower down the graph, then there are fewer errors, but if it is at the top of the graph, it indicates many errors and could prove more difficult to support; if this was the case, you would change your biometric system.

Security Tokens and Devices

There are different types of tokens that have different time limits; let us look at the difference between the Time-Based One-Time Password and HMAC-based One-Time Password:

- **Time-Based One-Time Password (TOTP)**: A TOTP requires time synchronization, because the password needs to be used in a very short period of time, normally between 30 and 60 seconds. Here, we can see the TOTP that has come to a phone—it can also come to a device similar to the RSA Secure ID shown earlier in this chapter. TOTP could be used when you want to access secure cloud storage:

Figure 18: TOTP

- **HMAC-based One-Time Password (HOTP)**: A HOTP is similar to TOTP in that a one-time password is issued; the main important factor is that there is no restriction on time but you can only use this password once.

Certification-Based Authentication

Certificate-based authentication is very popular as it provides two-factor authentication that makes it more secure than single-factor authentication such as a username and password. We will now look at various types:

- **Smart Card**: As previously mentioned in this book, a smart card looks like a credit card with a chip on it. The certificate is located on the chip itself and does not leave any trace (footprint) on the computer or laptop being used.

- **Common Access Card (CAC)**: CACs are used by governmental and military personnel as they provide both authentication and identification as it has a picture of the user on it. They are similar to smart cards. On the front side of a CAC is a picture of the user with their service; Army, Navy and Airforce and the reverse side shows their blood group and their Geneva Convention Category. To view a CAC card, please go to: http://www.cac.mil/Common-Access-Card/.
- **Personal Identity Verification (PIV)**: This is very similar to the CAC but is used by federal agencies rather than the military.

Port-Based Authentication

1EEE 802.1x is a port-based authentication protocol that is used when a device is connected to a switch or when a user authenticates to a wireless access point.

 Authentication with a password that has a short lifespan will be a TOTP.

Common Account Management Practices

Account management ranges from account creation on start up to its disablement when someone leaves the company. Fully understanding these concepts is crucial to obtaining the Security+ certification.

Account Types

Each user in a system needs an account to access the network in a Microsoft Active Directory environment; the user account has a **Security Identifier (SID)** linked to the account. When I create a user called Ian, they may have an SID of SID 1-5-1-2345678-345678. When the account is deleted, the SID is gone and a new SID is created.

For example, a member of the IT team has deleted a user account called Ian, it may have a SID of SID 1-5-1-2345678-345678, so he quickly creates another account called Ian but this account cannot access resources as it has a new SID of SID 1-5-1-2345678-3499999. The first portion from left to right identifies the domain and then the remainder is a serial number that is never reused.

There are various different types of user accounts and these are heavily tested in the Security+ exam; you must know when you would need each account:

- **User Account**: A user account, also known as a standard user account, has no real access. They cannot install software - they give users limited access to the computer systems. There are two types of user accounts: those that are local to the machine and those that access a domain. A domain is another name for a large group of users.

- **Guest Account**: A guest account is a legacy account that was designed to give limited access to a single computer without the need to create a user account. It is normally disabled as it is no longer useful and some administrators see it as a security risk.

- **Sponsored Guest Account**: A sponsored guest account is used for external speakers who may need access to the internet via a wireless router to show internet content whilst delivering their presentation to maybe a group of university students or company employees. For example, John Smith has been asked by Company A to deliver a presentation to company employees about a new pension plan. While he is delivering the presentation, he wants to show the latest share prices for the stock market. The finance department have asked the IT department to let John Smith access the company network to use the internet. The IT Director decided the best course of access was to create a sponsored guest account that would allow John to have access to the company guest Wi-Fi.

A guest speaker should be allocated a sponsored guest account.

- **Privilege Account**: User accounts do not have rights but privilege accounts have much higher access to the system and tend to be used by members of the IT team. Administrators are an example of privilege accounts.

- **Administrative Account**: An administrative account can install software and manage the configuration of a server or a computer. They also have the privileges to create, delete, and manage user accounts. An administrator should have two accounts: a user account for routine tasks and then an administrator account to carry out their administrative duties.

- **Service Account**: When software is installed on a computer or server, it needs higher levels of privilege to run the software, but at the same time, we need a lower level administrative account and the service account fits the bill. An example of this is an account to run an anti-virus application.

A service account is a type of administrator account used to run an application.

- **Shared Account**: When a group of people perform the same duties, such as members of customer services, they can use a shared account. The people monitoring this account can send a reply coming from the shared account. If you need to set up monitoring or auditing to individual employees, you must eliminate the practice of using shared accounts. For example, a multinational corporation that has 100,000 employees has five members of the **Human Resources** (**HR**) team that receive and process email applications from potential employees. They all use a shared account called `jobs@corporations.com` and between them they open and action the CVs they receive. Mr. Grumpy was one of the people who applied for a job within the company and has complained to the **Chief Executive Officer** (**CEO**) because he was not happy with how his application was handled. The CEO wanted to know which of the HR employees was responsible but could not identify the person responsible as all five members of the HR team denied dealing with the application.

When you need to monitor or audit to an employee level, you must eliminate the use of shared accounts.

- **Generic Accounts**: Generic accounts are default administrative accounts created by manufacturers for devices ranging from baby alarms, smart ovens, and smart TVS; they all have a default usernames and passwords. If you surf the web for the device that you have purchased, it is very easy to find the credentials to hack that device. As cybercrime is increasing each day, we should rename the default account name and its associated password. At the time of writing this book, *Security Week* has published an article on hacking a home oven; it can be viewed at `https://www.securityweek.com/security-flaw-could-have-let-hackers-turn-smart-ovens`. Here's another example. Baby monitors are getting more sophisticated and come with the ability to see and hear your baby from somewhere else in your home via a web browser. When the police have investigated such instances, they have found out that the baby monitors can be used to film children when they are asleep using the default user account and password; most parents are unaware that this is possible.

> If you do not change the default username and password for household devices, know as IoT, it is possible for a cybercriminal to hack into your home. This includes baby monitors, TVs, ovens, and refrigerators.

Account Creation

Multinational corporations will make hundreds of accounts annually and need to have a standardized format; this is called a standard naming convention. Account templates are copied and modified with the details of new employees. Some examples of standard naming conventions are as follows:

- **First name, last name**: John.Smith
- **Last name, first name**: Smith.John
- **First initial, last name**: J.Smith

If you have John Smith and Jack Smith you would have two J Smiths, therefore you may also use a middle initial J A Smith or a number at the end J Smith1, to make them unique.

All user accounts need to be unique so that each person is responsible for their own account. If you leave your computer logged on to the network whilst you go for a coffee and someone deletes data using your account then you are held responsible. A good practice would be to lock your screen while you are not at your desk to prevent this.

Without a standard naming convention, accounts would be created differently and cause chaos when you tried to find users in your directory service.

Employees Moving Departments

When employees move between departments, IT teams normally modify their account for the next department they move to; they don't generally get a new account. In the Security+ exam, when people move department, they are given new accounts and the old account remains active until it has been disabled.

Disabling an Account

There are a few times when the IT team will disable accounts as good practice; let us look at the reasons for this:

- **Employee Leaving**: A good practice when someone leaves the company is that human resources provide the employee with an exit interview to find out the reasons that they are leaving. The final step is that the IT team should disable their accounts and reset their passwords. These steps keep their email and certificate settings so that encrypted data can still be accessed and they can no longer access the network. If you delete the account, then you lose all of this.
- **Extended Absence Period**: When an employee is away from a company for a month or more, then it may be prudent to disable the account so that it cannot be accessed. It could well be that the employee is on maternity/paternity leave, seconded to another company, on a long course, or taking a gap year to fulfill one of their dreams. It then means that, while they are away, the account cannot be hacked and can be reactivated once they return.
- **Guest Account**: Guest account are designed for temporary users but are seldom used; they are disabled to prevent them being hacked.

 When an employee leaves a company, the first stage is that the account is disabled and not deleted. You will also reset the password so that the old account holder cannot use the account.

Account Recertification

Account recertification is a process where an auditor will review all of the user accounts. The auditor will have a matrix showing all of the active accounts and what privileges and access that they should have. If the auditor finds anything wrong, then they will report it to the management, who will then either write a new account policy or make changes to the management of accounts using change management. For the purpose of the exam, the auditor should be looked at as a snitch; they will never take any action but they will report their findings to the management.

Account Maintenance

Account maintenance is ensuring that accounts are created in accordance with the standard naming convention, disabled when the employee initially leaves, then deleted maybe 30 days later.

Account Monitoring

If you wish to find out when a user account has been granted a new set of privileges, then this can only be done via active monitoring of the accounts. This could be automated by using a **Security Information and Event Management (SIEM)** system that will create and alert you about changes to the system. You will not be alerted by user account review as there could be 6-12 months between the review—you may need to know immediately.

 If you want to know immediately when there is a change to a user account, such as it being given higher privileges, then you need active account monitoring or set up a SIEM system.

Security Information and Event Management

Security Information and Event Management (**SIEM**) is considered an IT best practice, and for regulated industries it is an audit compliance requirement. It supports IT service reliability by maximizing event log value and is used to aggregate, decipher, and normalize nonstandard log formats; it can also filter out false positives. The only time that an SIEM system will not provide the correct information is when the wrong filters are set in error:

- **Account Management**: In a multinational corporation that may have in excess of 50,000 users, it is very important that account management policies are in place so that the directory service is kept up to date. Let us look at different account management tools and policies. An Active Directory query can be run against the system to discover accounts that have not been used for a certain period of time.

- **Account Expiry**: When companies employ temporary employees such as sub-contractors during the account creation phase, an expiry date will be enabled. This is to prevent someone from trying to gain access to the company network once their contract has expired. Once the account hits the expiry state, the account is automatically disabled, however, the IT team can reset the expiry date if the contract is extended. Here is an example of account expiry:

Ian Neil Properties   ? ✕

| Dial-in | Environment | Sessions | Remote control |

| Remote Desktop Services Profile | Personal Virtual Desktop | COM+ |

| General | Address | Account | Profile | Telephones | Organization | Member Of |

User logon name:

| Ian | @Adatum.com ▼ |

User logon name (pre-Windows 2000):

| ADATUM\ | Ian |

[Logon Hours...]   [Log On To...]

☐ Unlock account

Account options:

☑ User must change password at next logon
☐ User cannot change password
☐ Password never expires
☐ Store password using reversible encryption

Account expires
○ Never
● End of: Wednesday, December 12, 2018 ▼

Figure 19: Account expiry

If a person moves department, they get a new account, if their old account is still being used, then we should get an auditor who will perform a user account review.

- **Time and Day Restriction**: Time and day restriction is set up for each individual user as a company may have many different shift patterns and may not wish their employees to access their network outside of their working hours. This prevents users coming in at 3 a.m. when nobody else is in at the company and stealing data:

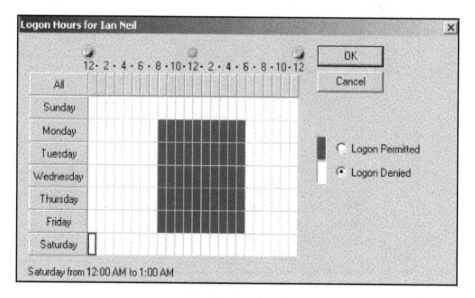

Figure 20: Time and day restrictions

For example, a toy factory may employ university students to work prior to the busy Christmas period with three different shift patterns, 6 a.m.-2 p.m., 2-10 p.m. and 10 p.m.-6 a.m. Each employee will have a time and day restriction in place so that they can log in only for their individual shift times.

- **Account Lockout**: To prevent dictionary and brute-force attacks, account lockout is enforced so that maybe three or five attempts to enter the password are allowed; once exceeded, the account is disabled. This prevent hackers guessing an account password.

If a time restriction is to be placed on a group of contractors, rule-based access control will be used. Time and day restriction can only be used for individuals.

Group-Based Access Control

When a company has a large number of users, it is difficult to give each user access to the resources that they need to perform their job. Groups are created and they will contain all users in that department. For example, the sales group will then contain all of the people working in sales and the group will be used to allow access to resources such as a printer or file structure. If you decide to use group-based access and you have new employees or interns, you may create another group for them with lower permissions.

For example, in a large corporation, there are 25 employees who work in marketing and need full access to the marketing file share. Next week, they will have three new interns start with the company but they need only read access to the same share. We therefore create the following:

- A global group called `marketing` is created; all 25 employees are added to the group. The group is given full control access to the data.
- A global group called `marketing interns` is created; the three interns are added to the group. The group is given read access to the data.

If group-based access is used in the exam question, then the solution will be a group-based access solution.

Credential Management

The details of usernames and passwords that someone uses to access a network or an application are called credentials. Users will sometimes have more than one set of credentials to access their local network, and their Facebook, Hotmail, or Twitter account. It would be a serious security risk to use the same account and password for any two of these. Windows 10 has a Credential Manager that can store credentials in two categories: generic credentials and Windows 10. When you log in to an account and you check the **Remember Password** box, these details could be stored inside credential management to consolidate them. It can be for generic accounts used to access web portals or Windows 10 credentials:

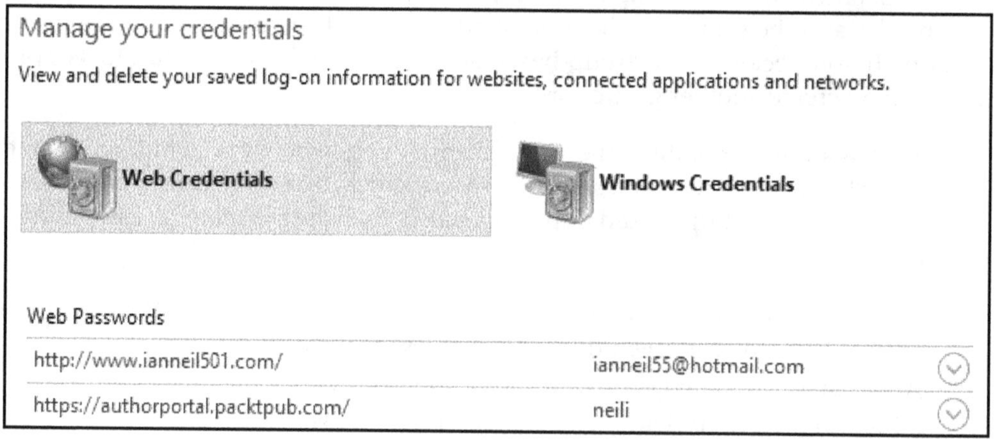

Figure 21: Credential manager

User Account Reviews

An auditor will carry out a user account review periodically to ensure that old accounts are not being used after an employee either moves department or leaves the company. The auditor will also ensure that all employees have the correct amount of permissions and privileges to carry out their jobs and that they don't have a higher level than they required. Least privilege is giving the person only the access that they require.

Practical Exercise – Password Policy

In this practical exercise, you need to prevent users from resetting their account by using the same password. The company should not allow the users to change their password more than once every three days and these passwords need to be complex. A user must use a minimum of 12 passwords before they can reuse the original password. You need to prevent a hacker using more than five attempts at guessing a password:

1. On a Windows 10 desktop, type `gpedit.msc` or, on a domain controller, go to **Server Manager | Tools | Group Policy management**. Edit the **Default Domain Policy**
2. Under **Computer Configurations**, expand **Windows Settings**
3. Select **Security Settings**
4. Select **Account Policy**, then select **Password Policy**
5. Select **Password History** and enter `12 passwords remembered`—press **OK**
6. Select **Minimum Password Age**. Enter `3 days`—press **OK**
7. Select **Password must meet complexity requirements**—select the radio button, **Enabled**, and press **OK**
8. Go back to **Account Policies** and select **Account Lockout Policies**
9. Select **Account Lockout Threshold** and change the value to five invalid login attempts—press **OK**

Review Questions

1. What is the most common form of authentication that is most likely to be enter incorrectly?
2. When I purchase a new wireless access point what should I do first?
3. What is password history?
4. How can I prevent someone from reusing the same password?
5. Explain what format a complex password takes.
6. How can I prevent a hacker from inserting a password multiple times?
7. What type of factor authentication is a smart card?
8. How many factors is it if I have a password, PIN, and date of birth?
9. What is biometric authentication?
10. What authentication method can be used by two third parties that participate in a joint venture?

11. What is an XML-based authentication protocol?

12. What is Shibboleth?

13. What protocol is used to store and search for Active Directory objects?

14. What is the format of a distinguished name for a user called Fred who works in the IT department for a company with a domain called Company A that is a dotcom?

15. What authentication factor uses tickets, timestamps, and updated sequence numbers and is used to prevent replay attacks?

16. Which Stratum time server is the reference time source?

17. What is a **Ticket Granting Ticket (TGT)** session?

18. What is single sign-on? Give two examples.

19. How can I prevent a Pass the Hash attack?

20. Give an example of when you would use Open ID Connect.

21. Name two AAA servers and the ports associated with them.

22. What is used for accounting in an AAA server?

23. What is the purpose of a VPN solution?

24. Why should we never use PAP authentication?

25. What type of device is an iris scanner?

26. What can be two drawbacks of using facial recognition?

27. What is Type II in biometric authentication and why is it a security risk?

28. What is a time-limited password?

29. How many times can you use a HOTP password? Is there a time restriction associated with it?

30. How does a CAC differ from a smart card and who uses CAC?

31. What is a port-based authentication that authenticates both users and devices?

32. What type of account is a service account?

33. How many accounts should a system administrator for a multinational corporation have and why?

34. What do I need to do when I purchase a baby monitor and why?

35. What is a privilege account?

36. What is the drawback for security if the company uses shared accounts?

37. What is a default account? Is it a security risk?

38. The system administrator in a multination corporation creates a user account using an employee's first name and last name. Why are they doing this time after time?

39. What two actions do I need to complete when John Smith leaves the company?

40. What is account recertification?

41. What is the purpose of a user account review?

42. What can I implement to find out immediately when a user is placed in a group that may give them a higher level of privilege?

43. What will be the two possible outcomes if an auditor finds any working practices that do not confirm to the company policy?

44. If a contractor brings in five consultants for two months of mail server migration, how should I set up their accounts?

45. How can I ensure that the contractors in Question 44 can only access the company network from 9 a.m.- 5 p.m. daily?

46. If I have a company that has five consultants who work in different shift patterns, how can I set up their accounts so each of them can only access the network during their individual shifts?

47. A brute-force attack cracks a password using all combinations of characters and will eventually crack a password. What can I do to prevent a brute-force attack?

48. The IT team have a global group called IT Admin; each member of the IT team are members of this group and therefore has full control access to the departmental data. Two new apprentices are joining the company and they need to have read access to the IT data, how can you achieve this with the minimum amount of administrative effort?

49. I have different login details and passwords to access Airbnb, Twitter, and Facebook, but I keep getting them mixed up and have locked myself out of these accounts from time to time. What can I implement on my Windows 10 laptop to help me?

50. I have moved departments but the employees in my old department still use my old account for access; what should the company have done to prevent this from happening? What should their next action be?

Answers and Explanations

1. A password is most likely to be entered incorrectly; the user may forget the password or may have the *Caps Lock* key set up incorrectly.

2. When purchasing any device, you should change the default username and password as many of these are available on the internet and could be used to access your device.

3. Password history is the number of passwords you can use before you can reuse your current password. Some third-party applications or systems may call this a Password Reuse list.

4. Password history could be set up and combined with minimum password age. If I set the minimum password age to one day, a user could only change their password a maximum of once per day. This would prevent them from rotating their passwords to come back to the old password.

5. A complex password uses three of the following; uppercase and lowercase letters, numbers, and special characters not used in programming.

6. If I set up an account lockout with a low value such as three, the hacker needs to guess your password within three attempts or the password is lockout, and this disables the user account.

7. A smart card is multi-factor or dual factor as the card is something you have and the PIN is something you know.

8. A password, PIN, and date of birth are all factors that you know, therefore, it is a single factor.

9. Biometric authentication is where you use a part of your body or voice for authentication, for example, your iris, retina, palm, or fingerprint.

10. Federated services are an authentication method that can be used by two third parties; this uses SAML and extended attributes such as employee or email address.

11. **Security Assertion Mark-up Language (SAML)** is an XML-based authentication protocol used with federated services.

12. Shibboleth is a small open source Federation Services protocol.

13. **Lightweight Directory Authentication Protocol (LDAP)** is used to store objects in an X500 format and search Active Directory objects such as users, printers, groups, or computers.

14. A distinguisher name in the ITU X500 object format is: *cn=Fred, ou=IT, dc=Company, dc=Com.*

15. Microsoft's Kerberos authentication protocol is the only one that uses tickets. It also uses timestamps and updated sequence numbers and is used to prevent replay attacks. It also prevents pass the hash attacks as it does not use NTLM.

16. Stratum 0 is the reference time source. Stratum 1 is set up internally to obtain time from Stratum 0.

17. A **Ticket Granting Ticket** (**TGT**) process is where a user logs in to an Active Directory domain using Kerberos authentication and receives a service ticket.

18. Single sign-on is where a user inserts their credentials only once and accesses different resource such as emails and files without needing to re-enter the credentials. Examples of this are Kerberos, Federated Services, and a smart card.

19. Pass the hash attacks exploit older systems such as Microsoft NT4.0, which uses NT Lan Manager. You can prevent is by enabling Kerberos disabling NTLM.

20. Open ID Connect is where you access a device or portal using your Facebook, Twitter, Google, or Hotmail credentials. The portal itself does not manage the account.

21. The first AAA server is Microsoft RADIUS, using UDP Port 1812 - it is seen as non-proprietary. The second is CISCO TACACS+ and uses TCP Port 49. Diameter is a more modern secure form of RADIUS that is TCP based and uses EAP.

22. Accounting in an AAA server is where they log the details of when someone logs in and logs out; this can be used for billing purposes. Accounting is normally logged in a database such as SQL. RADIUS Accounting uses UDP Port 1813.

23. A VPN solution creates a secure to connect from a remote location to your corporate network or vice versa. The most secure tunneling protocol is L2TP/IPSec.

24. PAP authentication uses a password in clear text; this could be captured easily by a packet sniffer.

25. An iris scanner is a physical device used for biometric authentication.

26. Facial recognition could be affected by light or turning your head slightly to one side; some older facial recognition systems accept photographs. Microsoft Windows Hello is much better as it uses infrared and is not fooled by a photograph or affected by light.

27. Type II in biometric authentication is Failure Acceptance Rate, where people that are not permitted to access a tour network are given access.

28. **Time-Based One-Time password** (**TOTP**) has a short time limit of 30-60 seconds.

29. HOTP is a one-time password that does not expire until it is used.

30. A CAC is similar to a smart card as it uses certificates, but the CAC card is used by the military, has a picture, and the details of the user on the front and their blood group and Geneva convention category on the reverse side.

31. IEE802.1x is port-based authentication that authenticates both users and devices.

32. A service account is a type of administrative account that allows an application to have the higher level of privileges to run on a desktop or server. An example of this is using a service account to run an anti-visas application.

33. A system administrator should have two accounts: a user account for day-to-day tasks and an administrative account for administrative tasks.

34. When I purchase a baby monitor, I should rename the default administrative account and change the default password to prevent someone using it to hack my home. This is known as an **Internet of Things (IoT)** item.

35. A privilege account is an account with administrative rights.

36. When monitoring and auditing are carried out, the employees responsible cannot be traced while more than one-person shared accounts. Shared accounts should be eliminated for monitoring and auditing purposes

37. Default accounts and passwords for devices and software can be found on the internet and used to hack your network or home devices. Ovens, TVs, baby monitors, and refrigerators are examples, therefore poses a security risk.

38. The system administrator is using a standard naming convention.

39. When John Smith leaves the company, you need to disable his account and reset the password. Deleting the account will prevent access to data he used.

40. Account recertification is an audit of user account and permissions usually carried out by an auditor; this could also be known as user account reviews.

41. A user account review ensures that old accounts have been deleted - all current users have the appropriate access to resources and not a higher level of privilege.

42. A SIEM system can carry out active monitoring and notify the administrators of any changes to user account or logs.

43. Following an audit, either change management or a new policy will be put in place to rectify any area not conforming to company policy.

44. The contractor's account should have an expiry date equal to the last day of the contract.

45. Rule-based access should be adopted so that the contractors can access the company network 9 a.m.-5 p.m. daily.

46. Time and day restrictions should be set up against each individual's user account equal to their shift pattern.

47. Account Lockout with a low value will prevent brute-force attacks.

48. Create a group called IT apprentices then add the apprentices accounts to the group. Give the group read access to the IT data.

49. The credential manager can be used to store generic and Windows 10 accounts. The user therefore does not have to remember them.

50. The company should have disabled the account and reset the password. A user account review needs to be carried out to find accounts in a similar situation.

5
Understanding Network Components

In this chapter, we are going to look at networking components and how they could affect the security of your network. We will look at firewalls, switches, and routers. We will start by looking at the OSI Reference model that was created to improve communications between devices.

We will cover the following exam objectives in this chapter:

- **Install and configure network components, both hardware–and software-based, to support organizational security**:
    - Firewall—ACL—application-based versus network-based—stateful versus stateless—implicit deny
    - VPN concentrator—remote access versus site-to-site—IPSec—tunnel mode—transport mode—AH—ESP—split tunnel versus full tunnel—TLS—always-on VPN
    - NIPS/NIDS—signature-based—heuristic/behavioral—anomaly—inline versus passive—in-band versus out-of-band—rules—analytics—false positive—false negative
    - Router—ACLs—antispoofing
    - Switch—port security—layer 2 versus layer 3—loop prevention—flood guard
    - Proxy—forward and reverse proxy—transparent—application/multipurpose

- Load balancer—scheduling—affinity—round-robin—active-passive—active-active—virtual IPs
- Access point—SSID—MAC filtering—signal strength—band selection/width—antenna types and placement—fat versus thin—controller-based versus standalone
- SIEM—aggregation—correlation—automated alerting and triggers—time synchronization—event deduplication—logs/WORM
- DLP—USB blocking—cloud-based—email
- NAC—Dissolvable versus permanent—host health checks—agent versus agentless
- Mail gateway—spam filter—DLP—encryption
- Bridge, SSL/TLS accelerators, SSL decryptors, and media gateway
- Hardware security module

- **Given a scenario, implement secure protocols**:
  - Protocols—DNSSEC—SSH—S/MIME—SRTP—LDAPS—FTPS—SFTP—SNMPv3—SSL/TLS—HTTPS—secure POP/IMAP
  - Use cases—voice and video—time synchronization—email and web—file transfer—directory services—remote access—domain name resolution—routing and switching—network address allocation—subscription services

- **Given a scenario, implement secure network architecture concepts**:
  - Zones/topologies—DMZ—extranet—intranet—wireless—guest—honeynets—NAT—ad hoc
  - Segregation/segmentation/isolation—physical—logical (VLAN)—virtualization—air gaps
  - Tunneling/VPN—Site-to-site—remote access
  - Security device/technology placement—sensors—collectors—correlation engines—filters—proxies—firewalls—VPN concentrators—SSL accelerators—load balancers—DDoS mitigator—aggregation switches—taps and port mirror
  - SDN

- **Given a scenario, install and configure wireless security settings**:
  - Cryptographic protocols—WPA—WPA2—CCMP – TKIP
  - Authentication protocols—EAP—PEAP—EAP-FAST—EAP-TLS—EAP-TTLS—IEEE 802.1x—RADIUS federation
  - Methods—PSK versus enterprise versus open—WPS—captive portals

OSI Reference Model (OSI)

The **Open Systems Interconnection (OSI)** reference model was created by the **Internet Standards Organization (ISO)** and is a reference model used for communication. Each of the seven different layers have different protocols and responsibilities. The Security+ exam focuses mainly on layers **2, 3,** and **7**:

Layer	Description	Example	Devices	Packet Structure
7	Application	HTTP, SMTP		
6	Presentation	Encryption, Formatting		
5	Session	Logging On/Off		
4	Transport	TCP, UDP		Datagrams
3	Network	IP, ICMP	Router	Packets
2	Data Link	IP Sec, VLAN, ARP	Switch	Frames
1	Physical	Cables	Hub	Bits - 01010101

Figure 1: OSI reference model

Here is a brief summary of each layer:

- **Application Layer**: Applications, such as HTTP for accessing the web or SMTP for accessing emails, are launched here. The **Web Application Firewall (WAF)**, whose job it is to protect web-based applications, operates at this layer.
- **Presentation Layer**: The presentation layer formats data into the character code, such as Unicode or ASCII. Encryption also works at this layer.
- **Session Layer**: This is where you would create a session, such as logging in and logging out.

- **Transport Layer**: Ports are either TCP or UDP. TCP is connection-orientated as it uses a three-way handshake and acknowledges the receipt of each packet, whereas UDP is connectionless and the application is responsible for checking the data has arrived. Most ports are TCP-based, video will use UDP as it is much faster than TCP.

- **Network Layer**: The network layer is responsible for **Internet Protocol** (**IP**) addressing and routing. A router whose function is to route packets works at this layer, and a Layer 3 switch that is a multifunction switch also operates at this layer. The format of data is called packets, hence we hear of IP packets. The **Internet Control Message Protocol** (**ICMP**) operates at this layer; when troubleshooting tools such as `ping`, `tracert,` or `pathing` are used, ICMP produces the replies.

- **Data Link Layer**: The three main functions of the data-link layer are to deal with transmission errors, regulate the flow of data, and provide a well-defined interface to the network layer. MAC addresses operate at this layer. This is the lowest layer that a switch operates at. When the exam talks about a *switch*, this is the Layer 2 switch. The Address Resolution Protocol that translates an IP into a MAC address; IPSec, an encryption-tunneling protocol; switches; and **Virtual Local Area Network** (**VLAN**), where you can segment traffic on a switch, all work at that layer.

- **Physical Layer**: Cables operate at the physical layer, such as Ethernet, coaxial, and wireless communication.

When protocols, such as the TCP/IP protocol suite, are created, it is based on some or all layers of this model.

Exam tip: When a switch is mentioned, it is a Layer 2 switch that can create VLANs. ARP operates at Layer 2 and an ARP attack must be done locally on the host.

Installing and Configuring Network Components

There are many network components and topologies (layouts) that we need to know about to maintain a secure environment. We are going to look at each of these in turn. We need to know how each device is configured and which device is the most appropriate in different scenarios. We will look at firewalls, the main job of which is to prevent unauthorized access to the network.

Firewall

A firewall prevents unauthorized access to the corporate network, and in the Security+ exam, we tend to use a back-to-back configuration, as shown here:

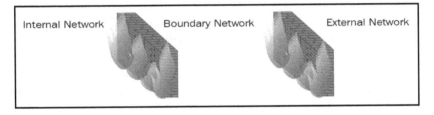

Figure 2: Back-to-back firewall configuration

You can see each of these firewalls is not letting traffic pass through them; this is because we need to open only the ports that we need. If Firewall 1 is traversed, then Firewall 2 will hopefully prevent access to the internal network known as the local area network. To enable applications to pass through the firewall, we must open the port number for each application. Each application has a different port number - if you think of someone who wants to watch the news, the Democrats watch CNN on channel 21 and the Republicans will watch Fox News on channel 29. Each TV program has a different channel number. If we want to enable internet access, we should make an exception to the Hypertext Transfer Protocol (HTTP) on TCP `port 80`. This is the port number that each web server works on no matter whether we use Internet Explorer, Microsoft Edge, Google Chrome, or Firefox; each of these applications uses TCP `port 80` to allow web traffic.

The direction of ports is outbound coming from the internal network going to the external network, or inbound coming from outside to the internal network. If we opened only the outbound port for `port 80`, the request would go out but the incoming response would be prevented.

The main purpose of a firewall is to prevent unauthorized access to the network. The default setting is to block all traffic allowed by exception. There are many different firewalls:

- **Host-Based Firewall:** This is an application firewall that is built into desktop operating systems, such as the Windows 10 operating system:

Figure 3: Host-based firewall

As the Host-Based Firewall is an application on a desktop, it is vulnerable to attack. If someone disables the service running the Windows firewall service, then the firewall is disabled and the computer becomes vulnerable. Remember from Chapter 4, *Delving into Identity and Access Management*, services are started using a service account, a type of administrative account. The following screenshot shows a running firewall service:

Figure 4: Windows firewall service

- **Network-Based Firewall**: This is a hardware product that keeps the network safe. It is vital that only the ports required are open. One of the configurations is the back-to-back configuration where two layers of firewall are rolled out. The network-based firewall is placed at the edge of the network to prevent unauthorized access.

- **Stateful Firewall**: This looks deep at the application and its traffic to see whether it is allowed through. For example, a packet arrives with the `Get <webpage>` command and, because the `Get` verb in HTTP is the request to view a web page, the traffic is allowed. However, if the HTTP verbs use the `PUT` verb that could be used to deface the web page, it is blocked. If `HEAD` is used, it tries to pull down the website header information and it is also blocked. The Stateful Firewall knows the size of each packet and will block traffic that is not the size that it should be.
- **Stateless Firewall**: The Stateless Firewall could also be called a packet-filtering firewall. It only looks at whether the packet is permitted and never looks in depth at the packet format.
- **Web Application Firewall (WAF)**: The WAF is placed on a web server and its role is to protect web-based applications running on the web server.
- **Unified Threat Management Firewall (UTM)**: The UTM is a multipurpose firewall: it does malware, content, and URL filtering. It is known as an all-in-one security appliance.

 Exam tip: A UTM firewall is an all-in-one security appliance that acts as a firewall and does content and URL filtering. It can also inspect malware.

Router

A router is a device that connects two different networks together when setting up a host machine; it is known as the default gateway. It is used by your company to give you access to other networks, for example, the internet. It has a routing table built into it, so it knows which route can be used to deliver network packets. The router is the IP equivalent of a post office sending letters around the world, but instead of letters, IP packets are being transported.

Access Control List (ACL): The router sits on the external interface and uses an ACL so it can also filter the traffic coming into the network using the following:

- Port number
- Protocol
- IP address

Anti-spoofing: An anti-spoofing filter is placed on the input side of a router interface and only allows packets through that are within the address range of that subnet. It excludes packets that have invalid source addresses.

Access Control List – Network Devices

The **Access Control List** (**ACL**) for network devices must not be confused with the ACL for files and folders - they are totally different. Two network devices that use ACL are firewalls and routers. The ACL prevents access by using port numbers, application names, or its IP address. When you install a new firewall or router, there are no rules except the last rules of deny all. The default for either a router or firewall is to block all access allowed by creating exceptions using allow rules for the traffic you want to allow through. If there are no allow rules, the last rule of deny applies - this is called an *Implicit Deny*.

For example, John has been doing some online shopping and bought a pair of shoes, but he cannot download the new book that he bought. He has used HTTP to gain access to a website, and then gone to the secure server for payment, using HTTPS for purchases to protect his credit card details; however, when trying to download the book, the traffic is being blocked by the firewall. The ACL allows TCP `port 80` (HTTP) and HTTPS, but there is no allow rule for the FTP that used TCP `port 21`:

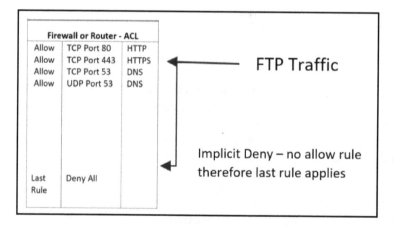

Figure 5: Implicit Deny

As there is no allow rule on the firewall for FTP traffic, when the FTP traffic arrives, it is checked against the allow rules, and if there is no matching rule, it then drops down to the last rule, denying all traffic, this is known as Implicit Deny. Although the example is for a firewall, an ACL is used by the router. Both devices are filtering incoming traffic.

Intrusion Prevention System

There are two types of **Intrusion-Prevention Systems** (**IPS**), the first is the Network Intrusion Prevention System (NIPS), which can only operate on your network and cannot work inside a host. The second is called the Host Intrusion Prevention System (HIPS), and it operates inside a host machine and cannot operate on the network.

NIPS is an internal network device whose role is to prevent access to the network, and it is placed on the perimeter of your network behind your firewall. Think of NIPS as Rambo with a big gun whose job it is to shoot the bad guys.

Intrusion Detection System

The **Intrusion-Detection System** (**IDS**) is the same as the IPS; there is the HIDS, which only works on a host, and the NIDS, which only works on the network. Think of the IDS as Sherlock Holmes, the famous detective; his job is to find different traffic patterns on the network and then inform Rambo, the NIPS, who will then remove them from the network.

 Exam tip: NIPS has the capability to detect as well as protect if there are no NIDS on your network. To protect a virtual machine from attack, you will install a HIPS.

Modes of Detection

There are three modes of detection used by the NIPS/NIDS. For the purpose of the exam, you must know them thoroughly:

- **Signature-Based**: Works off a known database of known exploits and cannot identify new patterns. If the database is not up to date, they will not operate efficiently.
- **Anomaly-Based**: Starts off the same as the signature-based with the known database but they have the ability to identify new variants.

- **Heuristic/Behavioral-Based**: Instead of trying to match known variants, the heuristic/behavioral starts off with a baseline and matches traffic patterns against the baseline. It could also be known as anomaly-based.

 Exam tip: Anomaly-based NIPS/NIDS detect new patterns and are much more efficient than signature-based, which can only work with known variants.

Modes of Operation

There are different modes of operation for the sensors of the NIPS/NIDS:

- **Inline**: The NIPS will be placed on or very near to the firewall as an additional layer of security; when the NIPS has been set up in inline mode, the flow of traffic goes through the NIPS. This is known as in-band.
- **Passive**: The traffic does not go through the NIPS; this mode is normally used by the NIDS as it detects changes in traffic patterns in the local network. This is known as out-of-band.

When sensors are placed inside the network, they can only detect traffic once it is inside your network and has passed through your firewall. If you wish to detect attacks before they come into your network, the sensor must be placed on the external network to the firewall.

Monitoring Data

When analytics (how we analyze the data) examine the information provided, it is based on rules that are set inside the IPS/IDS. However, no system is foolproof. They try their best but sometimes provide outcomes different than those expected. There are two different types:

- **False Positive**: The NIDS/NIPS has decided, based on the information gathered, that an attack is taking place, however, when the network administrator investigates it, they find that there is no attack.
- **False Negative**: The NIDS/NIPS is not updated and attacks have been taking place without detection.

Exam tip:
A false positive is a false alarm, however, a false negative doesn't detect anything while you are being attacked.

Switch

A switch is an internal device that connects all users in a local-area network. The switch has a table listing the MAC addresses of the host connected to it:

Figure 6: Cisco switch

Once the switch has been installed, it builds up a routing table; each host is identified by their MAC address. The switch delivers the packet only to the host that requires the packet. Switches can be stacked when there are more than 48 users connected to the network:

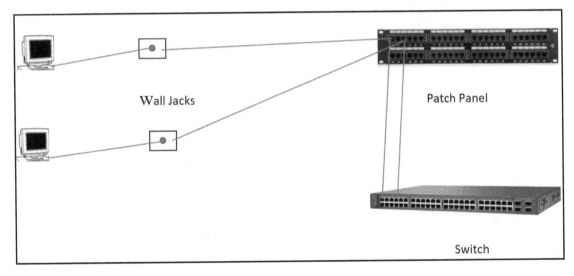

Wall Jacks

Patch Panel

Switch

Figure 7: Network connections

A computer has an Ethernet cable that plugs into a wall jack, then the wall jack is connected to the patch panel by cables that are laid under floors or above ceilings, a user cannot see them. From the patch panel, there is a cable that goes into one port on the switch. It is very easy to plug a cable into a wall jack the network administrator must place security on the switch. There are two types of port security, 802.1x, and other protection that can be configured:

- **Port Security**: When an authorized user plugs their laptop into one of the wall-jack ports, the network administrator can prevent this in the future by implementing port security. Port security turns the port off, so no matter who connects to it, they will not get a connection. The downside is that if you have a 48-port switch and put port security on 40 of the ports, it only leaves enough ports to connect eight users; this is not practical, therefore port security should be used sparingly.

- **802.1x**: When a network administrator uses 802.1x port security, the device itself is authenticated by a certificate before a connection is made. It will prevent an unauthorized device from connecting and allow an authorized device to connect. The benefit of 802.1x over port security is that none of the ports on the switch have been disabled and the switch has full functionality.

- **Flood Guard**: Prevents MAC flooding and Denial of Service attacks on a switch by identifying the attack and preventing it.

- **Loop Protection**: When two or more switches are joined together, they can create loops that create broadcasts. We need to use the Spanning Tree protocol to prevent this from happening by forwarding, listening, or blocking on some ports.

Exam tip:
If you want to prevent someone from plugging their laptop into a waiting area, we will use port security to shut that port down. But if you want to prevent a rogue server or a wireless access point from connecting to the network, we will use 802.1x port security, which authenticates the device.

Layer 3 Switch

Traditional switches work at Layer 2 of the OSI Reference Model and are susceptible to ARP attacks. However, a Layer 3 switch operates at the network layer using the IP address, and they route packets the same as a router and are high-performance switches. They operate using IP and not MAC addresses and this means that they are not affected by ARP attacks as they operate at Layer 2.

Proxy Server

A proxy server is a server that acts as an intermediary for requests from clients seeking resources on the internet or an external network. Think of it as a go-between who makes requests on behalf of the client, ensuring that anyone outside of your network does not know the details of the requesting host.

The flow of data is from internal to external and it has three main functions; URL filter, content filter and web page caching.

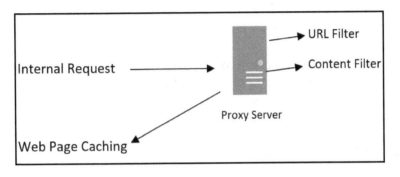

Figure 8: Proxy server

- **URL Filter**: When a user goes to a website, they type the URL, for example, `www.nfl.com`. Companies may not want their employees going to Facebook or Twitter during working hours, so these websites are placed on the default block page. The URL filter checks the default block page to see whether there is a website that should be blocked - you will get a warning stating the page is blocked and you cannot access it; additionally, your attempt to access it will be logged.
- **Content Filter**: Looks at the content on the requested web page. It will block the request if the site involves gambling or inappropriate content.
- **Web Page Caching**: Most companies within the same industry tend to go to certain websites related to their line of business, or at lunchtimes people look at the sport results. Each time they go to the internet, a session is opened through the firewall; this allows an unsecured session to be seen and also consumes bandwidth. A more secure way of doing this is to have a proxy server cache the pages, but they need to ensure that the frequency of caching ensures that the content is relevant. You could never cache the stock market as the price fluctuates second by second.

The purpose of caching is to reduce the bandwidth being used and also make the access to web pages faster as they are actually obtaining content from their Local Area Network (LAN). There are different types of caching:

- **Active Caching**: The IT team sets up jobs to cache web pages, for example, they cache www.nfl.com at 3 a.m local time to ensure it has the latest results.
- **Caching**: When new web pages are being requested (as long as they are not blocked by a filter), the pages are fetched and submitted to the requesting host and a copy is then placed in the cache. That way, the second time it is requested, it is retrieved from the cache.
- **Transparent Cache**: Intercepts the request by the host and does not modify the search.
- **Non-Transparent Cache**: Intercepts and verifies the request is valid. It looks at the URL filter to see whether the site is blocked. It is used to stop people from caching web pages that are restricted.
- **Application Proxy**: Deals with requests on behalf of another server. A page within an online shop that loads its content and displays data from another location outside of the shop.

Reverse Proxy

The flow of traffic from a reverse proxy is incoming traffic from the internet coming into your company network. The reverse proxy is placed in a boundary network called the Demilitarized Zone (DMZ). It performs the authentication and decryption of a secure session to enable it to filter the incoming traffic.

For example, if a company sets up a webinar through Skype or another video conference application, they can invite potential customers. All of the conferencing requests will pass through a reverse proxy that authenticates them and redirects their session to the relevant Skype server.

Remote Access

There are times when people who are working remotely need to access the company's network to access resources. There are two main types of remote access:

- **Remote Access Server (RAS)**: A legacy server where the dial-up networking is used, it is expensive as you need to pay the same cost as a telephone call. The server is located in the company network and the client has the software installed to allow communication. Each side has a modem that converts the digital communications in the computer to analog communication that can be transmitted over telephone lines. The speed of the modem is up to 56 Kbps - this makes the communication very slow. If you use dial-up networking to access the internet, the pages would load very slowly and look like a map; this is why it has been discontinued.

- **Virtual Private Network (VPN)**: This is located in the company's network and the client has software to allow the connection, but it utilizes the internet; this makes it cheaper to use. Most hotels offer free Wi-Fi and the sessions can be free. The downside is that the internet is the public highway and a secure tunnel is used to protect against attack. The main tunneling protocols are as follows:
  - **L2TP/IPSec**: This is the most secure tunneling protocol that can use certification, Kerberos authentication, or a preshared key. L2TP/IPSec provides both a secure tunnel and authentication.
  - **Secure Socket Layer (SSL) VPN**: This works on legacy systems and uses SSL certificates for authentication.

Exam tip:
L2TP/IPsec is the only tunneling protocol in the exam objectives; you need to know it thoroughly, especially how IPSec works, both the **Authenticated Header** (**AH**) and **Encapsulated Payload** (**ESP**). The only other VPN that is mentioned is the legacy SSL VPN that uses an SSL certificate. IPSec tunnel mode is used across external networks, where IPSec transport mode is used between server to server locally.

Virtual Private Network using L2TP/IPSec

Before we look at the tunneling protocols, we need to learn a little about encryption - there are two main types of encryption: asymmetric and symmetric. Encryption is the process of taking data in plain-text format and transferring it to cipher-text, a format that makes it unreadable. Encryption is covered in depth later in this book. The two main types are as follows:

- **Asymmetric Encryption**: Certificates are used for encryption and it uses two keys: a private key and a public key. The public key is used for encrypting data and the private key is used for decrypting data.

- **Symmetric Encryption**: This uses only one key, called either the private key or shared key, for both encrypting and decrypting data, making it much faster but less secure than asymmetric encryption. Having only one key makes it quicker for encrypting and decrypting large amounts of data; the downside is that it is less secure due to the fact that if someone obtains the private/shared key, they can both encrypt and decrypt the data. When we use symmetric encryption, we tend to create a secure tunnel using an asymmetric technique called Diffie Hellman to create a secure tunnel before the symmetric data is sent across the network or internet.

- **Key Length**: Certificate keys are formed in units called bits. The fewer the bits, the faster it is to encrypt and decrypt, while a higher number of bits means it is slower to encrypt or decrypt but it is more secure. Typically, we don't use asymmetric keys smaller than 4,096 bits.

Exam tip:
Symmetric encryption is used to encrypt and decrypt large amounts of data as it uses only one key, making it faster than asymmetric, which uses two keys.

A VPN creates a tunnel across the internet, normally from home or a remote site to your work. We need to look at the L2TP/IPSec tunnel that works at Layer 2 of the OSI Reference Model where IPSec is used to encrypt the data; an IPSec packet is formed of two different portions:

- **AH**: Consists of either SHA-1 (160 bits) or MD5 (128 bits) hashing protocols, which ensure that the packet header has not been tampered with in transit
- **ESP**: Uses either DES (56 bits), 3 DES (168 bits), or AES (256 bits); these are all symmetric encryption protocols, which means that they can transfer data much faster

IPSec

IPSec can be used to create a secure session between a client computer and a server. For example, you may have the financial data on a financial server. All members of the finance team will have IPSec tunnels created between their desktops and the financial server. This will prevent anyone using a packet sniffer stealing data from the financial server or any session across the network. This is known as IPSec Transport mode.

IPSec can also be used as a VPN protocol as part of the L2TP/IPSec tunneling protocol that is used by major vendors who create VPN solutions, such as CISCO, Microsoft, Sonic Wall, or Checkpoint. This is known as IPSec Tunnel mode.

IPSec – Handshake

The first stage of an IPSec session is to create a secure tunnel - this is known as a security association. In the Security+ exam, this is called **Internet Key Exchange** (**IKE**). Diffie Hellman is used to set up a secure tunnel before the data.

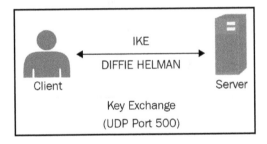

IKE

DIFFIE HELMAN

Client

Server

Key Exchange
(UDP Port 500)

Figure 9: Diffie Helman

The IKE phase of the IPSec session is using Diffie Hellman over UDP `port 500` to create what is known as quick mode. This creates a secure session so that the data can flow through it.

The second phase is where the data is encrypted with DES, 3 DES, or AES. AES provides the most secure VPN session as it uses 128, 192, or 256 bits. There are two different IPSec modes:

- **Tunnel Mode**: Tunnel mode is where the IPSec session is used across the internet as part of the L2TP/IPSec tunnel.
- **Transport mode**: Transport mode is where the IPSec tunnel is created with an internal network using client/server to server communication.

VPN Concentrator

The purpose of the VPN concentrator is to set up the secure tunnel during the IKE phase. It needs to create a full IPSec tunnel. This is normally when you have a site-to-site VPN.

Site-to-Site VPN

A site-to-site VPN is where you have two different sites, each with a VPN concentrator at each site and it acts as a leased line. The session is set to **Always On** as opposed to dial on demand:

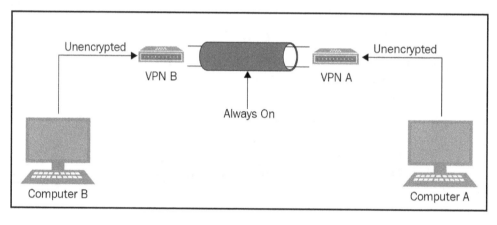

Figure 10: Site-to-site VPN

VPN Always On v On-Demand

There are two main session types: the first is **on-demand**, where a remote worker initiates a VPN session from home or a remote location, and when they finish the session the connection is dropped. The second is where a site-to-site VPN is set up and the session is known as **always on**, where the session is permanent.

SSL VPN

SSL VPN is a VPN that can be used with a web browser that uses an SSL certificate for the encryption. It has been replaced in recent times with **Transport Layer Security (TLS)**, which is a more modern version of SSL. In the Security+ exam, the SSL VPN is normally used for legacy VPNs that don't support L2TP/IPSec and use a SSL certificate.

Exam tip:
SSL VPN is the only VPN to use an SSL certificate, and it only needs a web browser to make a connection. It could also be replaced by the more secure TLS certificate.

Split Tunneling

Split tunneling is where a secure VPN session is connected and the user opens an unsecured session that would allow the hacker to come in through the unsecured session and gain access to your company's network:

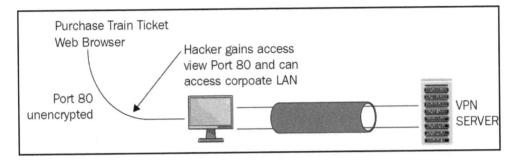

Figure 11: Split tunnel

For example, John connects his L2TP/IPSec session into the company network, then he realizes that he needs a train ticket for tomorrow. Instead of dropping the secure session and then going to the rail website, he leaves it connected. Once he opens up his web browser, he is using HTTP on TCP `port 80`, which is unsecured. This means that, while he has the web browser open, a hacker could access his desktop and use the secure tunnel to gain access to the company network.

Exam tip: A VPN should always set up a full tunnel; no other form of tunneling, such as split tunneling, should be used.

Load Balancer

A network load balancer is a device that is used when there is a high volume of traffic coming into the company's network or web server. It can be used to control access to web servers, video conferencing, or email.

In the Security+ exam, it is normally a high volume of web traffic. From *Figure 12*, you can see that the web traffic comes into the load balancer from the **Virtual IP address** (**VIP**) on the frontend and is sent to one of the web servers in the server farm:

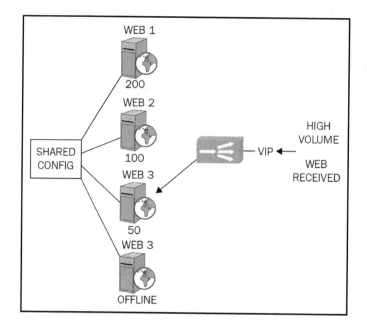

Figure 12: Load balancer

- **Least Utilized Host**: The benefits of a load-balancer are that it knows the status of all of the web servers in the server farms and knows which web servers are the least utilized by using a scheduling algorithm.

  The load balancer has selected to send the request to **Web 3**, which has the least number of requests (**50**), and **Web 4** will not be considered as it is currently offline. A user requesting three different pages may obtain them from different web servers but may not know this as the load balancer is optimizing the delivery of the web pages to the user.

- **Affinity**: When the load balancer is set to *Affinity*, the request is sent to the same web server based on the requester's IP address. The reason for this is that maybe in one region there is limited bandwidth for other web servers in the server farm.
- **DNS Round Robin**: The load balancer could be set to use DNS round robin as in *Figure 13*:

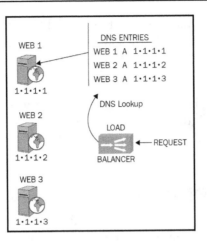

Figure 13: DNS Round Robin

While using DNS round robin when the request comes in, the load balancer contacts the DNS server and rotates the request based on the lowest IP address first, rotates around **Web 1**, **2**, and **3**, and then keeps the sequence going by going back to **Web 1** on a rotational basis.

Clustering

Clustering is where two servers share a quorum disk on the backend. The normal setup is the active-passive configuration, as shown in *Figure 14*, and it is commonly used for email or database servers:

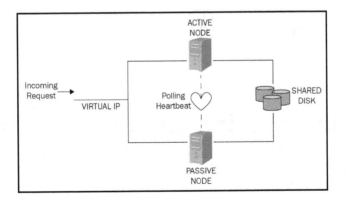

Figure 14: Clustering

In the above diagram, the request comes to the **Virtual IP** that sends the request to the active node that fulfills the request. In the background, the passive node is also connected to the shared disk, but has a heartbeat polling the active node. If the active node fails, the passive takes over.

The other mode of clustering is where both nodes are active in an active-active configuration. With this configuration, both nodes need to have enough resources to act as a dual active node without suffering from a bottleneck.

Data-Loss Prevention

Data-Loss Prevention (DLP) can stop unencrypted sensitive and **Personally Identifiable Information (PII)** from inadvertently leaving the company. It cannot scan encrypted data. There are two separate ways it can prevent data loss:

- **USB flash drive**: DLP can be set up on a file server to prevent data being copied onto a USB flash drive
- **Email**: Templates can be set up with regular expressions to stop data being sent out in email format

For example, an auditor has found that the credit card details of customers have been sent out of the company by email, and this needs to be prevented in the future. The company only accepts VISA, Mastercard, and American Express. The solution would be to set up a DLP template with the regular expression format for VISA, Mastercard, and American Express. As emails leave the company, they are scanned for this format and if it is included in an email, it is blocked and the security administrator is informed.

 Exam tip: DLP prevents PII and sensitive data from being inserted into an email or copied onto a USB flash drive.

Security Information and Event Management

A **Security Information and Event-Management (SIEM)** system automates the collection of log files from multiple hosts, servers, and network devices, such as firewalls, in real time to identify potential risks to the network.

The types of functionality from a SIEM system are as follows:

- **Aggregation**: The SIEM system can move log files and data from multiple sources to a common repository.
- **Event Correlation**: A SIEM system uses a correlation engine to correlate events from multiple systems. For example, if someone tried to log in to three separate devices, the SIEM server will notify the security administrator of a potential attack. When the same event is duplicated and is logged by different devices, the SIEM system will use event de-duplication to ensure that the event is logged only once.
- **WORM Drive Backup**: The logs from a SIEM system can be vital to the security team, therefore, they can be backed up onto a WORM drive, write-once, read-many. This allows log files to be backed up onto the WORM drive, but prevents the alteration or deletion of events.
- **Automated Alerting and Triggers**: A SIEM system could install agents on several devices so that the SIEM system is alerted when several events occur.
- **Time Synchronization:** A SIEM server relies on time synchronization from a Stratum Zero or the Atomic Clock time source so that time can be synchronized and events can be put into chronological order.

Mail Gateway

A mail gateway is a device that sits in a DMZ to scan incoming and outgoing email for viruses. It can also act as a spam filter, preventing spam emails from reaching the internal mail server.

Cloud-Based Email

Due to email being a critical function for businesses, more and more companies are moving away from in-house, server-based solutions, and are using Microsoft Office 365 or Google G Suite. The benefits of cloud-based email are that the cloud provider is responsible for scanning the incoming email as well as providing the hardware to run the mail servers.

Media Gateway

A media gateway is a translation device or service that converts media streams between disparate telecommunications technologies. An example of this is Karaka, which is an XMPP Gateway that allows communication between Jabber and Skype.

Hardware Security Module

A **Hardware Security Module** (**HSM**) is a physical device that stores the X509 certificates used on a network. These modules traditionally come in the form of a plug-in card or an external device that attaches directly to a computer or network server.

Software-Defined Network

Traditional networks route packets via a hardware router and are decentralized; however, in today's networks more and more people are using virtualization, including cloud providers. A **Software-Defined Network** (**SDN**) is where packets are routed through a controller rather than traditional routers, which improves performance.

Secure Network Architecture Concepts

Securing networks and protecting them is vital to protect a company's assets. We use different zones and topologies, network separation and segmentation, and install firewalls to prevent unauthorized access to the network. First of all, let's look at different zones and topologies. There are three main zones - LAN, WAN, and DMZ:

- **Local Area Network (LAN)**: A secure network with very fast links and a web server, called the intranet, that holds internal-only information, such as classified data, manufacturing price lists, or the internal forms library.
- **Demilitarized Zone (DMZ)**: A boundary layer between the LAN and the WAN that holds information that companies may want people from the internet to access. You may put your email server in the DMZ but never a domain controller. The web server inside the DMZ is called the extranet, which needs a username and password to access the site. It could be used for an area that a distributor log into to get a newly released price list.

- **Wide Area Network (WAN):** Open to the public and not a safe place, as it is freely accessible, the web server inside the WAN is the internet. The internet is an example of a WAN, and any data traversing the internet needs to be encrypted. It covers a very large geographic area and the links tend to be slower than the LAN and DMZ.

For example, an upscale store sells designer sneakers at $230, however, the shop's owner purchases them from the manufacturer by placing orders on the extranet server. Access to the extranet web server is via a unique username and password, and the price the shop purchases the sneakers at is $125, allowing for a profit of $105. On the intranet, the web server is the manufacturing price of the sneakers, which are made in China, for a mere $5 a pair:

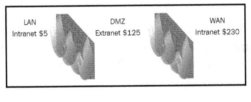

Figure 15: Zones

From this information, you should ask yourself three simple questions:

- What would happen if the customer knew that the shop owner was making a profit of $105? They would definitely want a discount.
- What would happen if the shop owner discovered the manufacturing price was $5? They would also like a discount.
- What would happen if the customer found out that their designer sneakers were made for $5? They may decide not to purchase them as they are really cheap sneakers in disguise and, through social media, the manufacturer would lose market share.

You can see why data in a LAN needs to be secure and not freely available to the general public.

Network Address Translation (NAT)

Network Address Translation (NAT) is where a request from a private internal IP address is translated to an external public IP address, hiding the internal network from external attack. See *Figure 16*:

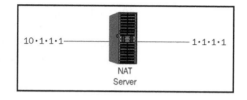

Figure 16: NAT

A NAT could be set up to hide a R&D network where new products are designed. Remember, a competitor may try to steal your new ideas and get them to market before you. A NAT could be set up on a firewall or a NAT server.

Port Address Translation (PAT)

Port Address Translation (**PAT**) is where multiple internal requests are translated to an external IP address; see *Figure 17*:

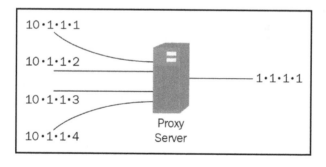

Figure 17: PAT

A proxy server could be used for PAT as it gets many internal requests that are translated to one external IP address.

Network Access Control (NAC)

If you have a Windows desktop or laptop and you go away on holiday for 2-3 weeks, when you come back your device may need multiple updates.

After a remote client has authenticated, NAC, then checks that the device being used is fully patched. See *Figure 18*:

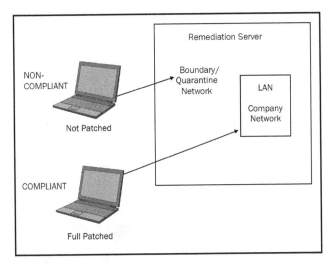

Figure 18: NAC

When the user is authenticated, the **Health Authority (HAuth)** checks against the registry of the client device to ensure that it is fully patched. A fully patched machine is deemed compliant and allowed access to the LAN. In the above diagram, the bottom **Laptop** is compliant. If the device is not fully patched, it is deemed noncompliant and is redirected to a boundary network, which could also be known as a quarantine network. The components of NAC are as follows:

- **Host Health Checks**: The Health Authority checks the health of the incoming device to ensure that it is fully patched.
- **Compliant/Non-Compliant Device**: A device that is fully patched is compliant, but a device that has missing patches is deemed non-compliant.
- **Agents**: Each device has an agent installed so that the HAuth can carry out health checks. The two types of agents are as follows:
  - **Permanent**: The agent is installed on the host
  - **Dissolvable**: A dissolvable agent is known as temporary and agentless and is installed for a single use

- **Remediation Server**: Sits on the boundary or quarantine network. When the non-compliant machine is connected to the boundary network, it can obtain the missing updates from the remediation server. Once the device is fully patched, it is then allowed to access the LAN.

Honeypot

When security teams are trying to find out the attack methods that hackers are using, they set up a website similar to the legitimate website with lower security, known as a honeypot. When the attack commences, the security team monitors the attack methods so that they can prevent future attacks. Another reason a honeypot is set up is as a decoy so that the real web server is not attacked. A group of honeypots is called a honeynet.

Exam tip: A honeypot can be used to examine the attack method that hackers use.

Secure Socket Layer Accelerators

Secure Socket Layer (SSL) is used to encrypt data so that when it is in transit it cannot be stolen or altered. SSL encryption is a processor-intensive operation and most servers, such as database servers, are working very hard as it is. SSL acceleration refers to offloading the processor-intensive SSL encryption and decryption from a server to a device, such as a reverse proxy, to relieve the pressure from the server.

SSL/TLS Decryptor

When traffic comes into your network from the internet and it is encrypted, the firewall, NIPS, NIDS, DLP, or any network device cannot examine the data. Therefore, after the traffic has passed through the external firewall, the SSL/TLS decryptor will decrypt the data before it passes through an inline NIPS. This then means that the NIPS can examine and prevent malicious traffic from accessing the local area network.

Sensor/Collector

A sensor/collector can be a device, tap, or firewall log whose purpose is to alert the NIDS of any changes in traffic patterns within the network. If you place your first sensor on the internet side of your network, it will scan all of the traffic from the internet.

Tap/Port Mirror

A tap or a port mirror is set up on a port of a switch so that when the data arrives at that port, a copy is stored on another device for later investigation or it is sent to a sensor who will investigate the traffic and, if needs be, inform the NIDS of changes in traffic patterns.

DDoS Mitigator

A **Distributed Denial of Service (DDoS)** attack is where a very large amount of traffic is sent to a switch or a server so that it is overwhelmed and cannot function. A DDoS mitigator is a device, such as a stateful firewall on the external interface of your DMZ or a flood guard on an internal switch, that can identify the DDoS attack at an early stage and prevent it from being successful.

Exam tip: Capturing the data flowing through a port on a switch can be done by port mirroring, also known as a tap.

Segregation/Segmentation/Isolation

Cyber crime is rife and is the largest growing criminal industry. In today's word, most businesses are interconnected and use the internet. Maintaining the security and integrity of data, including research and development, is paramount. We need to be able to isolate, segment, or segregate our network, both physically and virtually. Let's look at the options we have:

- **Physical Segmentation/Separation**: If we have data, such as email or a web server, that we want people to be able to access from the internet, whether it be a customer or one of our salespeople, we will physically separate it from our LAN by placing it in the DMZ, which is a boundary layer, so that users accessing this data do not need to come into our secure LAN. You would never place a domain controller or a database server in the DMZ.

- **Air Gaps**: Another physical method is to create air gaps between some systems that we use internally to separate confidential systems from normal systems:
  - **Example 1**: The US department of defense has two distinct networks: the **Secret Internet Protocol Router Network** (**SIPRNet**), where classified data such as top secret or secret documentation are accessed, and the **Non-classified Internet Protocol Router Network** (**NIPRNet**) where unclassified data is held. These two private networks have air gaps between them so that a desktop from the NIPRNet cannot access the SIPRNet or vice versa.
  - **Example 2**: In a finance department, there is one computer that would be used to make electronic payments, such as BACS or CHAPS transfers, and this machine would not be accessible by everyone in that finance department, therefore it would be isolated from the other departmental machines - this is also an example of an air gap.

- **Logical Separation - VLAN**: There is sometimes a need to create a separate logical network within the LAN to segment a department from the rest of the internal network. The device that connects all of the internal computers is called a switch, but within a switch we have the ability to create a **Virtual Local Area Network** (**VLAN**). If you look at *Figure 19*, you can see a switch with two separate VLANs:

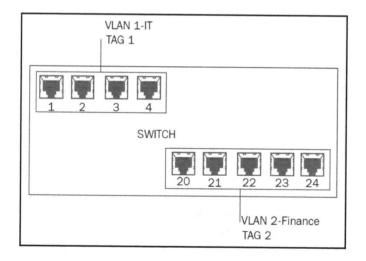

Figure 19: Two VLANS in a switch

A VLAN is created by using the software on the switch where you can bond a number of ports to work together as a separate logical network. If you look at *Figure 19*, you can see that port numbers 1-4 have been used to create a VLAN for the IT department, and then ports 20-24 have been used to create another VLAN for the finance department. Although both of these departments are on an internal device, creating the VLANs isolates them from other VLANs and the company's network. An important factor is that a VLAN tag is set up so that when traffic arrives at the switch, it knows where to send it.

- **Virtualization:** If we create a virtual network, we can isolate the users on that network from other users on the same virtual network using VLANs. On a virtual host, I can create many different isolated virtual networks. Virtualization is covered in Chapter 6, *Understanding Cloud Models and Virtualization*.

Security Device/Technology Placement

It is important for a security or network administrator to understand the functionality that each device provides and where best to place them to ensure that your network is safe. *Figure 20* shows the placement of each device:

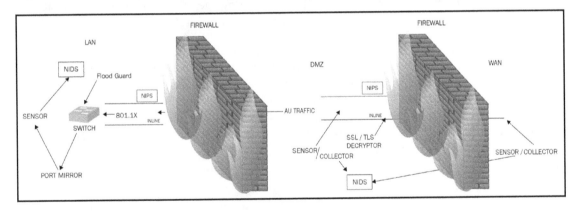

Figure 20: Security device placement

If we look at *Figure 20*, the first thing you will notice is that the three network zones that have been established are the LAN, DMZ, and WAN. These networks are divided by two firewalls that are in a back-to-back configuration so that, if traffic manages to get through the first firewall, we hope that the next firewall stops it. As resources, such as our website, are in the DMZ, the external firewall may have one or two ports open that the internal firewall between the DMZ and LAN does not have.

DMZ - Device Placement

Between the WAN and DMZ there is a network firewall. The purpose of this firewall is to prevent unauthorized access to the network. Directly behind the external firewall is an SSL/TLS decryptor that decrypts the traffic coming in so that other security devices can examine it.

The next stage is that the decrypted traffic is placed through an inline NIPS. As it is inline, all traffic must pass through it. The purpose of the NIPS is as an additional layer of security and should be placed close to the external firewall.

Behind the NIPS is the NIDS in passive mode, where traffic does not travel through it but it is scanning the network for changes in traffic patterns. The NIPS in the DMZ scans the network and has sensors/collection places in the DMZ to alert it to changes in traffic patterns.

LAN - Device Placement

The firewall dividing the DMZ and the LAN will be a stateful firewall that will prevent DDoS attacks and knows of the acceptable commands used by each application. Directly behind the firewall will be another inline NIPS examining the traffic as it comes into the LAN. Another NIDS and a set of sensors/collectors are placed in the LAN.

The internal switch connects all of the internal devices, and it will be a managed switch using 802.1x so that it authenticates all devices connecting to the network and stops unauthorized devices and rogue WAP from connecting to the network. The switch will have a flood guard installed to prevent DDoS and MAC flooding attacks. The switch may have a port mirror installed on one of the ports so that a copy of the traffic, stored on a backup device for later investigation, is sent to a sensor. Should the sensor identify anything abnormal, it will notify the NIDS in the LAN. A port mirror is also known as a tap.

Aggregation Switches

Depending on the number of users that reside in your LAN, you may need several switches to be operating, and these switches need to move traffic between each other. Therefore, rather than having a daisy chain, which would take more time to move the traffic around, we install an aggregation switch. The aggregation switch connects multiple switches in a mode called link aggregation:

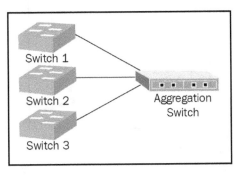

Figure 21: Aggregation switch

Link aggregation is a way of joining Ethernet links together so they act like a single, logical link. If you connect all of the switches together, you can balance the traffic among these links to improve performance. An important reason for using link aggregation is to provide fast and transparent recovery in case one of the individual links fails.

Implementing Secure Protocols Segregation/Segmentation/Isolation

A protocol is the rules required by different applications for the exchange of data where the application can perform actions such as running commands on remote systems, sending and receiving email, or maybe downloading files from the internet. Each application has a special port number it uses for communication. If you think of ports as being TV channels, if we want to watch sport we go to the sports channels, if we want to watch news we go to the news channel. Applications are the same; if we want to send an email, we use a mail application, and they all have a distinct port number for communication.

There are two types of ports: **Transmission Control Protocol** (**TCP**) and **User Datagram Protocol** (**UDP**). The main difference between the two is that the TCP is connection-orientated as it uses a three-way handshake, and UDP is faster but less reliable as it is connectionless. See *Figure 22* for the three-way handshake:

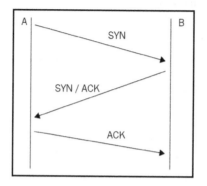

Figure 22: Three-way handshake

In a three-way handshake, the first packet that is sent is called a SYN packet, where the sending host informs the receiving host of the number of its next packet. The receiving host sends a SYN-ACK packet where it says what its next packet is. The ACK packet acknowledges both, and then the data is sent. The data is sent in chunks, and where it is received, an acknowledgment is sent that tells the sending host to send more packets. Once all of the data is sent, a three-way handshake confirms all of the data is intact and the session closes.

In a UDP session, the application is responsible for ensuring that everything is received, and because a three-way handshake is not used, the connection is faster but less reliable. You would use UDP for streaming video, where speed is paramount.

For the purpose of the Security+ examination, you will need to know when to choose the correct protocol and which port it uses. A list of common protocols is listed here with their uses later.

As most protocols use TCP ports, I will only mention the UDP ports and therefore you can assume if it is not labeled UDP, it is TCP:

Protocol	UDP	Port	Use
File Transfer Protocol (FTP)		21	File transfer - passive FTP
Secure Shell (SSH)		22	Run remote command - securely
Secure Copy Protocol (SCP)		22	Secure copy to UNIX/LINUX
Secure FTP (SFTP)		22	Secure FTP download
Telnet		23	Run remote command - unsecure
Simple Mail Transport Protocol (SMTP)		25	Transport mail between Mail Servers
Domain Name System (DNS)	TCP/UDP	53 53 53	Host name resolution Zone transfer Name queries
Dynamic Host Configuration Protocol (DHCP)	UDP	67/68	Automatic IP address allocation
Trivial File Transfer Protocol (TFTP)	UDP	69	File transfer using UDP
Hypertext Transport Protocol (HTTP)		80	Web browser
Kerberos		88	Microsoft authentication using tickets
Post Office Protocol 3		110	Pull mail from mail server, no copy left on mail server
NETBIOS	UDP	137-139	NETBIOS to IP address resolution
Internet Message Access Protocol (IMAP 4)		143	Pull mail from mail server
Simple Network Management Protocol (SNMP)	UDP	161	Notifies the status and creates reports on network devices
Simple Network Management Protocol Version 3 (SNMP v3)	UDP	162	Secure version of SNMP
Lightweight Directory Access Protocol (LDAP)		389	Stores X500 objects, searches for active directory information
Lightweight Directory Access Protocol Secure (LDAPS)		636	Secure LDAP where the session is encrypted

Secure Internet Message Access Protocol (IMAP 4)		993	Secure IMAP4
Secure Post Office Protocol 3		995	Secure POP3
File Transfer Protocol Secure (FTPS)		989/990	Download of large files securely
Remote Desktop Protocol (RDP)		3389	Microsoft remote access
Session Initiated Protocol (SIP)		5060/5061	Connects internet based calls
Secure Real Time Protocol (SRTP)		5061	Secure voice traffic

Exam tip: Knowing why we use each protocol is more important than knowing the port numbers. There will be a review at the end of this book testing port numbers.

Use Case

A use case is where everyone in a company tries to achieve a goal. An example would be if you called a company, their customer services take your order, their finance department processes the payment, production would make the product, and then dispatch would mail it to you. Another way of looking at use cases is that they are an example of how something is used. In the following examples, we will see use cases for different protocols.

File Transfer – Use Case

Transferring files is a common function. When we purchase an e-book, it is immediately available to download onto our Kindle. There are four different protocols that we can use for file transfers:

- **File Transfer Protocol (FTP)**: If I wish to upload files to a web server, I would use FTP on port 20, but the more common use is to download files using port 21, which is known as Passive FTP. The downside of using FTP is that the transfer is in clear text, so a packet sniffer could view the information.
- **Secure FTP (SFTP)**: This allows me to download files securely so that they cannot be tampered with. It is secure as it is packaged with SSH.

- **Trivial File Transfer Protocol (TFTP)**: The UDP version of a file transfer; it is faster than FTP as it does not use a three-way handshake, but it is not secure as the files are transferred in clear text. It is used when user authentication is not required.
- **File Transfer Protocol Secure (FTPS)**: FTPS is much faster than SFTP as it uses two ports, 989 and 990, and is used for downloading very large files securely.

> **Exam Tip**: SSH is a secure method of running a command on a router.

Remote Access – Use Case

There are various ways to obtain remote access; we are going to look at each in turn and decide when we would choose to use them:

- **Telnet**: A protocol that was first used, in 1973 to run remote commands on devices, such as routers. Unfortunately, the session is in clear text and therefore not secure. If you want to know whether port 25 is opening on a mail server called Mail1, you could run `telnet Mail1 25`. It is no longer used as it is unsecure but may be tested.
- **Secure Shell (SSH)**: Invented in 1991 to replace Telnet so that it could run commands securely; it is commonly used when you want to perform remote access onto routers.
- **Remote Desktop Protocol (RDP)**: A Microsoft product that allows you to run a secure remote access session on a Windows desktop or server. When you set up remote access using RDP, the service obtaining the session needs to allow access for incoming remote sessions and then place the users into the remote desktop users group. If these two actions are not taken, it will not work. As most routers are CISCO products, RDP cannot be used to remote into a router.
- **Remote Access Server (RAS)**: A legacy server that allows remote access via a modem and telephone line and therefore is very rarely used.
- **Virtual Private Network (VPN)**: Used to create a secure tunnel from home or a remote location into your work. The most common protocol is L2TP/IPSec, which is used in tunnel mode across the internet. If you have a legacy system pre-2000 VPN, you would use an SSL VPN that requires an SSL certificate.

Email – Use Case

There are different types of email, some are web-based and some use the MAPI client on the desktop. Let's look at each of them and understand when we would use them:

- **Simple Mail Transport Protocol (SMTP)**: Used to transfer files between different mail servers and is used for outbound emails.
- **Simple Mail Transfer Protocol Secure (SMTPS)**: Encrypts the mail being transferred between mail servers, making it very secure.
- **Post Office Protocol 3 (POP3)**: An email client that pulls email from the mail server, but when the email is downloaded it does not retain a copy on the mail server itself. It is not commonly used, but is tested in the Security+ exam. There is also a secure version of POP3.
- **Internet Message Access Protocol version 4 (IMAP4)**: A mail client that also pulls emails from the mail server, but it has more functionality than POP3 as a copy of the message is retained on the mail server. It can also provide tasks, calendars, and journaling. There is also a version of secure IMAP. An easy way to remember the port number for IMAP4 is to pretend the first letter of IMAP is number 1. Then take the last figure, which is 4, for the second digit, and then take 1 from 4 to get 3 for your third digit, giving you 143, the actual port number.
- **Web Mail (HTTPS)**: Web mail, such as Microsoft's Outlook Anywhere, is accessed via a secure web browser and uses the HTTPS protocol.
- **Secure/Multipurpose Internet Mail Extensions(S/MIME)**: Uses **Public Key Infrastructure** (PKI) to either encrypt the email or digitally sign the email to prove the integrity of the message. It is very cumbersome as it requires each user to exchange their public key with each other and does not scale very well.

Name Resolution – Use Case

There are two types of name resolution: hostname resolution, which is the most common, and NETBIOS, which is a legacy name resolution that is very rarely used.

Hostname

The most common form of name resolution is hostname resolution, a database of hostnames to IP addresses called DNS that uses a flat file called the hosts file:

- **Domain Name System** (**DNS**): This is a hierarchical naming system that takes a hostname and resolves it to an IP address. I don't need to know the actual IP Address. If I want to go to the Microsoft website, I know that I need to enter `www.microsoft.com` in my web browser and it will take me there. If I have a user called Ian in a domain called `ianneil501.com`, the hostname portion would be Ian and the **Fully-Qualified Domain Name** (**FQDN**) would be `ian.ianneil501.com`. Entries in the DNS database are as follows:
  - **A**: IPV 4 host
  - **AAAA**: IPV6 host
  - **CNAME**: Alias
  - **MX**: Mail server
  - **SRV records**: Finds services such as a domain controller

For example, a user would like to visit the website of `http://ianneil501.com`; to get there, they would enter `www.ianneil501.com` in their web browser as per *Figure 23*. The hostname resolution follows a strict process:

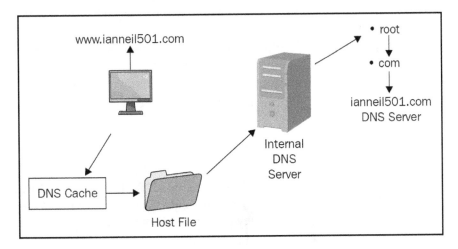

Figure 23: Hostname resolution

In *Figure 23*, the hostname resolution adopts a strict process and takes the first entry for that hostname no matter whether it is right or wrong—this is a pitfall of the process. Let's look at this process starting with the DNS cache:

- **DNS cache**: Stores recently resolved names; if the cache is empty, attackers will attempt to poison the DNS cache by putting in wrong entries to divert you to a server where they can attack you or poison the DNS cache so that you cannot get to a legitimate server.
- In the preceding example, the DNS cache is empty so it would move onto the host file located on the local computer. If you need to view the DNS cache, you would run the `ipconfig /displaydns` command, and if you wanted to clear the DNS cache, you would run the `ipconfig /flushdns` command.
- **Hosts file**: This is a flat file where entries are manually inserted and read from the top to the bottom. It takes the first entry, whether right or wrong. The purpose of a host file is that, if one user needs to go to a server called Sneaky Beaky, I would put an entry for that server in his local hosts file that would allow them to go there. If I put the entry in the DNS server, that would allow anyone to find that server. In the preceding example, the hosts file is empty so name resolution would move to the DNS server, whose IP address is in the local computer's network card.
- **DNS server**: Normally maintains only the hostnames for your domain and would then need to complete a referral process through the root server of the internet, which is represented by a dot.
- **Root server**: The root server would then refer the request to the .com server, who in turn refers the request to the authoritative DNS server for the `ianneil501.com` domain, which would then reply with the IP address of the website.
- **Cache the reply**: A copy of the name resolution is placed in the DNS cache for future use.

DNSSEC

To prevent someone from gaining access to DNS records, DNSSEC was introduced to protect the DNS traffic. Each DNS record is digitally signed, creating an RRSIG record to protect against attacks assuring you that they are valid and their integrity has been maintained.

Exam tip: DNSSEC produces a RRSIG record for each host.

NETBIOS

NETBIOS is a Microsoft legacy naming convention that has a flat namespace of a maximum of 15 characters with a service identifier. Each computer name has three separate entries in its database, called WINS, and it uses a flat file, called the LMHosts file.

The entry for PC1 as a WINS database would be as follows:

- PC1 <00>: The <00> represents the workstation service
- PC2 <03>: The <03> represents the messenger service
- PC3 <20>: The <20> represents the server service

Web – Use Case

The majority of people use the internet to make purchases and research information, so it is important that we know what are the protocols used when accessing websites:

- **Hypertext Transfer Protocol (HTTP)**: Used to access websites, no matter whether you are using Internet Explorer, Chrome, Firefox, or Microsoft Edge.
- **Hypertext Transfer Protocol Secure (HTTPS)**: When you are using HTTP and adding items to your shopping cart, you will then be diverted to a secure server that uses HTTPS so that your session is secure and you can then enter your credit or debit card details.
- **Transport Layer Security (TLS)**: An upgraded version of SSL that is used to encrypt communications on the internet and transfer data securely, such as email or internet faxing. HTTPS is a common instance of it, DNSSEC is another.

Voice and Video – Use Case

In the past, when companies wanted meetings, such as a sales meeting, a date was set and the salespeople kept their schedule open, traveling to the location of the meeting the night before and booked themselves into a hotel. This was very costly and time-consuming; nowadays, we use video-conferencing where everyone connects to the meeting, does not have to travel, and can free their schedule, making them more productive. In the Security+ exam, we need to be able to understand which protocols are used. There are three main protocols:

- **Session Initiated Protocol (SIP)**: Allows people from all over the internet, and those with VoIP, to communicate using their computers, tablets, and smartphones. An example would be of a secretary who could receive a Skype call for the boss: SIP allows them to put the caller on hold, speak to their boss, and, if needs are, put the person through.
- **Real Time Protocol (RTP)**: Once SIP has established the session, RTP transfers the video-conferencing traffic.
- **Secure Real Time Protocol (SRTP)**: Used to secure the video-conferencing traffic - it normally uses TCP **port 5061**.
- **VLAN**: Voice traffic is placed in a VLAN segments it from the rest of the network, to give it the bandwidth to operate.
- **Media Gateway**: Allows different methods of video and voice to communicate with each other, for example, if you use an XMPP gateway, you can connect Jabber clients to a Skype session.

 Exam tip: Voice traffic should be placed in its own VLAN to ensure reliability.

Network Address Allocation – Use Case

If you have a network with 10,000 computers and, every morning, you needed to manually insert an IP address into the machine, it would be very time-consuming and there would be a very high chance that you would insert a typo and the IP address would be incorrect. There are two different IP addressing schemes: IP Version 4 and IP Version 6. Let's look at each of these in turn.

IP Version 4

The format of an IP Version 4 address is dotted decimal notation, composed of four octets making it 32-bit addressing, for example, `131.107.2.1`. The IP address class is taken by looking at the number on the left-hand side. The last digit on the right-hand side cannot be a zero as it is the network ID and cannot end in `255` as this is the broadcast ID.

The network ID is like a zip code; one person cannot have a zip code used by multiple people. The broadcast ID is used to send traffic to all hosts, therefore, we cannot use an IP address that ends in a zero or `255`.

There are public addresses that you can lease and private addresses that are free, but can only be used internally. If you have a banger car, you can drive it around private land all day long, but as soon as you put it on a public road without any insurance, if you were caught by the police, they would impound the car. Private IP addresses can operate internally, but the routers on the internet will drop any private IP packets.

There are three private IP address ranges:

- **Class A**: The first number on the left starts with 1-126, although 127 is technically a Class A address - we cannot allocate it to a host as it is used for diagnostic testing.
- **Class B**: The range is `172.16.x.x` to `172.31.x.x`. It is only a partial address range.
- **Class C**: The range is `192.168.x.x`, and it is the complete address range.

Each IP Version 4 client needs an IP address and a subnet mask whose job is to determine whether the packet delivery is local or remote. If the packet is for a remote address, then the client needs to be configured with a default gateway - the router interface on the LAN. If the client does not have a default gateway, then it is restricted to communicating on the local network. There are two appendices at the back of this book on subnetting and CIDR notation.

IP Version 4 addresses are allocated on a regional basis throughout the world:

Registry	Area covered
AfriNIC	Africa area
APNIC	Asia/Pacific region
ARIN	Canada, USA, and some Caribbean islands
LACNIC	Latin America and some Caribbean islands
RIPE NCC	Europe, the Middle East, and Central Africa

The automatic way of allocating IP addresses is to use a server called the **Dynamic Host Configuration Protocol** (**DHCP**) server. This is a server with a database of IP addresses that can allocate to requesting hosts; there is a four-stage process and it is known as D-O-R-A.

IP Version 4 – Lease Process

IP Version 4 follows the following steps to perform the lease:

1. **Discover**: When the client boots up, it sends a broadcast to find a DHCP server and can be identified by inserting its **Media Access Control** (**MAC**) address into the broadcast packet.
2. **Offer**: If the client is lucky enough to find a DHCP server, it then receives an offer packet by the DHCP server. If there are two DHCP servers, it will receive two offers.
3. **Request**: The client replies back to the DHCP server that it wants to obtain the address from.
4. **Acknowledgment**: The final packet from the DHCP server is the acknowledgment that included the IP address, subnet mask, default gateway, and DNS address.
5. **Command line**: To release and renew an IP address using the command line, we would run the `ipconfig /release` command and then the `ipconfig/renew` command.

IP Version 4 Lease Process – Troubleshooting

A DHCP client will not always obtain an IP address because maybe it cannot connect to the DHCP server. An unlikely reason is that the address pool is exhausted; in that case, the local machine will allocate an **Automated Private IP Address** (**APIPA**) starting with `169.254.x.x`. This is an excellent aid to troubleshooting, as it lets the network engineer know that the client cannot contact the DHCP server.

There are many reasons that this happens, so let's look at the DHCP process:

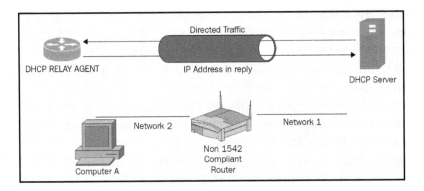

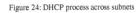

Figure 24: DHCP process across subnets

If the DHCP client is on another subnet, it can cause some problems:

- **RFC-1542 Compliant Router**: A device that connects different networks and subnets together. DHCP-broadcast traffic will pass through an RFC-1542-compliant router, but in *Figure 24*, the router is not a RFC-1542 compliant router, therefore broadcast traffic from **Computer A** will not get to the DHCP server, and an APIPA address will be allocated that will prevent the client from obtaining network resources.
- **Opening Ports**: If the router is a not an RFC-1542 compliant router, you could open UDP ports 67 and 68 by setting **allow** rules on the ACL of the router, otherwise the DHCP broadcast will suffer from an implicit deny.
- **DHCP Relay Agent**: A DHCP relay agent is programmed with the IP address of the DHCP server, therefore it contacts the server using unicast and not broadcast traffic. The DHCP relay agent acts as a set of ears listening for DHCP discover requests. It then acts as a proxy and obtains an IP address from the DHCP server to return to the requesting client.

IP Version 6 Addressing

IP Version 6 addresses are in a colon-hexadecimal format and comprise 8 blocks of 4 digits, making it a 128-bit address. The first 64 bits from the left-hand side are the routing or network portion, and the last 64 bits will be used for the host.

There are different address ranges and the main three are as follows:

- **Public**: The public addresses, just like the IP Version 4 addresses, can be used externally. They start on the right-hand side with `2001`, `2002`, or `2003` value. An example is `2001: ABCD:0000:0000:0000:0000:1230:0ABC`.
- **Link Local**: Link local are like the APIPA IP Version 4 address; they are restricted to one subnet and start with `fe80`.
- **Unique Local**: Unique local addresses are sometimes known as site-local addresses; they are restricted to a site and start with either `fc00` or `fd00`. A site is a number of IP subnets.
- **Simplify - Removing Leading Zeros**: An IP Version 6 address can be simplified by removing leading zeros and replacing a number of blocks of `0000` with a double colon. Here are two examples:

Example 1: We have an IP Version 6 address of `2001:ABCD:0000:0000:0000:0000:1230:0ABC` that we want to simplify; in this case, we will remove only the leading zeros:

- `2001:ABCD:0000:0000:0000:0000:1230:0ABC`
- `2001:ABCD::1230:ABC`

You will notice that we have replaced four blocks of zeros with double colons. We need to count the remaining blocks and, since there are four, we know that four blocks are missing.

Example 2: We have an IP Version 6 address of `2001:ABCD:0000:0000:ABCD:0000:1230:0ABC` that we want to simplify. In this case, we will remove only the leading zeros:

- `2001:ABCD:0000:0000:ABCD:0000:1230:0ABC`
- `2001:ABCD::ABCD:0:1230:ABC`

You will notice that this is trickier as there are blocks of zero in two places, but we replace the first blocks of zeros with the double colons, and then, if we have further blocks of zeros, we replace each of these with `:0:`. In the example, we count only six blocks, therefore we know we have only two blocks of zeros.

Subscription Services – Use Case

In the past, the traditional method for purchasing application software was to purchase the application on a DVD from a local store or wait 3-4 days for it to be delivered from Amazon. At that time, you would have to pay $300–$400 for the software. With the evolution of the cloud, there is now a tendency to obtain your applications through subscription services, where you pay a monthly fee and can download the application immediately. Two examples of this are as follows:

- **Office 365**: Office 365 from Microsoft, where you not only get your email but you also get Skype, SharePoint, and Office applications
- **Adobe Acrobat Pro**: Adobe Acrobat Pro is one of the premier applications that allows you to create and modify PDF files

Routing – Use Case

The purpose of a router is to connect networks together, whether it be internal subnets or external networks and route packets between them. A router sits at Layer 3 of the OSI Reference Model, where the data packets are known as IP packets, as Layer 3 of the OSI deals with IP addressing and delivery.

If we look at *Figure 25*, we can see five different routers that connect networks between **New York**, **Dublin**, **Paris**, **London**, and **Edinburgh**:

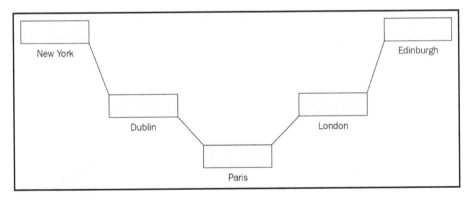

Figure 25: Routing packets

If we think of these routers as post offices delivering mail, it may make it easier to understand. If mail arrives at the Paris post office, the people working there have two sacks, one for Dublin and the other for London; they just need to know where to send the mail next. They cannot have sacks for every destination in the world, it is just not feasible.

For example, if mail arrives at the Paris post office and it is destined for Edinburgh, the post office staff know that they just need to put the mail in the London sack. Once the mail arrives in London, there will be two different sacks, one destined for Edinburgh and the other destined for Paris. The workers know to place the mail for Edinburgh in the Edinburgh sack. If they receive mail for New York, they know to place it in the Paris sack.

Routing packets is no more difficult than moving mail around the world; the router has many routes in a routing table and knows the next hop for packet delivery.

Several protocols are used in the management and control of IP packets going through the router:

- **Access Control List (ACL)**: The router will have to allow rules at the top of the ACL but the last rule is to deny all. It can restrict traffic based on IP addresses, protocols, and port numbers. If traffic that is not on the list arrives, then the last rule of deny will apply - this is known as Implicit Deny.
- **Secure Shell (SSH)**: SSH is used to remote into the router and run commands securely.

Time Synchronization – Use Case

Time is vital for SIEM systems, so that events can be placed in chronological order, and for Kerberos as it uses USN and timestamps to prevent replay attacks. In a modern network, the domain controller is synchronized with a time server or the atomic time clock, also known as a reference time source. Stratum has three main types of time servers:

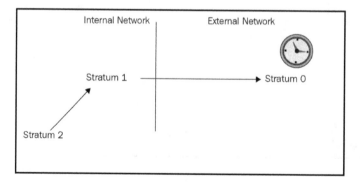

Figure 26: Time synchronization

From the diagram, you can see that the **Stratum 0** time server is the external time server and the internal **Stratum 1** time server will synchronize with **Stratum 0**. A domain controller or SIEM server will synchronize their times with either **Stratum 1** or **2**:

- **Stratum 0**: The atomic time clock or reference time server
- **Stratum 1**: An internal time server that synchronizes its time with a Stratum 0
- **Stratum 2**: An internal time server on a remote subnet that synchronizes its time with the Stratum 1 time server

Exam tip: A Stratum 0 time server is the ultimate authority in a Stratum time server environment. It is the atomic clock that time should be synchronized with.

Directory Services – Use Case

Directory services hold accounts for users, groups, and objects, such as printers, and they store these objects in the **International Telecommunications Union (ITU)** X500 objects format. There are only three main objects:

- **DC**: The DC object represents the domain, therefore if you have a domain, such as `ianneil501.com`, it is written as `dc=ianneil501` and `dc=com`, as there are two portions of the domain name separated by a dot.
- **OU**: The OU object represents an organization unit; this helps divide the users and computers in your domain into departments.
- **CN**: The CN object represents a common name, where if an item is neither a domain nor an organizational unit, it will be a common name. A common name represents anything other than the domain or organizational unit.

  For example, if I have a user called Ian who works in the IT department within a domain called `ianneil501.com`, the distinguished name in an X500 format starts at the bottom of the structure going left to right:

  ```
  cn=Ian, ou=IT, dc=ianneil501, dc=com
  ```

The user is a common name, the IT department is an OU, and `ianneil501.com` is the domain that is in two distinct portions.

Active Directory

Microsoft's Active Directory is a very common directory service and we are going to look at the components and protocols used:

- **Lightweight Directory Access Protocol (LDAP)**: When objects are created in Active Directory, it is done by completing a wizard, then LDAP stores it as X500 objects, therefore, it is the Active Directory store person. For example, LDAP is the same as a shopkeeper who sells shoes. When a delivery arrives, the shoes are unloaded and stored at the back of the shop. When a customer arrives and cannot see the size they want, they ask the shopkeeper, who goes to the storeroom to find the shoes. When a systems administrator opens up a wizard in Active Directory and creates a user account, LDAP creates and stores objects in an X500 format. If the administrator has 10,000 users and needs to find a user, they use the search facility and LDAP brings back the result of the search:

- **Lightweight Directory Access Protocol Secure (LDAPS)**: LDAPS performs the same function as LDAP, however, LDAP is not secure and could be attacked by an LDAP injection where an attacker tries to gain information from the directory service. Using LDAPS encrypts the session using SSL/TLS, this is known as LDAP over SSL, making it secure.

- **Kerberos**: Kerberos is the authentication system used to log into Active Directory and uses tickets for authentication. The user completes a session, called a **Ticket Granting Ticket** (**TGT**) session, and obtains a 10-hour service ticket. When the user tries to access email, their computer exchanges their service ticket for a session ticket therefore it is a mutual authentication.

Each update to an Active Directory object is done by giving the change an **Updated Sequence Number** (**USN**). For example, the next change must be USN 23 and the change after that is USN 24, and it is stamped with the time it happens, which is known as being timestamped.

All computers in an Active Directory domain must have their time synchronized to be within five minutes of the domain controller. A replay attack is where a man-in-the-middle attack is performed and the information is altered and replayed at a later date.

Due to Kerberos having each with a different update number, called a USN and timestamp, it will prevent a replay attack. Replay attacks are interception attacks that replay data at a later date, but the Kerberos traffic will not be sequential and, when this happens, the replayed data will be rejected.

Exam tip: Ensure you know the secure version of all of the protocols.

Switching – Use Case

A switch is an internal device that connects all of the users in the LAN so that they can communicate with each other. As we have seen in previous chapters, a computer connects to a wall jack into a patch panel, and then from the patch panel to the switch. Let's look at the functionality and protocols used by a switch:

- **801. Ix**: A managed switch is called 802.1x, where the switch identifies and authenticates devices connecting to the switch and blocks rogue devices, such as a rogue access point, without the need to switch the port off. It controls the flow of traffic from wireless to wired communication and can work in conjunction with a **Remote Authentication Dial-In User Service** (**RADIUS**) server for authentication. Each device has an X509 certificate for identification.
- **Port Security**: Port security is where a port in a switch is switched off to prevent someone from plugging their laptop into a wall jack.
- **Flood Guard**: A flood guard is used in a switch to prevent MAC flooding, where the switch is flooded with a high volume of fake MAC addresses and prevents DDoS attacks.
- **VLAN**: VLANs can be set up on a switch to segment the network traffic. For example, if the finance department wanted to be isolated from other departments within the LAN, a VLAN could be created. The VLAN tag must be set up, otherwise, the switch will not know where to send the traffic. You may also put machines that could be used for electronic bank transfer or credit card payments into their own VLAN for better security.
- **Spanning Tree Protocol (STP)**: When more than one switch is connected, you may have redundant paths and this causes looping that provides broadcast traffic; by using STP, it has an algorithm that sets up some ports to forward, listen, or block traffic to prevent looping.

Simple Network Management Protocol – Use Case

Networks are very large and have many different devices; there needs to be some sort of monitoring software to ensure that the devices are still functioning. We use two different versions of SNMP:

- **Simple Network Management Protocol (SNMP)**: Each network device has an agent installed and is programmed so that, if a trigger is met, the SNMP management console is notified. SNMP can monitor the status of network devices and provide reports if required.
- **Simple Network Management Protocol Version 3 (SNMP v 3)**: SNMP v 3 is the secure version of SNMP, as it authenticates and encrypts data packets.

Implementing Wireless Security

Wireless communication is now part of everyday life, from using 4G on your mobile phone to access the internet to using Bluetooth to listen to your music as you walk down the road. However, if your wireless device is insecure, it can lead to data loss and maybe someone stealing funds from your bank account. Let's first look at the different types of wireless networks:

- **WLAN**: A WLAN is an internal corporate wireless network that sits in your Local Area Network. Normally, in a WLAN, you would use WPA2 Enterprise or WPA2 CCMP as your encryption methods.
- **Guest**: A guest wireless network is a wireless network separate from your WLAN where contractors can access the internet; it may be used for training purposes. The guest wireless network can be used by members of staff to access the internet during their lunchtimes.
- **Infrastructure**: An infrastructure wireless network is where devices connect to a wireless network using a **Wireless Access point (WAP)**.
- **Ad hoc**: An ad hoc network is where wireless connectivity is enabled between two devices without a WAP.

Exam tip: A guest wireless network gives contractors access to the internet; it could also be used by employees at lunchtime.

Wireless Access Points (WAP) Controllers

Wireless access points (**WAPs**) help extend the wireless network and there are two different types of controllers:

- **FAT Controllers**: A FAT controller is a standalone WAP similar to that used at home. It has its own pool of DHCP addresses, and everything for the wireless network is installed on the WAP.
- **Thin Controllers**: A thin controller allows multiple WAPs to be controlled remotely by a single controller; this is ideal in a corporate environment where they are quite a few WAPs.

Exam tip: A thin controller is used to manage multiple wireless access points remotely.

Securing Access to your WAP

Without the use of encryption, there are three simple methods for securing access to your wireless access point:

- **Default Username and Password**: When a WAP is rolled out, it has the default setting of the username and password, both being set to `admin` in lowercase. One of the first steps is to change both of these and then set up an encryption method.

- **Disable the SSID**: The SSID is the network name for the wireless network and the default SSID is `default`, therefore, the first stage is to change the SSID. With the SSID changes, the WAP will still broadcast the name and devices, such as laptops, tablets, or smartphones, will be able to view the SSID. The best way to stop someone from seeing the SSID is to use the disable SSID function; after that is done, the only way to connect to the WAP is to enter the SSID manually:

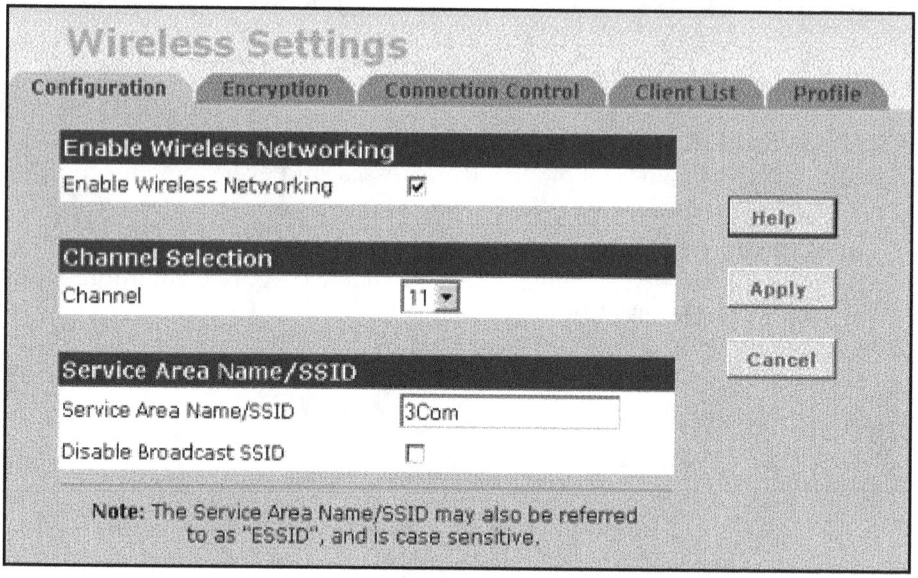

Figure 27: SSID

- **Discovering the Disabled SSID**: Even though the SSID has been disabled, it can still be found using a wireless packet sniffer. When the packets are being sent to the WAP, the SSID is embedded into the packet. Another method is to use a device called an SSID decloak, which will magically make the SSID appear to the device. To protect the WAP, we must use encryption.

- **MAC Filtering**: Every network device has a unique address, called the media access control address, embedded into its network interface. A method of restricting who can access the device is by using MAC filtering, where you enter the MAC addresses of the devices that are allowed to use the WAP. If you think of this, why did they not call it MAC addition, because that is basically what you are doing? If your MAC address is not entered into the WAP, then you do not get access:

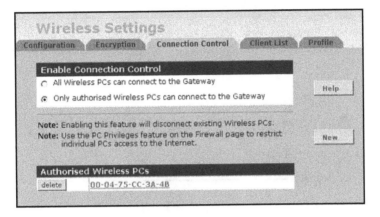

Figure 28: MAC filtering

Wireless Bandwidth/Band Selection

There are different wireless standards, and we need to know the limitations of each. The band selection is also known as the frequency:

Standard	Frequency	Speed	Remarks
802.11 a	5 GHz	54 Mbps	5 GHz channel bandwidth is 40 MHz
802.11 b	2.4 GHz	11 Mbps	2.4 GHz channel bandwidth is 20 MHz
802.11 g	2.4 GHz	54 Mbps	
802.11 n	2.4 GHz/5Hz	150 Mbps	MIMO - multiple input multiple output and travels the furthest distance

Wireless Channels

In the Security+ exam, the wireless channels go from channel 1 up to channel 11, and the device placement should be as follows:

- **Channel 1**: Your first wireless device
- **Channel 11**: Your second wireless device
- **Channel 6**: Your third wireless device

We place the devices as far apart as possible to prevent overlap of adjacent channels and interference. Wireless devices can suffer interference from elevators, baby monitors, cordless phones, metal racking, and load-bearing walls.

Wireless Antenna Types - Signal Strength

There are three main antenna types:

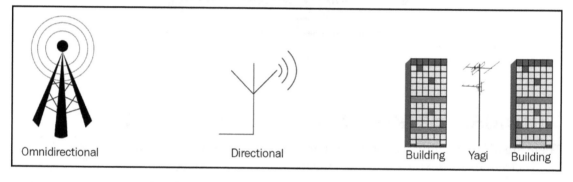

Figure 29

- **Omnidirectional**: Omnidirectional antennas provide the most coverage as they transmit over 360 degrees.
- **Directional**: Directional antennas transmit only in one direction, therefore, if the antenna is pointing in the wrong direction, there will be no connection to the wireless network.
- **Yagi**: Yagi fin is an antenna that can transmit in two directions, therefore it is suitable to be placed between two buildings. A way to remember this for the exam is: *Yagi Bear is between two buildings looking for food.*

Wireless Coverage

One of the security implications of having a wireless network is to ensure that wireless networks will have coverage that will give access to resources in a timely fashion without the coverage being extended outside of the companies' boundaries where it could be hacked. Let's look at each of these in turn:

- **Site Survey**: Before we install a wireless network, we need to complete a site survey so that we know what can cause interference with the wireless network. In certain areas, we may need an extra WAP because of potential interference with the network. If we install a wireless network and it does not function properly or runs at a slow speed, then we have not carried out a thorough-enough site survey.
- **Low-Power Directional Antennas**: If the wireless network goes outside of the boundary of a company's network, it may be hacked or attacked. To prevent these attacks, we turn down the power on the wireless access point and this reduces the distance of the wireless network coverage.
- **Wireless Speed Slow**: If the speed of the wireless network is very slow, we may be too far away from the WAP.

 Exam tip: If my newly installed WLAN is not fully functional, we may not have carried out the site survey properly.

Wireless Encryption

So that we can secure our wireless network, we need to choose a form of encryption, ranging from WEP, which is the weakest, to WPA2—CCMP, which is the strongest. Let's look at each of these in turn:

- **Wired Equivalent Privacy (WEP)**: WEP is the weakest form of wireless security, with a 40-bit key that is very easy to crack.
- **Wi-Fi Protected Access (WPA)**: WPA replaced WEP as it uses the **Temporal Key Integrity Protocol** (**TKIP**), which was designed to be more secure than WEP. WPA is backward compatible with WEP. TKIP is backward compatible with legacy wireless encryption.

- **Wi-Fi Protected Access version 2 (WPA2)**: WPA2 is much stronger than WPA and there are two main versions—one for the home user and the other for the corporate:

    - **WPA2-Pre-Shared Key (WPA2–PSK)**: WPA2-PSK was introduced for the home user who does not have an enterprise setup. The home user enters the password of the wireless router to gain access to the home network; this is very common nowadays.

    - **WPA2-Enterprise**: WPA2-Enterprise is a corporate version of WPA2 where a RADIUS server combines with 802.1x user certificates for authentication.

    - **WPA2-TKIP**: WPA2-TKIP could be used for backward compatibility with legacy systems, however, TKIP was replaced by a more secure CCMP that is not backward compatible.

    - **WPA2-CCMP**: WPA2-CCMP is the strongest version of WPA2 as it uses AES for authentication.

Wireless – Open System Authentication

If we want to set up a wireless network for the general public to access without any encryption or any passwords, we could use the Open System Authentication but the users would have to access the WAP at their own risk.

Wireless – WPS

When we access our wireless network or gaming console, we may use WPS where the password is already stored and all you need to do is to press the button to get connected to the wireless network. This could be attacked by a Brute Force attack.

Wireless – Captive Portal

When you join the wireless network at the airport, you are connected to the free Wi-Fi, yet you cannot access the internet right away. It redirects you to a captive portal where you need to enter your email address, put in your Facebook credentials, or pay for the premium wireless network.

Wireless Attacks

There are two main types of attacks relating to wireless networks:

- **Evil Twin**: An evil twin is where there is another WAP that looks like the legitimate WAP but it has no security; this is to lure you into using this WAP and is where your traffic will be captured.
- **Rogue Access Point**: A rogue access point is where an additional access point is joined to your corporate network, yet again with no security, to lure users into connectivity to it. This can be prevented by installing 802.1x-managed switches where all devices connecting to the network are authenticated.

Wireless Authentication Protocols

There are numerous wireless authentication protocols:

- **IEEE 802.1x**: IEEE 802.1x is transparent to users as it uses certificates and can be used in conjunction with a RADIUS server for enterprise networks.
- **RADIUS federation**: RADIUS Federation is a federation service where access to the network is gained by using WAPs.
- **EAP:** EAP is an authentication framework allowing point-to-point connections.
- **Protected Extensible Authentication Protocol (PEAP)**: The Protected Extensible Authentication Protocol is a version of EAP that encapsulated the EAP data and made it more secure for WLANS.
- **EAP-FAST**: EAP-FAST, also known as Flexible Authentication via Secure Tunneling, is an Extensible Authentication Protocol (EAP) developed by Cisco. It is used in wireless networks and point-to-point connections to perform session authentication. It replaced LEAP, which was insecure.
- **EAP-TLS**: EAP-TLS uses the TLS public key certificate authentication mechanism within EAP to provide a mutual authentication of client to server and server to client. We install an X509 certificate on the endpoint.
- **EAP-TTLS**: EAP-TTLS uses two phases; the first is to set up a secure session with the server utilizing certificates that are seamless to the client, which will then use a protocol such as MS-CHAP to complete the session. It is designed to connect older legacy systems.

Review Questions

1. What is the lowest layer of the OSI reference model that a switch operates?
2. What layer of the ISO does a router operate?
3. Which layer of the OSI Reference Model does a VLAN operate?
4. On which layer of the OSI Reference Model does a web application firewall work?
5. What is the purpose of a web application firewall and where is it normally placed?
6. What is the default setting for a firewall?
7. What is Implicit Deny and which two devices does it affect?
8. If traffic is not arriving at my VLAN, what should I do?
9. Which port type is connection-orientated and why?
10. Which type of port would I use for streaming video?
11. What is the firewall that does content filtering, URL filtering, and malware inspection?
12. Which network device connects two networks together?
13. Which type of internal device connects users on the same network?
14. Which type of device hides the internal network from hackers on the internet?
15. What is an inline NIPS?
16. Which type of IPS protects virtual machines from attack?
17. Which type of IPS is placed behind the firewall as an additional layer of security?
18. If I don't have a NIDS on my network, which device can passively monitor network traffic?
19. What is the difference between a signature and anomaly-based NIDS?
20. What is the passive device that sits on your internal network?
21. If I receive an alert that Server 1 has a virus and I inspect the server and there are no viruses, what is this known as?
22. How can I prevent someone from accessing the medical center's network by plugging their laptop into a port in the waiting room?
23. How can I prevent someone from plugging a rogue access point into my network?
24. How do 802.1x and port security differ? Which one gives me more functionality?
25. Which device can be installed on a switch to prevent a DDoS attack?
26. Which is the purpose of web caching on a proxy server?
27. Which type of proxy verifies that the request is valid before web caching?

28. What is the purpose of a VPN?
29. What happens in the IKE phase of a VPN session?
30. What is the purpose of a VPN concentrator?
31. What is the most secure VPN tunneling protocol?
32. What type of VPN uses SSL certificates?
33. How many keys does symmetric encryption use and what are the benefits over asymmetric encryption?
34. What modes would you use a L2TP/IPSec tunnel over the internet and then internally?
35. Which VPN session type would you use on a site-to-site VPN?
36. What network device should you use to manage a high volume of web traffic?
37. How does active/passive clustering work?
38. What type of network is used by a virtual network so that the route requests are forwarded to a controller?
39. How should I set up my voice traffic so that I can control the bandwidth across my internal network?
40. What is the purpose of a Demilitarized Zone (DMZ) and what type of web server is located there?
41. What is the difference between NAT and PAT?
42. If I want to find out what attack methods a potential hacker is using, what do I need to set up?
43. What is the purpose of network access control? Name the two agents that is uses.
44. What type of network device would check that there is no spam before the mail is delivered to the internal mail server?
45. What type of device can be used to automate the collection of log files across many different devices?
46. If I wanted to back up data to a backup device but at the same time prevent someone from deleting the data, what device do I need to use?
47. What can be used to ensure that someone cannot steal sensitive data by using a USB flash drive or emailing the data to their personal email account?
48. What is a port mirror that could also be called a tap?
49. Which protocol should I use to download very large files from the internet?
50. Which email client does not retain a copy on the mail server?
51. What type of records are created by DNSSEC?
52. When my Windows DNS server is not available, which Linux server could I use for name resolution and which port number does it use?
53. What is the protocol used for UDP ports 5060/5061?

54. Which ports does NETBIOS use?

55. If I want to access information from Active Directory securely, which protocol and port should I use?

56. If I want to run a command securely on a CISCO router, which protocol and port should I use?

57. Which secure protocol should I use to find out a report on the utilization of network devices?

58. What are the two portions of an IPSec packet?

59. Which authentication protocol can prevent replay attacks and how?

60. How can I tell whether my laptop fails to get an IP address from a DHCP server?

61. What type of IP address is `2001:123A:0000:0000:ABC0:00AB:0DCS:0023` and how can we simplify it?

62. Describe subscription services.

63. What type of wireless network does not use a WAP to connect two devices together?

64. What is the strongest version of wireless encryption?

65. Which Stratum time server is the atomic time server or reference time source?

66. If I disable SSID broadcasting from my wireless router, which two methods can I use to discover the SSID?

67. I have just installed a new tablet onto my network and it still cannot access the WAP. Other users can connect easily, I have checked the encryption types and login details and they are correct. What stage has been missed?

68. What type of wireless controller will allow me to administer seven WAPs?

69. What is the benefit of installing an omnidirectional antenna?

70. What could be a problem with installing a directional antenna?

71. What type of wireless method uses a password to connect to the WAP?

72. If I own a coffee shop and want to provide a wireless network for my customers that does not require any administration from my side, how should I set it up?

73. I have joined the wireless network at the airport, but I cannot connect to the internet. What is preventing this?

74. What type of wireless authentication protocol is encapsulated inside PEAP?

75. Why should I not use PAP?

Answers and Explanations

1. The data-link layer (Layer 2) is the lowest layer that a switch operates at.

2. A router works at Layer 3 of the OSI Reference Model as it works on IP addresses.

3. A VLAN is created on a switch that works at layer 2 of the OSI Reference Model.

4. A web application firewall works at Layer 7 of the OSI Reference Model.

5. The web application firewall is normally installed on a web server as its job is to protect web applications from attack.

6. The default setting for a firewall is block all, allow by exception.

7. Implicit deny is used by both the firewall and the router where the last rule is deny all. Should there not be an allow rule, then the last rule applies and it is known as implicit deny.

8. If the VLAN traffic is not arriving, check that the VLAN tag is set up properly as it tells the VLAN traffic where to go.

9. A TCP Port is connection-orientated as it uses a three-way handshake to set up the session. It also acknowledges when the packets arrive.

10. A UDP port would be used for streaming video as it is connectionless and faster than TCP.

11. The **Unified Threat Management** (**UTM**) is a firewall that provides value for money as it can provide URL filtering, content filtering, and malware inspection, as well as the firewall functionality.

12. A router connects different networks together and works at Layer 3 of the OSI Reference Model.

13. A switch connects users on an internal network, normally in a star topology

14. A **Network Address Translator** (**NAT**) hides the internal network from those on the external network.

15. An inline NIPS is where the incoming traffic passes through and is screened by the NIPS.

16. A **Host-based IPS** (**HIPS**) is installed inside the guest virtual machine to protect it from attacks.

17. A network-based IPS (NIPS) is placed behind the firewall as an additional layer of security. The firewall prevents unauthorized access to the network.

18. A NIPS can passively monitor the network as it can fulfill the functionality of a NIPS if there is no NIDS on your network.

19. A signature-based NIDS works off a known database of variants, whereas the anomaly-based one starts off with the database and can learn about new patterns or threats.

20. A passive device that sits inside your network is a NIDS.

21. If one of the monitoring systems reports a virus and you physically check and find no virus, this is known as a false positive.

22. If we enable port security, where we turn the port off on the switch, it will prevent further use of the wall jack.

23. To prevent a rogue access point attaching to your network, you would enable 802.1x on the switch itself. 802.1x ensures that the device is authenticated before being able to use the post.

24. A managed switch uses 802.1x that authenticates the device but does not disable the port when port security merely disables the port. 802.1x therefore provides more functionality.

25. A flood guard can be installed on a switch to prevent DDOS attacks.

26. Web caching on a web server keeps copies of the web pages locally, ensuring faster access to the web pages and preventing the need to open a session to the internet.

27. A non-transparent proxy ensures that all requests are validated before being carried out.

28. The purpose of a VPN is to create a tunnel across unsafe networks from home or a hotel to the workplace.

29. In the IKE phase of an IPSec session Diffie Hellman using UDP Port 500 sets up a secure session before the data is transferred.

30. The purpose of a VPN concentrator is to set up the secure session for a VPN.

31. The most secure VPN tunnel is L2TP/IPSec, which uses AES encryption for the ESP.

32. An SSL VPN is the only VPN to use SSL certificates.

33. Symmetric encryption only uses one key to encrypt and decrypt and can encrypt larger amount of data faster than asymmetric encryption, that uses two keys.

34. IPSEC in Tunnel Mode is used across the internet or external networks, and IPSec Transport Mode is used between hosts internally.

35. When setting the Site-to-Site VPN, it should be used in always-on mode as opposed to dial on demand.

36. A load-balancer should be used to manage a high volume of web traffic as it sends the requests to the least-utilized node that is healthy.

37. Both the active and passive node share the same quorum disk, the passive node polls the passive node and when the active node fails, the passive node takes over.

38. SDN is used in a virtual environment when the routing requests are forwarded to a controller.

39. A voice VLAN should be set up to manage the flow of voice traffic, isolating it from the rest of the network.

40. The DMZ is a boundary layer that hosts an extranet server; it is sometimes known as the extranet zone.

41. A NAT is one internal connection to one external connection that hides the internal network. PAT is multiple internal connections to one external connection.

42. If you setup a honeypot, which is a web site with lower security, you will be able to monitor the attack methods being used and then be able to harden your actual web server against potential attacks.

43. Network access control ensures that devices connecting to your network are fully patched. There are two agents: one that is permanent and the other than is dissolvable that is for a single use.

44. A mail gateway can be placed on the network before the mail server to prevent spam getting to the mail server.

45. A SIEM server can correlate log files from many devices and notify you of potential attacks.

46. If data is backed up to a WORM drive write-once read-many, the data cannot be deleted or altered.

47. **Data Loss Prevention (DLP)** prevents data from being emailed out or taken from a file server using a USB drive.

48. A port mirror is when a copy of the data going to a port on a switch can be diverted to another device for analysis; this is also called a tap.

49. FTPS that uses TCP ports 989/990 can download very large files quickly.

50. POP3 downloads the complete email and does not retain a copy on the mail server.

51. DNSSEC creates RRSIG records for each DNS host and a DNSKEY record used to sign the KSK or ZSK.

52. When a windows DNS Server is not available, host-name resolution can be carried out by a Linux/UNIX Bind server, as it does host name resolution, it uses the port 53.

53. **Session Initiated Protocol (SIP)** that establishes the interconnection for voice traffic uses UPD Ports 5060/5061.

54. NETBIOS uses UDP ports 137-139 and also a flat file called the LMHosts File.

55. LDAPS TCP port 636 accesses Active Directory information securely.

56. Secure shell (SSH) is used to run remote commands on a router.

57. SNMPv3 is the secure version of the simple network management protocol that collects reports and statistics from network devices.

58. An IPSec packet has the authenticated header that uses either SHA1 or MD5 and an **Encapsulated Payload** (**ESP**) that uses DES, 3DES, or AES.

59. Kerberos is an authentication protocol that uses **Updated Sequence Numbers** (**USN**) and timestamps to prevent replay attacks. It is also the only authentication protocol that uses tickets.

60. If you cannot get an IP address from a DHCP server, you would receive a 169.254.x.x IP address.

61. It is an IP Version 6 address and you can simplify it by removing the leading zeros to 2001:123A::ABC0:AB:DCS:23.

62. Subscription Services is where software is leased, for example, Office 365 where you get not only email but Office packages as well. Spotify is another example.

63. An ad hoc wireless network allows two devices to connect without a WAP.

64. The strongest version of wireless encryption is WPA2-CCMP as it uses AES.

65. The Stratum 0 is the ultimate time source; Stratum 1 requests to sync time with it.

66. A wireless packet sniffer or an SSID De-cloak device can discover the SSID even if the SSID broadcast has been disabled.

67. When connecting a new network device but everyone seemed to be right it could be that the MAC address has now been added to MAC filtering.

68. A thin wireless controller can control multiple WAP remotely.

69. An omnidirectional antenna broadcasts the signal in all directions.

70. A directional antenna only broadcasts in one direction, therefore, if it is pointing in the wrong direction, the users will not be able to connect to the network.

71. PSK is a method to connect to the wireless network using the WAP password.

72. Open System Authentication allows the public to connect to the WAP without any authentication.

73. In this scenario, the user has connected to the Captive Portal at the airport, which may need your email address, Google account, or Facebook account to connect to the free Wi-Fi network.

74. EAP is incorporated inside a PEAP authentication protocol.

75. PAP shows the password in cleat text, making it very insecure.

6
Understanding Cloud Models and Virtualization

In this chapter, we will be learning about the deployment and security issues of virtualization. We will get acquainted with the deployment and storage environments of the cloud models. We will also learn about different scenarios to learn when to use on-premises, hosted, and cloud environments.

We will cover the following exam objectives in this chapter:

- **Summarizing cloud and virtualization concepts**:
    - Hypervisor—Type I—Type II
    - Application cells/containers
    - VM sprawl avoidance—VM escape protection
    - Cloud storage—cloud deployment models—SaaS—PaaS—IaaS—private—public—hybrid—community
    - On-premises versus hosted versus cloud
    - VDI/VDE
    - Cloud access security broker
    - Security as a service

- **Explain how resiliency and automation strategies reduce risk**: Elasticity—scalability—distributive allocation—redundancy—fault tolerance—high availability—RAID.

Cloud Computing

The demand for cloud services has risen in recent years as the workforce has been more mobile; the cloud solution is very cost-effective and maintains the high availability of systems. Before you decide to move to a **Cloud Service Provider** (**CSP**), you need to ensure that you trust them 100%.

This section will look at different cloud models, coupled with cloud storage and how machines in the cloud are created. There are many good reasons why cloud computing has become popular:

- **Elasticity**: The cloud is like a pay-as-you-go model where one day you can increase resources and then the next day you can scale down the resources. You can even add more processor power, faster disks, more memory, or dual network cards whenever you want - there's no need to wait for delivery times, but the cost increases:
    - **Example 1**: A toy firm is hiring 50 temporary workers from October onward to deal with the rush for toys at Christmas. If the toy company were not on the cloud, they would have to purchase another 50, desktops, but instead, they lease virtual machines from a CSP. Once the Christmas rush has ended, the lease of their machines ends. You only pay for what you need.
    - **Example 2**: An IT training company uses 12 laptops for the delivery of different courses. Each week the image changes and they have to roll it out 12 times - this is time-consuming. Images are stored in a library on a file server.

        When they move to the cloud, they just roll out one image and the CSP clones it so they don't need to reimage each laptop. Today, they are delivering Word 2016, therefore the cloud machines need an i5 processor with 4 GB of RAM for two days. They go to a CSP and lease the hardware specification that they need.

        The next week, in another location, they will deliver Skype for Business, so there is no need to reimage the laptops but they now leave quad i7 processors with striped disk sets and 64 GB of RAM. The course is now for five days, so it is longer and more expensive. The image is uploaded and the cloud machines are upgraded, resulting in a much higher cost as they are using more resources. They do not need to purchase the additional hardware and the setup is more cost-effective.

- **Scalability**: Scalability is the ability of a company to grow while maintaining a resilient infrastructure. The cloud enables a company to grow and grow without the worry of needing to make capital expenditure while doing so. It enables the company to grow faster than an on-premises company that needs to invest more money into bricks and mortar. As the cloud allows elasticity, it goes hand in hand with becoming scalable. As your company grows, the cloud provider can allow you to lease more resources. If at any time you want to reduce the amount of resources needed, the cloud provider can also reduce resources.

  > For example, company A is a newly formed business that has hit the marketplace running; there is a need for the company to rapidly expand and open new offices in Chicago and London, as sales in those locations are astronomical. Normally, when a new site is opened, it needs to invest $50,000 in IT equipment, so the company has turned to a cloud model for the new equipment. They will lease the offices until sufficient sales have been made to invest in purchasing a property. All of the employees will have laptops and high-speed fiber broadband. The network infrastructure will be cloud-based, therefore there is no need to purchase physical servers that would have an impact in reducing their cash flow. Cash flow is maintained, even though new equipment has been provided.

- **No Capital Expenditure (capex)**: When you move your infrastructure to the cloud, there is no capital expenditure; normally IT resources have a maximum lifespan of 3-5 years. As technology keeps moving and hardware becomes obsolete, this means they may have to find $50-100,000 every five years just for hardware. For example, a company is looking to upgrade their desktops and servers with the cost of hardware being $250,000 and a disposal fee of $25,000 in five years' time. If they move to the cloud, it is going to cost them $60,000 a year. However, they don't need to find the whole $250,000 in one lump sum as the CSP will update their hardware perpetually so that the hardware will never be obsolete. It will also help the company maintain a better cash flow, as capital expenditure is not required. The difference in price is 1.8% higher per year, which could be justified as there are no maintenance fees or disaster recovery site required, making it very cost-effective. The CSP deals with maintenance and disaster recovery as part of the cloud plan.

- **Location-Independent**: As you are accessing the cloud through a browser, it is location-independent, therefore it offers faster recovery if your premises have a disaster. For example, one of your company offices is located in Northern California and recently was burned down by a wildfire, however, since your data and infrastructure are cloud-based, you can operate quickly from another location as long as you have internet access. If you had a traditional network, the infrastructure would have been burned down, your desktops would have been gone, and it could take a week or two to get back to an operational state.
- **Regional Storage of Data**: The cloud is regulated, therefore data from a country must be stored within that region as laws on data compliance can change from region to region.
- **No Maintenance Fees**: The CSP provides ongoing maintenance, so when the cloud contract is signed there are no hidden costs.
- **No Disaster Recovery Site Required**: The CSP provides a 99.999% availability of its IT systems, therefore, once your data is in the cloud, there is no requirement for a disaster recovery site as the CSP provides that as part of the contract.

Exam tip:
Private cloud = single tenant, Public cloud = multitenant.
Community cloud = same industry, sharing resources.

Implementing Different Cloud Deployment Models

We will first look at the different cloud models and their characteristics. The most common cloud model is the public cloud, so let's start with that:

- **Public Cloud**: This is the most common model, where the CSP provides cloud services for multiple tenants. This is like being one of many people who rent an apartment in an apartment block:

Figure 1: Public cloud

Just like in the public cloud, none of the tenants owns their apartment. For example, a small company does not want to invest $50,000 in IT systems, so they purchase their cloud package from a cloud provider where they and another company are hosted by the cloud provider. This is similar to someone renting one apartment in a block from a landlord - you lease but do not own the flat. This is a multitenant environment where the cloud provider has multiple companies on the same virtual host.

- **Private Cloud**: A private cloud is where a company purchases all of its hardware this gives them more control than other cloud models. They normally host their own cloud because they do not want to share resources with anyone else, but at the same time, their workforce has all of the mobile benefits of the cloud. It is similar to someone buying a house because they want privacy. The private cloud needs isolation from other companies, which is why it is known as single-tenant:

Figure 2: Private cloud

For example, an insurance company wants its sales staff on a cloud environment where they can access resources from anywhere—whether they are at home, at a customer's site, or in a hotel room. The problem they have is that they do not wish to share resources with other cloud tenants. Therefore, they purchase the hardware and their IT team hosts its own private cloud. The benefit of this is that the sales team can access any resources they want at any time of day or night. It is known as single-tenant but, like owning your own home, they buy the equipment.

- **Community Cloud**: The community cloud is where companies from the same industry collectively pay for a bespoke application to be written, and the cloud provider manufacturers host it:

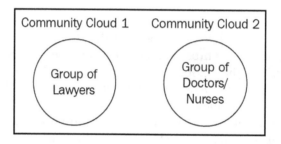

Figure 3: Community cloud

In the preceding diagram, you can see lawyers on the left-hand side and on the right-hand side is a group of medical people - doctors and nurses. The lawyers cannot share the same software package as medical people, since they have different requirements. Therefore, **Community Cloud 1** is for lawyers who have brainstormed and financed the perfect legal application, which is hosted in the cloud - this is private to them. **Community Cloud 2** is for a group of medical people, it could maybe be two hospitals, who have designed and shared the cost of making the perfect medical software package, which is hosted by the CSP.

For example, there is no application that can provide all of the functionality required for pawnbrokers to list the assets that have been pawned with the payment made against each asset. Then, they need assets that have not been reclaimed to be sold on the internet, as well as being sold in their shops.

Three of the largest pawnbroking companies enter into a business venture where they get together and design the perfect application to enable their companies to be more efficient and save labor costs over time. The cloud provider creates this application and hosts it. This saves them the costs of purchasing new hardware. The cloud provider will also back up the data each night and guarantee a 99.99% availability of the systems. This is known as a community cloud as the application is no good to anyone who is not a pawnbroker.

- **Hybrid Cloud**: Companies that decide not to host their company in the cloud are known as on-premises, but during their peak time they may expand into the cloud - this is known as cloud bursting. A mixture of both on-premises and cloud is known as a hybrid model:

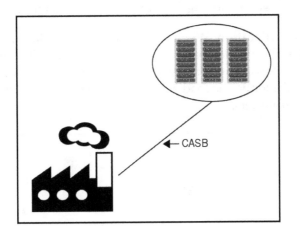

Figure 4: Hybrid cloud

In the bottom left-hand corner, we have a brick factory. This is known as on-premises, where the company owns a brick-and-mortar building. In the top-left corner are servers in the cloud. The **Cloud Access Security Broker** (**CASB**) enforces the company's policies between the on-premises situation and the cloud.

Cloud Service Models

There are different types of cloud services, and these are very heavily tested in the Security+ exam; therefore, we will show screenshots of the types of offerings. We will first look at infrastructure as a service, which is the model that you may have more control over:

- **Infrastructure as a Service (IaaS)**: If you think of a network infrastructure, you think of desktops, servers, firewalls, routers, and switches - the hardware devices for a network. When you purchase these devices, they have a default factory setting and these settings need to be configured. Desktops are bare-bones, meaning that they have no operating system installed. IaaS is the same; you need to preconfigure these devices, install an operating system, and maintain the patch management. See the pricing for IaaS in the screenshot that follows.

- **Distributive Allocation**: When you decide to use an IaaS model or IaaS models, you may install a virtual load balancer to provide a distributive allocation of some of your server capacity. As we know from previous chapters, a load balancer will allocate the load across multiple servers to ensure that no single server is overburdened:

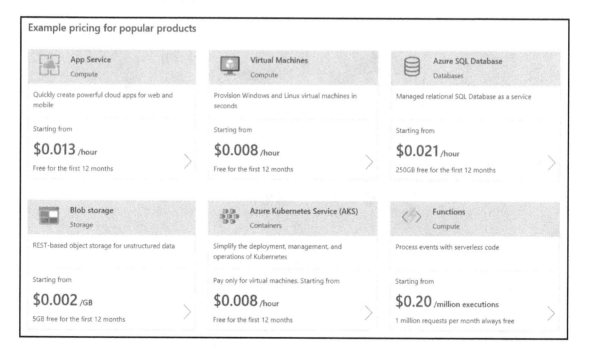

Figure 5: Microsoft's IaaS offering (July 2018)

Exam tip:
IaaS is where you will install the operating system and patch it. This is the service under IaaS you have more control over. Private Cloud is the cloud model that gives you more control.

- **Software as a Service (SaaS)**: This is where the CSP hosts a bespoke software application that is accessed through a web server. Let's look at three examples of this—Goldmine, Salesforce, and Office 365:
  - **Goldmine:** Goldmine is an SaaS package, that is, a **Customer Relationship Management (CRM)** package, which is used by companies that sell products and services. It will host lists of their customers, with contact numbers and addresses:

WHAT'S INCLUDED	SUBSCRIPTION
Contact management	YES
Email linking	YES
Web and mobile device access	OPTIONAL
Sales forecasting and opportunity management	YES
Marketing list management and group emails	YES
Integration for Constant Contact campaign downloads	YES
Customer service management	YES
Real time dashboards	YES
Customize fields	YES

GoldMine Cloud
powered by CloudJumper
No Server? No Problem.

Figure 6: Goldmine – SaaS

- **Salesforce**: Salesforce is an internationally used software package employed by sales teams to show a sales forecast over a period of time. It will allow salespeople to enter potential sales leads, categorize them, and hold any correspondence between the parties:

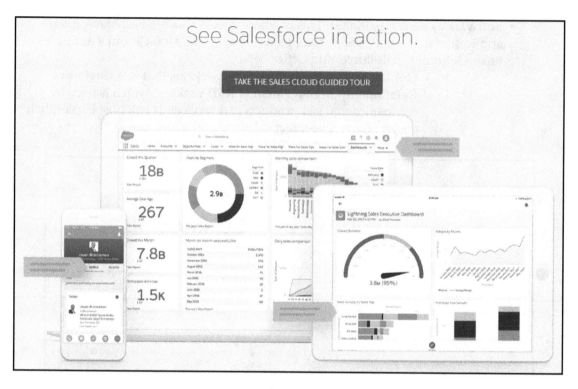

Figure 7: Salesforce—SaaS

- **Office 365**: Office 365 is a Microsoft product where the packages range from email to various Office applications that are all hosted in the cloud. Each user has a 1 TB storage space. The premium package comes with Skype, exchange for email, and SharePoint, which is a document management system:

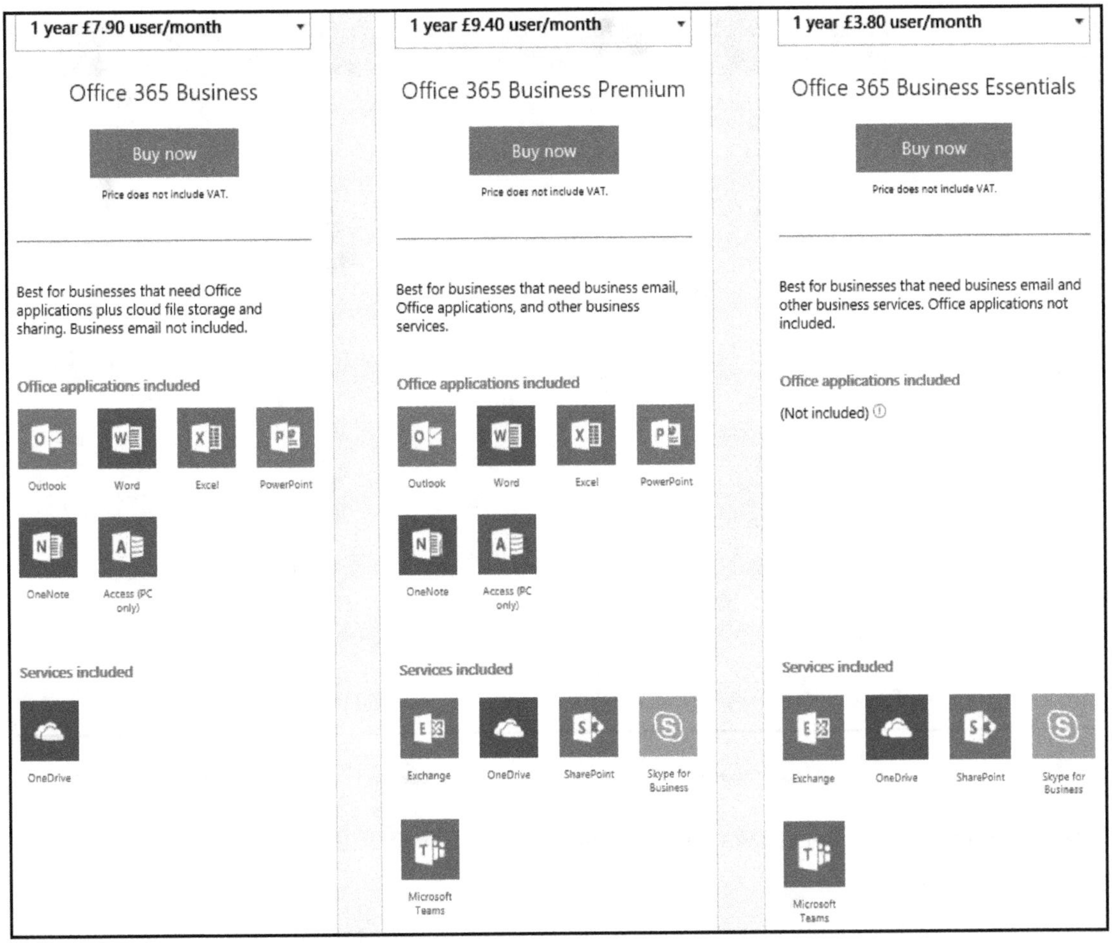

Figure 8: Microsoft Office 365 – SaaS

- **Platform as a Service (PaaS)**: This provides the environment for developers to create applications; an example of this is Microsoft Azure. The platform provides a set of services to support the easy development and operation of applications, rolling them out to iOS, Android devices, as well as Windows devices. You could host your bespoke applications under PaaS.

- **Security as a Service (SECaaS)**: SECaaS provides **Identity and Access Management** (**IAM**) that allows people to have secure access to applications from anywhere at any time:

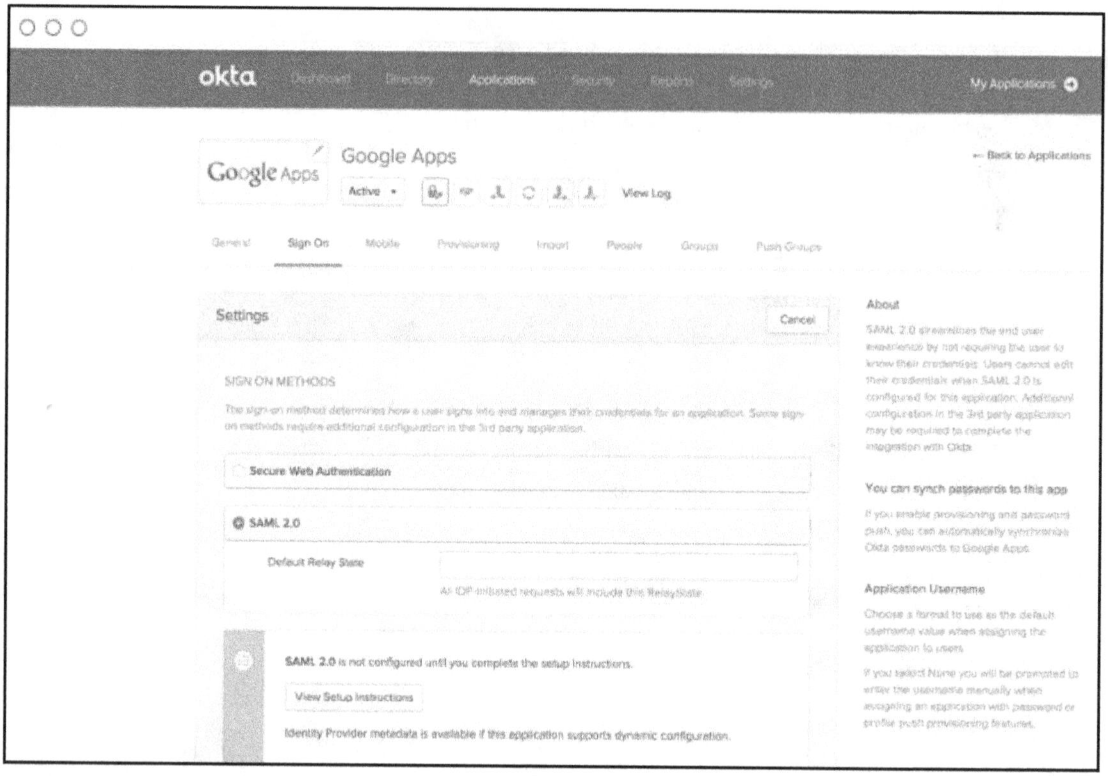

Figure 9: Okta security as a service (SECaaS) for Google Apps

The preceding screenshot shows Okta providing secure web authentication into Google Apps.

Disk Resiliency and Redundancy

We are going to look at different disk setups - some of which can provide fault tolerance or redundancy, meaning that, if a disk fails, then the data is still available. RAID 0 is used for faster disk access, but provides neither fault tolerance nor redundancy. Let's first look at the different RAID setups, as these will be heavily tested.

Redundant Array of Independent Disks

There is a need for the disk setup on servers to provide redundancy; this is where if one disk fails, the data is still available. We have already looked at failover clustering in `Chapter 5`, *Understanding Network Components*, where two servers share a quorum disk - the single point of failure in that scenario would be the shared disk. We are going to look at different **Redundant Array of Independent Disks** (**RAID**) levels and their characteristics:

- **RAID 0**: RAID 0 uses a minimum of two disks with a maximum of 32 disks:

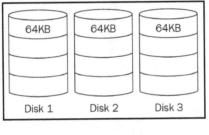

Figure 10: RAID 0

This is known as a stripe set, as the data is written across Disks 1-3 in 64 KB stripes. Should one disk fail, then all of the data will be lost, so RAID 0 does not provide fault tolerance or redundancy. The benefit of RAID 0 is its faster read access, so it may be used for the proxy server's cache.

- **RAID 1:** RAID 1 is two disks, known as a mirror set:

Figure 11: RAID 1

You can see from the preceding mirror set that the disk on the left has the original data and the disk on the right is a copy of that data. Should Disk 1 fail, you would "break the mirror" and then Disk 2 would provide the copy of the data for those who need access to it. At a later stage, we will add another disk and then re-establish the mirror set.

- **RAID 5:** RAID 5 has a minimum of three disks and is known as a stripe set with parity; it is written across the disks in 64 KB stripes just like RAID 0 but, when each stripe is written, one of the disks has a single parity block for each line of data, the parity is shown as shaded:

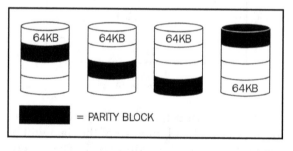

Figure 12: RAID 5

RAID 5 can suffer a single-disk failure but still allow access to the data, as the parity bits can recreate the missing data, but access will be slower than normal. This will give the IT team time to replace the missing disk.

For example, the preceding diagram represents a RAID 5 set but, in the following diagram, we are using a mathematical equation to represent the disk set so that you can see the impact of losing one disk and then losing two disks:

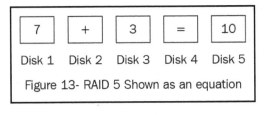

Figure 13: RAID 5 as a mathematical equation

Each of the disks has a numerical value. For example, if **Disk 3** fails, the equation would be $(7 + ? = 10)$ and the answer would be **3**. If we lose a second disk, **Disk 1**, the equation would then be $(? + ? = 10)$ and you could not work it out; the same happens if you lose two disks - parity cannot recreate the missing data.

- **RAID 6**: RAID 6 has a minimum of four disks and the same configuration as RAID 5, but it has an additional disk that holds another copy of the parity:

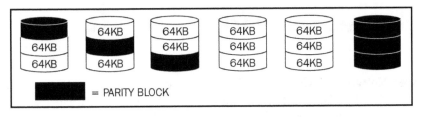

Figure 14: RAID 6

A RAID 5 disk set can afford to lose one disk but still be available as it is single parity. The good thing about a RAID 6 set is that it can lose two disks and still be redundant as it has double parity.

- **RAID 10**: RAID 10 is also known as RAID 1+0 - it is a RAID configuration that combines disk mirroring and disk striping to protect data. It requires a minimum of four disks, and stripes data across mirrored pairs. As long as one disk in each mirrored pair is functional, data can be retrieved:

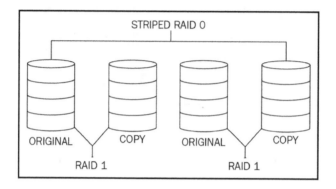

Figure 15: RAID 10

From this diagram, you can see a **RAID 1** on the left and then it is striped, so this will allow you to lose two disks.

Storage Area Network

A **Storage Area Network (SAN)** is a hardware device that contains a large number of fast disks, such as Solid-State Drives (SSDs), and is isolated from the LAN as it has its own network. A SAN typically has **Host Bus Adapters (HBAs)** (https://searchstorage.techtarget.com/definition/host-bus-adapter) and switches (https://searchnetworking.techtarget.com/definition/switch) attached to storage arrays and servers. The disks are set up with some form of redundancy, such as RAID 5 and upward, so that the storage space is redundant. Each switch and storage system on the SAN must be interconnected, and the physical interconnections must support bandwidth levels that can adequately handle peak data activities. There are two connection types:

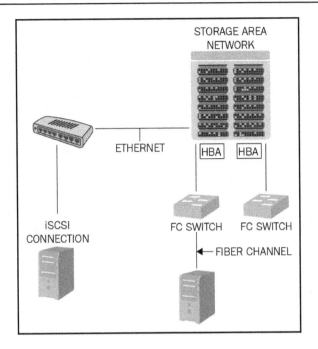

Figure 16: Storage area network

Each switch and storage system on the SAN must be interconnected, and the physical interconnections must support bandwidth levels that can adequately handle peak data activities. There are two connection types:

- **Fiber Channel**: Fast but expensive as it needs fiber channel switches
- **iSCSi Connector**: Runs **Small Computer System Interface (SCSI)** commands over Ethernet, and can connect through normal Ethernet switches and still offer good speed

The servers that use SAN storage are diskless but use the SAN storage as if they had disks installed, but you need very fast connection speeds so that the server does not suffer performance issues. For example, in the following diagram, **Server 1** is a virtual host and it needs another **200 TB** of data to host more virtual machines. It connects to the **SAN** using Ethernet and Ethernet switches; this connector is known as an iSCSi connector:

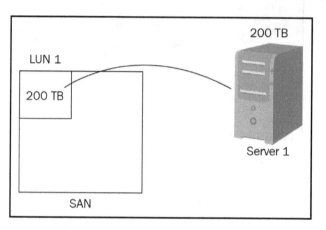

Figure 17: SAN—iSCSI Connector

The SAN allocates 200 TB by giving it a **Logical Unit Number** (LUN). This is known as an iSCSi target. Server 1, which has been allocated the space, is known as the iSCSi initiator. Server 1 is diskless but still sets up the disk space using disk management as if it were a physical disk. To prevent latency, the connection between Server 1 and the SAN must be fast.

Understanding Cloud Storage Concepts

It is quite common to use cloud storage to hold your data from the iCloud provided by Apple, Google Drive provided by Google, OneDrive provided by Microsoft, or Dropbox provided by Dropbox, Inc. The consumer versions of cloud storage allow you to have limited storage space, but offer to sell you a business version or additional storage by charging a monthly subscription fee. Let's look at the following diagram:

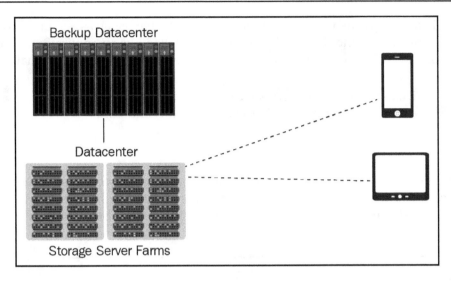

Figure 18: Cloud storage

In this diagram, you can see on the left-hand side a data center that has a vast amount of storage servers in a configuration called a server farm. The data center is a secure location where your data resides, but the data must stay within your world region. The data center has a backup data center to provide redundancy. The storage on these servers is likely to be diskless SAN storage.

Exploring Virtual Networks

A virtual network is very similar to a physical network in many ways but, for the Security+ exam, we must know the concepts of virtualization. To be able to host a virtual environment, we must install a hypervisor on a computer hosting the virtual machines. There are two different types of hypervisor:

- **Type 1 hypervisor**: This is an enterprise version that can be installed on a computer without an operating system, called bare metal. Examples are VMWare ESX, Microsoft's Hyper V, or Zen used by **Amazon Web Services** (**AWS**).

- **Type 2 hypervisor**: This needs an operating system, such as Server 2016 or Windows 10, and then the hypervisor is installed like an application. An example of a Type 2 hypervisor is Oracle's VM VirtualBox or Microsoft's virtual machine.

Exam tip: Type 1 hypervisor can be installed on a bare metal machine—examples are VMWare, Hyper V, and ESX.

The main server in a virtual environment is called a host and the virtual machines are called guests. This is very similar to a party where the person holding the party is a host and the people attending the party are called guests. There are various different components to virtualization:

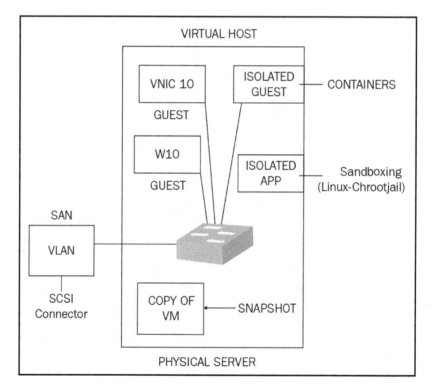

Figure 19: Virtualization

Now, we will look at each of the components:

- **Host**: The host may hold 100 virtual machines and therefore the main resources that the host needs are storage that normally uses a SAN, memory, and processor cores. These can be increased through time and so the host is scalable (it can grow). VM Sprawl is where the virtual host is running out of resources.

  For example, Server 1 is a virtual host, already has 50 guest machines, and is running out of physical disk space, but there is a requirement for Server 1 to host another 20 guest machines. There is enough memory and there are enough processing cores, but there is a lack of disk space. The solution would be to create a LUN on the SAN, giving Server 1 another 10 TB of disk space that it can allocate to the new virtual machines. Server 1 then connects to the SAN and configures the disk space allocated in disk management.

- **Guest**: Windows 10 is an example of a guest machine and needs the same amount of resources for a virtual machine as a physical Windows 10 machine. An isolated guest machine is known as a container. The following screenshot shows a virtual host with two guest machines, Server 2016 and Windows 10:

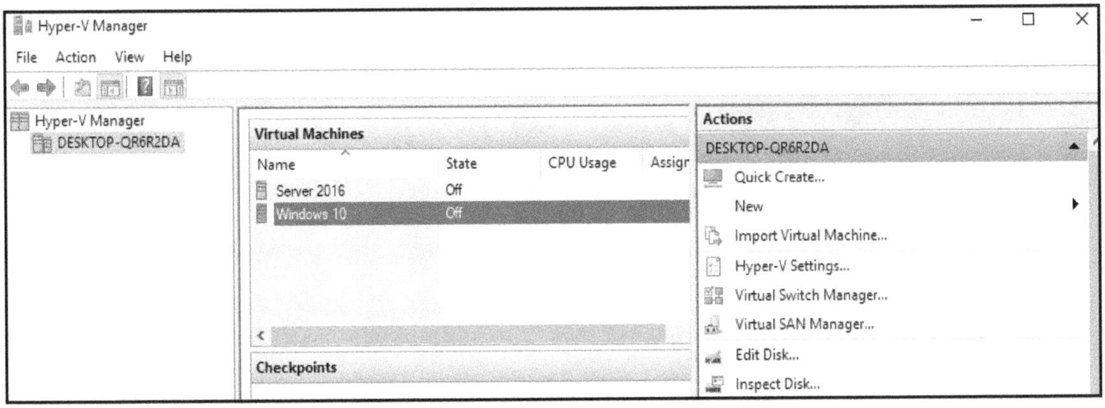

Figure 20: Virtual host with two guest machines

- **Containers**: Isolated guest virtual machines are called containers.

- **Virtual Switch**: Although a virtual switch can act like a switch connecting all of the machines, it can also create three different types of network: internet, external, and private. For each external network, the host needs a physical network card. Therefore, if you have two external networks, the host needs a minimum of two physical network cards. An internal network can create VLANs within this network:

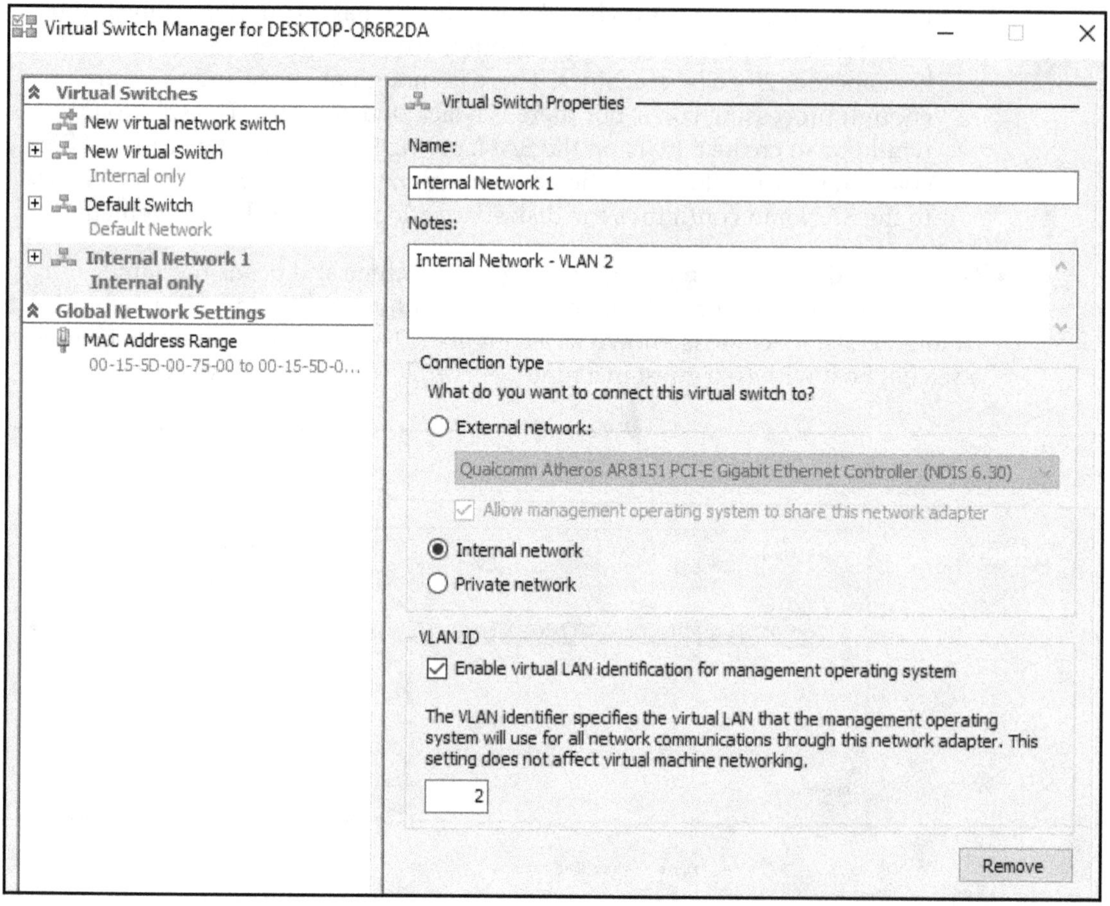

Figure 21: Virtual switch – Internal Network 1 with VLAN 2

- **Sandboxing**: Sandboxing is where an application is placed in its own virtual machine for patching and testing, or if it is a dangerous application that you don't want to roam across your network. In a Linux environment, this is known as a chroot jail.

- **Snapshot**: This is like taking a picture with a camera—whatever the virtual machine's setting is at that time is what you capture. You might take a snapshot before you carry out a major upgrade of a virtual machine so that, if anything goes wrong, you can roll the machine setting back to the original. If you have spent an hour upgrading and patching a virtual machine, you may snapshot it afterward to save the settings. Please see the following, a snapshot for Server 2016; Microsoft calls it a snapshot in Server 2008 but a checkpoint from Server 2012 R2 onward, but it is basically a snapshot:

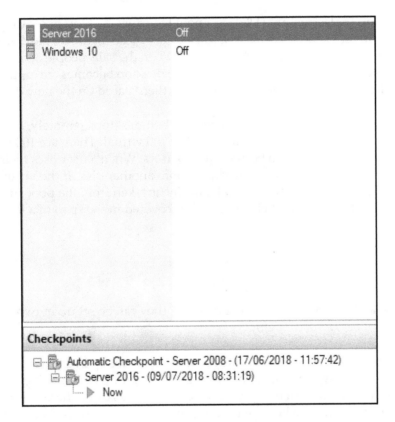

Figure 22: Snapshot of Server 2016

- **VLAN on a SAN**: When we create VLANs, we create these on switches in a physical environment. But, in the virtual environment, when the virtual switch is created on a SAN, the VLAN is said to be created on a SAN. A VLAN on a SAN uses an iSCSi connector.

Exam tip: When we create a VLAN on a SAN, we will always use an iSCSi connector.

Virtual Desktop Infrastructure

A **Virtual Desktop Infrastructure** (**VDI**) is a pool of virtual desktop pools for groups of users who share the same needs, such as a sales team whose members need access to the same applications and utilities on their desktops. When the salespeople access their desktops, their settings are copied elsewhere; if the desktop becomes corrupt, another desktop from the pool is taken and the settings are then placed on the new desktop.

For example, a company has 50 users, who access their desktops remotely, as they are hosted in a virtual environment. There are another 100 virtual. There are 100 virtual machines all set up and waiting to be allocated to users. When a user uses their virtual machine, all of their desktop settings are copied onto another disk. If the virtual machine that they are using fails, then a new virtual machine is taken from the pool and their settings are then applied so that their desktop is recovered in the span of a few minutes.

VDE

When users use a virtual machine as their desktop, they can be set up in two ways—permanent or non-permanent:

- **Example 1**: A college has desktops for students set up in a virtual environment. During the day, the teacher has four different groups all carrying out the same activity, however, each group needs a pristine desktop. Therefore, it is set up as non-permanent so when the user logs off, the image reverts back to the original setting.
- **Example 2**: Employees in a corporate environment are using virtual machines as their desktops. User A has just spent 10 hours working on a project, therefore, when they log in on the next day, they need to get the same desktop or productivity would be lost. Their desktop is therefore set up as permanent.

Heating, Ventilation, and Air-Conditioning (HVAC)

The servers for both cloud and virtualization, the storage servers and virtual hosts, are located in server farms that are in data centers. If these servers get too hot, the devices will fail. Therefore, in a data center, we have hot and cold aisles:

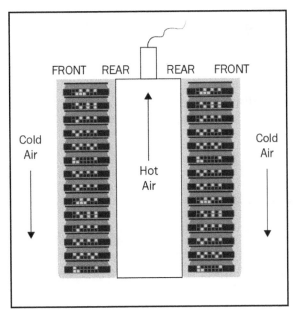

Figure 23: HVAC

The cold aisle is where the cold air comes in and that faces the front of the servers. The rear of the servers face each other, they push out hot air into the hot aisles, and this is allowed to escape through a chimney. This way, the temperature can be regulated and this ensures the availability of the IT systems.

Network Environments

Let's look at some of the network environments.

On-Premises

On-premises is where your company's network is inside a physical building; you will then have physical firewalls, routers, and switches. Each person will have a physical machine, the software is normally held on disks and, the IT team is on-site. You have total control and responsibility over your resources.

Hosted Services

Hosted services are technology services offered to you or your company by a provider that hosts the physical servers running that service somewhere else. Access to the service is usually provided through a direct network connection that may or may not run via the internet. The hosted services provider has full responsibility over your resources, including backup.

Cloud-Hosting Services

Cloud-hosting services provide hosting on virtual servers, which pull their computing resources from high-end servers that obtain their storage from a SAN. Access to resources is either via a lease line or the internet. The cloud provider has full responsibility over the hardware and availability of the IT systems:

- **Example 1**: A company that makes Easter eggs has its own on-premises where they manufacture the eggs, and delivery trucks to take them to their suppliers. They may need to take on additional staff around Easter, so they then have a small public cloud for the busy period—this is known as a hybrid model.
- **Example 2**: A new company cannot afford its own IT administrators as the turnover is limited, so they decide to subscribe to Microsoft's Office 365 for all of their needs. They adopt a cloud model and get email, Skype, and all of their Office 2016 applications. This is more cost-effective for them.

Practical Exercise – Is the Cloud Cost-Effective?

In this exercise, you are going to go to Amazon Web Services, which provides a calculator to see how much you could save by moving your infrastructure into the cloud. The instructions are accurate at the time of printing, but you may need to use them as a guideline if Amazon changes its website.

Search Google for the following: Amazon Web Services, pricing. Or go to Amazon Web Services and press the **Pricing** tab. Perform the following steps:

1. Select **Pricing**:

    - **AWS Pricing: Calculate My Cloud Savings**
    - **Currency: Euro**
    - **Environment**: Compare against on-premises
    - **AWS Region: EU (Ireland)**
    - **Server Type: db** (This means database)
    - **App Name: SQL**
    - **Number of VNs: 10**
    - **CPU Cores: 4**
    - **Memory: 64 GB**
    - **Hypervisor: VMWare**
    - **DB Engine SQL Server Enterprise**
    - **Storage: SAN**
    - **Raw Capacity: 100 TB**

2. Press **Calculate TCO**.
3. How much did you save? Was it cost-effective?
4. Now, search for another cloud provider and use their calculator to see who is more cost-effective.

Review Questions

1. In a cloud environment, what is elasticity?
2. In which cloud environment would I install the software and then have to update the patches?
3. Which cloud model is Office 365?
4. What is the major benefit of using a public cloud?
5. What is a cloud single-tenant model?
6. What is a cloud multitenant model?
7. Describe how a community cloud operates.
8. What are the limitations imposed on a CSP regarding data storage?
9. Who is responsible for the disaster recovery of hardware in a cloud environment?
10. What is a **Cloud Access Security Broker (CASB)**?
11. What model is it if you own the premises and all of the IT infrastructure resides there?
12. What is a hybrid cloud model?
13. What is distributive allocation?
14. What type of model deals with identity management?
15. What RAID model has a minimum of three disks? How many disks can it afford to lose?
16. What are the two RAID models that have a minimum of four disks?
17. What is the difference between RAID 5 and RAID 6?
18. Where will a diskless virtual host access its storage?
19. If you have a virtual switch that resides on a SAN, what connector will you use for a VLAN?
20. What type of disks does a SAN use?
21. Name a Type 1 hypervisor.
22. What type of hypervisor can be installed on bare-metal machines?
23. What is the machine that holds a number of virtual machines called?
24. What is a guest and what is it called if you isolate it?

25. In a virtual environment, what is sandboxing and how does it relate to chroot jail?
26. Which is faster for data recovery: a snapshot or a backup tape?
27. Why does HVAC produce availability for a data center?
28. Which cloud model is it if you decide to use Salesforce?
29. What do you call the cloud model where people from the same industry share resources and the cost of the cloud model?
30. What is an example of cloud storage for a personal user?

Answers and Explanations

1. Elasticity allows you to increase and decrease cloud resources as you need them.
2. **Infrastructure as a Service (IaaS)** requires you to install the operating systems and patch the machines. The CSP provides bare-metal computers.
3. Office 365 is a **Software as a Service (SaaS)** that provides email, Skype, and Office applications.
4. The major benefit of a public cloud is that there is no capital expenditure.
5. A private cloud is a single-tenant setup where you own the hardware.
6. Public cloud is multitenant.
7. A community cloud is where people from the same industry, such as a group of lawyers, design and share the cost of a bespoke application and its hosting, making it cost-effective.
8. A CSP must store the data within regions. It cannot even more backup data to another region for resiliency.
9. The CSP is responsible for the hardware fails.
10. The CASB ensures that the policies between the on-premises and the cloud are enforced.
11. On-premises is where you own the building and work solely from there.
12. A hybrid cloud is where a company is using a mixture of on-premises and cloud.
13. Distributive allocation is where the load is spread evenly across a number of resources, ensuring no one resource is over-utilized. An example of this is using a load balancer.
14. **Security as a Service (SECaaS)** provides secure identity management.
15. RAID 5 has a minimum of three disks and you can afford to lose one disk without losing data.

16. RAID 6 and RAID 10 both have a minimum of four disks.
17. RAID 5 has single parity and can lose one disk, where RAID 6 has double parity and can lose two disks.
18. A diskless virtual host will get its disk space from a SAN.
19. A VLAN on a SAN will use an iSCSi connector.
20. A SAN will use fast disks, such as SSDs.
21. Hyper V, VMware, and Zen are all Type 1 hypervisors.
22. Type 1 hypervisors can be installed on bare-metal machines.
23. A host holds a number of virtual machines - it needs fast disks, memory, and CPU cores.
24. A guest is a virtual machine, for example, a Windows 10 virtual machine, and if it is isolated it is called containers.
25. Sandboxing is where you isolate an application for patching or testing or because it is dangerous. A chroot jail is for sandboxing in a Linux environment.
26. A snapshot is faster at recovering than any other backup solution.
27. HVAC keeps the servers cool by importing cold air and exporting hot air. If a server's CPU overheats, it will cause the server to crash.
28. Salesforce is an online sales package, this is **Software as a Service (SaaS)**.
29. A community cloud is where people from the same industry share resources.
30. Cloud storage for personal users could be iCloud, Google Drive, Microsoft Onedrive, or Dropbox.

7
Managing Hosts and Application Deployment

In this chapter, we are going to look at different mobile devices and their characteristics and applications that run on these devices. In the Security+ exam, you need to know all of these aspects thoroughly. Let's first of all look at deploying mobile devices securely, followed by their management and security.

We will cover the following exam objectives in this chapter:

- **Explaining the impact associated with types of vulnerabilities**: Pointer dereference—race conditions
- **Given a scenario, deploying mobile devices securely**:
  - Connection methods—cellular—Wi-Fi—SATCOM—Bluetooth—NFC—ANT—infrared—USB
  - Mobile device management concepts—application management—content management—remote wipe—Geofencing—Geolocation—screen locks—push notification services—passwords and pins—biometrics—context-aware authentication
  - Containerization—storage segmentation—full device encryption
  - Enforcement and monitoring for: third-party app stores—rooting/jailbreaking—sideloading—custom firmware—carrier unlocking—firmware OTA updates—camera use—SMS/MMS—external media—USB OTG—recording microphone—GPS tagging—Wi-Fi direct/ad hoc—tethering—payment methods
  - Deployment models—BYOD—COPE—CYOD—corporate-owned—VDI

- **Explaining the security implications of embedded systems:**
  - SCADA/ICS—smart devices/IoT—wearable technology—home automation—HVAC—SoC—RTOS—printers/MFDs—camera systems
  - Special purpose—medical devices—vehicles—aircraft/UAV

- **Summarizing secure application development and deployment concepts:**
  - Development life cycle models—waterfall versus Agile
  - Secure DevOps—security automation—continuous integration—baselining—immutable systems—infrastructure as code
  - Version control and change management
  - Provisioning and deprovisioning
  - Secure coding techniques—proper error handling—proper input validation—normalization—stored procedures—code signing—encryption—obfuscation/camouflage—code reuse/dead code—server-side versus client-side—execution and validation—memory management—use of third-party libraries and SDKs—data exposure
  - Code quality and testing—static code analyzers—dynamic analysis (for example, fuzzing)—stress testing—sandboxing—model verification
  - Compiled versus runtime code

Deploying Mobile Devices Securely

Mobile devices are now used in our everyday lives and they pose problems for security teams as they are very portable and extremely easy to steal. In this section, we will look at some of the problems that you may face as a security professional. First, let's look at the different deployment models.

Mobile Device Management (MDM) sets policies on the use of these tools to protect the network. For example, they may prevent the camera being used on mobile devices and could also prevent a smartphone from being able to send/receive texts.

Bring Your Own Device

Bring Your Own Device (BYOD) is where an employee is encouraged to bring in their own device so that they can use it for work. Although it may save the employer money, it also has its pitfalls. BYOD needs two policies to be effective:

- **Acceptable Use Policy (AUP)**: An AUP outlines what the employee can do with the device during the working day; for example, they will not be allowed to play games or surf their personal email. If this is not acceptable, then the BYOD fails at the first hurdle and employees cannot bring their devices to work.
- **Onboarding Policy**: The onboarding policy would ensure that the device coming into the company's network is fully patched and secure before being attached to the network.

- **Offboarding Policy**: The offboarding policy covers such things as handing back the company's data as this could pose a problem. If the device owner does not agree, you may have to take them to court to get your data back. Some companies use storage segmentation, also called containerization, where they insert a storage card where the business data would be stored. During the offboarding, the employee would simply be asked to hand back the card:
  - **Example 1**: A new employee has brought their mobile device into the company and within 30 minutes one of the file servers has caught a virus. The security team tracks the source of the virus to the mobile device. How could this have been avoided? It's simple - the onboarding policy has not been carried out properly; if it had been, the virus would have been removed before connecting the device.

- **Example 2**: John, a member of the sales team, who has been using his tablet for BYOD, has just won the National Lottery and decided to leave the company. During the offboarding phase, he was asked to reset his tablet to its factory settings to ensure that the data was deleted. John has refused to do this as he has personal data and music files on the tablet. The company have called the local police and accused him of stealing their data. John informed the police officer that this is his personal device with his own data, and he produced a copy of the sales receipt for the device. The police officer was powerless and could do nothing further. The company would have to take John to court and prove that the data was theirs. John is now traveling the world, leaving the company with a further headache - they cannot take John to court because they don't know which country he is in. If they had used storage segmentation and asked John for the storage card on exit, this scenario would never have occurred.

Exam tip: BYOD relies on an Acceptable Use Policy and Onboarding/Offboarding policies being adopted.

Choose Your Own Device

Choose Your Own Device (**CYOD**) avoids problems of ownership because the company has a variety of tablets, phones, and laptops. When a new employee comes along, they merely choose one of these devices from a list. When they leave the company and offboard, the devices are taken from them as they belong to the company. The acceptable user policy would state that the devices can only store company data as they are corporate-owned devices.

Corporate-Owned Personally-Enabled

Corporate-Owned Personally-Enabled (**COPE**) is where the company purchases the device, such as a tablet, phone, or laptop, and allows the employee to use it for personal use. It is a much better solution for the company than BYOD. However, the IT team can limit what applications run on the devices as they are corporate-owned.

The COPE model can also help IT work within legal and regulatory parameters. Some European countries prohibit companies from wiping data on personal devices; if an employee loses a device, a remote wipe cannot be done. However, with COPE, the IT team has every right to wipe it remotely as it is corporate-owned and they remain compliant.

Virtual Desktop Infrastructure

A **Virtual Desktop Infrastructure** (**VDI**) is where an employee's desktop is based in the cloud or a virtual platform, and this can be accessed by using a mobile device, such as a tablet or laptop. This could provide a secure environment for contractors.

Mobile Device Connection Methods

There are various different connection methods for mobile devices:

- **Cellular**: This is where tablets and phones are using 3G, 4G, or 5G to connect to their provider without needing any other devices. Cellular connections are encrypted to prevent anyone seeing who is logging on or stealing your data. The problem that cellular faces is that, if there are no masts nearby and the device has a setting of no service, they will not work.

- **Wi-Fi**: Connecting to a wireless access point is a common method of gaining access to the internet. The connection needs to be encrypted to prevent man-in-the-middle attacks. Some wireless providers have hotspots in major cities and airports so that their customers can connect.

    If you live in an area where the cellular data shows no service, you could turn on your modern smartphone using Wi-Fi calling to connect to their network—but beware: this is only a method to connect to your carrier's network and they still charge you as normal for the calls.

    If you are connecting to a Wi-Fi hotspot in a hotel, you must be careful as most are insecure. Companies often have a guest wireless network that visitors can use, or their employees can use at lunchtime.

- **Bluetooth**: You may see someone walking down the street with a piece of gray plastic on one of their ears and they seem to be talking to themselves, but they are using their phone with a Bluetooth connection. Most Bluetooth devices have a range of about 10 meters. The devices are paired using a code to connect. For example, Ian is driving and has his phone set to hands-free. As he is driving, he receives a phone call from a friend and has him on loudspeaker; this is an example of using Bluetooth.

- **Near-Field Communication (NFC)**: NFC is normally used to make a wireless payment when the card must be within 4 cm of the card reader. You should store your NFC enabled card inside an aluminum pouch or wallet to prevent someone standing very close to you and skimming your card.

> **Exam tip**: Near-field communication is used for contactless payment within 4 cm of the card.

- **Infrared**: An infrared device is purely line-of-sight and has a maximum range of about 1 meter. This can be used to print from your laptop to an infrared printer. Infrared connections are not encrypted but you could see an attacker as they need to be within 1 meter.

- **USB**: Some mobile devices can be tethered to a USB dongle to gain access to the internet. A flash USB device can be used to transfer data between devices, as it is self-installing, and security teams tend to use group policy to prevent data being stolen by removable devices or use **Data Loss Prevention** (**DLP**).

- **Secure Satellite Communications (SATCOM)**: The secure satellite communications (SATCOM) equipment used by the US military is currently undergoing impressive capacity and performance advances. At the same time, it faces increasing security threats on several fronts. Military operations demand robust and flexible network-centric communication solutions for reliable information flow between frontline troops, support personnel, and commanders, both for operational control and situational awareness:

Figure 1: SATCOM

- **Adaptive Network Topology (ANT)**: ANT is a proprietary, open access, multicast wireless sensor network—very similar to Bluetooth low energy. It can provide secure access to wireless sensors.

Mobile Device Management Concepts

MDM is a software that allows security administrators to control, secure, and enforce policies on smartphones, tablets, and other endpoint devices. Let us look at the different aspects of MDM.

Push notification services can be used to inform the device owner that an email or a text has arrived. For example, if someone sends you a message to your LinkedIn account, a push notification can tell you that you have a new message.

Accessing the Device

Mobile devices are very small and very easy to steal, therefore, we need to look at how we can prevent someone from accessing the data even if the device's host has been lost or stolen. We will first look at screen locks and passwords, followed by biometrics, and then context-aware authentication:

- **Screen Locks**: Screen locks activate once the mobile device has not been accessed for a period of time. Then, after it is locked, the user gets a number of attempts to insert the PIN before the device is disabled.

- **Passwords and PINs**: Some mobile devices, such as smartphones, are very easy to steal and you can conceal them by putting them in a pocket. It is crucial that strong passwords and PINs with six or more characters are used. This makes decoding them more difficult and can lead to the device being disabled. For example, an iPhone gives you six attempts to log in, and after that it will disable the login for one minute. If you then fail on the seventh attempt, it locks you out for a further two minutes. If you continue to input the wrong PIN, you get locked out for 60 minutes on your ninth attempt.

Exam tip: Mobile devices need screen locks and strong passwords to protect them.

- **Biometrics**: Mobile devices can use biometrics, such as fingerprint or facial recognition. Apple uses Touch ID and Microsoft uses Windows Hello.

- **Context-Aware Authentication**: Context-aware security is location-based, where the user is located, who the user is, what the user is requesting, how the user is connected, and when the user is requesting information. The goal is to prevent unauthorized end users or insecure computing devices from being able to access corporate data. For example, Mary, a financial director based in London, is using context-aware authentication. For the authentication to be successful, the user must be Mary, the time has to be between 9 a.m.-5 p.m., Monday to Friday, and she needs to be in London. If all of these criteria are not met then authentication fails.

Device Management

Corporate devices need to be controlled so that employees cannot simply connect to an app store and download every application that they wish. For example, allowing games on corporate devices would have an adverse impact on productivity and security. We are now going to look at the downloads, applications, and content managers, and their characteristics, followed by remote wipe:

- **Download Manager**: The download manager controls the number of connections and the speed of downloading onto a mobile device
- **Application Management**: Application management uses whitelists to control which applications are allowed to be installed onto the mobile device
- **Content Management**: Content management stores business data in a secure area of the device in an encrypted format to protect it against attacks
- **Remote Wipe**: When a mobile device has been lost or stolen, it can be remote-wiped—the device will revert to its factory settings and the data will no longer be available

Exam tip: Geo-tracking will tell you the location of a stolen device.

Device Protection

Mobile devices are very easy to lose or steal, so we must have some way of finding those devices; we are going to look at the differences between geofencing, geolocation and using cable locks:

- **Geofencing**: Geofencing uses the **Global Positioning System** (**GPS**) or RFID to define geographical boundaries; once the device is taken past the defined boundaries, the security team will be alerted.
- **Geolocation**: Geolocation uses GPS to give the actual location of a mobile device. This is used when you lose your iPad and then use your iPhone to determine its location. This can be very useful if you lose or drop a device.
- **Cable locks**: Cable locks on laptops and tablets prevent them being stolen.

Exam tip:
Geofencing prevents mobile devices from being taken off the company's premises.

Device Data

To protect the data that is stored on a device, we should implement **Full Device Encryption (FDE)**. The device requires a **Trusted Platform Module** (**TPM**) chip to store the encryption keys.

For example, a salesperson has just received a new company laptop where the operating system had been hardened. The device used Bitlocker encryption, where the whole device is encrypted to protect the data stored on the hard drive. In the Security+ exam, this is known as FDE.

Containerization offers organizations the ability to deploy and manage corporate content securely in an encrypted space on the device. All corporate resources, such as proprietary applications, corporate emails, calendars, and contacts, reside within this managed space. We could also place an application inside a virtual machine to segregate it from the laptop.

Storage segmentation is where an external device is connected to a laptop, for example, a USB flash drive or **Secure Data card** (**SD card**). This allows the data on storage segmentation to be separate from any application or data already on the device.

For example, you are using your own smartphone as a BYOD but your company has asked you to separate the business data that they give you from your personal data, for example, pictures of family and friends that you already have stored on the phone. The easiest way to do this is to install an SD card on the phone where you will store the company data. This makes offboarding your data pretty easy—all you would have to do is eject the SD card and surrender it to the company.

Mobile Device Enforcement and Monitoring

There are many different tools and features that roll out with mobile devices. As a security professional, you need to know the security threats that they pose. Some of the features that a security professional should be well-versed in are mentioned here:

- **Network Access Control**: Network Access Control ensures that mobile devices that connect to your network are fully patched and compliant before obtaining access to the internal network.
- **Firmware Over-The-Air (OTA) updates**: Firmware is software that is installed on a small, read-only memory chip on a hardware device and is used to control the hardware running on the device. Firmware OTA updates are pushed out periodically by the vendor, ensuring that the mobile device is secure. An example is when the mobile device vendor sends a notification that there is a software update; this will include a firmware update.
- **Custom Firmware - Android Rooting**: Custom firmware downloads are used so that you can root your mobile device. This means you are going to give yourself a higher level of permissions on that device. The main benefit is the ability to remove any unwanted apps and games that your carrier or phone maker installs, as rooting can grant you a full uninstallation. Deleting apps that you will never use can also free up some additional storage capacity. However, be aware that your downloads from an unknown vendor may pose security risks.

 Exam tip: Rooting and jailbreaking remove the vendor restrictions on a mobile device to allow unsupported software to be installed.

- **Carrier unlocking**: Carrier unlocking is where a mobile device is no longer tied to the original carrier. This will allow you to use your device with any provider.
- **Jailbreaking**: Jailbreaking is similar to rooting, only this time the operating system is Apple's iOS – this allows you to run unauthorized software on Apple devices and remove device restrictions placed on the device. You can still access the Apple App Store even though jailbreaking has been carried out.
- **Third-party app stores**: There is a danger of downloading apps from third-party app stores as there is no guarantee of the quality of the app being installed. This could pose a security risk, later you could find that it had embedded monitoring software.

- **Sideloading**: Sideloading is having an application package in a `.apk` format and then installing it on a mobile device. This is useful for developers who want to trial third-party apps, but also allow unauthorized software to be run on a mobile device.

- **USB On-The-Go (USB OTG)**: USB OTG allows USB devices, such as tablets and smartphones, to act as a host, allowing other USB devices, such as USB flash drives, digital cameras, mice, and keyboards, to be attached to them. Apple does not allow USB OTG. Attaching USB devices can pose security problems as it makes it easy to steal information.

- **Camera Use**: Smartphones and tablets roll out with very good quality camera and video recorders whose media can be circulated on social media within seconds. This poses a security risk to companies, as trade secrets could be stolen very easily. Research and development departments ban the use of personal smartphones in the workplace. MDM polices may disable the cameras on company-owned smartphones.

- **Recording Microphones**: Smartphones and tablets can record conversations with their built-in microphones. They could be used to take notes, but they could also be used to tape conversations or record the proceedings of a confidential meeting.

- **SMS/MMS**: **Short Message Service** (**SMS**) is known as text messaging and has become a common method of communication. These messages can be sent between two people in a room without other people in the room knowing about their communication; these text messages could be used to launch an attack. The **Multimedia Messaging Service** (**MMS**) is a standard way to send messages that include multimedia content.

- **GPS Tagging**: When you take a photograph, GPS tagging inputs the location where the photograph was taken. Most modern smartphones do this by default.

- **Payment Methods**: Smartphones allow credit card details to be stored locally so that the phone can be used to make contactless payments. If this is a BYOD, it needs to be carefully monitored as someone could leave the company with a company credit card and continue to use it. MDM may prevent the payment function by disabling this tool in the mobile device management policies.

- **Wi-Fi direct/ad hoc**: The Wi-Fi direct wireless network allows two Wi-Fi devices to connect to each other without requiring a wireless access point. It is single-path, therefore it cannot be used for internet sharing. An ad hoc wireless network is where two wireless devices can connect with a wireless access point, but it is multipath and can share an internet connection with someone else.

- **Tethering**: Tethering is where a GPS-enabled smartphone can be attached to a mobile device to provide internet access. Microsoft's Windows 10 is capable of tethering. The danger of this is if someone uses a laptop to connect to the company's network and then tethers to the internet; it could result in split tunneling. This is where a user has a secure session via VPN to the corporate LAN, and then opens up a web browser with an insecure session that could be hacked and gives the attacker a gateway to a secure session to your LAN. MDM must ensure that this does not happen. When tethering, to ensure security, we must only create one session at one time.

Industrial Control System

The **Industrial Control System** (**ICS**) is a general term that encompasses several types of control systems and instrumentation used for industrial process control. They are controlled by a SCADA system and are used for the following:

- Electricity production and distribution
- Water supply and treatment
- Food production
- Oil and gas production and supply
- Chemical and pharmaceutical production
- Telecommunications
- Manufacturing of components and finished products
- Paper and pulp production

Supervisory Control and Data Acquisition

Supervisory Control and Data Acquisition (**SCADA**) systems are *automated control systems* that are crucial for industrial organizations since they help to maintain efficiency, process data for smarter decisions, and communicate *system* issues to help mitigate downtime.

The SCADA system can be used for water, oil or gas refineries where there are multiple phases of production. Iran had a uranium enrichment facility that was a SCADA system, but it suffered an attack from the Stuxnet virus that attacked the centrifuges. The Stuxnet virus was discovered in 2007, but many believe it could have been there in 2005:

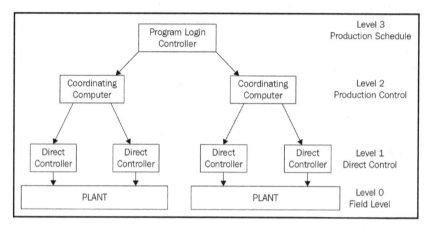

Figure 2: SCADA system

The security of the SCADA system is paramount. A network firewall prevents unauthorized access to the network, then they will use a NIPS as an additional layer. If further segmentation is required, they could use VLANs internally. This is no different from protecting a corporate network.

Mobile Devices – Security Implications of Embedded Systems

An embedded system is an electronic system that has software and is embedded in computer hardware. Some are programmable and some are not. Embedded systems are commonly found in consumer, cooking, industrial, automotive, medical, communications, commercial, and military applications. Following are some examples:

- **Household Items**: These include microwave ovens, washing machines, dishwashers, refrigerators, baby monitors, printers, MP3 players, video game consoles and cameras, and audio/video surveillance to wireless devices that control lighting.

- **IT Infrastructure**: These include telephone switches at the network end to cell phones at the consumer end; dedicated routers and network bridges to route data; and HVAC systems that use networked thermostats to control temperature and CCTV security systems.

Let's now look at each of these:

- **Smart Devices/IoT**: Smart devices, such as a smart TV, can connect to a home network and gain access to the internet. IoT comprises small devices, such as ATM cash machines, small robots, and wearable technologies, that can use an IP address and connect to internet-capable devices. We must ensure that we change the default usernames and passwords for these devices to prevent someone hacking them. From a security point of view, supporting IoT items is a nightmare because of the diversity of the devices:

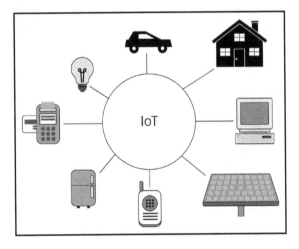

Figure 3: IoT devices

- **Home Automation**: A home automation system will control lighting, climate, entertainment systems, alarm systems, and appliances.
- **Wearable Technology**: The use of wearable technology has increased in recent years from monitoring health and performance to sending texts and receiving calls on your watch.
- **System On a Chip (SoC)**: An integrated circuit (`https://en.wikipedia.org/wiki/Integrated_circuit`) that integrates all components of a computer or other electronic systems. Wearable technology and most embedded systems may include a SoC. Life support devices uses SoC.

- **Real Time Operating System (RTOS)**: Intended to serve real-time applications that process data as it comes in, typically without buffer delays. Processing time requirements are measured in tenths of seconds or shorter increments of time. If a task or process does not complete within a certain time, the process will fail. This could be employed when robots are being used in production to ensure that the processes are being completed in a timely fashion.
- **Multifunctional Devices (MFD)**: Consists of at least two of the following: printer, scanner, fax, or photocopier in an all-in-one device. The weakness of each of these is that they all have a network interface and could be attacked through that interface. Any default setting or passwords must be changed.
- **Camera systems**: Camera systems now tend to be networked and used for home automation or for security systems to protect premises. For example, the police are dealing with a riot. The police are dressed in riot gear and there are vans with camera systems installed that are being used to tape the event in real time. The footage can be sent back to an incident control room where the police can see whether any of the rioters are on their internal police systems. This footage may also be used in court.

Exam tip: Multifunctional devices can be attacked through their network interfaces, not all of them have printing capabilities.

- **Heating, Ventilation, Air Conditioning (HVAC)**: Can be networked and centrally controlled by a security team. They can set the temperature in every room and can ensure that the data center is kept at a regulated temperature. The controllers can also view the usage to see which offices are occupied and which are empty.

Special-Purpose Devices

Special-purpose devices are more expensive bespoke devices that provide a unique purpose. For example, there are man overboard devices that detect someone falling into the water—we are going to look at a defibrillator.

Mobile Medical Devices can include infusion devices that measure fluids that are given to patients in hospital. (See the following photograph). Ambulances will carry life-support systems, such as defibrillators, that are used to save a person's life if they have just suffered from cardiac arrest. The defibrillators will have an SoC installed as it gives out instructions on how to use it, but if it detects a pulse, it will not send a charge:

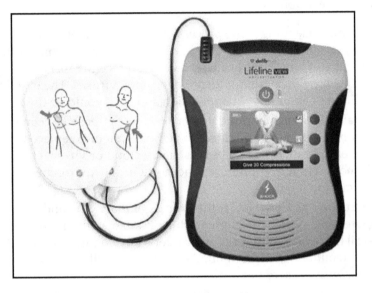

Figure 4: Defibrillator

Some luxury **vehicles** have embedded systems that produce a wireless hotspot in the car so that, when you are driving along, your passengers can connect to the internet. Others have the ability to carry out automatic self-parking. There have been many trials recently of self-driving cars; vendors, such as Google, are still trying to perfect their systems.

For many years, people have been flying model aircraft that also have embedded systems, but in the past 2-3 years, unmanned aerial vehicles called drones (Aircraft/**Unmanned Aerial Vehicles (UAV)**) have been making the headlines. The military can use these drones to carry out surveillance of areas where it is too dangerous to send manned aircraft. Some drones can be as large as a mini-aircraft, and some can be as small as a model aircraft but can have a camera attached so that aerial photographs can be taken.

Secure Application Development and Deployment Concepts

Some of the concepts used while securing an application during the development and deployment phases are as follows:

- **Baselining**: Baselining is the process of recording all of the applications that are installed on a mobile device. At a later stage, you could run another baseline that would tell you which applications have been recently installed. If you have an up-to-date baseline, you can identify zero-day viruses. The baseline would show an addition of an unknown application and this would be the zero-day exploit.

- **Immutable Systems**: Immutable systems are composed of components so that every time a system is upgraded, the whole system is replaced as a clean install and never upgraded. This is best used in a cloud or virtual environment, but it would not work for on-premises and non-virtual environments as it would take more time and labor.

- **Infrastructure as Code**: IaC is the process of managing and provisioning computer data centers through machine-readable definition files, rather than physical hardware configuration or interactive configuration tools. An example of these would be to create a number of PowerShell scripts to automate processes that you wish to carry out.

- **Version Control and Change Management**: Change Management normally occurs when software is getting either outdated or an audit has been carried out that highlights weak security with the software being used. Version control is used to identify the most up-to-date copy of software; for example, the first change would be version 1, the second would be version 2, and so on.

- **Provisioning and Deprovisioning**: Provisioning and deprovisioning have two different meanings. The first is when a new user arrives and we provision (create) their new account, then when they leave we deprovision (disable) their account. Software is very similar; if we create a new app that is designed for smartphones and tablets, when we provision it, this means we roll it out, and when it is no longer useful, we deprovision it.

Development Life Cycle Models – Waterfall v Agile

The **Software Development Life Cycle (SDLC)** is a structure followed by a development team within the software organization. It consists of a detailed plan describing how to develop, maintain, and replace specific software. There are two main models that are adopted. One is the traditional method, which is called waterfall, and the more dynamic method is called Agile.

Waterfall

The waterfall model is the traditional method used in the SDLC as it has a linear and sequential pattern to it. The development of the software moves from the top to the bottom, with each phase needing to be completed before the next phase can begin:

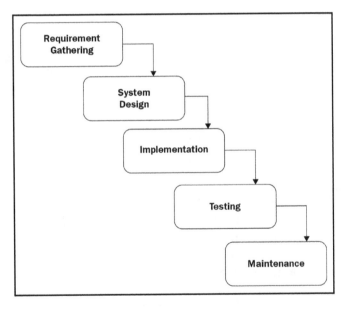

Figure 5: Waterfall model

It starts with gathering information about the requirement, then it is put into the design phase, and then it is implemented. The testing phase is carried out before it goes into production; any testing carried out will be rolled back prior to deployment. The maintenance phase is for patching and fixing any bugs.

Agile

The Agile method anticipates change and breaks down each project into prioritized requirements, delivering each individually within an iterative cycle. Adaptability and customer satisfaction by rapid delivery are the key concepts of this model:

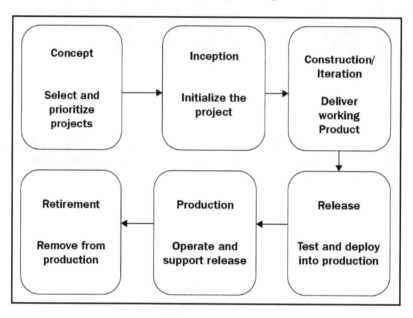

Figure 6: Agile model

Agile v Waterfall

Waterfall is a structured software development methodology, and can often be quite rigid, whereas the Agile methodology is known for its flexibility. Waterfall must finish one process completely before it can begin another. Agile is dynamic and is geared for rapid deployment to ensure customer satisfaction.

Exam tip: Waterfall is an SDLC model that requires each step to be completed before starting the next step.

DevOps

DevOps is where the IT operations and developers work together in the entire service life cycle, from design to rollout to production support. They use many of the same techniques as developers for their systems work.

Secure DevOps

Secure DevOps is where the security team, IT operations, and developers work together on software development; the focus is on reducing the time it takes for the software to get into production, which is why they adopt an Agile SDLC. There are processes that help them:

- **Security Automation**: This is the automatic handling of tasks by a computer rather than a security administrator. Orchestration is the connecting and integrating of various security applications and processes together. For example, security automation could be set up to scan for vulnerabilities at 6 p.m. without any human intervention
- **Continuous Integration (CI)**: CI requires developers to copy code into a shared repository several times a day. Each check-in is then verified by an automated build, allowing teams to detect problems early.

Secure Coding Techniques

Although most people that work in networking or security are not application developers, CompTIA has introduced secure coding into the syllabus. This section needs to be understood so it is written in the simplest format we could think of:

- **A Race Condition** is where two instructions from a different thread access the same data at the same time. When the developer wrote the application, the threads should have been programmed to access the data sequentially.

  For example, two guys buy tickets for the Super Bowl final, and when they arrive at the stadium they find that they have been allocated the same seat. That's a great profit for those selling the ticket, but a bad deal for those purchasing the ticket.

- **Proper Error Handling**: When we develop IT systems, we want the errors that are sent back to users to be very short and generic so that an attacker has very little information to use and launch further attacks. However, we want the information logged on errors to be as detailed as possible so that the security administrators know why the error occurred.

- **Proper Input Validation**: Input validation is controlled by using either wizards or web pages where the following are laid out:
  - Is it alphabetical?
  - Is it numerical?
  - Is it a certain format, such as a zip code or telephone number?
  - What are the minimum and maximum numbers of characters?

If the data is not input in the correct format, it will not be accepted. Input validation on web pages lists errors in red at the top of the page of the incorrect entries; this prevents SQL injection, integer overflow, and buffer overflow attacks.

Exam tip:
System errors to the users should be generic, but the logging of errors for administrators should log the full details.

- **Normalization**: Each database has a list of tables that are broken down into rows and columns. In a large relational database, data may be retained in multiple places. The goal of normalization is to reduce and eliminate the redundancy to make fewer indexes per table and make searching much faster.
- **Stored Procedures**: Transact SQL is used to query an SQL server database and can suffer from SQL injection attacks where attackers attack some code into the query. To avoid this, a developer may write an SQL query and then save it as a stored procedure, called Procedure 1. Instead of retyping all of the code, they just execute Procedure 1, which then executes the SQL query inside. Stored procedures are used to prevent SQL injection attacks.

Exam tip: Stored procedures and input validation can prevent an SQL injection attack. SQL injection can be identified by the phrase 1=1.

- **Code Signing**: Code signing hashes the code so that you know it is the original code and it has not been tampered with.
- **Encryption**: Encryption is the technique to protect the code from being stolen. To use the code, you must have the private key to decipher it.
- **Obfuscation/Camouflage**: Obfuscation or camouflage turns lines of code into an obscure format so that, if the code is stolen, it cannot be understood.

Exam tip: Obfuscation makes code obscure so that if it is stolen, it cannot be understood.

- **Code Reuse/Dead Code**: Developers like to keep code libraries where they store their source code. If they need to develop an application, they may start with old code then modify it for the new application. Dead procedures make up the most important part of dead code; it is code that is never executed. They inflate the executables, make systems harder to understand, and might even introduce new errors later in the life cycle of the program. They also consume resources and should be removed as they serve no purpose.

- **Memory Management**: It is important that, when a developer writes an application, they control how much memory it can consume as it can create performance issues. Memory leaks occur when object references that are no longer needed are unnecessarily maintained, and this causes the computer to gradually run out of memory.

- **Use of Third-Party Libraries**: The use of apps on mobile devices is a fierce marketplace where, as soon as you purchase a domain name, someone has emailed you offering you a good deal on mobile apps for your business. There are many third-party libraries that have many pieces of code, and although they not be perfect, it is a fast way to get your application to market. There are many third-party libraries for Android and JavaScript that have grown in popularity.

- **Software-Developer Kits (SDKs):** An SDK is a set of software development tools that allows the creation of applications for a certain software package, computer system, operating system, or similar development platform:
    - **Example 1 - Microsoft**: There is a Windows 10 SDK from Microsoft that provides the latest headers, libraries, metadata, and tools for building Windows 10 apps.
    - **Example 2 - Oracle**: There is a Java Standard Edition Development Kit. The JDK is a software development environment used for developing Java applications and applets. It includes the **Java Runtime Environment (JRE)**, an interpreter/loader (Java), a compiler (`javac`), an archiver (`jar`), a documentation generator (`javadoc`), and other tools needed in Java development.

- **Data Exposure:** Sensitive data is normally encrypted to prevent it from being stolen by attackers; this would include passwords and credit card details. We should limit the amount of data allocated to a user who is using an application; we should also use input validation and DLP to protect our data.

Code Quality and Testing

When an application developer writes an application, it needs to go through thorough testing before it is put into production. We need to ensure that the code does not have flaws or bugs that could be exploited by threat actors:

- **Pointer Dereference:** A pointer is an object in programming that stores the memory address of another value located in computer memory. When it retrieves the value, it is known as dereferencing the pointer. A failed pointer dereference means that the value has not been obtained.
- **Null Pointer Exception:** A `null` pointer exception is thrown when an application attempts to use an object reference that has the `null` value. A developer may think that an object was created previously, but since it does not appear, the code will show a `null` value as there is no object to point to:

```
String s=null;
String s1="a";
String s2=s1+s;// null pointer exception
```

Exam tip: A `null` pointer exception points to an object that is stored as a `null` value.

- **Static Code Analyzers**: When developers use static code analyzers, the code is not executed locally. Instead, they launch the static code analyzer tool, then the source code is run inside the tool that reports any flaws or weaknesses.
- **Dynamic Code Analysis**: When developers use dynamic analysis, the code is run and then they use a technique called fuzzing where a random input is inserted into the application to see what the output will be. White box pen testers use fuzzing to see the flaws and weaknesses in an application before it is rolled out to the production environment.
- **Stress Testing**: Stress testing is where a load is put through an application to see how its processors, memory, and disks can deal with the load. For example, Microsoft has a tool called Jetstress that simulates a storage load on an Exchange email server. The administrator defines the number of users and, when Jetstress runs, it gives an output relating to the disk I/O and storage usage. The test results in a pass or fail.
- **Sandboxing**: Sandboxing is where an application is run inside a virtual machine for testing purposes before it is put into production.

- **Model Verification**: Model verification and validation are the primary processes to ensure that an application has no bugs that need to be fixed and that it conforms to the specifications that were written.

- **Compiled versus Runtime Code**: Code is written in either C, C++, Python, or JavaScript. Once it is written, turn on a compiler that identifies weaknesses in the code. When the code is runtime, it means that the developer is evaluating the code for errors as it runs. Compiled and runtime products are both used to find application errors.

Server-Side v Client-Side Execution and Validation

Website scripts run in one of two places:

- **Server Side - called the backend**: Server-side validation is where the input by the user is being sent to the server and being validated with the response being sent back to the client. Programming languages such as C# and .NET are server-side.

- **Client Side - called the frontend**: Client-side validation does not require a round trip to the server, so the network traffic will help your server perform better. This type of validation is done on the browser side using script languages such as JavaScript, VBScript, or HTML5 attributes.

Client-side validation is much quicker, but an attacker can exploit the JavaScript and bypass the client side. Server-side validation takes much longer, and can use input validation to check that the input is valid and to stop the attacker who has just bypassed the client side. There is more control over server-side validation and it is more secure.

Review Questions

1. What is the purpose of MDM?
2. What is BYOD?
3. What two policies need to be agreed upon before BYOD is implemented?
4. How do BYOD and CYOD differ, and what are the benefits of CYOD to a company?
5. Name three types of mobile device connection methods.

6. What is used when we make a contactless payment using our debit card?

7. Which services allows your mobile device to be notified when an email message arrives in your inbox?

8. What two measures should I take to secure my mobile device?

9. What will prevent my laptop from being stolen when I am in a meeting with my boss?

10. What can I do to protect the data at rest on my mobile device?

11. What can I implement if I want to keep my personal data and pictures separate from my corporate data on my smartphone?

12. Once I have been authenticated by the VPN server, what method can be implemented to ensure that my mobile device is fully patched?

13. What is rooting and which operating system does it affect?

14. What is the purpose of jailbreaking and which operating system does it affect?

15. If my smartphone is with T-Mobile, what can be done at the end of my two year contract so that I can use Verizon as my provider?

16. What is the purpose of sideloading an application?

17. What is the benefit of USB OTG?

18. If I work in the R&D department, what are the two dangers when I take my cellphone to work?

19. When I go on holiday with friends from school, how can people on my social media know where the photograph was taken?

20. If I have been working in the sales department and have been using my cellphone to make work-related contactless payments, what does my company need to ensure happens during offboarding?

21. What two methods can I use to set up a wireless connection with another mobile device without using a WAP?

22. What is the purpose of tethering?

23. What is an embedded electronic system? Give two examples.

24. What is the purpose of a SCADA system?

25. What category of device are my smart TV and wearable technology?

26. What is home automation?

27. What is the purpose of SoC?

28. If a process is not carried out within a specified period of time, which causes the process to fail, what method am I using?

29. What is the most likely way an attacker would gain control of an MFD?

30. What is the purpose of the security team controlling the HVAC in a data center?

31. Someone at work has suffered from a cardiac arrest and the first aid delegate takes out a defibrillator that give instructions of the steps to take. What had been built into the device to give these instructions?

32. Give an example of embedded systems that can be used with vehicles.

33. What is a UAV? Give two examples.

34. What is the purpose of baselining?

35. What type of system am I using if I totally destroy the system and create a new system when an update takes place?

36. What software development life cycle is a traditional method that needs the previous stage to be complete before the next stage can start?

37. What software development life cycle is fast and customer-focused?

38. What is the purpose of secure automation in secure DevOps?

39. What is the benefit of using continuous integration in secure DevOps?

40. What is the main problem with a race condition when using an application?

41. What is the perfect way to set up error handling in an IT system?

42. Explain input validation and name three types of attacks that this could prevent.

43. How can I prevent an SQL injection attack other than with input validation?

44. What is the purpose of code signing?

45. What is the purpose of obfuscation?

46. What is dead code and how should it be treated?

47. If I am an Android developer, what can I obtain from the internet to help me make an application and get it to market quickly?

48. Explain how pointer dereference works.

49. What is a `null` pointer exception?

50. What is the technique used by developers to ensure that the application written conforms to the original specifications given by the customer?

Answers and Explanations

1. MDM sets and enforces policies to protect the network from mobile devices.
2. BYOD is where you bring your personally owned device to use in the workplace.
3. The acceptable use policy and onboarding/offboarding policies need to be agreed upon before you can implement BYOD.
4. BYOD are personally owned devices, whereas CYOD are company-owned devices. Using CYOD allows the security administrators to remotely wipe the device if it is stolen and can make offboarding very easy as they own the device, so data ownership will never be an issue.
5. Mobile devices can connect through cellular, wireless, and Bluetooth connections.
6. Near-field communication is used to make a contactless payment; the device must be within 4 cm of the card.
7. Push notification services notify your mobile device when an email message arrives at your inbox.
8. Screen locks and strong passwords are needed to secure a mobile device.
9. A cable lock will prevent my laptop from being stolen when I am in a meeting with my boss.
10. **Full Device Encryption** (**FDE**) is used to protect the data at rest on my mobile device.
11. Storage segmentation will allow you to keep personal data separate from business data on a cellphone. It is also known as containerization.
12. **Network Access Control** (**NAC**) ensures that devices are fully patched before they enter the corporate network.
13. Rooting can be carried out on Android devices where custom firmware is downloaded that removes restrictions that the vendor puts on the mobile device. This then allows you to run unauthorized software on the device.
14. Jailbreaking is the same as rooting as it lifts the restriction on Apple's iOS devices. You can then install unauthorized software but can still access the Apple App Store.
15. Carrier unlocking will allow me to use my smartphone on another carrier's network.
16. Sideloading allows you to install third-party, unauthorized software on your mobile device.
17. USB **On-The-Go** (**OTG**) allows you to connect a USB device to your mobile device. Apple does not allow USB OTG.

18. If I work in a sensitive area, my cellphone will allow me to take pictures and post them on my social media. I could also make a video or record conversations of confidential meetings.

19. Most modern smartphones use GPS tracking to store the location where pictures were taken.

20. When they offboard people who use contactless payment on a smartphone, they need to ensure that the business credit card details have been removed from the wallet.

21. Wi-Fi direct and an ad-hoc network allow wireless connections with another mobile device without a WAP.

22. Tethering allows you to use a cellphone on a laptop to provide internet.

23. Embedded electronic systems have software embedded into the hardware, some are using SoC. Examples are microwave ovens, gaming consoles, security cameras, wearable technology, smart TVs, medical devices such as defibrillators, or self-driving cars.

24. SCADA systems are industrial control systems used in the refining of uranium, oil, gas or the purification of water.

25. Smart TVs and wearable technology are classified as IoT devices.

26. Home automation is where you can control temperature, lighting, entertainment systems, alarm systems, and many appliances.

27. An SoC is a low-power integrated chip that integrates all of the components of a computer or electronic system. An example would be the controller for a defibrillator. Think of it as an operating system stored on a small chip.

28. The **Real-Time Operating System (RTOS)** processes data as it comes in without any buffer delays. The process will fail if it is not carried out within a certain period of time.

29. An attacker would most likely gain control of an MFD through its network interface.

30. When a security team controls the HVAC in a data center, they can ensure that the temperature is regulated and the servers remain available. They also know which rooms are occupied based on the use of air-conditioning and electricity.

31. An SoC gives instructions of the steps to take when using a defibrillator; however, if it detects a pulse, it will not send a charge.

32. An example of embedded systems is vehicles that are either self-parking or self-driving.

33. Unmanned aerial vehicles are drones or small, model aircraft that can be sent to areas where manned aircraft cannot go. They can be fitted with a camera to record events or take aerial photographs; an example of these would be to determine the spread of a forest fire.

34. Baselining is the process of recording all applications on a mobile device. You could then run the baseline at a later stage to find out what applications have been added since the last baseline.

35. An immutable system is totally destroyed when an update is made. This is ideal for the cloud or virtual environment.

36. Waterfall is a software development life cycle model that is traditional and needs each stage to be completed before the next stage can proceed.

37. Agile is a software development life cycle model that is fast and customer-focused.

38. Secure automation is where tasks, such as vulnerability scanning, are done by the computer and not the security administrator.

39. Continuous integration is where the developer will send code to a central repository two or three times a day so that it can be validated.

40. A race condition is when two threads of an application access the same data, but if it is a purchase only one is made.

41. The perfect way to set up error handling is for the user to get generic information but for the log files to include a full description of the error.

42. Input validation is where data that is in the correct format is validated prior to being inserted into the system. SQL injection, buffer overflow, and integer overflow are prevented by using input validation.

43. Other than input validation, a stored procedure can prevent an SQL injection attack.

44. Code signing confirms that the code has not been tampered with.

45. Obfuscation is taking code and making it obscure so that, if it is stolen, it will not be understood.

46. Dead code is never used, but could introduce errors into the program life cycle; it should be removed.

47. Using a third-party library will help a developer obtain code from the internet to help make an application and get it to market quickly. There are many for Android and JavaScript.

48. When an object in programming has its value retrieved, this is known as a dereference.

49. A null pointer exception is a runtime exception where the application has tried to retrieve an object with a `null` value.

50. Model verification is a process used by developers to ensure that the application conforms to the original specifications.

Protecting Against Attacks and Vulnerabilities

8

In this chapter, we are going to look at attacks and vulnerabilities. Each type of attack will have its unique characteristics. This is probably the most heavily tested subject in the Security+ exam. This chapter needs to be thoroughly understood because, sometimes, questions about attacks are very vague, so if you do not understand the concepts fully, you may not understand what is being asked.

We will cover the following exam objectives in this chapter:

- **Given a scenario, analyze indicators of compromise and determine the type of malware**: Viruses—crypto-malware—Ransomware—worm—Trojan—rootkit—keylogger—adware—spyware—bots—RAT—logic bomb—backdoor

- **Comparing and contrasting types of attacks**: Social engineering—phishing—spear phishing—whaling—vishing—tailgating—impersonation—dumpster diving—shoulder surfing—hoax—watering hole attack—principles (reasons for effectiveness)—authority—intimidation—consensus—scarcity—familiarity—trust—urgency. Application/service attacks—DoS—DDoS—man-in-the-middle—buffer overflow—injection—cross-site scripting—cross-site request forgery—privilege escalation—ARP poisoning—amplification—DNS poisoning—domain hijacking—man-in-the-browser—zero day—replay—pass the hash. Hijacking and related attacks—clickjacking—session hijacking—URL hijacking—typo squatting. Driver manipulation—shimming—refactoring. MAC spoofing—IP spoofing. Wireless attacks—Replay—IV—evil twin—Rogue AP—Jamming—WPS—Bluejacking—Bluesnarfing—disassociation—RFID—NFC . cryptographic attacks—birthday—known plain text/cipher text—dictionary—Brute force—rainbow tables—online versus offline—collision—downgrade—replay—weak implementations
- **Explaining penetration testing concepts:** Active reconnaissance—passive reconnaissance—pivot—initial exploitation—persistence—escalation of privilege—penetration testing versus vulnerability scanning—black box—white box—gray box
- **Explaining vulnerability scanning concepts:** Passively test security controls—identify vulnerability—identify lack of security controls—identify common misconfigurations—intrusive versus non-intrusive—credentialed versus non-credentialed—false positive

Virus and Malware Attacks

In today's world, viruses and malware are rife; there are many different variants and we will look at each of these in turn:

- **Virus**: A virus is a program that embeds itself in another program and can be executed in many different ways, for example, by clicking on a link on a web page or opening up an email attachment. Once it has been activated, it replicates itself, going from host to host. A lot of viruses use `port 1900`.

- **Ransomware**: Ransomware involves the attacker encrypting the files on a user's computer and then displaying a link asking for money to release the files. An example of this is shown in the following screenshot. Another example of ransomware is when you download a free program and it says that you have problems with your computer so you need to purchase the full version of the software. This is quite subtle. Remember—the rule of thumb is that, if you have to part with money, then it is ransomware:

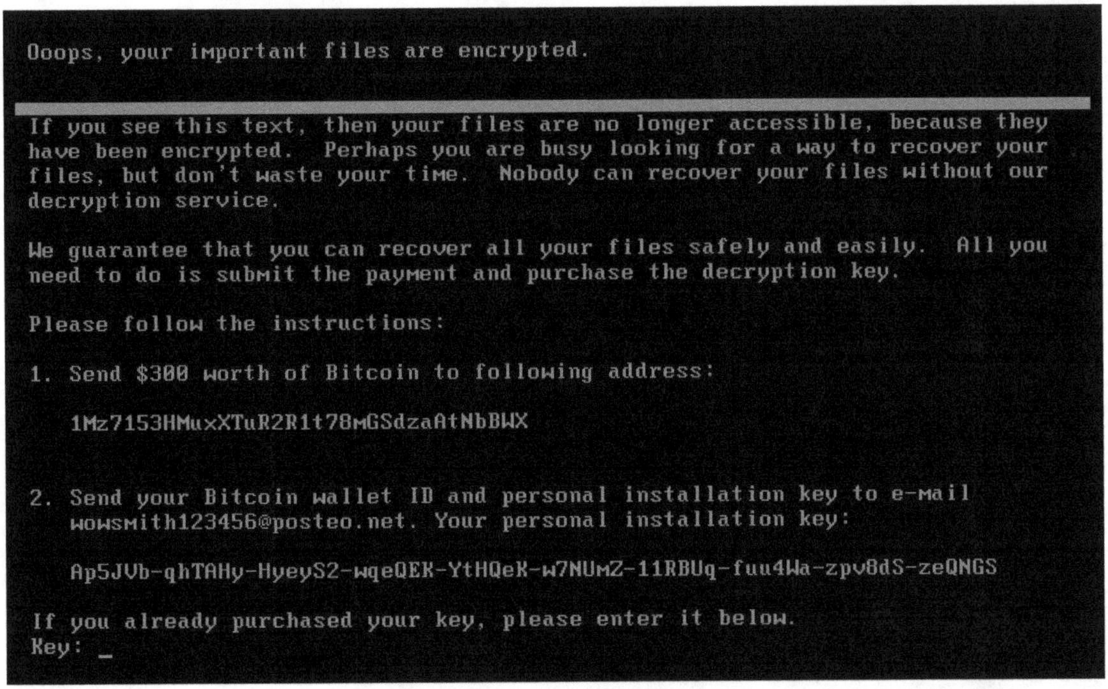

```
Ooops, your important files are encrypted.

If you see this text, then your files are no longer accessible, because they
have been encrypted.  Perhaps you are busy looking for a way to recover your
files, but don't waste your time.  Nobody can recover your files without our
decryption service.

We guarantee that you can recover all your files safely and easily.  All you
need to do is submit the payment and purchase the decryption key.

Please follow the instructions:

1.  Send $300 worth of Bitcoin to following address:

    1Mz7153HMuxXTuR2R1t78mGSdzaAtNbBWX


2.  Send your Bitcoin wallet ID and personal installation key to e-mail
    wowsmith123456@posteo.net. Your personal installation key:

    Ap5JVb-qhTAHy-HyeyS2-wqeQEK-YtHQeK-w7NUmZ-11RBUq-fuu4Wa-zpv8dS-zeQNGS

If you already purchased your key, please enter it below.
Key: _
```

Figure 1: Ransomware

- **Crypto-Malware**: Crypto-malware is a type of ransomware that encrypts a user's files and demands a ransom. Sophisticated crypto-malware uses advanced encryption methods so that files cannot be decrypted without a unique key.

- **Worm**: A worm is a program that replicates itself to spread to other computers, exploiting security weaknesses. Common ports are `1098`, `4444`, and those in the 5000 range. An example of a worm is Nimda. The Nimda virus was released in September 2001; its name is admin spelt backward and refers to a file called `admin.dll`. When it runs, it continues to propagate itself. The main target of Nimda was Microsoft's IIS web server and file servers. It would create a Denial-of-Service attack and its job was to simply slow networks down to a halt. When it accessed a server, it would run down mapped network drives to everyone connected to the server, then it rewrote the system files so that they had an EML extension. Once it had totally destroyed a machine, a huge white envelope appeared on the desktop; this meant that it would no longer function.

- **Trojan**: Trojans are known for creating a backdoor on your computer that gives malicious users access to your system, allowing them to steal confidential or personal information. They try to exploit `system32.exe` and then run a DLL file to attack the operating system kernel - this is the management part of the operating system. The Trojan will try to find password information and set up an SMTP engine that uses a random port to send those details to the attacker.

- Trojans attack the `/System 32` and `SysWOW64` directories by placing a `.dll` file there.

- `Trojan.BHO.H File C:\WINDOWS\SysWOW64\fezegepo.dll`
- `Trojan.Vundo File C:\WINDOWS\system32\fezegepo.dll`

For example, Gh0st RAT is a remote access Trojan that was originally designed by threat actors in China. A user clicks on a link and a dropper program called `server.ex` installs Gh0st RAT with `svchost.dll`, which then allows the attacker to take control of the computer. It can then log keystrokes, download and upload files, and run a webcam and microphone feeds.

- **Remote Access Trojan (RAT)**: A RAT is a program that sends login details to the attacker to enable them to take full control of the computer.

- **Rootkit**: A rootkit is designed to enable access to a computer or areas of its software which are not otherwise allowed. For example, you might reinstall the OS
but it is keeps coming back. It could be launched using `c:\windows\system32` for a Windows computer or `bin/` and `/usr/bin/` for Linux/Unix computers.
- **Backdoor**: A backdoor is a piece of software or a computer system is created by program developers in case someone locks themselves out of the program; they are generally undocumented. Attackers use these to gain access to systems.
- **Logic bomb**: A logic bomb is a virus that is triggered by either an action or at a specific date, for example, the Fourth of July or Christmas Day. On March 20, 2013, in South Korea, a logic bomb was triggered and malware began erasing data from machines to coordinated the act of destruction with multiple victims. The malware consisted of four files, including one called `AgentBase.exe`, which triggered the wiping. Contained within that file was a hex string (`4DAD4678`) indicating the date and time the attack was to begin - March 20, 2013 at 2 p.m. local time (2013-3-20 14:00:00). As soon as the internal clock on the machine hit 14:00:01, the wiper was triggered to overwrite the hard drive and master boot record on Microsoft Windows machines and then reboot the system. It attacked the government and banking sector.

In a Linux environment, a rootkit virus attacks the `/usr/bin` directory.

- **Keylogger**: The main idea behind keyloggers is to track and log keystrokes. You can install a keylogger by putting it on a very small, thin USB drive at the rear of a desktop computer.
- **Adware**: Adware is an unwanted program that keeps popping up with unwanted advertisements. One way to stop adware is to enable a popup blocker.
- **Spyware**: Spyware is renowned for slowing down computers as it uses your computer's processing power and RAM resources to continually track what you are doing on your computer and sends the information to a third party.
- **Botnet**: A bot is a program that takes control of a computer. A botnet is a collection of bots that have been set up for malicious purposes, normally to carry out a DoS attack.

Social Engineering Attacks

Social Engineering attacks are based on the exploitation of someone's personality. There are various types of social engineering attacks; let's look at each of them and the principles of why they are effective:

- **Phishing and Spear Phishing**: Phishing attacks are carried out by emailing someone telling them that their bank account needs updating, so they need to complete the attached form. Such forms ask for personal details that could later be used for identity fraud. Such emails often look as though they have come from a legitimate body, so users are fooled into carrying out the instructions they contain: Spear Phishing targets a group of people.

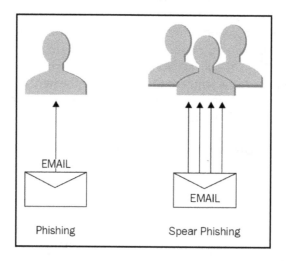

Figure 2: Phishing attack

- **Whaling**: A whaling attack is a kind of phishing attack that targets either a chief executive officer or a high-level executive. CEOs and high-level executives have intense days, so they might action what *looks* like a minor request quickly so that they can move on to their next task, but end up being attacked.
- **Vishing**: A vishing attack involves the use of a VoIP phone or another telephone, or someone leaving a voicemail to try and extort information.
- **Tailgating**: Tailgating is when someone opens a door using their ID badge and then someone follows them in before the door closes. This can be especially effective if the person going through first is a middle-aged man and the tailgating person is a pretty lady - they may be old school and keep the door open for the lady.

- **Impersonation**: Impersonation can involve someone putting on a uniform - of a traffic warden or police officer, for example. Imagine you are driving down the street and get flagged down by a police officer - they are holding something that looks like a speed gun. Another form of impersonation is that someone pretends to be from the help desk asking you for information about your department or tells you that you need to change your password because of problems with the IT systems.

- **Dumpster Diving**: Dumpster diving is when someone removes the trash from your trash can in the hope that a letter holds **Personally Identifiable Information** (**PII**) that can be used later to commit fraud. The best way to prevent this is to shred all mail that has PII before you dispose of it. This is effective, most people just throw letters in the bin without a second thought.

- **Shoulder Surfing**: Shoulder surfing involves a person standing behind someone who's using a computer so that they can see sensitive information. Another example is someone using an ATM machine while the person behind them is using their smartphone to video the transaction. This is effective as the victim is concentrating on withdrawing their money and is not aware that they are being watched.

- **Hoax**: The `jdbgmgr.exe` virus hoax in 2002 involved email spam (`https://en.wikipedia.org/wiki/Email_spam`) that advised computer users to delete a file named `jdbgmgr.exe` because it was a computer virus (`https://en.wikipedia.org/wiki/Computer_virus`); see the following figure:

jdbgmgr.exe

Figure 3: Hoax virus

The email said that this cute little bear was a virus and should be deleted, as anti-virus software from anti-virus vendors would not find it; this was true, as it was not a virus. It was an operating system file and to delete it would damage your computer. The reason why this attack worked was that the bear was there and the anti-virus software did pick it up on a scan, therefore, it looked real. Another example of a hoax would be purchasing fake anti-virus software that does not work.

- **Watering Hole Attack**: Companies in the same industry visit very similar websites, therefore, attackers identify a website that people in a particular industry are likely to visit and then infects it with a virus. This is effective as the people targeted have often been using the website for years and trust its content.
- **Authority**: An email may be sent out by someone of authority, such as the CEO or HR manager, ordering you to complete a form that can be accessed by clicking on a link; see the following email. This is effective because nobody wants to defy the **Chief Executive Officer (CEO)**:

> *From: Ian Neil (CEO)*
>
> *To: All Staff*
>
> *Subject: UPDATE YOUR FINANCIAL DETAILS*
>
> *Dear All,*
>
> *The finance team are moving to a new finance application and have told me that personnel within the company have not updated their bank details. You need to click on this link and update your details:* `http://update.details.wehackyou.com`.
>
> *Failure to do so by the end of play today will result in disciplinary action against those individuals that do not comply.*
>
> *Kind Regards,*
>
> *Ian Neil*
>
> *Chief Executive Officer*

- **Intimidation**: An example of intimidation is someone pretending to be someone of high authority, for example, a policeman; they then threaten the person that, if they don't do as they are told, they will be in trouble. This is effective because victims of this kind of attack are made to believe that they have no other choice but to do as they are asked.

An email from your CEO, a high-level executive, or the HR manager telling you to fill in a form or click on a link is an authority attack.

- **Urgency**: An example of an urgency attack is someone arriving at a reception desk and demanding access quickly; they could target a new receptionist, who may get flustered and let them in. Another good example is a "fireman" demanding access to the server room before the building burns down. This is effective because the receptionist panics, believing that there is a fire.

Allowing a fireman into your server room is an urgency attack.

- **Scarcity**: An example of this kind of attack is trying to rent a room for a weekend away; you and 10 friends pick a hotel and go onto the website and it says **Only one room left!** in red. You purchase the last room, and so do 10 of your friends, and guess what? There is still only one room left! Another example is a personal secretary receiving a phone call from someone claiming to be in charge of domain names while the CEO is at a conference. The caller tells the secretary that they are calling to renew the domain name and that it must be done in the next 30 minutes or else the company will lose the domain name; they state that the renewal will be $45. The secretary knows that the company website and email addresses cannot operate without the domain name. This attack is effective because the secretary cannot disturb the CEO during an important meeting, so they purchase the domain name renewal. It may well be 3-4 months away.
- **Familiarity and Trust**: In preparation for these attacks, hackers make themselves familiar to their victims; they come around a lot, and eventually they become trusted. At that point, they can begin working their way inside a company, for example, gaining access to areas of the company that they should not be able to access. This is effective as they become part of the furniture and nobody questions their actions.
- **Consensus**: People like to be accepted by their peers and coworkers. An attacker might ask for some information and state that they obtained it last week from a coworker and just need an update on it. This works as the person supplying the information does not want to be seen as acting differently from other members of the team. Sometimes, this is referred to as **social proof**.

Common Attacks

If you are going to gain the CompTIA Security+ qualification, you need to know the different types of attacks that you may encounter; there are numerous attacks and you need to know about each of them, their characteristics, and how they can be prevented. Let's look at each in turn.

Application/Service Attacks

- **Denial-of-Service (DoS) Attack**: A DoS attack is where the victim's machine or network is flooded with a high volume of requests from another host so that it is not available for any other hosts to use. A common method is to use SYN flood attacks, where the first two parts of the three-way handshake occur and the victim holds a session waiting for an ACK that never comes.

 A SYN flood attack is where only the first two parts of the three-way handshake take place, leaving your computer in a state of limbo. DDoS attacks often involve a high volume of these.

- **Distributed Denial of Service (DDoS) attack**: A DDoS attack is where a botnet is set up to flood a victim's system with an enormous amount of traffic so that is taken down; you can see in *Figure 4* that an attack originating from China took out the Facebook network. Look at the enormous amount of traffic! Luckily enough, Facebook is very well-organized and was back up and running within 30 minutes. Stateful firewalls can be set up to prevent DDoS attacks from gaining access to your network:

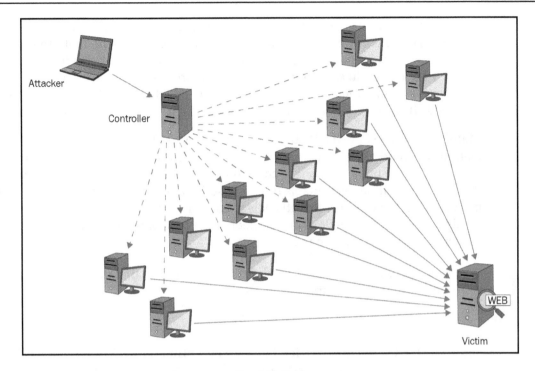

Figure 4: DDoS attack

- **Amplification Attack**: A DNS amplification is a DDoS attack in which the attacker exploits vulnerabilities in DNS servers to turn initially small queries into much larger payloads, which are used to bring down the victim's servers.
- **Man-in-the-Middle (MITM) attack**: An MITM attack is where the attacker intercepts traffic going between two hosts and then changes the information in the packets in real time. See *Figure 5*, where Mary is contacting Carol, but John is the man-in-the-middle and changes the conversation as it goes backwards and forwards. A Man-in-the-Middle can inject false information between the two hosts:

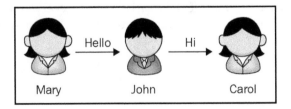

Figure 5: Man-in-the-middle

For example, a hacker is imitating the conversations of two parties to gain access to funds. The attacker intercepts a public key and with that can put in their own credentials to trick the people on both sides into believing that they are talking to each other in a secure environment. While online shopping from home or a mobile device, victims think that they are buying goods from a legitimate source, but instead their money is being stolen.

- **Man-in-the Browser (MITB) attack**: MITB attacks use the same approach as man-in-the-middle attacks (`https://www.owasp.org/index.php/Man-in-the-middle_attack`), but a Trojan is used to intercept and manipulate calls between the main application's executable (the browser) and its security mechanisms. The most common objective of this attack is to commit financial fraud by manipulating the transactions of internet banking systems, even when other authentication factors are in use.

Exam tip: Kerberos prevents replay attacks, as it uses updated sequence numbers and timestamps.

- **Padding Oracle On Downgraded Legacy Encryption (POODLE)**: A POODLE attack is a man-in-the-middle attack that exploits the use of SSL 3.0 on legacy systems; this is extremely insecure. Encryption in SSL 3.0 uses either the RC4 stream cipher or a block cipher in CBC mode. A downgrade attack is when you abandon a higher level of security for an older, low-level security system; in this case, we are downgrading the computer's browser to an older version of the browser's SSL 3.0 using CBC.
- **Replay Attack**: A replay attack is a MITM attack that intercepts data but replays it at a later date. Kerberos, a Microsoft authentication protocol, can prevent this as each entry has updated sequence numbers and timestamps. For example, communication takes place between two hosts on a Windows network that uses Kerberos authentication; data is being transmitted with USN 7 appearing and then USN 10 appears; the receiving host will then realize the data is not as it should be. When USN and USN 8 or USN 9 are received the next day, they will be rejected as being out of sequence, preventing the replay attack.

A POODLE attack is an MITM downgrade attack using SSL 3.0 in CBC mode.

- **Zero-Day Attack**: A Zero-Day attack is when an exploit is found but, at that time, there is no solution to prevent it, so the attackers attack more, unless you have previously taken a baseline. If you look at *Figure 6*, you will see a time line of a Zero-Day attack. It takes two more days for a solution to prevent it - no anti-virus, SIEM, NIDS, or NIPS will be able to stop a Zero-Day attack, as vendors don't have the ability to detect it that day. Vendors will be waiting for an update.

		Days		
0	1	2	3	4
Exploit found	Information Gathered	Send to AV Vendor	AV Solution made	Update rolled out

Figure 6: Zero day exploit

The only way to detect a Zero-Day exploit is when you have previously taken a baseline of your computer, then you can check the changes since the baseline; this will identify a Zero-Day exploit. If you have no previous baseline, then you will not detect it.

- **Pass-the-Hash Attack**: The attacker first obtains the hashes from a targeted system that is using an **NT Lan Manager** (**NTLM**) using any number of hash-dumping tools. They then use a pass-the-hash tool to place the obtained hashes on a Local Security Authority Subsystem service. A Windows-based authentication system believes that the attacker is a legitimate user, and automatically provides the required login credentials. This can all be accomplished without the need for the original password, and account lockout cannot be enforced as this attack is operating on a lower layer. You need to disable NTLM or enable Kerberos to prevent the pass-the-hash attack.

- **Domain hijacking**: Domain hijacking is when someone tries to change the domain registration of a domain with the internet authorities so that they can control it for profit. For example, an attacker manages to re-register the domain name of a well-known company and can access the control panel with the original domain's company, Hosting A. They then take out a hosting package with Hosting B, where they copy over all of the files from Hosting A and move them into Hosting B. They then point the DNS records to Hosting B, where they can take sales from customers who believe they are trading with the original company.

A Zero-Day virus cannot be traced or discovered by any security device, as it may take up to five days before a patch or update is released.

- **DNS Poisoning**: When DNS resolution occurs, the first place that is checked is the DNS cache on the local machine; after that, it goes to the hosts file and then onto the DNS server. DNS Poisoning is the process of putting bad entries into the **DNS cache**, diverting requests to a fraudulent website that has been made to look like the legitimate website (See *Figure 7*):

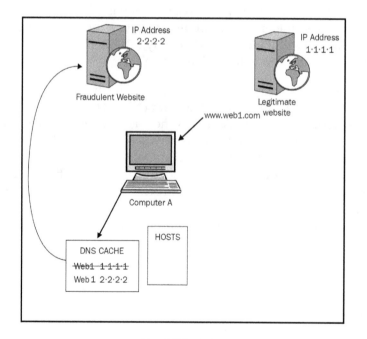

Figure 7: DNS poisoning

If we look at *Figure 7*, **Computer A** has already visited the legitimate website, called Web 1, and its proper IP address of 1.1.1.1 has been placed in its DNS cache. When DNS resolution is performed, the DNS cache is searched first, then the hosts file is next, followed by the internal DNS server. The attacker has now deleted the entry for Web 1 and inserted their entry for Web 1 with an IP address of `2.2.2.2`. Now, when the user enters the `www.web1.com` URL, the only entry in the DNS cache is `Web1 2.2.2.2` and the user is diverted to a website that looks like the legitimate website. When they enter their card details to make a purchase, their account is emptied.

- **DNSSEC**: DNSSEC encrypts DNS traffic and is designed to prevent DNS spoofing attacks, DNS cache poisoning, and your DNS traffic from being captured. DNSSEC produces RRSIG records for each entry in the DNS database.
- **ARP Poisoning**: ARP operates at **Layer 2** of the OSI reference model and operates using MAC addresses. ARP poisoning is an attack that must be done locally. ARP cache poisoning, or ARP poison routing, is when an attacker sends (spoofed) **Address Resolution Protocol** (**ARP**) messages to a local area network. ARP spoofing may allow an attacker to intercept data frames on a network, modify traffic, or stop all traffic. ARP poisoning can be prevented by using IPSec tunnels across your internal network.
- **MAC Spoofing Attack**: MAC spoofing is the theft of the Media Access Control (MAC) address of another networked device, which is then used to gain access to the network, for example, a wireless access point that uses MAC filtering.
- **IP Spoofing**: IP spoofing is the creation of **Internet Protocol** (**IP**) packets with a false source IP address to hide the identity of the sender or to impersonate another computing system so that they cannot be traced when they carry out a malicious attack.
- **Privilege Escalation**: A privilege escalation attack is where an attacker wants to grant themselves more permissions than they are entitled to. With a higher level of privilege, they will be able to run unauthorized code or make changes to the IT infrastructure. They may try to use someone else's account to access the Active Directory and allocate themselves a higher level of privilege. For example, John, an administrator, leaves his laptop unattended when his boss asks him to go into their office. Mary, who is a normal user, goes into John's laptop, clicks on the shortcut to the directory service and makes herself a member of the administrator's group. When John comes back, he does not realize anything has happened, as his laptop seems the same as when he left it.

Programming Attacks

Programming attacks use scripts or overload the characters or integers expected. Let's look at these in turn:

- **Christmas Tree Attack**: A Christmas Tree attack is where the packet has a number of flags or settings set to open. An example is that the flags are set to one; for example, the URG, PUSH, and FIN flags are all set to a value of 1, meaning that they are open. A large number of these data-heavy packets can slow down or overload a network. As the URG is set to 1, this means that this packet should have a higher priority over other packets.

- **Dynamic Link Library (DLL) Injection**: This is a technique used for running code within the address space of another process by forcing it to load a DLL. This makes the application run differently from how it was designed to. For example, you could install a malware DLL in another process.

- **Cross-Site Request Forgery (XSRF)**: An XSRF attack is when a user clicks on a link to a legitimate website where embedded programming is executed. An XSRF attack can be used to modify firewall settings (`https://searchsecurity.techtarget.com/definition/firewall`), to post unauthorized data on a forum, or to conduct fraudulent financial transactions. A compromised user may never know that such an attack has occurred until the loss of money is discovered.

 Exam tip: In a Christmas Tree attack, the URG, PUSH, and FIN flags are all set to 1, meaning that they are open. As URG is set to 1, it says that this packet has a high priority over other traffic.

- **Cross-Site Scripting (XSS)**: XSS is when a user injects malicious code into another user's browser. It uses both HTML tags and JavaScript. The following is a very simple server-side script to display the latest comments:

```
print "<html>"
print "Latest comment:"
print database.latestComment
print "</html>"
```

- The attacker could alter the comment to have HTML tags for a script, as follows:

```
<html>
Latest comment:
<script>   (Javascript code is placed here)   </script>
</html>
```

- When the user loads the page into the browser, it will now launch the JavaScript and then the attack will be successful. Here are some examples using JavaScript.

Example 1 - JavaScript - Creating a Money Variable

JavaScript can use the `var` command, which means variable. An example would be to set a variable for money then allocate it a value of `300.00`. You can see we use `var` for the variable and then use `money` as its label. In the next row, we use the `money` variable and give it a value of `300.00`:

```
<script type="text/javascript">
<!--
var money;
money = 300.00;
//-->
</script>
```

Example 2 - JavaScript - Setting the Day of the Month

We will use JavaScript to set the day of the month; you will notice the JavaScript code between the `<html>` tags: `<script>` to start the script and `<\script>` to end the script. The `var` command is very common in JavaScript:

```
<!DOCTYPE html>
<html>
<body>
<p>Click the button to display the date after changing the day of the
month. </p>
<button onclick="myFunction()">Try it</button>
<p id="demo"></p>
<script>
```

```
function myFunction() {
var d = new Date();
d.setDate (15);
document.getElementById("demo").innerHTML = d;
}
</script>
</body>
</html>
```

An XSS attack can be identified by looking for the `var` command and for a variable with the `<html>` tags `<script>` and `</script>`. Scripts with `var` are likely to be JavaScript. This is a very popular exam topic:

- **Buffer Overflow**: A Buffer Overflow occurs when a program tries to store more data than it can hold in a temporary memory storage area. Writing outside the allocated memory into the adjacent memory can corrupt the data, crash the program, or cause the execution of malicious code, which could allow an attacker to modify the target process address space:

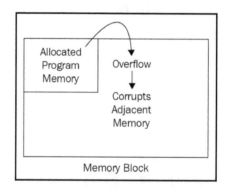

Figure 8: Buffer overflow

In the example here, we are going to set up a buffer to be a maximum of 64 characters, then we are going to use `strcpy` to copy strings of data. A string of data is used to represent a number of text characters. The problem that arises is that `strcpy` cannot limit the size of characters being copied. In the example here, if the string of data is longer than 64 characters, then a buffer overflow will occur:

```
int fun (char data [256]) {
int i
char tmp [64];
strcpy (tmp, data);
}
```

- **Integer Overflow**: An Integer Overflow is a condition that occurs when the result of an arithmetic operation, such as multiplication or addition, exceeds the maximum size of the integer type used to store it. It is similar to Buffer Overflow but uses numerical values. It will not overflow into memory, as it is not being written to memory, but can lead to unexpected values being stored. An integer data type allows integers up to two bytes or 16 bits in length (or an unsigned number up to decimal 65,535); when two integers are to be added together that exceed the value 65,535, the result will be an integer overflow.

- **SQL Injection Attack**: When you use a SQL database, you can run queries against the SQL database using transact SQL. An example is if I want to know the customers that I have in my SQL database. I can run the following transact SQL query: `Select* from Customers`. This will display all of the customers in my SQL database. An SQL Injection attack is where the SQL command is modified to gain information from the database by ending the statement with 1=1. Since one equals one, the statement is true and information will be gained.

Exam tip: `strcpy` could create a buffer overflow as it cannot limit the size of characters.

- **Stored Procedure**: A Stored Procedure is a pre-written SQL script that might ask you for a list of all the customers that have purchased items over $1,000 in the last 7 days. When this is written, it is saved as a Stored Procedure called `ABC`. When I run the `ABC` Stored Procedure, it will give me all of the information I require, and an attacker won't be able to modify the script inside.

- **Input Validation**: Input validation is where data is entered either using a web page or wizard; both are set up to only accept data in the correct format within a range of minimum and maximum values. Have you ever completed a web form quickly and maybe put your zip code into another field? This results in an error in the form and it fails to process the submit button. The web form then has a list at the top, in red, of the incorrect parameters, with a red star next to each of them. Once you have corrected the entries, the form will accept these and submit. Input Validation can prevent SQL Injection, Buffer Overflow, and Integer Overflow attacks.

Hijacking Related Attacks

In this section, we will look at attacks where a hacker hijacks either a device, cookie, or piece of software. Let's look at these in turn:

- **Bluejacking**: Bluejacking is where an attacker takes control of a Bluetooth device such as a phone. They are then able to make phone calls and send text messages.
- **Bluesnarfing**: Once again, an attacker hijacks a Bluetooth phone, but in this scenario, they extract contact details and any sensitive information.

> Input Validation could prevent SQL Injection, Buffer Overflow, and Integer Overflow attacks.

- **Session Hijacking**: When you visit a website, your desktop can store your browsing information in a file called a cookie. This is a security risk as it can be used to identify you. For example, the second time you visit a website, it may say **Good Morning, Mr Smith** at the top. If someone copies your cookie and places it on their machine, the website will also see them as Mr Smith. This is known as Session Hijacking.
- **URL Hijacking**: URL Hijacking is a process in which a website is falsely removed from the results of a search engine and replaced by another web page that links to the remote page. Another form of this is Typosquatting.
- **Typosquatting:** When someone types the URL of a website into their browser, they may transpose two characters of the website name if they have typed it very quickly. Typosquatting is where an attacker creates websites with characters transposed to redirect a user's session to a fraudulent website. This is also known as URL Hijacking.

> A Stored Procedure could prevent a SQL injection attack as it is a pre-written script that is executed and cannot be altered when executed.

- **Clickjacking**. Clickjacking is a malicious technique for tricking a web user into clicking on an icon or link. The outcome of which is different from what the user perceives they are clicking on, thus potentially revealing confidential information or taking control of their computer. An attacker establishes a malicious website that invisibly embeds the Facebook like or share button in a transparent iframe. When the victim clicks within the malicious site, the click is directed to the invisible like or share button.

Driver Manipulation

Device drivers allow an operating system such as Windows to talk to hardware devices such as printers. Sophisticated attackers may dive deep into device drivers and manipulate them so that they undermine the security on your computer. They could also take control of the audio and video of the computer, stop your anti-virus software from running, or your data could be exposed to someone else. There are two main techniques for Driver Manipulation, and these are as follows:

- **Shimming**: A `shim` is a small library that transparently intercepts API calls and changes the arguments passed. They can also be used to run programs on different software platforms than they were developed for. Normally, it is used to help third-party software applications work with an operating system.
- **Refactoring**: Refactoring is the process of changing a computer program's internal structure without modifying its external functional behavior or existing functionality.

Cryptographic Attacks

There are a variety of cryptographic attacks, and we will now look at these in turn. You need to thoroughly know these for the Security+ exam. We will start with the birthday attack and finish with key stretching:

- **Birthday Attack**: The birthday paradox states that in a random gathering of 23 people, there is a 50% chance that two people will have the same birthday. If we store passwords as hashes, then all passwords that are the same will produce the same hash if we use the same hashing algorithm. The birthday paradox looks for collisions in hashes; if it finds two hashes of the same value, the attacker also knows that the password is the same.
- **Digital Signatures**: Digital signatures are susceptible to a Birthday Attack.

- **Rainbow Tables**: Rainbow Tables are lists of pre-computed passwords with a corresponding hash; you can obtain free rainbow tables from the internet. Some larger Rainbow Tables are 460 GB in size. These tables speed up the cracking of passwords that have been hashed.
- **Collision Attack**: A Collision Attack on a cryptographic hash tries to find two inputs producing the same hash value; this is known as a Hash Collision.
- **Salting Passwords**: Salting password values is where a random set of characters is inserted into or appended to a password hash. This prevents duplicate passwords being stored and prevents Rainbow Tables and Collision Attacks. This also creates a longer password, slowing down brute force attacks.
- **Key Stretching**: Key Stretching is similar to salting a password by inserting random strings to prevent rainbow table and collision attacks. `Bcrypt` and `PBKDF2` can be used for Key Stretching. For example, a company has a password policy of not using complex passwords and have therefore suffered many attacks. To prevent this in future, they use `Bcrypt` to key stretch weak passwords, making them more difficult to crack. They should have introduced both complex passwords and Key Stretching to make passwords more secure.

Password Attacks

The two most common password attacks are dictionary attacks and brute force attacks; let's look at these in turn:

- **Dictionary Attack**: For a Dictionary Attack, we could start by using all of the words in the Oxford English Dictionary and use them to try and crack passwords, but misspelled names or passwords with special characters such as $ or % can't be cracked, as they don't appear in the dictionary.

Which of the following passwords would a Dictionary Attack crack?

- `elasticity`
- `el@ST1city`
- `fred123`
- `blueberry`

It would crack `elasticity` and `blueberry`, but `el@STcity` features numbers and characters not in a dictionary, therefore, it will fail. It wouldn't crack `fred123` either, as it ends in numbers.

- **Brute Force Attack:** A Brute Force attack runs through all of the different combinations of letters and characters and will eventually crack a given password. The length of the password may slow down such an attack, but it will eventually be cracked. This is the fastest type of password cracker which will crack all different combinations. Salting a password with randomized characters will only slow a brute force attack down. There are two types of brute force attacks:
  - **Online mode**: The attacker must use the same login interface as the user's application.
  - **Offline mode**: This attack requires the attacker to steal the password file first, then it will give them unlimited attempts at guessing the password.

Which of the following passwords would a brute force attack crack?

- `elasticity@abc123`
- `el@ST1city`
- `fred12redrafg`
- `blueberryicecream12345`

It would crack them all - eventually:

- **Hybrid Attack**: A Hybrid Attack is a combination of both a dictionary attack and a brute force attack.
- **Account Lockout**: Account Lockout refers to the number of attempts a user can make to insert their password before being locked out of the system. If I set account lockout at three attempts, it will stop both Dictionary and Brute Force attacks.
- **Minimum Number of Characters**: Should Account Lockout not be an option, the best way to prevent the password being cracked is Salting or Key Stretching, where randomized characters are inserted into the password. This will prevent a Dictionary Attack, but will only slow down a Brute Force attack.

Setting account lockout as a low value will prevent a Brute Force attack.

- **Login Errors**: Inserting an incorrect password because you rushed inserting it or have *Caps Lock* on/off will create password errors. If we look at certificates, smart cards, TOTP, and passwords, passwords are the most likely to be inserted incorrectly.
- **Weak Implementations**: Weak implementations of passwords are as follows:
    - Using the most common passwords
    - A low number of characters (less than seven characters)
    - Simple passwords such as `123456` or `abcdef`
    - Default passwords for devices

These are very easy to guess using a password cracker. `Password` is the most common password to be used. The following list shows some of the most common passwords over the years:

- `123456`
- `Password`
- `123456789`
- `qwerty`
- `letmein`
- `iloveyou`
- `abc123`
- `football`

Wireless Attacks

Over the past few years, the use of wireless internet in our daily lives and in the workplace has increased to the extent that, if I am booking a hotel room and there is no wireless internet, then I look for another hotel. Most rail companies provide complimentary Wi-Fi. Let's look at different types of wireless attacks:

- **Evil Twin**: An Evil Twin is a wireless access point with no security that is made to look like a legitimate wireless access point; when a user connects to it, all of their traffic is scanned and the user is unaware of this:

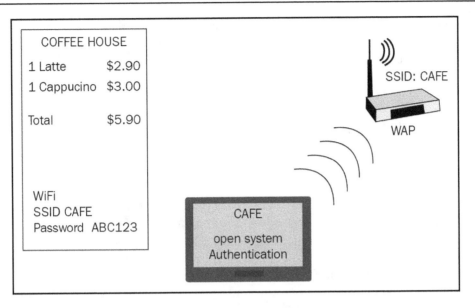

Figure 9: Evil twin

The diagram in *Figure 9* helps to explain an evil twin wireless access point. The victim has gone to a coffee shop to purchase some coffee; the coffee shop provides Wi-Fi free of charge; the SSID is hidden, and the WAP password is included on the receipt. However, when the customer sits down at the table to hook up their tablet, they find an SSID called CAFÉ; they then think that this is the Wi-Fi that they have the details for and click to join the network, but instead of requiring them to enter a Wi-Fi password, it is set to open system authentication, so it connects immediately. The user then thinks to themselves, *"What was the purpose of printing the Wi-Fi details on the receipt?"* They can connect automatically and are unaware that they have just joined an Evil Twin WAP where all of their data will be intercepted by a wireless packet sniffer. The legitimate WAP will not appear, as the SSID is hidden.

- **Rogue Access Point (AP)**: A Rogue AP refers to someone entering your network and connecting their own open system authentication wireless access point. Users think that it is great, as they connect and get fast Wi-Fi. The way to prevent a Rogue WAP is to use an 802.1x managed switch, as it authenticates the device before it can be functional, therefore, the Rogue AP will be blocked.

Implementing an 802.1x managed switch prevents Rogue WAPs from accessing your network, as the AP needs to be authenticated to first.

- **Jamming**: Anyone with a transceiver can eavesdrop on ongoing transmissions, inject spurious messages, or block the transmission of legitimate ones. The simplest form of jamming is where an attacker corrupts transmitted messages by causing electromagnetic interference in the network's operational frequencies close to the targeted receivers.

Exam tip: A wireless jamming attack uses interference.

- **WPS Attack**: WPS is where a password is already stored and to connect to the wireless network you simply push the button. Susceptible to Brute Force Attacks.
- **WEP IV attack**: An Initialization Vector (IV) is an arbitrary number that can be used along with a secret key for data encryption. The use of an IV prevents repetition in data encryption, making it more difficult for a hacker using a dictionary attack to find patterns and break a cipher. It is very common with WEP. Once an attacker learns the plain text of one packet, they can compute the RC4 key stream generated by the IV used.
- **Disassociation**: A Wireless Disassociation attack refers to when you are using your Wi-Fi network and then all of a sudden you are disconnected and can no longer see the WAP. This is similar to a DDoS attack, where every time you connect you are disconnected. The only way to prevent this is to put a cable straight into the WAP.
- **RFID**: RFID systems, like most electronic devices and networks, are susceptible to both physical and electronic attacks. RFID prevents the theft of electronic items.
- **Near-Field Communication (NFC)**: NFC is used to make a wireless payment, but a credit/debit card needs to be within 4 cm of the reader. NFC is built into most bank cards, and if someone with a skimmer is close to you they could steal your details to make a fraudulent transaction. You can prevent this by placing your card into an aluminum pouch or wallet. When you take your card out, remember to ensure that nobody is too close to you.

Penetration Testing

A penetration test is an intrusive test where a third party has been authorized to carry out an attack on a company's network to identify weaknesses. Intrusive scan used by them can cause damage to your systems.

Penetration testing is commonly known as pen testing. Pen testers are given different amounts of information:

- **Black Box**: Black Box pen testers are given no information on the company
- **Gray Box**: Gray Box pen testers are given some information
- **White Box**: White Box pen testers know everything about the system

For example, a pen tester is about to carry out a pen test but has not been given any information on the system. As they arrive at the company, the IT manager offers them a cup of coffee and then gives them the Local Admin account of Server 1. What type of pen test is this? It is a gray box, as he has been give some information?

Penetration Testing Techniques

Let's now look at the types of techniques that a pen tester may adopt:

- **Initial Exploitation**: This is where the pen tester assesses the information that they already know and devises a plan so that they can exploit the system. They will look for the weakest point in the company's security at the initial point of exploitation.
- **Active Reconnaissance**: Active Reconnaissance is where someone actively tries to gain information about the system. For example, an attacker finds a username left on one of the corporate desktops; they then ring up the active directory team, pretending to be that person and ask for a password reset. This is active reconnaissance, as they have carried out an action.

- **Passive Reconnaissance**: Passive Reconnaissance is where an attacker is constantly gathering information, with the victim's knowledge. For example, an attacker is sitting in a coffee shop when they realize that two members of Company A's security team are having lunch. The attacker listens to every word that is said, and the security team is unaware of the eavesdropping, this is passive reconnaissance.

 Listening is Passive Reconnaissance. Resetting a password is Active Reconnaissance.

- **Pivot**: A pivot attack is when an attacker gains access to a desktop computer inside a company that they then use to attack another computer or server.
- **Persistence**: An advanced persistent threat is an attack in which an unauthorized user gains access to a system or network and remains there for an extended period of time without being detected.
- **Escalation of Privilege**: Escalation of privilege is where an attacker exploits a weakness in a system so that they can gain a higher level of privileges on it.

Vulnerability Scanning Concepts

A vulnerability scanner is a passive scanner that identifies vulnerabilities or weaknesses in a system. For example, there could be missing updates for the operating system, anti-virus solutions, or there could be only one administrator account on the system. Microsoft has a vulnerability scanning tool called Microsoft **Baseline Security Analyzer** (**MBSA**). A Zero-Day exploit cannot be traced by a vulnerability scanner; it has not yet been identified and has no updates or patches available.

Let's look at the type of output a vulnerability scanner could produce:

- **False Positive**: A False Positive is where the scan believes that there is a vulnerability but when you physically check it is not there.
- **False Negative**: A False Negative on the other hand is more dangerous, there is a vulnerability but the scanner does not detect it. An example of a False Negative is a Zero-Day exploit that is attacking the system without there being a way of detecting it.

A pivot is gaining access to one computer so that an attack can be launched on another computer.

- **Identify Common Misconfigurations**: A vulnerability scanner looks at the architecture and design of the flow of data - is it flowing as it should be? Have services been enabled that should be disabled? Are the firewall rules as they should be? Have the correct permissions been set or are the default usernames and passwords being used, or has someone given themselves a higher level of permissions than they should have?
- **Security controls**: A vulnerability scanner will passively test security controls such as:
    - **Code Review**: A vulnerability scanner can passively test the source code of programs and applications to find vulnerabilities before the applications are put into production.
    - **Attack Surface**: A vulnerability scanner can identify services that should not be running, applications that should not be installed, and missing patches, so that the attack surface is as secure as it can be at that time.
    - **Permissions**: Have permissions been set correctly, or has a user or application been granted a much higher level than they need? Have short, weak, or simple passwords been allowed when they should not have been?
    - **Baselines**: The computer baseline can be checked to ensure that unauthorized applications have not been installed on any IT system.

Credentialed v Non-Credentialed scans

There are two types of scans, credentialed and non-credentialed. Let's look at these in turn:

- **Non-Credentialed**: A Non-Credentialed scan will monitor the network and see any vulnerabilities that an attacker would easily find; we should fix the vulnerabilities found with a Non-Credentialed scan first, as this is what the hacker will see when they enter your network. For example, an administrator runs a Non-Credentialed scan on the network and finds that there are three missing patches. The scan does not provide many details on these missing patches. The administrator installs the missing patches to keep the systems up to date as they can only operate on the information produced for them.
- **Credentialed scan**: A Credentialed scan is a much safer version of the vulnerability scanner. It provides more detailed information than a Non-Credentialed scan. You can also set up the auditing of files and user permissions.

Exam tip: A Credentialed scan can produce more information and can audit the network. A Non-Credentialed scan is primitive and can only find missing patches or updates.

Penetration Testing v Vulnerability Scanning

A penetration test is more intrusive as it tries to fully exploit the vulnerabilities that it finds and could cause damage to IT systems, whereas vulnerability scanners are non-intrusive, as they scan for vulnerabilities. Even a credentialed scan only scans the registry/permissions and finds missing matches - it is informational and does not exploit the system, therefore, is less likely to cause damage to systems.

Practical Exercise - Running a Credentialed Vulnerability Scanner

In this exercise, we are going to download the **Microsoft Baseline Security Analyzer (MBSA)** tool and run it against our local computer to look for vulnerabilities:

1. Go to Google and search for the Microsoft Baseline Security Analyzer tool. You can just enter MBSA and Google will find it.
2. Click on `MBSASetup-x64-EN`. The **MBSA** Setup wizard appears. Press **Next**, as shown in the following screenshot:

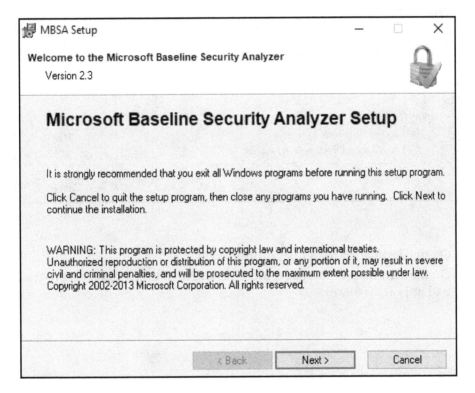

Figure 10

3. Click on **I accept the license agreement**, then press **Next**:

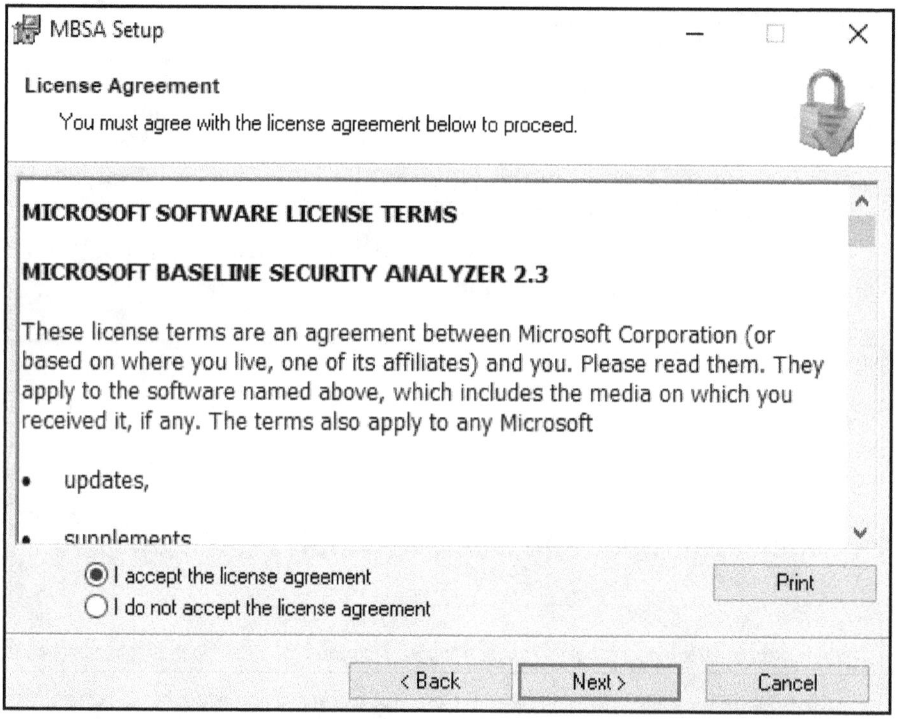

Figure 11

4. On the destination folder page, press **Next**.
5. On the start installation page, press **Install**, then the installation progress page will appear, as follows:

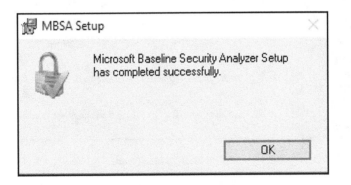

Figure 12: Installation progress

6. Then, the setup will finish:

Figure 13: Installation complete

7. A shortcut is placed on the desktop. Double-click it. The UAC prompt appears; click **Yes**:

Figure 14: MBSA shortcut

8. The **MBSA Management console** appears; click **Scan a computer**, then, at the bottom-right, click **Start Scan**:

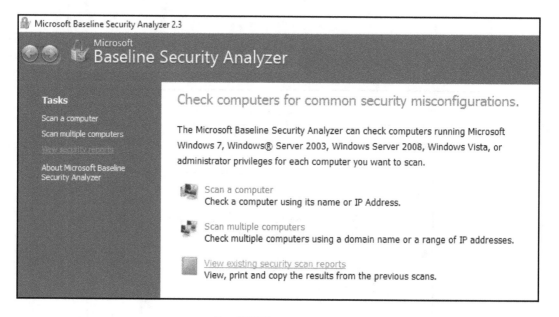

Figure 15: MBSA management console

9. The **scan** starts and downloads security update information from Microsoft. As it compares computer updates against the latest updates for Windows 10, this will take about 10-15 minutes:

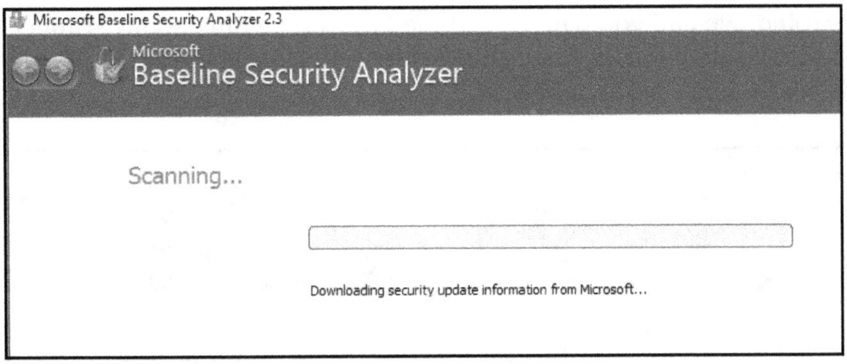

Figure 16: Obtaining security updates from Microsoft

10. The scan results page comes up; you will notice that the default is **Score (worst first)**:

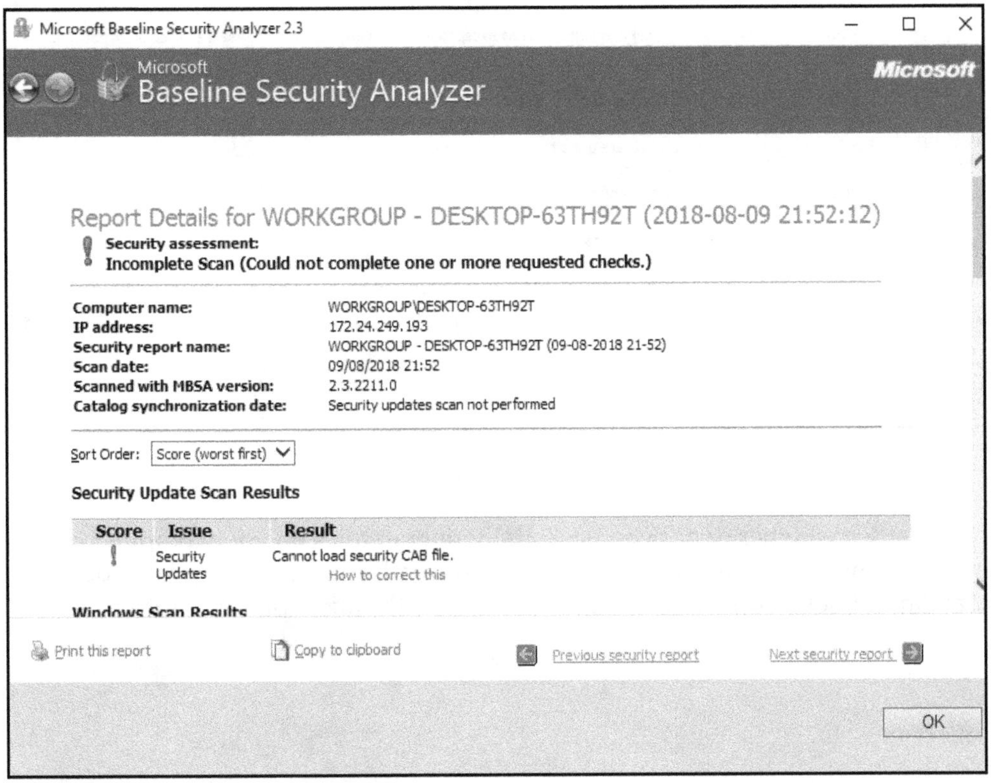

Figure 17

11. Scroll down and you will see that the MBSA is a vulnerability scanner that is used as a credentialed scan, and that it produces some good results. However, it is passive and informational, and did not try to exploit the computer at all:

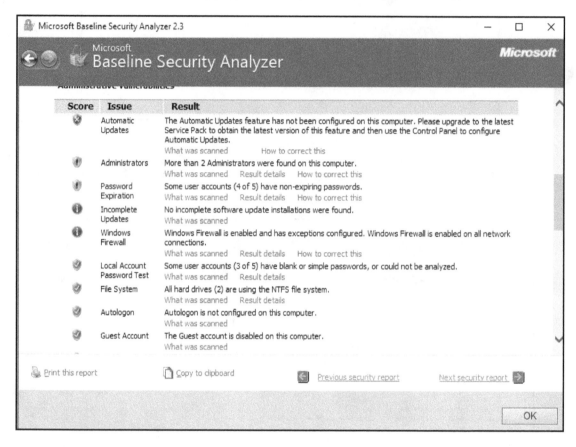

Figure 18: Credentialed vulnerability scan

You can now see whether or not you have any vulnerabilities on your computer. There are hyperlinks below each item listed, giving you information on how to update your vulnerabilities. Look at each of these in turn and take the appropriate actions.

Review Questions

1. If I install a freeware program that analyses my computer and then finds 40,000 exploits and asks me to purchase the full version, what type of attack is this?
2. What is crypto-malware?
3. What type of virus replicates itself and uses either ports 4444 or 5000?
4. What type of virus inserts a .dll into either the SysWOW64 or System 32 folder?
5. What is a RAT?
6. What type of virus attacks the windows/system 32 folder on Windows, or the bin/ and /usr/bin/ on Linux?
7. How does a logic bomb virus work?
8. What is the purpose of a keylogger?
9. What is a botnet?
10. Explain a phishing attack.
11. How does spear phishing differ from a phishing attack?
12. What is a whaling attack?
13. What type of attack can include leaving voicemail?
14. What is social engineering tailgating?
15. What is social engineering?
16. What type of attack could involve dressing as a police officer?
17. What type of attack is it if a fireperson arrives and you let them into the server room to put out a fire?
18. What type of attack is it if I am in an ATM queue and someone has their phone to one side so that they can film the transaction?
19. What type of attack is distributing fake software?
20. What is a watering hole attack?

21. What type of attack is it if I receive an email from my company's CEO, telling me to complete the form attached by clicking on a link in the email?

22. One of my bosses asks me to give them information that one of my peers gave them last week. I am not too sure, but I give them the information. What type of attack is this?

23. What type of attack is a multiple SYN flood attack on a well-known website that takes it down?

24. Explain a man-in-the-middle (MITM) attack.

25. How does a replay attack differ from a man-in-the-middle attack?

26. What type of attack is a man-in-the-middle attack using an SSL3.0 browser that uses a **Chain Block Cipher** (**CBC**)?

27. What type of attack is a man-in-the-browser attack?

28. How can I prevent a replay attack in a Microsoft environment?

29. How can I prevent a pass-the-hash attack?

30. What type of attack uses HTML tags with JavaScript?

31. What type of exploit has no patches and cannot be detected by NIDS or NIPS?

32. What is domain hijacking?

33. What is bluejacking?

34. What is bluesnarfing?

35. What type of attack does an attacker need to be local and how can I prevent that attack?

36. For what type of attack would I use the strcpy tool?

37. What is an integer overflow attack?

38. What type of attack uses the phrase `1=1`?

39. Name two methods to prevent the type of attack in question 38.

40. What type of attack is session hijacking?

41. If I misspell a website but still get there, what type of attack is this?

42. What type of attack would I use shimming or refactoring for?

43. What type of system is susceptible to a birthday attack?

44. What are rainbow tables?

45. How can I store passwords to prevent a dictionary attack?

46. Name two tools that can be used for key stretching.
47. What is the fastest password attack that can crack any password?
48. What is the only way to prevent a brute force attack?
49. What can we do to slow down a brute force attack?
50. What type of authentication is the most prone to errors?
51. What is an evil twin?
52. How can I prevent an attack by a rogue WAP?
53. I am trying to use the internet but my wireless session keeps crashing—what type of attack is this?
54. How close does an attacker need to be for an NFC attack?
55. If I have no information on the system but at the last minute the IT manager gives me the local admin account, what type of penetration test is this?
56. How much information does a black box pen tester have?
57. How much information does a white box pen tester have?
58. Which type of vulnerability scan can I use for auditing?
59. If I carry out a non-credentialed vulnerability scan, what will I find?
60. What type of reconnaissance is it if I try to obtain a password reset?
61. What type of reconnaissance is it if I actively listen?
62. What is a pivot?

Answers and Explanations

1. Because you have parted with money, this is a subtle form of ransomware.

2. An example of crypto-malware is ransomware where the victim's hard drive is encrypted and held to ransom, it could also have pop ups.

3. A worm replicates itself and can use either ports `4444` or `5000`.

4. A Trojan inserts a `.dll` into either the `SysWOW64` or `System 32` folder.

5. A remote access Trojan is a Trojan that sends the user's username and password to an external source so that a remote session can be created.

6. A rootkit virus attacks the root in Windows in the `/system 32` folder, or in Linux in the `/usr/bin/` directory. Windows you may reinstall the OS but the virus is still there.

7. A logic bomb virus is triggered off by an event; for example, a Fourth of July logic bomb would activate when the date on the computer was July 4.

8. A keylogger is a piece of software that could run from a USB flash drive plugged into the back of a computer, which then records all of the keystrokes being used. It can capture sensitive data that is typed in, such as bank account details and passwords.

9. A botnet is a group of computers that have been infected so that they can be used to carry out malicious acts without the real attacker being identified. They could be used for a DDoS attack.

10. A phishing attack is when a user receives an email asking them to fill in a form requesting their bank details.

11. Spear phishing is a phishing attack that has been sent to a group of users.

12. A whaling attack targets a CEO or a high-level executive in a company.

13. A vishing attack can use a telephone or leave a voicemail.

14. Social engineering tailgating is where someone has used a smart card or entered a pin to access a door, then someone behind them passes through the door before it closes, entering no credentials.

15. Social engineering exploits an individual's character in a situation that they are not used to.

16. Dressing as a police officer could be part of be an impersonation attack.

17. If you let a fireperson into the server room to put out a fire, that is a social engineering urgency attack.

18. If I am using an ATM and someone films the transaction, this is a subtle shoulder surfing attack.

19. Fake software that will not install is a hoax. An email alert telling you to delete a system file as it is a virus is also a hoax.

20. A watering hole attack infects a trusted website that a certain group of people visit regularly.

21. An email that looks like it has come from your company's CEO, telling you to carry out an action is a social engineering authority attack.

22. This is a social engineering consensus attack, where the person being attacked wants to be accepted by their peers.

23. An attack with multiple SYN flood attacks is a DDoS attack.

24. A man-in-the-middle (MITM) attack is where a connection between hosts is intercepted, conversation changed, then replayed, but the people involved still believe that they are talking directly to each other.

25. A reply attack is similar to a man-in-the-middle attack, except the intercepted packet is replayed at a later date.

26. A POODLE attack is a man-in-the-middle attack using an SSL3.0 browser that uses Chain Block Cipher (CBC).

27. A man-in-the-browser attack is a Trojan that intercepts your session between your browser and the internet; it aims to obtain financial transactions.

28. Kerberos authentication uses USN and timestamps and can prevent a replay attack, as the USN packets need and the timestamps need sequential.

29. Enabling Kerberos or disabling NTLM would prevent a pass-the-hash attack.

30. XSS uses HTML tags with JavaScript.

31. A zero-day virus has no patches and cannot be detected by NIDS or NIPS as it may take the anti-virus vendor up to five days to release a patch.

32. Domain hijacking is where someone tries to register your domain, access your hosted control panel, and set up a website that is similar to yours.

33. Bluejacking is hijacking someone's bluetooth phone so that you can take control of it and send text messages.

34. Bluesnarfing is when you steal someone's contacts from their bluetooth phone.

35. An ARP attack is a local attack that can be prevented by using IPSec.

36. Strcpy can be used for a buffer overflow attack.

37. An integer overflow inserts a number larger than what is allowed.

38. An attack that uses the phrase 1=1 is an SQL injection attack.

39. Input validation and stored procedures can prevent an SQL injection attack.

40. Session hijacking is where your cookies are stolen so that someone can pretend to be you.

41. Typosquatting is where an attacker launches a website with a similar name to a legitimate website in the hope that victims misspell the URL.

42. Shimming and refactoring are used for driver manipulation attacks.

43. Digital signatures are susceptible to a birthday attack.

44. Rainbow tables are pre-computed lists of passwords with the relevant hash in either MD5 or SHA1.

45. Salting passwords inserts a random value and prevents dictionary attacks, as a dictionary does not contain random characters.

46. Two tools that can be used for key stretching are `bcrypt` and `PBKDF2`.

47. A brute force attack is the fastest password attack that will crack any password as it uses all combinations of characters, letters, and symbols.

48. An account locked with a low value is the only way to prevent a brute force attack.

49. If account lockout is not available, the best way to slow down a brute force attack is to make the password length longer or to salt passwords.

50. Using passwords for authentication is more prone to errors as certificates and smart cards don't tend to have many errors.

51. An evil twin is a WAP that is made to look like a legitimate WAP.

52. Using an 802.1x authentication switch can prevent an attack by a rogue WAP, as the device needs to authenticate itself to attach to the switch.

53. A wireless disassociation attack is where the attacker prevents the victim from connecting to the WAP.

54. An attacker needs to be within 4 cm of a card to launch an NFC attack.

55. This is a gray box pen test; although the pen tester has no information that would make it black box, at the last minute, they are given a password, making it gray box. They are given some information.

56. A black box pen tester has no information.

57. A white box pen tester has all of the information available.

58. A credentialed vulnerability scan can be used for auditing.

59. A non-credentialed vulnerability scan can only see missing patches of the systems on your network.

60. If I try to obtain a password reset, it is active reconnaissance.

61. Listening is a passive reconnaissance technique; active listening means that you are concentrating on what is being said, and you are not taking any action.

62. A pivot is where you gain access to a network so that you can launch an attack on a secondary system.

Implementing the Public Key Infrastructure

9

Certificates are used for both encryption and authentication, and in this chapter, we are going to look at different encryption types and how certificates are issued and used. This is the most difficult module for students to understand, so we have focused on making the most difficult aspects seem easy. If you are going to be successful in the Security+ exam, you must know this module thoroughly. We will start with the **Public Key Infrastructure** (**PKI**), covering both the public and private keys. It is an asymmetric form of encryption.

We will cover the following exam objectives in this chapter:

- **Comparing and contrasting the basic concepts of cryptography**: We will cover symmetric algorithms, modes of operation, asymmetric algorithms, hashing, salt, IV, nonce, elliptic curves, weak/deprecated algorithms, key exchange, digital signatures, diffusion, confusion, collision, steganography, obfuscation, stream versus block, key strength, session keys, ephemeral keys, secret algorithms, data-in-transit, data-at-rest, and data-in-use. We also look at random/pseudo-random number generation and key stretching. We then move on to implementation versus algorithm selection. We deal with crypto service providers and crypto modules. We look at perfect forward secrecy and security through obscurity. We cover common use cases, low-power devices, low latency, high resiliency, supporting confidentiality, supporting integrity, supporting obfuscation, supporting authentication, and supporting non-repudiation. We finally go into resources versus security constraints.

- **Explaining cryptography algorithms and their basic characteristics**: We will explore symmetric algorithms, AES, DES, 3DES, RC4, and Blowfish/Twofish. We then study cipher modes, CBC, GCM, ECB, CTR, and stream versus block. We then go into asymmetric algorithms, RSA, DSA, Diffie-Hellman, groups, DHE, ECDHE, elliptic curves, PGP/GPG, hashing algorithms, MD5, SHA1-HMAC, and RIPEMD. We'll look at key-stretching algorithms, BCRYPT, PBKDF2, obfuscation, XOR, ROT13, and substitution ciphers.
- **Implementing a PKI given a certain scenario**: Here we'll cover components, CA, intermediate CA, CRL, OCSP, CSR, certificates, public keys, private keys, and **Object Identifiers** (**OIDs**). We also look into concept s, online versus offline CA, stapling, pinning, trust models, key escrow, and certificate chaining. Then we'll delve into types of certificates, wildcards, SAN, code signing, self-signed, machine/computer, email, users, root, domain validation, and extended validation. Finally, we'll get into certificate formats, DER, PEM, PFX, CER, P12, and P7B.

PKI Concepts

The PKI provides asymmetric techniques using two keys: a public key and a private key. There is a certificate hierarchy, which is called the certificate authority, that manages, signs, issues, validates, and revokes certificates. Let's first look at the components of the certificate hierarchy. A certificate is known as an X509 certificate.

Certificate Hierarchy

The **Certificate Authority** (**CA**) is the ultimate authority as it holds the master key, also known as the root key, for signing all of the certificates that it gives the **Intermediary**, which then in turn issues to the requester:

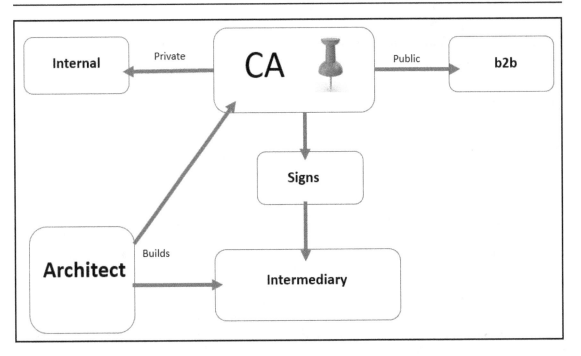

Figure 1: Certificate hierarchy

- **Online CA**: An internal online CA is always up and running so that people in the company can request a certificate at any time of the day or night. This would not be the case in a government or top-security environment.
- **Offline CA**: An offline CA is for a military or secure environment where clearance and vetting must be completed before someone can be issued a certificate. The CA is kept offline and locked up when it is not being used, but is taken out and switched to issue new certificates. After it issues a certificate, it goes back to being offline and is stored in the secure area.

Exam tip
For **Business-to-Business** (**b2b**) transactions and working with other commercial companies, your X509 certificates need to come from a public CA.

There are different types of CA:

- **Public CA**: A public CA is also known as a third-party CA and is commercially accepted as an authority for issuing public certificates; examples include Comodo, Symantec, and Go Daddy. There are many more. The benefit of using a third-party CA is that all of the management is carried out by them; once you purchase the certificate, all you have to do is install it. They keep an up-to-date **Certificate Revocation List** (**CRL**) where you can check whether your certificate is valid. A certificate that is not valid will not work if you are going to sell goods and services to other companies; this is known as a B2B transaction, which requires a public CA.

  For example, I put petrol in my car and go to pay for the petrol. I give the attendant some monopoly money but they refuse to take it; this would be the equivalent of a private CA. Businesses will not accept it as payment. I then go to the cash machine outside and withdraw $100 and I give this to the attendant; he smiles and accepts it and gives me some change. This is the equivalent of a public CA.

  If you wish to trade and exchange certificates with other businesses, you need to get your certificate from a public CA. The certificate that follows has been issued to the Bank of Scotland from a public CA called DigiCert Global CA; you can see on the front of the certificate the purpose for use and also the dates that it is valid for. The X509 has an OID, which is basically the certificate's serial number - the same way that paper money has serial numbers:

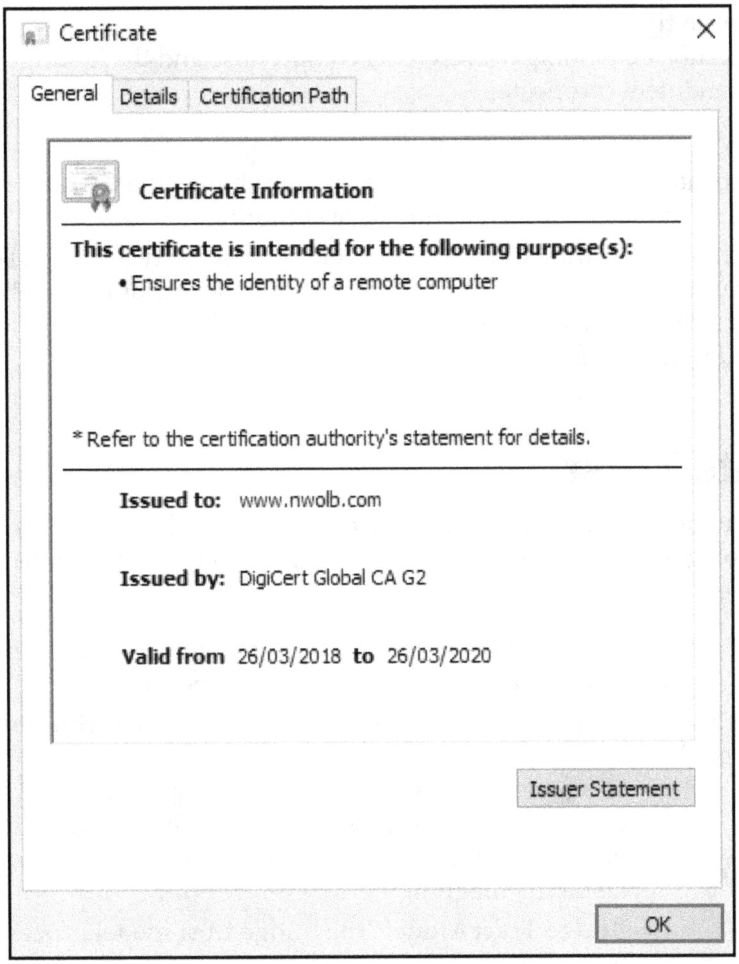

Figure 2: Public CA-issued certificate

- **Private CA**: A private CA can only be used internally; however, although it is free, you must maintain the CA. Hopefully, your company has the skill set to do so.
- **Certificate Pinning**: Certificate pinning prevents the compromise of the CA and the issuing of fraudulent X509 certificates.
- **Intermediary Authority**: The intermediary authority accepts the incoming requests for certificates and issues them once the CA has signed them. The certificates that are issued are known as X509 certificates.

Exam tip
Certificate pinning prevents CA compromise and the issuing of fraudulent certificates.

- **Certificate Architect**: The certificate architect builds the CA, and if it is already present, he will build the intermediary authority.
- **Certificate Chaining**: Certificates in computer security are digital certificates that are verified using a chain of trust where the trust anchor for the digital certificate is the root CA. This chain of trust is used to verify the validity of a certificate as it includes details of the CRL.

Certificate Trust

Certificates have some form of trust where the certificate can check whether or not it is valid. We are going to look at different trust models; you need to ensure that you know when each is used:

- **Trust Anchor**: A trust anchor in a PKI environment is the root certificate from which the whole chain of trust is derived; this is the root CA.
- **Trust Model**: A trust model proves the authenticity of a certificate; there are two trust models:
    - **Hierarchical Trust Model**: This uses a hierarchy from the root CA down to the intermediary (also known as a subordinate); this is the normal PKI model. An example can be seen in the certificate hierarchy diagram.
    - **Bridge Trust Model**: The bridge trust model is peer to peer, where two separate PKI environments trust each other. The certificate authorities communicate with each other, allowing for cross certification; sometimes, it is referred to as the trust model.
- **Certificate Chaining**: Certificates in computer security are digital certificates that are verified using a chain of trust where the trust anchor for the digital certificate is the root CA. This chain of trust is used to verify the validity of a certificate as it includes details of the CRL.

Exam tip
When two separate CAs trust each other, they will use a trust model called the bridge of trust.

- **Web of Trust**: A web of trust is a concept used in PGP or various versions of PGP to establish the authenticity of the certificate being used. In PGP, two people are going to encrypt data between themselves; the first stage would be to give each other a public key so that they can encrypt the data being sent to the other party. It works with the same concepts as asymmetric encryption although it is on a smaller scale.

Exam tip
A bridge trust model is used so that two separate CAs can work with each other.

Certificate Validity

Each time a certificate is used, the first thing that must happen is it must be checked for validity. There are three separate processes that you must know thoroughly, and these are as follows:

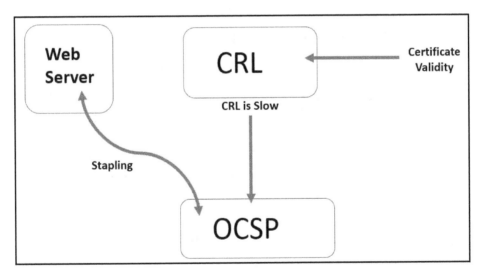

Figure 3: Certificate validity

- **Certificate Revocation List (CRL)**: The first stage in checking whether a certificate is valid, no matter the scenario, is to check the CRL. If the X509 is in the CRL, it is no longer valid and will not be accepted. No matter how obscure the question posed in the exam, unless it is going slow or it is a web server looking for a faster lookup, it will be the CRL that provides certificate validity.

- **Online Certificate Status Protocol (OCSP)**: Only when the CRL is going slow will the OCSP come into play; it is much faster than the CRL and can take a load from the CRL in a very busy environment.
- **OCSP Stapling/Certificate Stapling**: Certificate stapling, also known as OCSP stapling, is used when a web server bypasses the CRL to use the OCSP for a faster confirmation whether or not a certificate is valid.

> The validation of a certificate is done by the CRL unless it is going slow - then it will be the OCSP doing this.

Certificate Management Concepts

We are now going to look at the different ways certificates are managed in a PKI environment, starting with the request for a new certificate and ending with different certificate formats. You must learn all of this information thoroughly as these aspects are heavily tested:

- **Certificate Signing Request (CSR)**: This is the process of requesting a new certificate; the process for the exam is that two keys are generated and the public is sent to the CA, which then returns a file, the X509:

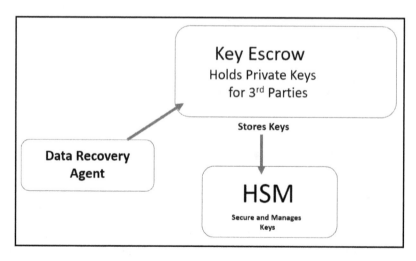

Figure 4: Key escrow

- **Key Escrow**: The key escrow holds the private keys for third parties and stores them in a **Hardware Security Module (HSM)**.
- **Hardware Security Module (HSM)**: The HSM can be a piece of hardware attached to the server or a portable device that is attached to store the keys. See the preceding diagram for more on this. It stores and managed certificates.
- **Data Recovery Agent (DRA)**: If a user cannot access their data because their private key is corrupted, the DRA will recover the data. The DRA needs to get the private key from the Key Escrow.

The Key Escrow stores private keys for third parties.

- **Certificates**: There are two main certificate types: the public key and the private key. The public key is sent to third parties to encrypt the data, and the private key decrypts the data. If you think of the private key as your bank card, that's a thing you wouldn't give away. The public key is the deposit slip that is tied to your account - if you were in a room with 20 people who wanted to pay $20 into your account, you would definitely give them your deposit slip. You will always give your public key away because when you are encrypting data you will always use someone else's public key.

A web server will use certificate stapling to bypass the CRL and use the OCSP for faster certificate validity. This is also known as OCSP stapling.

- **OIDs**: The OID on a certificate is similar to a serial number on a bank note. Bank notes are identified by their serial number. The certificate is identified by its OID.
- **Certificate Formats**: There are different certificate formats, and these are as follows:

Certificate type	Format	File extension
Private	P12	.pfx
Public	P7B	.cer
PEM	Base64 format	.pem
DER	Extension for PEM	.der

The certificate equivalent of a serial number is the OID located on the X509 itself.

Certificate Types

As a security professional, you will be responsible for purchasing new certificates, and therefore you must learn the certificate types thoroughly to ensure that you make the correct purchases. We will start with the self-signed certificate, which can roll out with applications such as Microsoft Exchange Server or Skype and finish with extended validation where the certificate has a high level of trust:

- **Self-Signed Certificate**: A self-signed certificate is issued by the same entity that is using it. However, it does not have a CRL and cannot be validated or trusted.
- **Wildcard**: For a wildcard certificate for a domain called `ianneil501.com`, the wildcard certification would be `ianneil501.com` and could be used for the domain and a subdomain. For example, in the `ianneil501.com` domain, there are two servers called `web` and `mail`. The wildcard certification is `ianneil501.com`, and when installed it would work for the **Fully Qualified Domain Names** (**FQDNs**) of both of these - these would be `web.ianneil501.com` and `mail.ianneil501.com`. A wildcard can be used for multiple servers in the same domain.

PEM uses a Base64 certificate.

- **Domain Validation**: A **Domain-Validated** (**DV**) certificate is an X.509 (`https://en.wikipedia.org/wiki/X.509`) certificate that's typically used for **Transport Layer Security** (**TLS**) (`https://en.wikipedia.org/wiki/Transport_Layer_Security`) where the domain name (`https://en.wikipedia.org/wiki/Domain_name`) of the applicant has been validated by proving some control over a DNS domain (`https://en.wikipedia.org/wiki/Domain_name`).
- **Subject Alternative Name (SAN)**: A SAN certificate can be used on multiple domain names, such as `abc.com` or `xyz.com`. You can also insert other information into a SAN certificate such as IP Address.

- **Code Signing**: Code-signing certificates are used to digitally sign software so that its authenticity is guaranteed.
- **Computer/Machine**: A computer or machine certificate is used to identify a computer within a domain.
- **User**: A user certificate provides authenticity to a user for the applications that they use.

> A wildcard certificate can be used on several servers in the same domain. A SAN certificate can be used on servers in different domains.

- **Extended Validation**: Extended validation certificates provide a higher level of trust in identifying the entity that is using the certificate. It would normally be used in the financial arena. You may have seen it in action where the background of the URL turns green. Companies applying for the certificate would have to provide more detailed information about the company. See the following screenshot:

Figure 5: Extended validation

Asymmetric and Symmetric Encryption

There are two main types of encryption that use certificates, and these are asymmetric and symmetric; we need to learn about each thoroughly. Let's start by explaining what encryption is; please remember that you are taking plaintext and changing it into ciphertext.

Encryption Explained

Encryption is where we take plaintext that can be easily read and convert it into ciphertext that cannot be easily read. For example, if we take the word `pass` in plaintext, it may then be converted to UDVV; this way, it is difficult to understand:

- **Substitution Cipher**: Julius Caesar, who died in 44 BC, invented the first substitution cipher, where he moved each letter of the alphabet three places one way or another. This way, he could make his military plans unreadable if they had been intercepted. What he forgot about was that most people in those days could not read! This was called ROT 13, after the thirteen-letter rotation, and is now known as the Caesar cipher. For example, if I take the word "echo" and move each letter it on thirteen places to the right in the alphabet sequence, you will get the word "RPUB"—that would be difficult for someone to read.

- **ROT 13**: ROT 13 is a variation of the Caesar cipher; as there are 26 letters in the alphabet, we are rotating the letters 13 times. The key to ROT 13 would be as follows:

Letter	A	B	C	D	E	F	G	H	I	J	K	L	M
ROT 13	N	O	P	Q	R	S	T	U	V	W	X	Y	Z

Letter	N	O	P	Q	R	S	T	U	V	W	X	Y	Z
ROT 13	A	B	C	D	E	F	G	H	I	J	K	L	M

When receiving the message - GVZR SBE GRN - then we would apply ROT 13, but instead of going forward 13 places to decipher, we would simply go back 13 places, and the message would be TIME FOR TEA.

Exam tip
Encryption is taking plaintext and changing it into ciphertext so that it cannot be read.

There are two types of encryption that use certificates: asymmetric and symmetric; let's look at each of these in turn:

- **Symmetric Encryption**: Symmetric encryption only uses one key, which is known as the private or shared key. The same key encrypts and decrypts the data. The danger of symmetric encryption is that if the key is stolen, the attacker gets the keys to the kingdom. The main reason for using symmetric encryption is that it can encrypt large amounts of data very quickly. The Security+ exam does not focus on key exchange because it only uses one key, but instead looks at which is the fastest or strongest symmetric key, and which is used for the encryption of large amounts of data.
- **Diffie Hellman** (**DH**): When symmetric data is in transit, it is protected by Diffie Hellman, whose main purpose is to create a secure tunnel for symmetric data to pass through. He does not encrypt data but created a secure tunnel.
- **DH groups**: DH groups specify the strength of the key. For example, group 1: 768-bit, group 2: 1024-bit, group 5: 1536-bit, group 14: 2048-bit, and so on. DH group 19: 256-bit elliptic curve is acceptable, and so is group 20: 384-bit elliptic curve.
- **Asymmetric Encryption**: Asymmetric encryption uses two keys - a private key and a public key - and is also known as a PKI, complete with its CA and intermediary authorities. The Security+ exam tests the use of both the private and public keys very thoroughly. I have created a diagram to help you understand the purpose of each key. We use the mnemonic **South-East-Distinguished-Visitor (SEDV)**.

The first stage in encryption is the key exchange; you will always keep your private key and give away your public key. You will always use someone else's public key to encrypt:

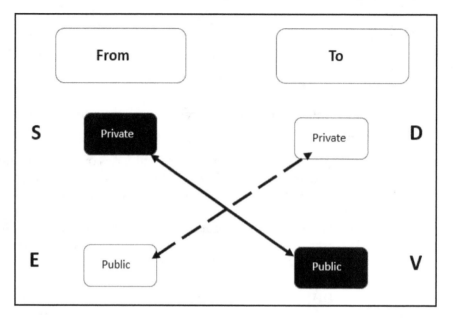

Figure 6: Asymmetric key exchange

In the preceding diagram, there are two different key pairs: the black key pair and the white key pair. These work together. Remember: the private key is your bank card, but the public key is your deposit slip - you will give it away so that people can pay money into your account.

The person who is sending the data is on the **From** side and the person receiving the data is on the **To** side.

A good way to remember the labels would be to think of South-East on the left-hand side and Distinguished-Visitor on the right. These labels stand for the following:

- **S**: Sign (digital signature)
- **E**: Encryption
- **D**: Decryption
- **V**: Validation

For example, Bob wants to encrypt data and send it to Carol; how is this done? Let's look at the following diagram. We can see that Bob owns the black key pair and Carol owns the white key pair. The first thing that needs to happen before encryption can happen is that they each give the other person their public key:

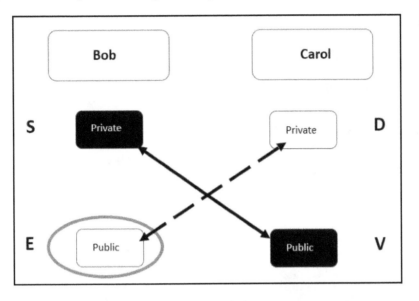

Figure 7: Bob encrypting data

You can see the under the column for **Bob** that he has his private key, which he will always keep, and the public key that Carol has given him. In the preceding diagram, you can see the label **E**, for encryption, and therefore Bob uses Carol's public key to encrypt the data. Then, under **Carol**, you can see the letter **D**, for decryption; therefore, when the encrypted data arrives, Carol uses the other half of the white key pair, the private key, to decrypt the data.

Exam tip
Encryption stops the data being read by changing plaintext to ciphertext. A digital signature ensures that the data has not been altered as it creates a hash of the message, but the original data can be read.

Digital Signatures Explained

When we send an email or document to someone, it could be intercepted in transit and altered. Your email address could be spoofed and someone could send an email as if it was from you, but there is no guarantee of integrity. Do you remember in Chapter 1, *Understanding Security Fundamentals*, that we used hashing to provide the integrity of data, but in emails we use a digital signature. We sign the email or document with our private key and it is validated by our public key.

The first stage in digital signatures is to exchange public keys - the same principle as encryption.

For example, George wants to send Mary an email and he wants to ensure that it has not been altered in transit. See the following diagram:

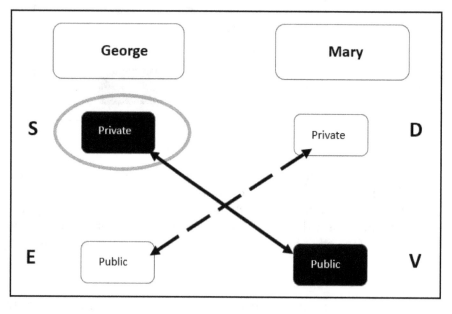

Figure 8: Digital signature

In the above diagram, you can see that George is going to sign the email with his private key when he sends it to Mary; she validates it with the public key that George has already given to her. When the email has been validated, she knows that the email has not been tampered with. It could be read in transit, but not tampered with.

When people are asked to sign contracts, they sometimes use a third-party provider that asks them to digitally sign the contract; this then makes the contract valid as the digital signature proves the identity of the signatory.

Then there's non-repudiation. When I complete a digital signature, I am using my private key, which I should never give away to sign the email or document, proving that it has come has come from me. Non-repudiation means that I cannot deny that it was me who signed the document. I could not say it was done by someone else. In the early 6th century, King Arthur would send messages to his knights on a parchment scroll and then would put his wax seal on the scroll to prove it came from him. The digital signature in modern life is doing the same - it is proving who it came from. The digital signature creates a one-way hash of the entire document, so it also provides integrity similar to hashing.

Exam tip
Always use someone else's public key to encrypt data. Never give your private key away.

Cryptography Algorithms and Their Characteristics

If we look at symmetric and asymmetric keys, they use a cipher that has a number of bits attached to it—the lower the number, the faster and the higher the bits. The slower one, however, the one with the higher number of bits, is stronger. And more secure.

For example, we have two people who are going to complete a challenge - they are Usain Bolt, who is DES, a 56-bit key; and we have King Arthur wearing armor, who has an RSA of 4,096 bits. The first part of the challenge is a 100-meter dash, in which Usain Bolt wins and King Arthur is held back by the weight of his armor, 90 meters behind. The second part of the challenge is a boxing match, and Usain keeps hitting King Arthur, who keeps laughing at him as he is being protected by his armor. Then, out of the blue, King Arthur lands a knockout blow to Usain. Since the challenge was for charity and the result was a draw, they are both happy.

Concept
The smaller the key, the faster it is, but the more insecure it is. The higher the key, the slower it is, but the more secure it is.

Symmetric Algorithms

For the Security+ exam, you must know the characteristics of each of the symmetric algorithms, from when it is used to its key length. Remember, they will never ask you which key encrypts or decrypts, as the answer would always be the private key, also known as the shared key. Let's look at each of these characteristics in turn:

- **Advanced Encryption Standard (AES)**: AES comes in three key strengths: 128-, 192-, and 256-bits. AES is commonly used for L2TP/IPSec VPNs.
- **Data Encryption Standard (DES)**: DES groups data into 64-bit blocks, but for the purpose of the exam it is seen as a 56-bit key, making it the fastest but weakest of the symmetric algorithms. This could be used for L2TP/IPSec VPNs, but is weaker than AES.
- **Triple DES (3DES)**: 3DES applies the DES key three times and is said to be a 168-bit key. This could be used for L2TP/IPSec VPNs, but is weaker than AES.
- **Rivest Cipher 4 (RC4)**: RC4 is 40 bits and is used by WEP and is seen as a stream cipher.
- **Blowfish/Twofish**: Blowfish is a 64-bit key and Twofish is a 128-bit key, and both were originally designed for encryption with embedded systems. How can you remember which of these is faster as they have similar names? Easy. I have a pond with fish inside and I have a challenge with a guy called Tom. I need to catch two fish from the pond and he only needs to blow into the air. Guess what? He will win each time. Therefore, remember, Blowfish is faster than Twofish.
- **Diffie Hellman**: When using symmetric encryption, symmetric algorithms need DH to create a secure tunnel before they can transfer encrypted data. DH is asymmetric as it uses public and private keys; it does not encrypt data, but its role is to create a secure session.

Asymmetric Algorithms

Asymmetric algorithms use a PKI environment as they use two keys: a private key and a public key. Let's now look at different asymmetric techniques.

Diffie Hellman (DH) does not encrypt data; its main purpose is to create a secure session so that symmetric data can travel down it. The DH handshake is shown in the following diagram:

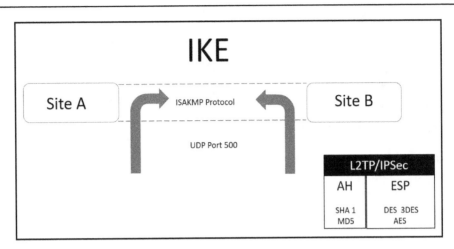

Figure 9: Diffie Hellman

DH creates the keys used in the **Internet Key Exchange** (IKE); it uses UDP port 500 to set up the secure session for the L2TP/IPSec VPN. Once the secure tunnel has been created, then the symmetric encrypted data flows down the tunnel.

- **Rivest, Shamir, and Adelman (RSA)**: RSA is named after the three people who invented the algorithm. The keys were the first private and public key pairs, and they start at 1,024, 2046, 3,072 and 4,096 bits. They are used for encryption and digital signatures.
- **Digital Signature Algorithm (DSA)**: DSA keys are used for digital signatures; they start at 512 bits, but their 1,024-bit and 2046-bit keys are faster than RSA for digital signatures.
- **Elliptic Curve Cryptography (ECC)**: ECC is a small, fast key that is used for encryption in small mobile devices; however, AES-256 is used in military mobile telephones.
- **Ephemeral keys**: Ephemeral keys are short-lived keys; they are used for a single session, and there are two of them:
  - **Diffie Hellman Ephemeral (DHE)**
  - **Elliptic Curve Diffie Hellman Ephemeral (ECDHE)**
- **Pretty Good Privacy (PGP)**: PGP is used between two users to set up an asymmetric encryption and digital signatures. For PGP to operate, you need a private and public key pair. The first stage in using PGP is to exchange the keys. It uses RSA keys.
- **GnuPG**: GnuPG is a free version of the OpenPGP; it is also known as PGP. It uses RSA keys.

Symmetric v Asymmetric Analogy

If we think of encryption as playing table tennis where each person has just one bat and the pace is extremely fast, this is similar to asymmetric encryption as it uses one key.

Then, if we change the game and we give the players two bats – the first bat to stop the ball and the second bat to turn the ball – this would be much slower.

The same can be said for encryption; asymmetric encryption is much more secure as it has two keys and uses DH, an asymmetric technique for setting up a secure tunnel for the symmetric data. Symmetric encryption uses a block cipher and encrypts large blocks of data much faster than the asymmetric technique.

XOR Encryption

The binary operation **Exclusive OR (XOR)** is a binary operand from Boole algebra. This operand will compare two bits and will produce one bit in return:

- Two bits that are equal: 0
- Two bits that are different: 1

This is the opposite to binary. For example, we are going to use the word `tread` in ASCII format and then we are going to insert a key using the word `hello` so that we can complete an XOR operation. See the following diagram:

	T	R	E	A	D
XOR (Original Input)	01010100	01110010	01100101	01100001	01100100
Key	01101000	01100101	01101100	01101100	01101111
Output	00111100	00010111	00001001	00001101	00001011

Figure 10: XOR

XOR encryption is commonly used with AES, several symmetric ciphers, and a one-time pad.

Key Stretching Algorithms

The concept of key stretching is to insert a random set of characters to increase the size of the password hash, making things harder for a brute-force attack:

- **BCRYPT**: BCRYPT is a password-hashing algorithm based on the Blowfish cipher. It is used to salt the passwords; a random string is inserted to increase the password length to help protect against rainbow table attacks. It also has an adaptive function where the iteration count can be increased to make it slower, so it remains resistant to attacks even with increasing computation power.
- **PBKDF2**: PBKDF2 stores passwords with a random salt and with the password hash using HMAC; it then iterates, which forces the regeneration of every password and prevents any rainbow table attack.

Cipher Modes

There are different cipher modes; most symmetric keys use a block cipher and can encrypt a large amount of data quicker than asymmetric encryption. Let's look at these in turn:

- **Stream cipher**: A stream cipher (https://searchsecurity.techtarget.com/definition/cipher) is a method of encrypting text (to produce ciphertext (https://whatis.techtarget.com/definition/ciphertext)) in which a cryptographic key and algorithm (https://whatis.techtarget.com/definition/algorithm) are applied to each binary digit (https://whatis.techtarget.com/definition/bit-binary-digit) in a data stream, one bit at a time. In this mode, only one key is used. It uses symmetric encryption but is not commonly used today as it is easy to crack.
- **Block cipher**: A block cipher is where a block of data is taken and then encrypted; for example, 128 bits of data may be encrypted at a time. This is the method used today as it is much faster than a stream cipher.

Stream v Block Cipher Analogy

We have two teams of four people who have been tasked with unloading a five-ton lorry full of skittles and placing them in a room on the bottom floor of a building.

There are skittles in boxes and there are skittles that have been placed loose. One of the teams has loose skittles that need to be bagged and the other lorry has boxes of skittles. It is obvious that the team with boxes of skittles will win:

- **Initialization Vector (IV)**: This is an arbitrary number that can be used along with a secret key for data encryption. This number, also called a nonce, is employed only one time in any session. The IV length is usually comparable to the length of the encryption key or the block of the cipher in use. Sometimes, this is also known as a starter variable.
- **Cipher Block Chaining (CBC)**: CBC adds XOR to each plaintext block from the ciphertext block that was previously produced. The first plaintext block has an IV that you XOR; you then encrypt that block of plaintext. See the following diagram:

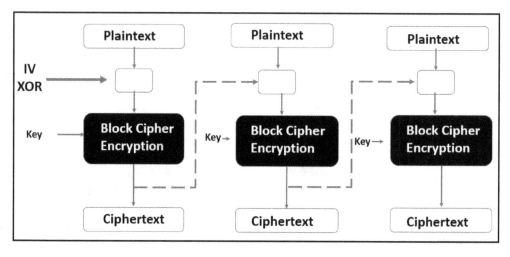

Figure 11: CBC

> The next block of plaintext is XOR'd against the last encrypted block before you encrypt this block. When decrypting a ciphertext block, you need the XOR from the previous ciphertext block. If you are missing any blocks, then decryption cannot be done.

- **Electronic Code Book (ECB)**: ECB replaces each block of the clear text with the block of ciphertext. The same plaintext will result in the same ciphertext. The blocks are independent from the other blocks. CBC is much more secure.

- **Galois/Counter Mode (GCM)**: This is a block cipher mode of operation that uses universal hashing over a binary Galois field to provide authenticated encryption. It can be implemented in hardware and software to achieve high speeds with low cost and low latency.
- **Counter Mode (CTR)**: CTR turns a block cipher into a stream cipher. It generates the next key stream block by encrypting successive values of a counter rather than an IV.

Hashing and Data Integrity

Hashing is where the data inside a document is hashed using an algorithm, such as a **Secure Hash Algorithm version 1 (SHA1)** or MD5. This turns the data inside the file into a long text string known as a hash value; this is also known as a message digest.

While you are hashing the same data, if you copy a file and therefore have two files containing the same data, then hash them with the same hashing algorithm, it will always produce the same hash value. Please look at the following example:

- **Verifying Integrity**: During forensic analysis, a scientist takes a copy of the data prior to investigation. To ensure that they have not tampered with it during investigation, they will hash the data before starting and then compare the hash to the data when finished. If the hash matches, then they know that the integrity of the data is intact.
- **One-Way Function**: For the purpose of the exam, hashing is a one-way function and cannot be reversed.
- **HMAC Authentication**: In cryptography, an HMAC (sometimes known as either keyed-hash message authentication code or hash-based message authentication code) is a specific type of **Message Authentication Code** (**MAC**) involving a cryptographic hash function and a secret cryptographic key. We can have HMAC-MD5 or HMAC-SHA1; the exam looks at both data integrity and data authentication.
- **Digital Signatures**: Digital signatures are used to verify the integrity of an email so that you know it has not been tampered with in transit. The private certificate used to sign the email creates a one-way hash function, and when it arrives at its destination, the recipient has already been given a public key to verify that it has not been tampered with in transit. This will be covered in more depth later in this book.

Can you read data that has been hashed? Hashing does not hide the data, as a digitally signed email could still be read; it only verifies integrity. If you wish to stop someone reading the email in transit, you need to encrypt it.

- **RIPEMD**: This is a 128-bit hashing function. RIPEMD has been replaced by RIPEMD-160, RIPEMD-256, and RIPEMD-320. For the purpose of the exam, you need to know that it can be used to hash data.

Comparing and Contrasting the Basic Concepts of Cryptography

The most common **asymmetric algorithms** include the DH algorithm, which creates a secure session so that symmetric data can flow securely. An example of this would be the L2TP/IPsec VPN. RSA is the most commonly used asymmetric algorithm, and was the very first of its kind, creating public and private key pairs. ECC is an asymmetric algorithm used for the encryption of small mobile devices.

Asymmetric – PKI

Asymmetric keys are obtained from a CA. If you are selling products or services with external entities, then you need to obtain your X509s from a public CA, otherwise your internal certificates will not be accepted.

Asymmetric – Weak/Depreciated Algorithms

An SSL should now be depreciated as it is weak; an example of an exploit is the POODLE attack, which is a man-in-the-middle attack that exploits the vulnerabilities of SSL 3.0 and SSL 3.0 (CBC). Asymmetric algorithms should not be using a key whose strength is 2,046 or lower. However, an SSL VPN is the only VPN that uses an SSL certificate and works with legacy clients.

Asymmetric – Ephemeral Keys

Ephemeral keys are short-lived keys that are used for a one-time only session. There are two types of Diffie Hellman: **Ephemeral (DHE)** and **Elliptic Curve Diffie Hellman Ephemeral (ECDHE)**. The other keys, used for other asymmetric and symmetric encryption, are known as static keys, as they have about a two-year lifespan.

Symmetric Algorithm – Modes of Operation

Symmetric encryption involves a stream cipher that encrypts data one bit at a time; this is easy to crack and is much slower than a block cipher. Block cipher mode takes blocks of data depending on the key and encrypts that data in blocks—this makes the encryption of a large amount of data much faster.

In an L2TP/IPSec VPN tunnel, we have a choice of three different versions of symmetric encryption; the weakest is DES, which has a 56-bit key, followed by 3DES, which has a 168-bit key. The most secure is AES, as it can go from 128 bits up to 256 bits. Remember, symmetric encryption has only one key. It is much faster for encrypting a larger amount of data, but it needs DH, an asymmetric technique, to create a secure tunnel before it is used.

Symmetric Encryption – Streams v Block Ciphers

Symmetric encryption uses a block cipher, where blocks of data are encrypted. The key size determines how large the block of data is; for example, if I use DES, then I can only encrypt blocks of 56 bits, whereas AES can encrypt blocks of data of up to 256 bits.

Asymmetric encryption encrypts one bit at a time, therefore it is slower but more secure than symmetric encryption as it uses a larger key size and uses two keys: public and private.

Symmetric Encryption – Confusion

Confusion massively changes the input to the output by putting it through a non-linear table created by the key.

Symmetric Encryption – Secret Algorithm

A secret key is the piece of information that is used to encrypt and decrypt messages in symmetric encryption.

Symmetric – Session Keys

A session key is an encryption and decryption key that is randomly generated to ensure the security of a communications session between a user and another computer or between two computers. A RADIUS server could create a session key for a user being authenticated.

Hashing Algorithms

A hashing algorithm takes the data from a document and generates a hexadecimal value from that input. If you take the same data and hash it with the same algorithm, it will generate the same hash. In the Security + exam, the hashing algorithms are SHA-1, which is 160 bits, and MD5, which is 128 bits. Hashing is a one-way function to ensure that the integrity of the data is intact.

Crypto Service Provider

A crypto service provider is a software library. For example, Microsoft uses the CryptoAPI and has providers such as the following:

- **Microsoft AES cryptographic provider**: This service provider provides support for the AES algorithm.
- **Microsoft DDS and DH/channel cryptographic provider**: This supports hashing and data signing with DSS and key exchanging for DH.

Crypto Module

A crypto module is a combination of hardware and software that implements crypto functions such as digital signatures, encryption, random number generation, and decryption.

Protecting Data

One of the key functions of a security team is protecting a company's data, as it is difficult to put a price on lost data. Let's look at three types of data: at rest, in use, and in transit:

- **Data-at-Rest**: Data-at-rest is data that is not being used and is stored either on a hard drive or external storage; let's look at the different devices:
    - **Desktops and laptops**: We could use Bitlocker, which is known in the Security+ exam as **Full Disk Encryption** (**FDE**). The desktop or laptop would need a TPM chip built into the motherboard. We could also use **Data Loss Prevention** (**DLP**) to prevent someone stealing the data with a USB drive.
    - **Tablets/phones**: Tablets and phones will need **Full Device Encryption** (**FDE**) to encrypt the device so that data cannot be stolen.
    - **USB or Removable Drive**: We should use **Full Disk Encryption** (**FDE**) so that if the drive is lost or stolen, the data is unreadable.
- **Data-in-Transit**: When purchasing items, we use `https` to encrypt the session before we enter the credit card details. If we are remote users we would use a VPN session to tunnel into the workplace to access data. TLS will be used to encrypt emails as they travel between mail servers.
- **Data-in-Use**: When we use memory on a device, it is in the **Random Access Memory** (**RAM**) or a faster block of memory called the CPU cache. We can protect this data by using full memory encryption.

Basic Cryptographic Terminology

The Security+ exam is full of cryptographic terminology, and in this section, we are going to look at this terminology, starting with obfuscation, which makes the code obscure. Try asking your family and friends to say the word "obfuscation" and watch them struggle. It is aptly named as the word itself is very obscure! You must know the terminology thoroughly.

Obfuscation

Obfuscation is the process where you take source code and make it look obscure, so that if it was stolen, it would not be understood.

Pseudo-Random Number Generator

Pseudo-Random Number Generator (**PRNG**) refers to an algorithm that uses mathematical formulas to produce sequences of random numbers. Random numbers can be used when generating data encryption keys.

Nonce

A nonce is an arbitrary number that can be used just once; it is often a random (https://en.wikipedia.org/wiki/Randomness) or pseudo-random (https://en.wikipedia.org/wiki/Pseudorandomness) number issued in an authentication protocol (https://en.wikipedia.org/wiki/Authentication_protocol) to ensure that old communications cannot be reused in replay attacks (https://en.wikipedia.org/wiki/Replay_attack).

Perfect Forward Secrecy

When a VPN makes a secure connection, a key exchange is made for each secure session, but it links to the server's private key. With perfect forward secrecy, there is no link between the session key and the server's private key; therefore, even if the VPN server has been compromised, the attacker cannot use the server's private key to decrypt the session.

Security Through Obscurity

The concept of security through obscurity is to prevent anyone from outside the organization from knowing the architecture or design of the system or any of its components. The internal people are aware of the weaknesses of the system, but you want to prevent an outside person from knowing anything about the system. Obfuscation is a technique that makes stored source code unreadable.

Collision

If you hash the same data or password with MD5 or with SHA-1, then it will always create the same hash. Hashes are used to store passwords or digitally sign documents. A collision attack is where the attacker tries to match the hash; if the hash is matched, it is known as a collision, and this could compromise systems.

Steganography

Steganography is where a document, image, audio file, or video file can be hidden inside another document, image, audio file, or video file.

Diffusion

Diffusion is a technique where you change one character of the input, which will change multiple bits of the output.

Implementation Decisions

In today's world, security administrators need to look at how the company operates to ensure it is more secure. Do they want to implement smart cards for multifactor authentication or implement a VPN so that remote users can connect to the company securely? Do they need to implement a DLP template to ensure that sensitive data cannot be emailed from the company?

Once the company vision has been decided, the security team needs to look at the algorithms that they need. Normally, this would be the strongest possible; however, we need to ensure that the server has enough processing power to deal with any increase in key length. We should not be using a key of less that 2,046 bits, they are too insecure.

Common Use Cases for Cryptography

In the Security+ exam, "use case" just means examples of when something is used. We are now going to look at examples of when different cryptography techniques are used.

Supporting Confidentiality

A company's data cannot be priced, and the disclosure of this data could cause grave danger to the company. If your competitors stole your secrets, they could beat you to the market and you would not get the rewards that you deserved. To prevent data from being accessed, we will encrypt the data to prevent it from being viewed and prevent any protocol analyzer from reading the packets. When people access the company's network from a remote location, they should use a L2TP/IPSec VPN tunnel, using AES, as the encryption method to create a secure tunnel across the internet and to prevent man-in-the-middle attacks. Encryption could be coupled with mandatory access control to ensure that data is secure and kept confidential.

Supporting Integrity

There are two main reasons for ensuring integrity. The first would be to hash data stored on a file server so that whether or not that the data has been tampered with can be proved. This could also be the case for a forensic examination of a laptop seized by the police - the forensic scientist could hash the data before the examination and then re-hash it at the end to prove that they had not tampered with the data. The hash values should match.

Another method of proving integrity would be to digitally sign an email with your private key to prove to the recipient that it has not been tampered with in transit. Prior to this, you had to send them your public key to validate the email. This proves that the email has maintained its integrity and has not been tampered with in transit.

Supporting Non-Repudiation

When you digitally sign an email with your private key, you cannot deny that it was you, as there is only one private key; this is known as non-repudiation. When two separate parties decide to do a business deal together, they may use a third party to create a digital contract, but parties would log in to where the contract was stored - once they digitally sign it, then it is legally binding.

Supporting Obfuscation

When companies store their source code, they use obfuscation to make it obscure so that it cannot be read by anyone who steals it. This is also known as security by obscurity, where you want to prevent third parties knowing about your IT systems and identifying any weaknesses in the system.

Low-Power Devices

Small **Internet of Things (IoT)** devices will need to use ECC for encryption, as it uses a small key - they do not have the processing power for conventional encryption.

Low Latency

When using encryption, we should use symmetric ciphers, such as 3DES or AES, to encrypt large amounts of data because they both use block cipher encryption with a small key length, compared to asymmetric keys, which have a minimum of 1,024 bits. The server will not have to use as much processing power, as the larger the key length is, the more processing and possible latency there can be. We should implement network accelerator cards where there is a lot of encryption and decryption.

High Resiliency

We should be using the most secure encryption algorithm to prevent the encryption key from being cracked by attackers. The more secure the encryption key, the longer and more processing power it will take to gain the encryption key. In an RSA encryption environment, we should use a key with at least 3,072 bits. We should also look at implementing accelerator cards to reduce the amount of latency on the encryption or decryption.

Supporting Authentication

A corporate environment should not use a single-factor username and password as they are not as secure as multifactor usernames and passwords. We should adopt at least two-factor authentication and use a smart card and PIN to make authentication more secure. Installing a RADIUS server adds an additional layer to authentication to ensure that authentication from the endpoints is more secure.

Resource v Security Constraints

The more secure the encryption used and the higher the key length, the more processing power and memory the server will need. If there are not enough resources on the server, it could be vulnerable to a resource exhaustion attack, which causes the systems to hang or even crash - it is like a DoS attack. We must strike a balance between the hardware resources that the server has and the amount of processing power we use.

Practical Exercises

For these three practical exercises, you need a 2012/2016 server that is a domain controller. If you are a home user and have access to a desktop with Windows 7, Windows 8.1, or Windows 10 and do not have a server, you can still complete the second exercise.

Practical Exercise 1 – Building a Certificate Server

1. Log in to your 2012/2016 domain controller and open **Server Manager**.
2. Select **Manage**, then **Add Roles and Features**; click **next** three times.
3. On the **Select Server Roles** page, check the top box, **Active directory certificate server**. Select the **Add Features** button. Click **Next** three times. Check the **CA** box, then click **Next**, and then **Install**. This will take a few minutes; when it is finished, press **Close**.
4. On the **Server Manager** toolbar, double-click on the yellow triangle; this is a notification. In the post-deployment configuration wizard, double-click on the blue hyperlink, and click **Configure active directory certificate service**. Click **Next**, then in the role services wizard, check the **CA** box. You need to wait a few seconds, then the **Next** button comes alive. Press **Next** twice. In the CA Type wizard, select **Root CA** and click **Next** three times. For the CA name under **Common name for this CA**, enter the name MyCA, click **Next** three times, then click **Configure**. After it is configured, press **Close**.
5. On the **Server Manager** toolbar, press **Tools**, then **CA**. Expand **MyCA** on the left-hand side, then expand **Issued Certificates**, which should be blank, as no certificates have been issued. See the following screenshot:

Certification Authority (Local)	Request ID	Requester Name	Binary Certificate	Certificate Template	Serial Number
⊿ MyCA			There are no items to show in this view.		
Revoked Certificates					
Issued Certificates					
Pending Requests					
Failed Requests					
Certificate Templates					

Figure 12: Certificate authority

Practical Exercise 2 – Encrypting Data with EFS and Stealing Certificates

Follow these steps:

1. Go to the desktop; create a folder called `test`.
2. Inside the folder, create a text document called `data`.
3. Right-click the folder called `data`, then select **Properties**.
4. On the **General** tab, click **Advanced**, then check the box against encrypt content to secure data. The `data` folder should turn green; that means it is encrypted with EFS.
5. Go to the **Start** button, then type `mmc` and select the icon with the red suitcase.
6. Console 1 should open. Select **File** | **Add remove snap in**, then select **Certificates**, select **Add**, click **Next**, and then **Finish**.
7. Expand **Certificates** | **Current User** | **Personal**. You should see an entry for an EFS certificate.
8. Right-click the certificate. Select **All tasks** | **Export**.
9. The certification export wizard appears. Press **Next**. On **Export Private Key**, select **Yes**, export the private key, and press **Next**. You will see that it is the P12 format. Press **Next**, check the **Password** box, enter the password `123` twice, and then press **Next**. In the file to export, call it `PrivKey` and save it to the desktop. Press **Next** and then **Finish**.
10. A box telling you the export was successful should appear.
11. Repeat the exercise and export the public key as `PubKey`.
12. You should notice the two files on the desktop; the public key has a `.cer` extension and looks like a certificate. The private has a `.pfx` extension and looks like a letter being inserted into an envelope.

Practical Exercise 3 – Revoking the EFS Certificate

1. Go to **Server Manager** | **Tools** and select **Certificate Authority.**
2. Expand **Issued Certificates** and you should see an EFS certificate.
3. Right-click the certificate and select **All Tasks.**
4. Revoke the certificate.

You will now notice it has moved from **Issued Certificates** to **Revoked Certificates**.

Review Questions

1. What type of certificate does a CA have?
2. If I am going to use a CA internally, what type of CA should I use?
3. If I want to carry out B2B activity with third-party companies or sell products on the web, what type of CA should I use?
4. Why would I make my CA offline when not in use?
5. Who builds the CA or intermediary authorities?
6. Who signs X509 certificates?
7. What can I use to prevent my CA being compromised and fraudulent certificates being issued?
8. If two entities want to set up a cross certification, what must they set up first?
9. What type of trust model does PGP use?
10. How can I tell whether my certificate is valid?
11. If the CRL is going slow, what should I implement?
12. Explain certificate stapling/OCSP stapling.
13. What is the process of obtaining a new certificate?
14. What is the purpose of the key escrow?

15. What is the purpose of the HSM?

16. What is the purpose of the DRA and what does it need to complete its role effectively?

17. How can I identify each certificate?

18. What format is a private certificate and what file extension does it have?

19. What format is a public certificate and what file extension does it have?

20. What format is a PEM certificate?

21. What type of certificate can be used on multiple servers in the same domain?

22. What type of certificate can be used on multiple domains?

23. What should I do with my software to verify that is it original and not a fake copy?

24. What is the purpose of extended validation of an X509?

25. What type of cipher is the Caesar cipher and how does it work if it uses ROT 4?

26. What is encryption and what are the inputs and outputs called?

27. What type of encryption will be used to encrypt large amounts of data?

28. What is the purpose of DH?

29. What is the first stage in any encryption, no matter whether it is asymmetric or symmetric?

30. If Carol is encrypting data to send to Bob, what key will they each use?

31. If George encrypted data four years ago with an old CAC card, can he un-encrypt the data with his new CAC card?

32. If Janet is digitally signing an email to send to John to prove that it has not been tampered with in transit, what key will they each use?

33. What two things does digitally signing an email provide?

34. What asymmetric encryption algorithm should I use to encrypt data on a smartphone?

35. What shall I use to encrypt a military mobile telephone?

36. Name two key-stretching algorithms.

37. What is the purpose of key stretching?

38. What is the difference between stream and block cipher modes, and which one will you use to encrypt large blocks of data?

39. What happens with cipher block chaining if I don't have all of the blocks?

40. If I want to ensure the integrity of data, what shall I use? Name two algorithms.

41. If I want to ensure the protection of data, what shall I use?

42. Is a hash a one-way or two-way function, and is it reversible?

43. What type of man-in-the-middle attack is SSL 3.0 (CBC) vulnerable to?

44. Explain why we would use **Diffie Hellman Ephemeral (DHE)** and **Elliptic Curve Diffie Hellman Ephemeral (ECDHE)**.

45. What are the strongest and weakest methods of encryption with an L2TP/IPSec VPN tunnel?

46. What is the name of the key used to ensure the security of communication between a computer and a server or a computer to another computer?

47. What should I do to protect data at rest on a laptop?

48. What should I do to protect data-at-rest on a tablet or smartphone?

49. What should I do to protect data-at-rest on a backend server?

50. What should I do to protect data-at-rest on a removable device, such as a USB flash drive or an external hard drive?

51. What two protocols could we use to protect data in transit?

52. How can you protect data in use?

53. What is the purpose of obfuscation?

54. What is the purpose of perfect forward secrecy?

55. What type of attack tries to find two has values that match?

56. What is the purpose of rainbow tables?

57. Explain the concept of steganography.

58. What are the two purposes of Data Loss Protection (DLP)?

59. What is the purpose of salting a password?

Answers and Explanations

1. A CA has a root certificate, which it uses to sign keys.

2. I would use a private CA for internal use only; these certificates will not be accepted outside of your organization.

3. I would use a public CA for B2B activities.

4. If you were a military, security, or banking organization, you would keep the CA offline when it is not being used to prevent it from being compromised.

5. An architect would build the CA or intermediary authorities.

6. The CA would sign the X509 certificates.

7. Certificate pinning can be used to prevent a CA from being compromised and fraudulent certificates being issued.

8. If two separate PKI entities want to set up a cross certification, the root CAs would set up a trust model between themselves, known as a bridge trust model.

9. PGP uses a trust model known as a web of trust.

10. A **Certificate Revocation List** (**CRL**) is used to determine whether a certificate is valid.

11. If the CRL is going slow, an OCSP is used as it provides faster validation.

12. Certificate stapling/OCSP stapling is where a web server uses an OCSP for faster certificate authentication, bypassing the CRL.

13. A **Certificate Signing Request** (**CSR**) generates two keys; the public key is sent to the CA and then sent back the X509.

14. The key escrow stores and manages private keys for third parties.

15. A hardware security module is used by the key escrow as it securely stores and manages certificates.

16. When a user's private key becomes corrupt, the DRA recovers the data by obtaining a copy of the private key from the key escrow.

17. Each certificate can be identified by its OID, which is similar to a serial number.

18. A private certificate is in a P12 format with a `.pfx` extension.

19. A public certificate is in a P7B format with a `.cer` extension.

20. A PEM certificate is in Base64 format.

21. A wildcard certificate can be used on multiple servers in the same domain.

22. A **Subject Alternative Name** (**SAN**) certificate can be used on multiple domains.

23. Code-signing software is similar to hashing the software and ensuring the integrity of the software.

24. Extended validation is normally used by financial institutions as it provides a higher level of trust for the X509; when it is used, the URL background turns green.

25. The Caesar cipher is a substitution cipher; an example would be ROT 4, where each letter would be substituted by a letter four characters along in the alphabet.

26. Encryption is when plaintext is taken and turned into ciphertext.

27. Symmetric encryption is used to encrypt large amounts of data as it uses one key.

28. DH is an asymmetric technique that creates a secure tunnel; during a VPN connection, it is used during the IKE phase and uses UDP port 500 to create the VPN tunnel.

29. The first stage in encryption is key exchange. During asymmetric encryption, each entity will give the other entity their public key. The private key is secure and never given away.

30. Carol uses Bob's public key to encrypt the data and then Bob will use his private key to decrypt the data. Encryption and decryption are always done by the same key pair.

31. George must obtain the old private key to decrypt the data as the encryption was done with a different key pair.

32. Janet will digitally sign the email with her private key and John will check its validity with Janet's public key, which he would have received in advance.

33. A digital signature provides both integrity and non-repudiation.

34. ECC will be used to encrypt data on a smartphone as it is small and fast and uses the DH handshake.

35. AES-256 will be used to encrypt a military mobile telephone.

36. Two key-stretching algorithms are BCRYPT and PBKDF2.

37. Key stretching salts the password being stored so that duplicate passwords are never stored, and it also increases the length of the keys to make things harder for a brute-force attack.

38. Streams encrypt one bit at a time and block ciphers take blocks of data, such as 128-bit modes. A block cipher will be used for large amount of data.

39. CBC needs all of the clocks of data to decrypt the data, otherwise it will not work.

40. Hashing ensures the integrity of data; two examples include SHA-1 (160 bit) and MD5 (128 bit).

41. Encryption is used to protect data so that it cannot be reviewed or accessed.

42. A hash is one-way and cannot be reversed.

43. POODLE is a man-in-the-middle attack on a downgraded SSL 3.0 (CBC).

44. DHE and ECDHE are both ephemeral keys that are short-lived, one-time keys.
45. The strongest encryption for an L2TP/IPSec VPN tunnel is AES and the weakest is DES.
46. A session key ensures the security of communications between a computer and a server or a computer and another computer.
47. Data-at-rest on a laptop is protected by FDE.
48. Data-at-rest on a tablet or smartphone is protected by FDE.
49. Data-at-rest on a backend server is stored on a database, so it needs database encryption.
50. Data-at-rest on a USB flash drive or external hard drive is done via full disk encryption.
51. Data-in-transit could be secured by using TLS, HTTPS, or an L2TP/IPsec tunnel.
52. Data-in-use could be protected by full memory encryption.
53. Obfuscation is used to make the source code look obscure so that if it is stolen, it cannot be understood.
54. Perfect forward secrecy ensures that there is no link between the server's private key and the session key. If the VPN server's key was compromised, it could not decrypt the session.
55. A collision attack tries to match two hash values to obtain a password.
56. Rainbow tables are a list of precomputed words showing their hash value. You will get rainbow tables for MD5 and different rainbow tables for SHA-1.
57. Steganography is used to conceal data; you can hide a file, image, video, or audio inside another image, video, or audio file.
58. DLP prevents sensitive or PII information from being emailed out of a company or being stolen from a file server using a USB device.
59. Salting a password ensures that duplicate passwords are never stored and makes things more difficult for brute-force attacks by increasing the key size (key stretching).

10
Responding to Security Incidents

In this chapter, we will be looking at incident response, particularly with regard to the collection of volatile evidence for forensic analysis.

We will cover the following exam objectives in this chapter:

- **Using the appropriate software tools to assess the security posture of an organization, given a scenario:** Coverage here will include protocol analyzers, network scanners, rogue system detection, network mapping, wireless scanners/crackers, password crackers, vulnerability scanners, configuration compliance scanners, exploitation frameworks, data sanitization tools, steganography tools, honeypot, backup utilities, banner grabbing, command-line tools, ping, netstat, `tracert`, `nslookup/dig`, ARP, `ipconfig/ip/ifconfig`, `tcpdump`, Nmap, and Netcat.
- **Analyzing and interpreting the output from security technologies, given a certain scenario:** Here we will cover HIDS/HIPS, antivirus, file integrity checks, host-based firewalls, application whitelisting, removable media control, advanced malware tools, patch management tools, UTM, DLP, data execution prevention, and web application firewalls.
- **Following incident response procedures, given a certain scenario:** We will look at response plans, documented incident types/category definitions, roles and responsibilities, reporting requirements/escalation, cyber incident response teams, exercises, the incident response process, preparation, identification, containment, eradication, recovery, and lessons learned.

- **Summarizing the basic concepts of forensics:** This will involve the order of volatility, chain of custody, legal hold, data acquisition, capturing system images, network traffic and logs, capturing video, record time offset, taking hashes, screenshots, witness interviews, preservation, recovery, strategic intelligence/counterintelligence gathering, active logging, and tracking man hours.

- **Explaining the concepts of disaster recovery and continuity of operations:** Here we will look at backup concepts and full, differential, and incremental backups and snapshots.

Incident Response Procedures

There are many different incidents, and each of them requires a different incident response plan. For example, dealing with a flood is totally different to dealing with the failure of a server's hardware. The first stage of an incident response plan is to collect any volatile evidence so that the source of that incident can be identified, followed by containment of the incident itself, followed by the recovery procedures. Let's look in more detail at the components required to make incident response successful:

- **Documented Incident Types**: We should already have documentation about each incident that shows the steps required for a positive response. These types of incidents are laid down under different category definitions.

- **Category Definitions**: Your company should have an outline of a plan for dealing with most incidents ranging from the following categories:
  - Unauthorized access
  - Loss of computers or data
  - Loss of availability
  - Malware attacks
  - DDoS attacks
  - Power failure
  - Natural disasters, such as floods, tornadoes, hurricanes, and fires
  - Cyber security incidents

- **Roles and Responsibilities**: When an incident occurs, it is important to get an incident response team together to deal with the incident, which is made up of members in the following roles:
    - **Incident response manager**: A top-level manager who takes charge
    - **Security analyst**: Technical support to the incident
    - **IT auditor**: Checks that the company is compliant
    - **Risk analyst**: Evaluates all aspects of risk
    - **HR**: Sometime employees are involved in the incident
    - **Legal**: Gives advice and makes decisions on legal issues
    - **Public relations**: Deals with the press to reduce the impact

- **Reporting Requirements/Escalation**: Depending on the incident itself, you may have to report it to the authorities and/or your customer base should their credit card details be stolen. Your help desk must identify the incident response plan that deals with each particular incident so that it can be escalated to the team that has the skill set to deal with it.
- **Cyber Incident Response Teams**: Cybercrime is very prominent in today's world. It ranges from a single criminal trying to steal some money to organized criminal gangs through to advanced persistent threats, sometimes from national states. The cyber incident response team must move rapidly and have up-to-date training for the variety of incidents that they may face, and may have to use third-party specialists in some aspects of cybercrime.
- **Incident Response Exercises**: Companies will need to invoke each incident response plan periodically, very similar to fire drills that have been carried out for many years. This will allow your different incident response teams to gain the skill set necessary for dealing with future incidents.

Incident Response Process

While responding to an incident, the following processes are followed:

1. **Preparation**: The preparation phase is where the different incident response plans are written and kept up to date.
2. **Identification**: Once an incident has occurred, it is important that the appropriate incident response plan is invoked and the necessary personnel are notified.

3. **Containment**: When dealing with the incident, it is important that the volatile evidence is secured and the incident is prevented from spreading any further.

4. **Eradication**: In the eradication phase, we want to destroy the source of the incident. For example, if it is a virus, we want it totally removed.

5. **Recovery**: In the recovery phase, we are getting the company back to an operational state, hopefully within the **Recovery Point Objective** (**RPO**). For example, imaging machines and restoring data within one day.

6. **Lessons Learned**: Lessons learned is a detective phase where we pull together all of the facts and plan to prevent a re-occurrence in the future. Failure to carry this out will lead to a re-occurrence. The incident response process is shown here:

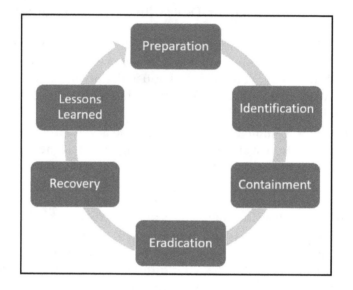

Figure 1: Incident response process

Understanding the Basic Concepts of Forensics

Forensics is used by the police when they are investigating crimes and need to find as much evidence as they can to secure a conviction. We will be looking at computer and web-based attacks. There are many different components, therefore we will look at each of them in turn:

- **Order of Volatility**: You are a firefighter and you arrive at a house on fire; you can only save items one at a time and there are two items inside. The first is a snowman, and the second is a rib of beef; you now have a dilemma: which one shall you choose? Easy! You save the snowman first as it is melting and you let the rib of beef cook some more so that the other firefighters can have a nice supper! So, when we want to ascertain the order of volatility, we are looking to secure the most perishable evidence first. We do not try and stop the attack until we have secured the volatile evidence so that the source can be identified. This is known as the order of volatility:
  - **Example 1 - Web-Based Attack**: An attacker is attacking the company website and the security team are trying to capture the network traffic to find the source of the attack. This is the most volatile evidence.
  - **Example 2 - Attack Inside a Computer**: When someone has attacked your computer, you need to capture the evidence in accordance with the order of volatility:
    - **CPU cache**: Fast block of volatile memory used by the CPU
    - **Random Access Memory (RAM)**: Volatile memory used to run applications
    - **Swap/page file**: Used for running applications when there is no RAM left
    - **Hard drive**: Data at rest for storing data
  - **Example 3 - Removable Storage Drive Attached to a Computer/Server**: Someone has left a USB flash drive plugged into your file server. When it is in use, programs such as Word are launched in RAM, so we would capture the volatile memory first.

- **Example 4 - Command-Line Tools**: You need to know which command-line tool provides information that could disappear if you reboot the computer, and that would be netstat. With **netstat -an**, the listening and established ports are shown. If you reboot the computer, all of the established connections will be lost.

Exam tip
The order of volatility is to do with collecting the most perishable evidence first.

Five-Minute Practical

Open up the Command Prompt on your computer and type **netstat -an**. You should now see the listening and established ports; count them, and write the numbers down. Run the **shutdown /r /t 0** command to immediately reboot the machine. Log back in, go to the Command Prompt, and run **netstat -an**; what is the difference? You will see that you have lost information that could have been used as evidence:

Volatile Evidence Summary			
Web-Based Attack	**Computer Attack**	**Removable Drive**	**Command**
Capture network traffic	CPU cache then RAM	Volatile memory using RAM	**netstat-an**

Exam tip
Capturing network traffic is the first step in remote or web-based attacks so that you can identify the course of action to take.

- **Chain of Custody**: The Chain of Custody starts when the evidence has been collected, bagged, and tagged. It lists the evidence and who has handled it along the way. For example, Sergeant Smith handed 15 kg of cocaine to Sergeant Jones following a drugs raid. However, when it is handed in to the property room, 1 kg is missing. In this event, we would need to investigate the Chain of Custody; in this scenario, Sergeant Jones would be liable for the loss. The Chain of Custody is shown here:

Date	From	TO	Evidence
1 August	Sergeant Smith	Sergeant Jones	15 kg cocaine
2 August	Sergeant Jones	Property room	14 kg cocaine

- **Example 1 - Missing entry on the chain of custody document**: On Monday 15, laptops were collected by the system administrator. The next day, the system administrator passes them on to the IT manager. On Wednesday, the IT director presents the 15 laptops as evidence to the court. The judge looks at the chain of custody document and notices that there was no formal handover between the IT manager and the IT director. With the handover missing, the judge wants to investigate the Chain of Custody.
- **Example 2 - Evidence leaves the detective's possession**: The FBI arrest a known criminal and collect 43 hard drives that they bag and tag, before placing them in two bags. They arrest the criminal and take them from Arizona to New York. One detective is handcuffed to the criminal while the other carries the two bags. When they arrived at check-in, the airline clerk tells them that the carry-on bags are more than the 8 kg allowance, and therefore they are too heavy and need to go in the hold. The detective does this, but locks the suitcases to prevent theft. Because the evidence is not physically in their possession at all times, the Chain of Custody is broken as there is a chance for someone working for the airline to tamper with the evidence. Therefore, they cannot prove to the court that the integrity of the evidence has been kept intact at all times.

Exam tip
The Chain of Custody must show who has handled the evidence until it is presented to the court. The evidence must not leave the possession of the person who has signed for it, otherwise it needs to be investigated.

- **Legal Hold**: Legal Hold is the process of protecting any documents that can be used in evidence from being altered or destroyed. Sometimes, this is also known as litigation hold.

    Example: Dr. Death has been prescribing new drugs to patients in a large hospital who have been dying. An auditor has been sent to investigate the possibility of foul play, and then following the audit, the FBI are notified. The doctor has been emailing a pharmaceutical company that has been supplying the drugs for a trial. The FBI does not want the doctor to be alerted, so they have the hospital's IT team put his mailbox on Legal Hold. When the mailbox is on Legal Hold, the mailbox limit is lifted; the doctor can still send and receive email, but cannot delete anything. This way, they are not alerted to the fact that they are under investigation.

- **Data Acquisition**: This is the process of collecting all of the evidence from devices, such as USB flash drives, cameras, and computers; as well as data in paper format, such as letters and bank statements. The first step in data acquisition is to collect the volatile evidence so that it is secured. The data must be bagged and tagged, and included in the evidence log.

Exam tip
Recording the time offset is used for time normalization across multiple time zones.

- **Record Time Offset**: When we collect evidence from computers, we should record the time offset. This is the regional time, so that in a multinational investigation we can put them into a time sequence - this is known as time normalization.

    Example: The police in three separate countries are trying to identify where the data started from in a chain, then who handled the data along the line. They have the following information of when it was first created:

    - **New York**: Created 3 a.m
    - **London**: Created 4 a.m
    - **Berlin**: Created 4.30 a.m

Without recording the time offset, it looks as if it started off in New York, but if we apply regional times, when it is 4 a.m. in London, the time in New York is 11 p.m. the day before, so it cannot be New York. When it is 4.30 a.m. in Berlin, it is only 3.30 a.m. in London; therefore, it originated in Berlin. However, with the record time offset, it looked the least unlikely before the time offset was applied.

- **Forensic Copies**: If we are going to analyze removable data that we have acquired, we would first of all take a forensic copy and keep the original data intact. We would then use the copy to analyze the data so that we keep the original data unaltered, as it needs to be used in its original state and presented as evidence to the courts.
- **Capturing System Images**: When the police are taking evidence from laptops and desktops, they take a complete system image. The original image is kept intact and the system is analyzed to find evidence of any criminal activity.

Exam tip
Taking a system image or a forensic copy of a hard drive is the first stage in any forensic investigation.

- **Screenshots**: You may also take screenshots of applications or viruses on the desktops and keep them as evidence. A better way of doing this would be to use a modern smartphone that would geotag the evidence.
- **Taking Hashes**: When either the forensic copy or the system image is being analyzed, the data and applications are hashed at the beginning of the investigation. At the end, it is re-hashed and should match the original hash value to prove data integrity. If, during the investigation, the officer believes that they have made a mistake, they can re-hash the data; if it has been altered, they should note it down and then carry out the investigation as best they can.

Exam tip
Hashing data before and after the investigation can prove data integrity.

- **Network Traffic and Logs**: When investigating a web-based or remote attack, we should first capture the volatile network traffic before stopping the attack. This will help us identify the source of the attack. In addition to this, we should look at different log files from the firewall, NIPS, NIDS, and any server involved. If we use a SIEM system, this can help collate these entries and give a good picture of any attack.

  > **Example:** Your company uses an account lockout of three attempts. If an attacker tries to log in once to three separate computers, each computer would not identify it as an attack, as it is a single attempt on each computer, but an SIEM system would pick up these attempts as three failed login attempts and alert the administrators in real time.

- **Capturing Video**: CCTV traffic can be a good source of evidence for helping to identify the attackers and the time the attack was launched. This can be vital in apprehending suspects.
- **Witness Statements**: The police may also take witness statements to try and get a picture of who was involved and maybe then use photo-fits so that they can be apprehended.
- **Preservation**: Data needs to be preserved in its original state so that it can be produced as evidence in the court. This is why we take copies and analyze the copies so that the original data is not altered and is pristine. Putting a copy of the most vital evidence in a **Write-Once-Read-Many** (**WORM**) drive will prevent any tampering with the evidence, as you cannot delete from a WORM drive.
- **Recovery**: When the incident has been eradicated, we may have to recover the data from a backup; a faster method would be a hot site that is already up and running with data less than one-hour old. We may also have to purchase additional hardware if the original hardware was damaged during the incident.

Exam tip
Re-imaging computers and restoring data is part of the recovery phase.

- **Strategic Intelligence/Counterintelligence Gathering**: This is where different governments exchange data about cyber criminals so that they can work together to reduce threats. It is also possible for companies who have suffered an attack to log as much information as they can and have a third party who specializes in incident response to help them find a way to prevent re-occurrence.
- **Active Logging**: To track incidents, we need to be actively monitoring and actively logging changes to patterns in our log files, or traffic patterns in our network. Installing an SIEM system can help collate all entries in the log files, ensuring that duplicate data is not used so that a true picture can be taken. Alerts based on certain triggers can be set up on our SIEM system so that we are notified as soon as the event happens.
- **Tracking Man Hours**: Companies should track man hours to realize the costs incurred during incidents. This may make them realize that they may have to spend more money on resources to protect against incidents.

Software Tools for Assessing the Security Posture of an Organization

Security teams are constantly under attack from cyber criminals and threat actors, and they therefore need to be able to use a mixture of different security tools so that they can identify attacks before they have a chance to cause grave damage to the business. We will now look at each of these tools to see the benefits of each:

- **Protocol Analyzer**: A protocol analyzer, such as Wireshark, can capture the traffic flowing through the network, including passwords in clear text and any commands being sent to network-based applications. A protocol analyzer can identify the three-way handshake between two hosts and the verbs being used with applications, such as the HTML GET verb for fetching a web page. But if we see the PUT or HEAD verb, we could recognize this as an attack.

Example: Someone within the company is not working as they should be but has been surfing the web, and the manager has called you in as the security administrator to gather evidence. You decide that a protocol analyzer or packet sniffer is the best tool for tracking the information. You run a Wireshark session and capture visits to the NFL website. When you analyze the trace, you notice that the request is using the HTTP GET verb. This is the request for a page on www.nfl.com. When we drill down further into the analysis of the request, we are looking at a page with an article, *Josh Hobbs and Mike Glennon drawing trade interest*, as shown here:

Figure 2: Protocol analyzer

Exam tip

A protocol analyzer can detect the operating system of a host and commands being sent across the network to any applications.

- **Network Scanners**: A network scanner can be used to map out your network for you so that you can see the network devices and can also show performance data and packet loss; see the following screenshot:

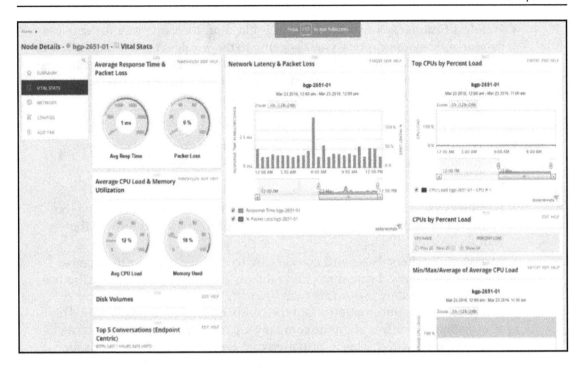

Figure 3: Network scanner

- **Rogue System Detection**: Rogue system protection tools, such as those made by McAfee, can detect rogue and unmanaged devices on your network and help you protect your network. If we also adopt 802.1x managed switches, we can prevent these devices from connecting to our network.

- **Network Mapping**: A network mapper can show all the devices on your network along with their operating systems and the services running on them. These tools will be banned from use on a corporate network because of the vast amount of information that can be gathered.

- **Wireless Scanners**: A wireless scanner is like a protocol analyzer for wireless networks. They can capture packets going to the wireless router. Embedded in the wireless packets is the name of the wireless network SSID. This means that even if you disable SSID broadcasting, the SSID can still be discovered. You could also use a SSID de-cloak device to find the SSID.

Exam tip
A network mapper can identify the operating systems and services running on a computer.

- **Wireless Crackers**: Tools, such as Fern Wi-Fi Cracker, are written using the Python programming language and can be used to crack and recover the WEP/WPA and WPS keys.
- **Password Crackers**: Password crackers are tools that can perform the most common dictionary, brute-force, and rainbow table attacks. They can also use guessing, where they use words such as *qwerty*, *password*, and *12345*; or spidering, where information about the company is used in passwords. This information can be found on the company's social media websites, such as Facebook and Twitter. This information can then be turned into words for password cracking.
- **Vulnerability Scanner**: There are two types of vulnerability scanner:
  - **Credentialed**: This basically involves running as an administrator and can find vulnerabilities and even audit files and permissions.
  - **Non-Credentialed**: This is the most basic, running with limited permissions and scanning hosts to find missing patches.

The vulnerability scanner is passive and does not cause damage to the systems. An example is Microsoft Baseline Analyzer (see the following screenshot). Although the computer was fully patched, as it was a credentialed scan, it gave me some information:

Microsoft Baseline Security Analyzer 2.3 — □ ✕

Microsoft
Baseline Security Analyzer

Microsoft

Windows Scan Results

Administrative Vulnerabilities

Score	Issue	Result
	Automatic Updates	The Automatic Updates feature has not been configured on this computer. Please upgrade to the latest Service Pack to obtain the latest version of this feature and then use the Control Panel to configure Automatic Updates. What was scanned How to correct this
	Administrators	More than 2 Administrators were found on this computer. What was scanned Result details How to correct this
	Password Expiration	Some user accounts (4 of 5) have non-expiring passwords. What was scanned Result details How to correct this
	Incomplete Updates	No incomplete software update installations were found. What was scanned
	Windows Firewall	Windows Firewall is enabled and has exceptions configured. Windows Firewall is enabled on all network connections. What was scanned Result details How to correct this
	Local Account Password Test	Some user accounts (3 of 5) have blank or simple passwords, or could not be analyzed. What was scanned Result details
	File System	All hard drives (2) are using the NTFS file system. What was scanned Result details
	Autologon	Autologon is not configured on this computer. What was scanned

🖨 Print this report   📋 Copy to clipboard   ◀ Previous security report   Next security report ▶

Figure 4: Credentialed vulnerability scan

Exam tip
A credentialed vulnerability scanner can audit files and examine permissions.

- **Configuration Compliance Scanner**: Compliance scanning focuses on the configuration settings (or security hardening) being applied to a system in accordance with a compliance framework. This means we are ensuring that all of the settings of a system are configured properly.
- **Exploitation Frameworks**: Exploitation framework tools, such as the open source Metasploit Framework, can develop and execute exploit code against a remote target computer. This can be used to harden your IT systems before they are attacked.

- **Data Sanitization Tools**: When you delete data and then use the `format` command to reformat your hard drive, professional packages exist to recover the data (depending on how old the data is, as it deteriorates over time). Using professional data sanitization tools ensures that this data will never be recovered.
- **Steganography Tools**: Steganography tools can be used for encoding and decoding images, such as JPEGs, and audio files, such as WAV file. You can hide data inside all sorts of files, including audio, video, and image file.

Exam tip

A compliance scanner can ensure that all of the settings on computers are compliant and as they should be.

- **Honeypot**: A honeypot is a website made to look like a legitimate website with lower security to distract attackers away from the legitimate website. Additionally, the security team can monitor the method that the attackers are using so that they can prevent such attacks in the future.

Backup Utilities

Backing up data is very important, because if the system fails, then a copy of the data can be obtained from a previous backup. A company cannot put a cost on its most critical data, and if it were to lose it, this would cause grave damage to the company (especially if the data was from the financial department or the research and development department, which makes new prototypes of products).

There are various ways that we can back up the data: we can take snapshots of virtual machines, back up to a network, back up to tape, or back up to a removable device. Let's look at these in turn:

- **Creating a Snapshot**: When using virtualization, a snapshot can be created so that the virtual machine can be rolled back to a previous state. This is the fastest backup to recover from as it can be done in a matter of seconds.

- **Network Location**: A backup can be performed to a file share on a server in the network. The server would have some sort of RAID redundancy or the storage would be part of a SAN.
- **Backing Up - To Tape**: A backup can be backed up to magnetic tape, and this would be the slowest form of restore. Additionally, a copy of the backup tape can be stored offsite in case the company has a fire and burns down.

Backup Types

There are various types of backups: Full, Incremental, and Differential. Let's look at these in turn:

- **Full Backup**: A full backup is a backup of all of your data. However, some companies might only be able to back up all of their data over the weekend, so they will use either an incremental or differential backup in the middle of the week. This is seen in the exam as the **fastest physical backup**.
- **Incremental**: An incremental backup backs up the data since the last full backup or the last incremental backup. An incremental backup will need the full backup from the start and then all of the incremental backups.
- **Differential**: A differential backup will back up the data since the last full backup. The problem with this is if we have a full backup at the start of the week and then a differential backup every day, they will grow progressively larger each day. A differential backup will always be two tapes: the full backup from the start and the latest differential.

  Example: We will compare the different types of backup. We will start the backup every day, but will suffer data loss on the Friday, and we will see for how many tapes we need to recover our data. Our full backup will be 50 GB of data, and every day, we will produce 5 GB of data. You can see this from the following table; how many tapes are needed for each type of backup to recover your data?:

  - **Full**: The latest full backup is 65 GB; every day, we back up more and more.
  - **Incremental**: Starts off with the full backup but needs all of the incremental backups.

- **Differential**: Starts off with the full backup but needs the latest differential backup:

Backup	Mon	Tues	Wed	Thurs	Fri	Tapes to recover
Full (F)	F 50 GB	F 55 GB	F 60 GB	F 65 GB	X	F 65 GB Thurs
Incremental (I)	F 50 GB	I 5 GB	I 5 GB	I 5 GB	X	F 50 GB Mon 3 X I—Tues, Wed, Thurs
Differential (D)	F 50 GB	D 5 GB	D 10 GB	D 15 GB	X	F 50 GB Mon D 15 GB Thurs

 Exam tip: Symptoms of steganography include an image being lighter than it should be or a file being larger than it should be.

- **Banner Grabbing**: Banner grabbing is a technique used to gain information about a remote server and is often used as part of a fingerprinting attack. This could be where you are looking for details on remote systems such as a web server. If you are looking for the patch level of a web server, we would use banner grabbing to collect this information. Tools like Netcat , Dimitri and Telnet are used for banner grabbing.

Command-Line Tools

Command-line tools are used every day by security professionals; therefore, for the Security + exam, you must be familiar with them, and so I have provided a screenshot for many of them. We are going to see when we would use each of them in turn:

- **Internet Control Message Protocol (ICMP)**: ICMP brings back the replies when you use command-line tools; therefore, if you block incoming ICMP on the network firewall, none of the tools will work externally.
- **Ping**: Ping is used to test connectivity to another host. In the following screenshot, you can see that we have pinged the hostname, `ianneil501.com`, and we have received four replies. The **Total Time to Live (TTL)** is a maximum of 128 seconds; in this case, it is 47 seconds—see the following screenshot:

```
C:\WINDOWS\system32>ping ianneil501.com

Pinging ianneil501.com [46.30.213.45] with 32 bytes of data:
Reply from 46.30.213.45: bytes=32 time=42ms TTL=47
Reply from 46.30.213.45: bytes=32 time=44ms TTL=47
Reply from 46.30.213.45: bytes=32 time=42ms TTL=47
Reply from 46.30.213.45: bytes=32 time=43ms TTL=47

Ping statistics for 46.30.213.45:
    Packets: Sent = 4, Received = 4, Lost = 0 (0% loss),
Approximate round trip times in milli-seconds:
    Minimum = 42ms, Maximum = 44ms, Average = 42ms
```

Figure 5: Ping

- **Continuous Ping**: Continuous ping uses the `ping -t` command and is used for diagnostic testing. Normally, we run `ping -t` when we cannot connect and then, once we can connect, we will get replies—see the following screenshot:

```
C:\WINDOWS\system32>ping -t www.ianneil501.com

Pinging www.ianneil501.com [46.30.213.45] with 32 bytes of data:
Reply from 46.30.213.45: bytes=32 time=42ms TTL=47
Reply from 46.30.213.45: bytes=32 time=43ms TTL=47
Reply from 46.30.213.45: bytes=32 time=41ms TTL=47
Reply from 46.30.213.45: bytes=32 time=41ms TTL=47
Reply from 46.30.213.45: bytes=32 time=47ms TTL=47
Reply from 46.30.213.45: bytes=32 time=49ms TTL=47
Reply from 46.30.213.45: bytes=32 time=45ms TTL=47
Reply from 46.30.213.45: bytes=32 time=43ms TTL=47
Reply from 46.30.213.45: bytes=32 time=44ms TTL=47
Reply from 46.30.213.45: bytes=32 time=46ms TTL=47
Reply from 46.30.213.45: bytes=32 time=42ms TTL=47
Reply from 46.30.213.45: bytes=32 time=43ms TTL=47
Reply from 46.30.213.45: bytes=32 time=42ms TTL=47
Reply from 46.30.213.45: bytes=32 time=43ms TTL=47
Reply from 46.30.213.45: bytes=32 time=43ms TTL=47
Reply from 46.30.213.45: bytes=32 time=41ms TTL=47
Reply from 46.30.213.45: bytes=32 time=46ms TTL=47
```

Figure 6: Continuous ping

- **Netstat**: Netstat is used to see the established connections and the listening ports. If you reboot the computer, all of the established ports will disappear - see the following screenshot:

```
C:\WINDOWS\system32>NETSTAT

Active Connections

  Proto  Local Address          Foreign Address        State
  TCP    127.0.0.1:5939         DESKTOP-QR6R2DA:49758   ESTABLISHED
  TCP    127.0.0.1:7778         DESKTOP-QR6R2DA:49793   ESTABLISHED
  TCP    127.0.0.1:49669        DESKTOP-QR6R2DA:49670   ESTABLISHED
  TCP    127.0.0.1:49670        DESKTOP-QR6R2DA:49669   ESTABLISHED
  TCP    127.0.0.1:49758        DESKTOP-QR6R2DA:5939    ESTABLISHED
  TCP    127.0.0.1:49793        DESKTOP-QR6R2DA:7778    ESTABLISHED
  TCP    127.0.0.1:49794        DESKTOP-QR6R2DA:49795   ESTABLISHED
  TCP    127.0.0.1:49795        DESKTOP-QR6R2DA:49794   ESTABLISHED
  TCP    192.168.0.118:49672    r-54-45-234-77:https    CLOSE_WAIT
  TCP    192.168.0.118:49677    DE-HAM-PLS-R012:5938    ESTABLISHED
  TCP    192.168.0.118:49748    ams10-004:http          ESTABLISHED
  TCP    192.168.0.118:49753    40.67.255.199:https     ESTABLISHED
```

Figure 7: Netstat

- **Tracert**: Tracert is used to trace the route between your computer and a target. This is at a maximum of 30 hops. If you have a reading of less than 2 ms, it is a great connection, but less than 25 ms is still a good connection. If you get a reading of over 800 ms, it means that you have poor connectivity; this could mean that a router is starting to fail - see the following screenshot:

```
C:\WINDOWS\system32>tracert www.ianneil501.com

Tracing route to www.ianneil501.com [46.30.213.45]
over a maximum of 30 hops:

  1    <1 ms    <1 ms    <1 ms  192.168.0.254
  2     1 ms     1 ms     1 ms  209.134-31-62.static.virginmediabusiness.co.uk [62.31.134.209]
  3     *        *        *     Request timed out.
  4    20 ms    19 ms    17 ms  perr-core-2a-ae16-0.network.virginmedia.net [62.253.138.245]
  5     *        *        *     Request timed out.
  6    29 ms    26 ms    26 ms  86.85-254-62.static.virginmediabusiness.co.uk [62.254.85.86]
  7    34 ms    33 ms    32 ms  ldn-b1-link.telia.net [213.248.84.25]
  8    30 ms    27 ms    26 ms  ldn-bb4-link.telia.net [62.115.143.26]
  9    42 ms    41 ms    37 ms  hbg-bb4-link.telia.net [62.115.122.160]
 10    46 ms    42 ms    49 ms  kbn-bb4-link.telia.net [213.155.135.121]
 11    53 ms    52 ms    45 ms  kbn-b3-link.telia.net [62.115.114.69]
 12    43 ms    43 ms    43 ms  onecom-ic-307407-kbn-horsk-i1.c.telia.net [62.115.47.242]
 13    43 ms    42 ms    44 ms  ae1-200.dr3-cph3.pub.network.one.com [46.30.210.17]
 14    43 ms    50 ms    43 ms  xe-0-2-0-200.ar1.pub.webpod1-cph3.one.com [46.30.210.31]
 15    41 ms    41 ms    41 ms  webcluster46.webpod1-cph3.one.com [46.30.213.45]
```

Figure 8: Tracert

Exam tip
Netstat shows the established and listening port, but if you reboot the computer, the established connections disappear.

- **Nslookup**: Nslookup is a diagnostic tool for verifying the IP address of a hostname in the DNS server database. We can also use the `set type=MX` command, which brings back the DNS details on all mail servers in the domain - see the following screenshot:

```
C:\Users\Administrator>nslookup www.ianneil501.com
Server:   cache2.service.virginmedia.net
Address:  194.168.8.100

Non-authoritative answer:
Name:     www.ianneil501.com
Addresses: 2a02:2350:5:100:8b40:0:7611:8566
          46.30.213.45
```

Figure 9: Nslookup

- **Dig**: Dig is the equivalent of `nslookup` in a Linux/Unix environment. As we can see in the following screenshot, the IP address of Google is `216.58.220.100`:

```
[root@centos7 ~]# dig google.com

; <<>> DiG 9.9.4-RedHat-9.9.4-29.el7_2.3 <<>> google.com
;; global options: +cmd
;; Got answer:
;; ->>HEADER<<- opcode: QUERY, status: NOERROR, id: 32702
;; flags: qr rd ra; QUERY: 1, ANSWER: 1, AUTHORITY: 0, ADDITIONAL: 1

;; OPT PSEUDOSECTION:
; EDNS: version: 0, flags:; MBZ: 0005 , udp: 4000
;; QUESTION SECTION:
;google.com.                    IN      A

;; ANSWER SECTION:
google.com.            5        IN      A       216.58.220.110

;; Query time: 27 msec
;; SERVER: 192.168.12.2#53(192.168.220.2)
;; WHEN: Tue Sep 04 11:18:22 AEST 2018
;; MSG SIZE  rcvd: 55
```

Figure 10: Dig

- **Address Resolution Protocol (ARP)**: ARP is used to translate the IP address to a MAC address; the `arp -a` command shows the ARP cache. You can also use `arp -s` to add a static entry into the ARP cache - see the following screenshot. You could prevent ARP poisoning by using IPSec:

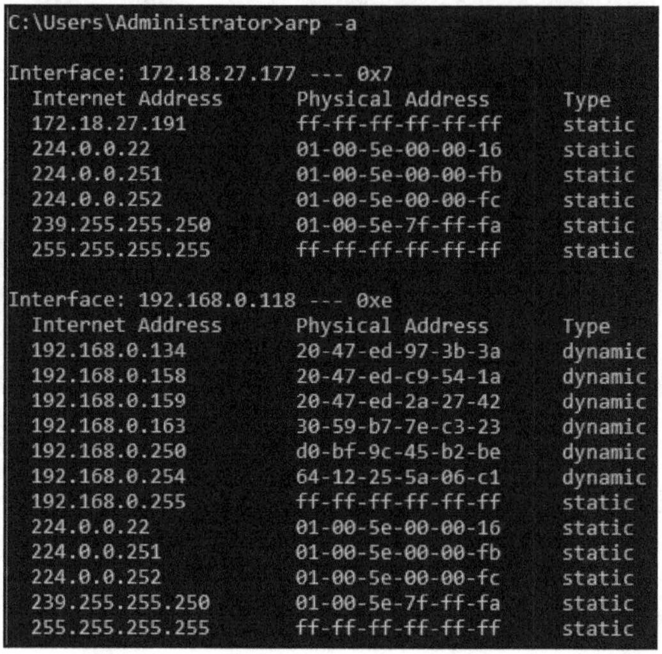

```
C:\Users\Administrator>arp -a

Interface: 172.18.27.177 --- 0x7
  Internet Address      Physical Address      Type
  172.18.27.191         ff-ff-ff-ff-ff-ff     static
  224.0.0.22            01-00-5e-00-00-16     static
  224.0.0.251           01-00-5e-00-00-fb     static
  224.0.0.252           01-00-5e-00-00-fc     static
  239.255.255.250       01-00-5e-7f-ff-fa     static
  255.255.255.255       ff-ff-ff-ff-ff-ff     static

Interface: 192.168.0.118 --- 0xe
  Internet Address      Physical Address      Type
  192.168.0.134         20-47-ed-97-3b-3a     dynamic
  192.168.0.158         20-47-ed-c9-54-1a     dynamic
  192.168.0.159         20-47-ed-2a-27-42     dynamic
  192.168.0.163         30-59-b7-7e-c3-23     dynamic
  192.168.0.250         d0-bf-9c-45-b2-be     dynamic
  192.168.0.254         64-12-25-5a-06-c1     dynamic
  192.168.0.255         ff-ff-ff-ff-ff-ff     static
  224.0.0.22            01-00-5e-00-00-16     static
  224.0.0.251           01-00-5e-00-00-fb     static
  224.0.0.252           01-00-5e-00-00-fc     static
  239.255.255.250       01-00-5e-7f-ff-fa     static
  255.255.255.255       ff-ff-ff-ff-ff-ff     static
```

Figure 11: ARP

- **ipconfig/ip/ifconfig**: These commands show the IP configuration. The Windows version is **ipconfig**, but Unix/Linux can use **ip** or **ifconfig**.

  The **ipconfig /displaydns** command is run in the following screenshot, and it shows the DNS cache on a computer:

```
C:\Users\Administrator>ipconfig /displaydns

Windows IP Configuration

    177.27.18.172.in-addr.arpa
    ----------------------------------------
    Record Name . . . . . : 177.27.18.172.in-addr.arpa.
    Record Type . . . . . : 12
    Time To Live  . . . . : 86400
    Data Length . . . . . : 8
    Section . . . . . . . : Answer
    PTR Record  . . . . . : DESKTOP-QR6R2DA.mshome.net


    mssplus.mcafee.com
    ----------------------------------------
    No records of type AAAA


    mssplus.mcafee.com
    ----------------------------------------
    Record Name . . . . . : mssplus.mcafee.com
    Record Type . . . . . : 1
    Time To Live  . . . . : 86400
    Data Length . . . . . : 4
    Section . . . . . . . : Answer
    A (Host) Record . . . : 0.0.0.1
```

Figure 12: DNS cache

`ipconfig /flushdns` is used to clear out all entries in the DNS cache—see the following screenshot:

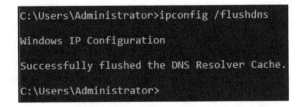

```
C:\Users\Administrator>ipconfig /flushdns

Windows IP Configuration

Successfully flushed the DNS Resolver Cache.

C:\Users\Administrator>
```

Figure 13: Clear DNS cache

- **tcpdump**: This is used by Linux/Unix as a packet sniffer command.

  tcpdump -i eth0 shows information on the first Ethernet adapter, as shown in the following screenshot:

```
# tcpdump -i eth0
tcpdump: verbose output suppressed, use -v or -vv for full protocol decode
listening on eth0, link-type EN10MB (Ethernet), capture size 65535 bytes
11:33:31.976358 IP 172.16.25.126.ssh > 172.16.25.125.apwi-rxspooler: Flags [P.], seq 3500440357
:3500440553, ack 3652628334, win 18760, length 196
11:33:31.976603 IP 172.16.25.125.apwi-rxspooler > 172.16.25.126.ssh: Flags [.], ack 196, win 64
487, length 0
11:33:31.977243 ARP, Request who-has tecmint.com tell 172.16.25.126, length 28
11:33:31.977359 ARP, Reply tecmint.com is-at 00:14:5e:67:26:1d (oui Unknown), length 46
11:33:31.977367 IP 172.16.25.126.54807 > tecmint.com: 4240+ PTR? 125.25.16.172.in-addr.arpa. (4
4)
11:33:31.977599 IP tecmint.com > 172.16.25.126.54807: 4240 NXDomain 0/1/0 (121)
11:33:31.977742 IP 172.16.25.126.44519 > tecmint.com: 40988+ PTR? 126.25.16.172.in-addr.arpa. (
44)
11:33:32.028747 IP 172.16.20.33.netbios-ns > 172.16.31.255.netbios-ns: NBT UDP PACKET(137): QUE
RY; REQUEST; BROADCAST
11:33:32.112045 IP 172.16.21.153.netbios-ns > 172.16.31.255.netbios-ns: NBT UDP PACKET(137): QU
ERY; REQUEST; BROADCAST
11:33:32.115606 IP 172.16.21.144.netbios-ns > 172.16.31.255.netbios-ns: NBT UDP PACKET(137): QU
ERY; REQUEST; BROADCAST
```

Figure 14: tcpdump

- **Nmap**: Nmap is a free and open source network mapper that can be used for network discovery and security auditing. Many systems and network administrators also find it useful for tasks, such as network inventory, managing service upgrade schedules, and monitoring host or service uptime.
- **Netcat**: Netcat, or nc, is a utility for showing network connections in a Linux/Unix environment. The netcat -z command is being used to scan ports 78-80, and from this you can see that ports 78 and 79 are closed, but port 80, being used by HTTP, is open. The -v switch means verbose and shows all information—see the following screenshot:

```
$ netcat -z -v ianneil501.com 78-80

nc: connect to ianneil501.com port 78 (tcp) failed: connection refused
nc: connect to ianneil501.com port 79 (tcp) failed: connection refused

Connection to ianneil501.com port 80 (tcp/html) succeeded!
```

Figure 15: Netcat

Analyzing and Interpreting Output from Security Technologies

There are various applications that security administrators can use to analyze and stop various attacks. Let's look at these here:

- **HIDS/HIPS**: HIDS/HIPS are both used inside host computers; the HIDS is used to detect attacks and the HIPS is used to protect the computer against attacks. Both have filters set up to choose an alert type to filter. Look at the following screenshot, where we are setting a filter for insecure SSH connection attempts:

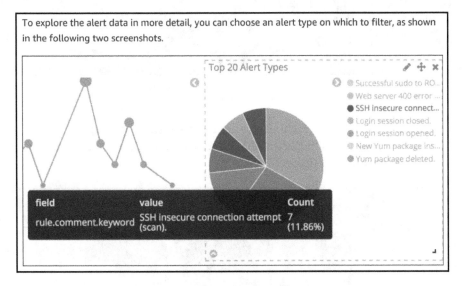

Figure 16: HIDS output

- **Antivirus/Advanced Malware Tools**: There are quite a few antivirus/anti-malware tools that will scan the computer on a regular basis and then produce reports. The following is a list of viruses that have been quarantined. The AVG free antivirus software has quarantined the four viruses so that they cannot cause any damage:

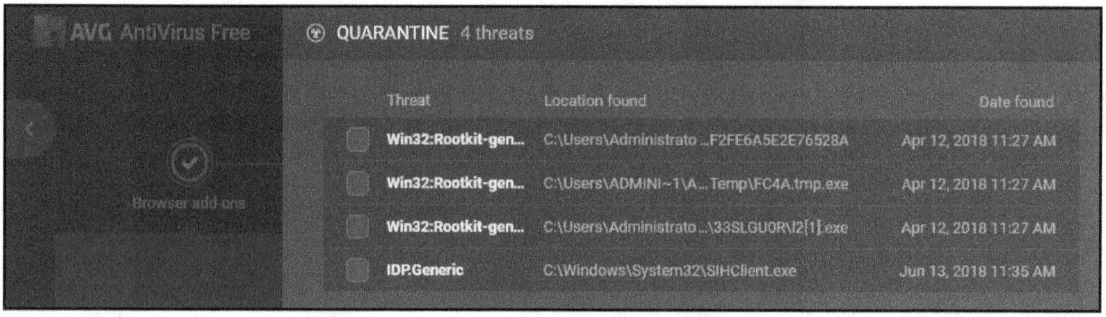

Threat	Location found	Date found
Win32:Rootkit-gen...	C:\Users\Administrato ...F2FE6A5E2E76528A	Apr 12, 2018 11:27 AM
Win32:Rootkit-gen...	C:\Users\ADMINI~1\A...Temp\FC4A.tmp.exe	Apr 12, 2018 11:27 AM
Win32:Rootkit-gen...	C:\Users\Administrato ...\33SLGU0R\I2[1].exe	Apr 12, 2018 11:27 AM
IDP.Generic	C:\Windows\System32\SIHClient.exe	Jun 13, 2018 11:35 AM

AVG AntiVirus Free — ⊛ QUARANTINE 4 threats — Browser add-ons

Figure 17: Quarantined viruses

The following screenshot shows a scan for vulnerable sensitive documents held on a desktop, and you can see that 135 documents have been found. We may need to install **Data Loss Prevention** (**DLP**) to protect these:

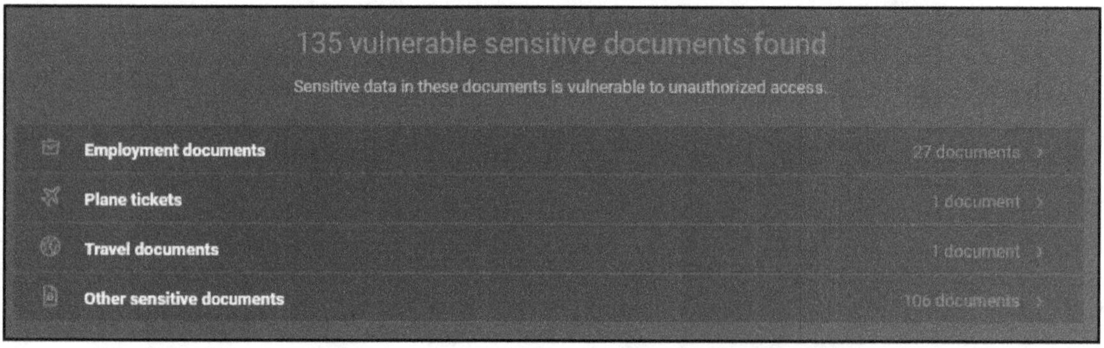

135 vulnerable sensitive documents found

Sensitive data in these documents is vulnerable to unauthorized access.

Employment documents		27 documents >
Plane tickets		1 document >
Travel documents		1 document >
Other sensitive documents		106 documents >

Figure 18: Sensitive documents scan

- **File Integrity Checker**: Microsoft has a **System File Checker** (**SFC**) that can replace corrupted files by replacing them with a copy held in a compressed folder with `system32`. You run it with the `sfc /scannow` command, as shown in the following screenshot:

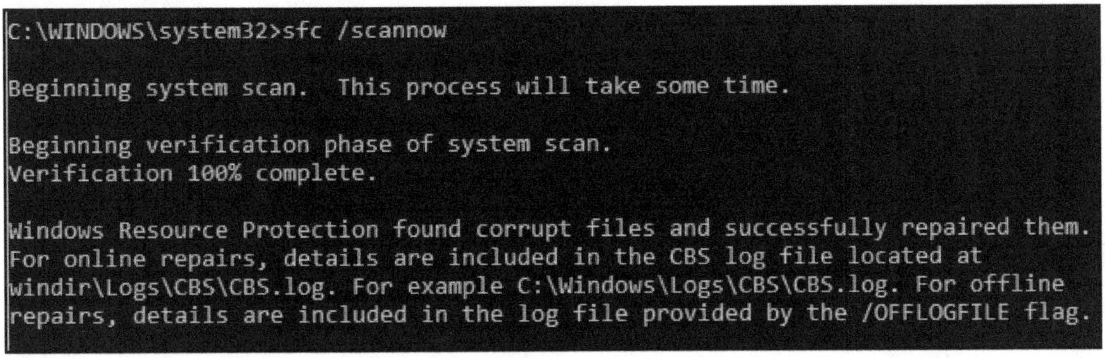

```
C:\WINDOWS\system32>sfc /scannow

Beginning system scan.  This process will take some time.

Beginning verification phase of system scan.
Verification 100% complete.

Windows Resource Protection found corrupt files and successfully repaired them.
For online repairs, details are included in the CBS log file located at
windir\Logs\CBS\CBS.log. For example C:\Windows\Logs\CBS\CBS.log. For offline
repairs, details are included in the log file provided by the /OFFLOGFILE flag.
```

Figure 19: System file checker

- **File Checksum Integrity Verifier (FCIV)**: This is a Microsoft utility that can generate MD5 or SHA-1 hash values for files to compare values against a known good value. FCIV can compare hash values to make sure that the files have not been changed. This can help you identify changes that have been made to your computer system.
- **Host-Based Firewall:** A host-based firewall can be used to prevent unauthorized access to the desktop, and we can set up allowed rules for those applications that we wish to use. The firewall in the following screenshot allows antivirus updates, checkpoints, VPN DNS name resolution, Firefox, and Java:

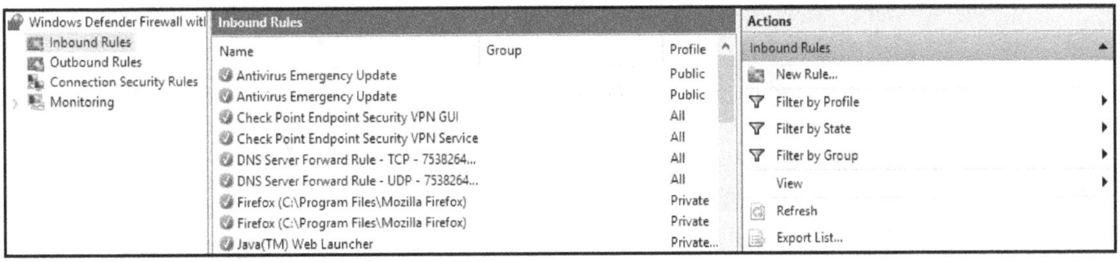

Figure 20: Host-based firewall

- **Application Whitelisting**: Application whitelisting determines the rules on what applications are allowed to be run on a computer. We can add applications, executable file names or dll binaries to the whitelist. The following is an example of application whitelisting using a Microsoft Application Control Policy tool called Applocker. This would then mean that the end user could only install and use these approved applications; if the application is not on the list, it is not allowed to be installed:

Action	User	Name	Condition
Allow	Everyone	Microsoft Office 2016	Publisher
Allow	Everyone	McAfee Security Scan	Publisher
Allow	Everyone	Mozilla Firefox	Publisher
Allow	Everyone	Internet Explorer	Publisher
Allow	Everyone	Wireshark	Publisher
Allow	Everyone	Adobe Acrobat Pro	Publisher

Figure 21: Application whitelisting

- **Removable Media Control**: Removable media are at a very high security risk as it is easy to steal data using them. However, we can prevent this by using a group policy; you can see one of the following options in the screenshot is **Prevent installation of removable devices**. This would prevent someone inserting a USB drive or another form of removable media to steal data:

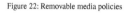

- Prevent installation of removable devices
- Prevent Media Sharing
- Prevent restoring previous versions from backups
- Prevent Windows Media DRM Internet Access
- Prohibit connection to non-domain networks when connec...
- Provide the unique identifiers for your organization
- Removable Disks: Deny execute access
- Removable Disks: Deny read access
- Removable Disks: Deny write access

Figure 22: Removable media policies

- **Patch Management Tools**: Microsoft has got a patch management tool called **Windows Server Update Services** (**WSUS**) that allows you to pull down the latest updates from the Microsoft website for different products.

Exam tip
Applications must be added to the whitelist so that they can be approved to be used.

- **Unified Threat Management (UTM)**: UTM is a firewall that can also prevent URL filtering, content filtering, and malware inspection. The following screenshot shows the setting of the Sophos UTM firewall version 9, where you can see the various information that it provides:

SOPHOS UTM 9 | admin

Dashboard for Thu Jul 3 2014 | 16:39:16

Dashboard
Management
Definitions & Users
Interfaces & Routing
Network Services
Network Protection
Web Protection
Email Protection
Endpoint Protection
Wireless Protection
Webserver Protection
RED Management
Site-to-site VPN
Remote Access
Logging & Reporting
Support
Log off

Resource usage
CPU ☐ 6%
RAM ☐ 71% of 2.8 GB
Log Disk ☐ 4% of 15.8 GB
Data Disk ☐ 2% of 12.0 GB

utm.sophos-exchange.virtual
Model: ASG Software
License ID: 405633
Subscriptions: Base Functionality
Email Protection
Network Protection
Web Protection
Webserver Protection
Wireless Protection
Endpoint AntiVirus
Uptime: 0d 18h 43m

Today's threat status
Firewall: 101 674 packets filtered
IPS: 195 attacks blocked
Antivirus: 5 items blocked
AntiSpam: 30 657 emails blocked
AntiSpyware: 7 items blocked
Web Filter: 468 URLs filtered
WAF: 11 attacks blocked
Endpoint: 0 attacks blocked
0 devices blocked

Version information

Interf...	Name	Type	State	Link	In	Out
all	All Interfaces				39.0 kbit	57.6 kbit
eth0	Internal Lan	Ethernet	Up	Up	34.7 kbit	54.6 kbit
eth1	SUM MGMT Interface	Ethernet	Up	Up	<0.1 kbit	0.6 kbit
eth2	WAN Interface	Ethernet DHCP	Up	Up	4.2 kbit	2.1 kbit
wlan2	Guest Wifi	Ethernet	Up	Up	0	0.2 kbit

Advanced Threat Protection
Botnet/command and control traffic detected — 120 Infected Hosts

Current system configuration
- Firewall is active with 22 rules
- Intrusion Prevention is active with 6019 of 17661 patterns
- Web Filtering is active, 57718 requests served today
- Network Visibility is active, 3 Application Control rules active
- SMTP Proxy is active, 41 095 emails processed, 32 940 emails blocked
- POP3 Proxy is active, 10 390 emails processed, 8 289 emails blocked
- RED is active, 5 servers (0 online), 0 clients (0 online)
- Wireless Protection is active, 0 APs connected
- Endpoint Protection is active, Sophos LiveConnect is enabled, 0 endpoints, 0 threat alerts, 0 out-of-date alerts
- Site-to-Site VPN is inactive
- Remote Access is active with 0 online users
- Web Application Firewall is active, 412 314 requests served today
- Sophos UTM Manager is connected to SUM
- Sophos Mobile Control is active, with 0 of 0 devices non-compliant
- HA/Cluster is inactive

Figure 23: Sophos UTM 9

- **Data Loss Prevention (DLP)**: DLP templates can be set up to prevent emails with sensitive and PII data from being emailed out of the company. DLP can prevent the removal of documents on a file server.

  Example: We wish to set up a template to prevent Visa, Mastercard, Diners Club, JCB, Discover, and American Express details from being emailed out. This is done by creating a template that consists of a regular expression. Should the pattern be matched, the email will be blocked and an administrator will be notified. The regular expression is shown here:

  ```
  ^(?:4[0-9]{12}(?:[0-9]{3})?|[25][1-7][0-9]{14}|6(?:011|5
  [0-9][0-9])[0-9]{12}|3[47][0-9]{13}|3(?:0[0-5]|[68][0-9])
  [0-9]{11}|(?:2131|1800|35\d{3})\d{11})$
  ```

  Figure 24: Regular expression for credit cards

- **Data Execution Prevention (DEP)**: When DEP is enabled, it prevents harmful programs, such as viruses, and other threats from trying to execute in restricted areas of the operating system. From the Command Prompt, you can run the **wmic OS GetDataExecutionPrevention_SupportPolicy** command. The values will either be 0.1.2 and 3. The following screenshot shows that it has a value of 2, which means it is enabled:

  ```
  C:\WINDOWS\system32>wmic OS Get DataExecutionPrevention_SupportPolicy
  DataExecutionPrevention_SupportPolicy
  2
  ```

  Figure 25: Data execution prevention

- **Web Application Firewall (WAF)**: A WAF is used to prevent attacks on web servers and the applications that they host. The following screenshot is an example of the log file from a Sonic Wall web application firewall log:

Time ▼	Priority	Category	Source	Destination	User	Location	Message
2013-02-01 08:29:21	Info	Web Application Firewall	76.93.6.176	10.203.23.180	dtelehowski		WAF threat detected: Cookie Tampering (_mkto_trk)
2013-02-01 05:02:47	Info	Web Application Firewall	95.143.243.150	10.203.23.180	tnaghmouchi		WAF threat detected: Cookie Tampering (_mkto_trk)
2013-02-01 05:02:34	Info	Web Application Firewall	95.143.243.150	10.203.23.180	tnaghmouchi		WAF threat detected: Cookie Tampering (_mkto_trk)
2013-02-01 05:02:25	Info	Web Application Firewall	95.143.243.150	10.203.23.180	tnaghmouchi		WAF threat detected: Cookie Tampering (_mkto_trk)
2013-02-01 05:02:07	Info	Web Application Firewall	95.143.243.150	10.203.23.180	tnaghmouchi		WAF threat detected: Cookie Tampering (_mkto_trk)
2013-02-01 05:01:42	Info	Web Application Firewall	95.143.243.150	10.203.23.180	tnaghmouchi		WAF threat detected: Cookie Tampering (_mkto_trk)
2013-02-01 04:59:43	Info	Web Application Firewall	95.143.243.150	10.203.23.180	tnaghmouchi		WAF threat detected: Cookie Tampering (_mkto_trk)
2013-02-01 04:59:39	Info	Web Application Firewall	95.143.243.150	10.203.23.180	tnaghmouchi		WAF threat detected: Cookie Tampering (_mkto_trk)

Figure 26: WAF log file

Review Questions

1. What is the purpose of an incident response plan?
2. Name three different categories of incident.
3. Name three different roles required to deal with an incident.
4. What should the help desk do when an incident has just been reported?
5. What is the purpose of an incident response exercise?
6. What is the first phase of the incident response process and what happens there?
7. What is the last phase of the incident response process?
8. What would happen if the last process of the incident response process was not carried out?
9. What is the order of volatility?
10. What is the first action you should take if your company experiences a web-based or remote attack?
11. What should you do if you find a USB flash drive in one of the servers?
12. What is the process of chain of custody and why would you investigate it?
13. What is the purpose of a legal hold?
14. What is the purpose of record time offset?
15. What is the first stage a forensics officer should carry out when they have just taken possession of a laptop computer?

16. What is the first stage a forensics officer should carry out when they have just taken possession of a hard drive or removable drive?

17. Why would a forensics officer take hashes of data before they start their investigation?

18. What are the benefits of a security administrator using an SIEM system?

19. Can I delete data that I have copies of on a WORM drive?

20. Why would we carry out active monitoring?

21. What tools can you use to find the operating system running on a computer?

22. If you are using an unencrypted media package that runs across my network, how can you capture the passwords?

23. If you want to find information about the operating system of a remote web server, what is the best tool to use?

24. What is the purpose of a network mapper?

25. If you have disabled the SSID on your wireless access point, can someone still find the SSID?

26. What type of vulnerability scanner can audit files and find out account vulnerabilities?

27. What is the most basic vulnerability scanner, which can only find missing patches?

28. What tools can you use to ensure that the settings on your server are correct?

29. What is the purpose of using the technique of steganography?

30. How can you find the attack method a hacker would use to exploit your website?

31. What is the quickest form of backup?

32. What is the quickest form of tape backup?

33. What are the most common types of backup? Name two.

34. How many tapes would you need to recover your data if you use a differential backup?

35. What would happen to command-line troubleshooting tools if you block incoming ICMP on the network firewall?

36. What tool is used to test connectivity and what command would you use to make it continuous?

37. What is normally the maximum value of a packet's TTL?

38. What does the `netstat -an` command-line tool provide and what would happen if you rebooted the computer?

39. What tool can you use in a Windows environment to verify the hostname entry in the DNS server?

40. What are the commands for displaying the DNS cache and then clearing all entries from it?
41. What command-line tool displays the route to a remote web server?
42. What is a packet tracing tool used in a Linux/Unix environment?
43. What is the command-line tool for showing the session between two hosts in a Linux/Unix environment?
44. What is the purpose of a file integrity checker?
45. If an application is neither on the blacklist or the whitelist, how can you ensure that you can install it on your computer?
46. How could you prevent 4,000 people from installing USB flash drives on their computers?
47. What tool is a firewall that can URL filter, content filter, and provide malware inspection?
48. What tool can prevent PII and sensitive data from leaving your network via email or from being copied onto a USB flash drive?
49. What is the tool that can prevent malicious programs from accessing the registry?
50. What tool would you use to prevent an attack on a web-based application?

Answers and Explanations

1. An incident response plan is written for a particular incident and lays out how it should be tackled and the key personnel required.

2. The different categories of incidents are as follows:
    - Unauthorized access
    - Loss of computers or data
    - Loss of availability
    - Malware attack
    - DDoS attack
    - Power failure
    - Natural disasters, such as floods, tornadoes, hurricanes, and fires
    - Cyber security incidents

3. The different roles required to deal with an incident are as follows:
    - Incident response manager—a top level manager takes charge
    - Security analyst—technical support to the incident
    - IT auditor—checks that the company is compliant
    - Risk analyst—evaluates all aspects of risk
    - HR—sometimes employees are involved in the incident
    - Legal— gives advice and makes decisions on legal issues
    - Public relations—deals with the press to reduce impact

4. The help desk identifies the incident response plan required and the key personnel that need to be notified.

5. An incident response exercise is for carrying out the incident response plan and planning for any shortfalls.

6. The first phase of the incident response process is the preparation phase, where the plan is already written in advance of any attack.

7. The last phase of the incident response process is lessons learned, where we review why the incident was successful.

8. If we do not carry out lessons learned, the incident may re-occur. Lessons learned is a detective control where we try to identify and address any weaknesses.

9. Collecting the most volatile evidence first.

10. The first action would be to capture the network traffic so that we can identify the source of the attack.

11. You should collect the data in the volatile memory first.

12. The chain of custody lists who has handled the evidence before it goes to court. Any break in the chain or the evidence leaving your site is a breach of the chain of custody and the judge would ask for it to be investigated.

13. Legal hold is a process for ensuring the security of data so it cannot be deleted; one such measure would be putting someone's mailbox on hold. This is sometimes called litigation hold.

14. Record time offset is used for time normalization across multiple time zones.

15. They should take a system image so that it can be used for investigation.

16. They should take a forensic copy so that it can be used for investigation.

17. To ensure that when they are finished, they can prove the integrity of the data.

18. An SIEM system can be used to correlate logs from multiple places and enable real-time reporting of incidents.

19. Data cannot be deleted from a WORM drive, as it is write-once, read many.

20. Active monitoring is used to identify an incident in real time.

21. You can use a protocol analyzer to find the operating system running on a computer.

22. You can use a protocol analyzer to capture the data and commands going to a network-based application.

23. Banner grabbing is the best tool to use if you want to find information about the operating system of a remote web server.

24. A network mapper can identify all hosts on your network, their patch level, and any services running on them.

25. You can use a wireless packet sniffer or a SSID de-cloak device to find the SSID of your WAP, as it is embedded in the network traffic going to the WPA.

26. A credentialed vulnerability scanner can audit files and find out account vulnerabilities.

27. A non-credentialed vulnerability scanner can only find missing patches.

28. A compliance scanner ensures that the settings on your server are correct.

29. Steganography allows you to hide a file – be it an audio, video, or image file – inside another file (be it an audio, video, or image file). A larger file or a faded image are the tell-tale signs of steganography.

30. You would set up a honeypot to find the attack method a hacker would use to exploit your website.

31. The quickest form of backup is a snapshot of a virtual machine.

32. The quickest form of tape backup is a full backup, as all backups need a full backup to start with.

33. The two most common tape backups are full and incremental.

34. You would need two tapes to perform a differential backup.
35. If incoming ICMP was blocked on the network firewall, none of your command-line tools would work as ICMP brings back the replies.
36. Ping is the tool that is used to test connectivity, and the `ping -t` command is used for continuous ping.
37. The normal maximum value of a packet's TTL is 128 seconds or less.
38. `netstat -an` shows listening and established ports. If you reboot your computer, the established sessions will disappear.
39. DNS lookup is used in a Windows environment to verify the hostname entry in the DNS server. Dig is the Unix/Linux equivalent.
40. `Ipconfig /displaydns` displays the DNS cache and `Ipconfig /flush` clears all entries.
41. Tracert is used to display the route to a remote web server over a maximum of 30 hops.
42. `tcpdump` is a packet tracer used in a Linux/Unix environment.
43. Netcat or `nc` shows the session between two hosts in a Linux/Unix environment.
44. A file integrity checker can determine whether a file has been altered by an application or is corrupt.
45. If an application is neither on the blacklist or the whitelist, you need to add it to the whitelist so that you can install it on your computer.
46. You can use a group policy to prevent 4,000 people from installing USB flash drives on their computers.
47. A UTM is a firewall that can URL filter, content filter, and provide malware inspection.
48. DLP can prevent PII and sensitive data from leaving your network via email or from being copied onto a USB flash drive.
49. DEP can prevent malicious programs from accessing the registry by restricting the area that programs can access.
50. A web application firewall can prevent an attack on a web-based application.

Managing Business Continuity

11

In this chapter, we will be looking at our business environment to provide systems availability, selecting the most appropriate method for disaster recovery. This will be broken down into four distinct sections, and you must understand each of them:

- Implementing secure systems design
- The importance of the secure staging deployment concepts
- Troubleshooting common security issues
- Disaster recovery and the concepts of continuity of operations
- Exam domain mapping

We will cover the following topics in this chapter:

- **Troubleshooting common security issues, given a certain scenario**: We'll cover unencrypted credentials/clear text, logs and events anomalies, permission issues, access violations, certificate issues, data exfiltration, misconfigured devices, firewalls, content filters, access points, weak security configurations, personnel issues, policy violation, insider threats, social engineering, social media, personal email, unauthorized software, baseline deviation, license compliance violation, availability/integrity, asset management, and authentication issues.

- **Implementing a secure systems design, given a certain scenario**: We'll look at hardware/firmware security, FDE/SED, TPM, HSM, UEFI/BIOS, secure boot and attestation, supply chains, hardware root of trust, EMI/EMP, OSes, types, networks servers, workstations, appliances, kiosks, mobile OS, patch management, disabling unnecessary ports and services, least functionality, secure configurations, trusted OSes, application whitelisting/blacklisting, disabling default accounts/passwords, peripherals, wireless keyboards, wireless mice, displays, Wi-Fi-enabled MicroSD cards, printers/MFDs, external storage devices, and digital cameras.

- **Explaining the importance of the secure staging deployment concepts**: Here we'll get into sandboxing, environments, development, testing, staging, production, secure baselines, and integrity measurement.
- **Explaining disaster recovery and the continuity of operations concepts**: We'll be covering recovery sites, hot sites, warm sites, cold sites, order of restoration, geographic considerations, off-site backups, distance, location selection, legal implications, data sovereignty, continuity of operations planning, exercises/tabletop, after-action reports, failover, alternative processing sites, and alternative business practices.

Implementing Secure Systems Design

IT systems range from desktops and servers used internally within an organization, to mobile devices, such as laptops, that can be used externally in unsecured environments (such as hotels and airports). We therefore need to harden systems and OSes so that they are as secure as we can possibly make them. There are various aspects that we need to look at, depending on the functionality of the device and where it is used. Let's look at all of the aspects that we need to take into consideration, starting with a system booting up:

- **Basic Input Output System (BIOS)**: The BIOS on every computer is different, depending on the manufacturer, with the BIOS chip on the motherboard giving instructions on how the computer boots up.
- **Unified Extensible Firmware Interface (UEFI)**: The UEFI is a modern version of the BIOS that is more secure and is needed for a secure boot of the operating system.
- **Secure boot and attestation**: Some newer OSes, such as Windows 10, can perform a secure boot at startup where the OS checks that all of the drivers have been signed—if they have not, the boot sequence fails. This can be coupled with attestation, where the integrity of the operation is also checked before booting up.

Example: Your company is a multinational company that requires an OS that can be used by both desktops and laptops and can provide both secure booting and attestation. What OS and feature will you choose and why? At the moment, we are using a BIOS to boot up from.

The first thing that we would do is upgrade the BIOS to UEFI so that it can provide a secure boot. The OS selected would be Windows 10 as it provides secure booting, where the drivers need to be signed to allow booting. We would then enable Device Guard, which logs the setting of the OS and checks the integrity of the software and hardware, otherwise the boot sequence fails.

Hardware/Firmware Security

We need to protect our computer systems against someone stealing the data by stealing the device, re-installing the operating system, and stealing the data. We need to be able to secure the OSes and hardware by encrypting them using products such as Microsoft's Bitlocker. Let's look at some encryption methods:

- **Hardware root of trust**: When we use certificates for FDE, they use a hardware root of trust that verifies that the keys match before the secure boot process takes place.
- **Full Disk Encryption (FDE)**: FDE uses X509 certificates to encrypt the full disk, but needs a TPM chip on the motherboard to store the keys. Sometimes, these can be referred to as self-encrypting devices. When you boot up from the computer, you are asked for a password to access the system.
- **Trusted Platform Module (TPM)**: The TPM chip is stored on the motherboard and is used to store the encryption keys so that when the system boots up, it can compare the keys and ensure that the system has not been tampered with. If the system thinks that tampering has happened, it locks itself up. The only way that it is accessed is by entering the recovery keys; for example, with Bitlocker, it is a 48-character password.
- **Hardware Security Module (HSM)**: An HSM is similar to TPM chips except that it is removable. The key escrow uses an HSM to store and manage private keys, but smaller ones can be used for computers.

Exam tip
FDE needs either a TPM chip on the motherboard or an HSM.

- **Supply chain**: It is vital that you have vetting for your supply chain as those in your supply chain may be given limited access to your network and may be able to install hardware into your network. You need to ensure that the people working for them have been cleared and the systems that they put in place have a certain level of security. You also need to ensure that the company doesn't have a bad credit rating and can always supply the hardware and services, even if a disaster occurs.

- **Electromagnetic Interference (EMI)**: EMI coming from motors, fluorescent lights, and radio frequencies could affect a system's performance and could cause jamming and prevent IT systems from working.

- **Electromagnetic Pulse (EMP)**: An EMP is a strong burst of electric energy that can damage electronic systems; an electrostatic discharge can cause permanent damage. Other forms include military weapons that can cause nuclear explosions, and lightning strikes. Surge protectors, uninterruptible power supplies, shielding, and Faraday cages can be used to protect against EMPs.

Operating Systems

There are various OSes, such as Linux, that are used by the cloud and many network appliances, and Microsoft has Windows 10 for desktops and laptops, and Server 29016 for servers. There is also Android for many phones, as well as Apple's iOS for iPhones and iPads. Let's look at the different uses of these:

- **Networks**: Network devices such as switches, routers, and firewalls all have some sort of OS installed so that they can be configured. Normally, these are different versions of Linux, such as FreeBSD, Red Hat, CentOS, and Ubuntu.

- **Servers**: A server OS needs to be secure as these can be used for databases, such as SQL Server, or a mail server, such as Exchange Server 2016. The domain controller runs on OSes such as Windows Server 2016 and has a secure boot.

- **Workstations**: Workstation OSes, such as Windows 10, are the most secure client OSes. Windows 10 has a secure boot and has the ability to use Bitlocker, a version of FDE for protecting against data theft.

- **Appliances**: Security appliances include firewalls and intrusion detection systems; intrusion detection systems are used to protect against attacks.

- **Kiosk**: A kiosk is a computer in a reception area or foyer; it is used to gain access to the building that you are visiting. Their functionality is limited and they would normally be a workgroup and not connected to the network.
- **Trusted operating system**: A trusted operating system is a secure system, normally used by the military, that has multiple layers of security, as it is used to access classified data. It is tied down tightly and changes to the OS are highly controlled.
- **Mobile OS**: Apple's iOS is an OS for Apple's mobile devices, such as the iPhone and the iPad, and Android is used by other mobile telephones, such as those produced by Samsung.

Securing IT Systems

It is important that we secure all of our IT systems against attacks. Let's now look at ways of hardening the OS to reduce the surface attack:

- **Disable default accounts/passwords**: The first step when we receive an IT system or an IoT device would be to disable the default administrative accounts and then reset the default passwords to prevent unauthorized access to the system.
- **Disabling unnecessary ports and services (principle of least functionality)**: A secure system should only have the minimum number of services enabled and should have a secure firewall to block all ports, with the exception of those required for the applications running on them. The secure system should have only the functionality required for business purposes. It should not have any applications running except those that are authorized to do so.

Exam tip
When administering a new IT system or IoT device, you need to change the default administrator account and password.

- **Secure configurations**: The military uses a STIG that outlines what setting should be enabled or disabled for a military system. Another cause to secure the configuration of an OS is for compliance reasons, and periodically, you can use a compliance scanner to ensure that the configuration is still secure.

- **Application whitelisting/blacklisting**: Application whitelisting involves a list of approved applications that can be installed onto an IT system. The application blacklist is a list of named applications that are forbidden. The most common reason why someone cannot run an application on an IT system is that it has not been added to the whitelist and not the fact that it is on the blacklist.
- **Patch management**: Patch management is where updates are downloaded and tested on an isolated system, such as in sandboxing, and when they have been thoroughly tested, they are then rolled out to the IT systems. This ensures that the IT systems have no vulnerabilities.

Peripherals

Now that we have looked at the security of the IT systems, we need to look at the vulnerabilities of the peripherals to see where they are vulnerable:

- **Wireless keyboards/wireless mice**: Wireless keyboards/wireless mice should not be used on secure systems as they are not encrypted and could easily be intercepted by a wireless packet sniffer.
- **Displays**: We need to ensure that we use display filters and do not have displays facing external windows. This is to prevent shoulder surfing.
- **Wi-Fi-enabled MicroSD cards**: Wi-Fi-enabled MicroSD cards have the same vulnerabilities as wireless keyboards and mice, where data can be intercepted by a wireless packet sniffer.
- **Printers/Multifunction Devices (MFDs)**: Printers/MFDs are very vulnerable. For example, a printer may have data in the spooler waiting to be printed off and a scanner may have an image stored in its internal memory.
- **External storage device**: External storage devices normally operate with a USB interface and therefore are easy to steal data from. The best way to protect against data theft would be to use Bitlocker-to-go, which encrypts the whole drive, or use a self-encrypting device.
- **Digital cameras**: Digital cameras store information on memory cards that are very easy to remove from the camera. They may have pictures of documents that could be printed off very easily.

The Importance of the Secure Staging Deployment Concepts

Before applications can be used in a production environment, we must ensure that they are as secure as possible to mitigate the risk of being attacked by an outside agency. We are going to look at three different aspects: sandboxing, environment, and secure baseline. Let's look at these in turn:

- **Sandboxing**: Sandboxing is where we can install an application in a virtual machine environment isolated from our network so that we can patch, test, and ensure that it is secure before putting it into a production environment. In a Linux environment, this is known as Chroot Jail.
- **Environment**: When we are designing an application, we need a secure staging environment for development, testing, and staging before moving the application into production. Such an environment is shown in the following diagram:

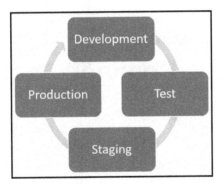

Figure 1: Environment

- **Development**: The first stage of developing an application is to use the most secure programming language for the task at hand. The application will go through different versions before it is complete, and these can be tracked by using version numbers.
- **Testing**: Software testers ensure that the functionality of the program fulfills the specifications. They may also employ a secure coding freelancer to carry out regression testing to ensure that the application is fit for production. At this stage, we are not looking at how it affects the production environment, as this is completed at staging.

- **Staging**: Staging is the process of rolling out the application to simulate a production environment; an end user will be asked to use the application to ensure that the data output is correct before the application is rolled out to the production environment. Those supporting the application will be trained on supporting the application when it is rolled out to production.
- **Production**: The production environment is where the application goes live and end users have the support of the IT team. The end users will be asked to give as much feedback as they can should the application have any problems that were not picked up beforehand.

- **Secure baseline/integrity**: A secure baseline is a list of applications, the configurations of the applications, and the patches of the applications that improves the security posture of the IT systems. We can use vulnerability scanners to identify any changes that might affect the integrity of the systems. A **File Checksum Integrity Verifier** (**FCIV**) and a **System File Checker** (**SFC**) can identify changes in the integrity of the application.

Troubleshooting Common Security Issues

On a day-to-day basis, the security team will come across some of the following issues; we will look at how the team can mitigate them:

- **Unencrypted credentials/clear text**: Unencrypted credentials/clear text are a security risk as they can be intercepted by a packet sniffer or protocol analyzer. We should be using an authentication protocol, such as Kerberos, that is encrypted and encrypts data in transit.
- **Logs and events anomalies**: There are many logs in a company (such as firewall logs, antivirus logs, and event viewers on computers and servers), showing attempts to log into the network. The best way to prevent duplications of events and get real-time monitoring would be to install an SIEM system.
- **Permission issues**: Permissions that are incorrectly set can give users more permissions than they need to do their jobs, but someone with more permissions will not let anyone know that this is the case. Audit user accounts and permissions on a regular basis to identify this.
- **Access violations**: Access violations are where users are accessing data that they are not allowed to see; for example, someone may have access to the payroll file and can see the salaries of everyone in the company. Audit user accounts and permissions on a regular basis to identify this.

- **Certificate issues**: When a new certificate is not working, we should first of all ensure that the certificate is valid and then check that it has been added to the **Trusted Root Certification Authorities** folder so that the computers trust the certificate provider—see the following screenshot:

	Issued To	Issued By	Expiration Date	Intended Purposes	Friendly Name	Status
Console Root						
Certificates - Current User	Actalis Authentication Root CA	Actalis Authentication Root CA	22/09/2030	Server Authenticati...	Actalis Authenticati...	
Personal	AddTrust External CA Root	AddTrust External CA Root	30/05/2020	Server Authenticati...	The USERTrust Net...	
Certificates	Baltimore CyberTrust Root	Baltimore CyberTrust Root	13/05/2025	Server Authenticati...	DigiCert Baltimore ...	
Trusted Root Certification Authorities	Certum CA	Certum CA	11/06/2027	Server Authenticati...	Certum	
Certificates	Certum Trusted Network CA	Certum Trusted Network CA	31/12/2029	Server Authenticati...	Certum Trusted Net...	
Enterprise Trust	Class 3 Public Primary Certificat...	Class 3 Public Primary Certificatio...	02/08/2028	Server Authenticati...	VeriSign Class 3 Pu...	
Intermediate Certification Authorities	COMODO RSA Certification Au...	COMODO RSA Certification Auth...	19/01/2038	Server Authenticati...	COMODO SECURE™	
Active Directory User Object	Copyright (c) 1997 Microsoft C...	Copyright (c) 1997 Microsoft Corp.	31/12/1999	Time Stamping	Microsoft Timesta...	
Trusted Publishers	DESKTOP-QR6R2DA	DESKTOP-QR6R2DA	23/08/3017	Server Authenticati...	<None>	
Untrusted Certificates	DESKTOP-QR6R2DA	DESKTOP-QR6R2DA	24/09/3017	Server Authenticati	<None>	
Third-Party Root Certification Authorities	DigiCert Assured ID Root CA	DigiCert Assured ID Root CA	10/11/2031	Server Authenticati...	DigiCert	
Trusted People	DigiCert Global Root CA	DigiCert Global Root CA	10/11/2031	Server Authenticati...	DigiCert	
Client Authentication Issuers	DigiCert Global Root G2	DigiCert Global Root G2	15/01/2038	Server Authenticati...	DigiCert Global Roo...	
Other People	DigiCert High Assurance EV Ro...	DigiCert High Assurance EV Root	10/11/2031	Server Authenticati...	DigiCert	
Smart Card Trusted Roots	DigiCert Trusted Root G4	DigiCert Trusted Root G4	15/01/2038	Server Authenticati...	DigiCert Trusted Ro...	
	DST Root CA X3	DST Root CA X3	30/09/2021	Secure Email, Serve...	DST Root CA X3	
	D-TRUST Root Class 3 CA 2 2009	D-TRUST Root Class 3 CA 2 2009	05/11/2029	Server Authenticati...	D-TRUST Root Clas...	
	Entrust Root Certification Auth...	Entrust Root Certification Authority	27/11/2026	Server Authenticati...	Entrust	
	Entrust Root Certification Auth...	Entrust Root Certification Authori...	07/12/2030	Server Authenticati...	Entrust.net	
	Entrust.net Certification Author...	Entrust.net Certification Authority...	24/07/2029	Server Authenticati...	Entrust (2048)	
	Equifax Secure Certificate Auth...	Equifax Secure Certificate Authority	22/08/2018	Secure Email, Serve...	GeoTrust	
	GeoTrust Global CA	GeoTrust Global CA	21/05/2022	Server Authenticati...	GeoTrust Global CA	

Figure 2: Trusted Root Certification Authorities

- **Data exfiltration**: Data exfiltration can be carried out by steganography, and the way to prevent this would be to use a stateful firewall to deeply inspect the data passing through it. Files becoming larger and images becoming lighter are symptoms of steganography at work. We can also prevent someone from stealing data via email or by putting it on an external device; this would be by using **Data Loss Prevention** (DLP).

Exam tip

If a certificate does not work, ensure that it is valid and add it to the **Trusted Root Certification Authorities** folder.

- **Asset management**: One of the problems a company could face is the loss or theft of assets. The first stage would be to create an asset register and have all asset devices tagged. We could use cable locks for desktops, laptops, and tablets. We could use mobile device management to remotely wipe stolen data and RFID to stop small devices leaving the company. We could use Geotracking on the mobile devices so that devices can be found.

- **Authentication issues**: One of the most common authentication issues faced by the security team is passwords, where people either forget their password or input the password with the caps lock on and then try it three times and get locked out. Also, as it is a single factor, it is no longer secure enough on its own. Another method would be using biometrics, but even then, the biometric device could suffer from FAR and FRR. One of the best solutions to this would be to use two-factor authentication using smart cards and certificates, as this would cause the lowest amount of support calls.

Misconfigured Devices

It is vital that all network appliances are properly configured, else the company could be vulnerable to attack. Let's look at some of the appliances for this:

- **Firewalls**: The purpose of a firewall is to prevent unauthorized access to the network, and it is vital that no one employee is responsible for maintaining the rules. When new rules are added, a second member of the IT team should confirm that the rule is correct.
- **Content filters**: If the UTM or proxy server has the incorrect content filter set up, then employees may be able to access gaming sites while at work, which would then reduce the productivity of the workforce.
- **Access points**: If the wireless access point was not set up properly, then it could mean that people would be able to access the company network from outside the building. The wireless access point should be set up using WPA2-CCMP encryption coupled with the disabling of the SSID and the enabling of MAC filtering.
- **Weak security configurations**: In general, if we set up IT systems with a weak security configuration, then we are leaving the company open to attack. We should ensure that none of the systems use the default username and password and that we use a compliance scanner to ensure that the system is set up as securely as it can be.

Personnel Issues

Most of the cybercrime is successful due to the actions of people that work for the company, and therefore we need to set up policies to mitigate against any attack. Let's look at some of the personnel security issues facing the security team:

- **Policy violation**: Companies write policies so that all employees know what is expected of them so that risks can be mitigated. During the induction period, the HR team has the new personnel read and sign the company policies. For example, if I am going to use my email account, there will be an email policy to guide me; or, if I am a remote user, I am expected to use a VPN to gain remote access to the company. Company employees should be reminded that failure to comply with company policies will be seen as a policy violation and could lead to disciplinary action and even being dismissed.

- **Insider threat**: The insider threat is the hardest threat to stop, as the insider may use someone else's credentials. You could install CCTV in all offices so that when the attack is carried out, you can see who is using the source computer at that time.

Exam tip
Accessing the company network externally with a secure connection or VPN is a policy violation.

- **Social engineering**: The most common social engineering attacks that affect a business are tailgating and familiarity. We need to give users annual training, reminding them about the dangers of tailgating; and no matter how friendly reception staff get with other employees, they should be aware of familiarity, where people will try and access areas that they are not allowed to get into by exploiting relationships. The security team could give each person a smart card that could be used with a smart card access control system.

- **Social media**: Data that is posted on social media can be used in social engineering attacks, and such data can sometimes be used to try and crack passwords. Annual security awareness training should warn employees of the danger of posting information about the company.

- **Personal email**: We can use DLP templates to prevent sensitive and PII information from leaving the company by email, but we cannot control use of personal email accounts, such as Gmail or Hotmail accounts. The security team should use either UTM or a proxy, and block the URLs of personal email providers.

Software Issues

Software is no longer run locally, as some of it is now run or downloaded from the internet. Therefore, the security team needs to be aware of unauthorized software being installed on their IT systems. Let's look at some software issues:

- **Unauthorized software**: One symptom of someone using unauthorized software is that the internet bandwidth is increasing while the disk space on the IT system is reducing. One of the best ways to stop this from happening it to use an application whitelist, where only approved applications can be installed.

Exam tip
Someone downloading unauthorized software will increase the bandwidth and reduce the disk space.

- **Baseline deviation**: When we roll out an image to desktops, we know that they have the same baseline, but we need to ensure that we run a baseline visualizer tool that can detect changes to the original baseline. We could also use a manual method of baseline comparison on a regular basis.
- **License compliance violation**: The company purchases 10 licenses for an application and then installs it onto the approved desktops. When another member of the company manages to steal the license key and puts it in their desktop, the company has violated the license agreement and the company could face a regulatory fine. We could prevent this violation by installing the software on a share and limiting the number of people using the share to equal the number of licenses that we have purchased. Another license violation would be someone installing a cracked copy of software on a company's desktop. We could prevent the installation of unauthorized applications by implementing application whitelists.

Disaster Recovery and the Continuity of Operations Concepts

It is important that if a company suffers from a disaster, they can be up and running as soon as possible. Disasters range from natural disasters, such as hurricanes and floods, to hardware failure, malicious insider attacks, and accidental deletion of data. The main aim of a disaster recovery plan is getting the company back up and running so that it can generate income. Let's look at the different aspects of disaster recovery:

- **Business Impact Analysis (BIA)**: A BIA looks at the monetary loss if a company is not up and running, coupled with the purchase of new equipment so that the business can continue to operate.
- **Recovery sites**: There are three main types of recovery site: these are hot, cold, and warm sites. Let's look at each of them:
    - **Hot site**: This site is up and running with staff loading data into live systems on an hourly basis. This makes it the most expensive to maintain, but it has the fastest recovery. We may also use a cloud provider to host our hot site, as it would allow us to be back up and running immediately.
    - **Warm site**: A warm site is similar to a hot site but data is backed up on a daily basis, so it will take a little bit longer to get up and running than a hot site.
    - **Cold site**: A cold site is the cheapest to maintain as it has power and water but no staff or equipment, making this the slowest site to get up and running.
- **Order of restoration**: Once a disaster has happened, it is important that we look at the services necessary for getting a company back up and running. We would rank them as critical, essential, or non-essential, and we would work on getting the most crucial service up and running first. However, if you are restoring from a differential or incremental backup, you would have to restore the full backup first before the differential and incremental tapes.

Exam tip
Cloud providers and multinational companies can only store data within the region that it was created in.

- **Geographic considerations**: Where your data is located has a major impact on the restoration phase following a disaster, so this impact must be accounted for. We will look at distance, off-site backups, and location selection:
    - **Distance**: We know that the fastest site to restore is a hot site, but if the hot site is 200 miles away, think of the logistics in getting company personnel to that site. This may take a few days to organize.
    - **Location selection**: The location of the hot site is critical to how fast we can recover our data and systems. If it is very far away and if one region suffers a power failure or is hit by a hurricane, can we get the site back up and running? This is why the cloud would be a good choice.
    - **Off-site backups**: When we back up our data, we should be storing backup tapes in a fire-proof safe and keeping our latest copy off-site, in case we suffer from a natural disaster.
- **Data sovereignty**: Data that has been created and turned into digital data is subject to the laws and regulations of the company that created it. It cannot be moved to another region—even for a backup-related reason. This affects both cloud providers and multinational corporations, as they cannot simply move data where they want to.
- **Legal implications**: Digital data is subject to the laws and regulations of the company in which it is created. The company creating the data must be compliant; for example, they may need to hold medical data for 25 years, financial data for 5 years, and normal data for 2 years.
- **Continuity of operations planning**: Companies need to look at each type of disaster and put processes in place for the company to be back up and running as quickly as possible. For example, your hot site could be in the cloud or you may have two different sites, and when the disaster happens, you would failover to the other site, keeping the business running.
- **Disaster recovery exercises**: There are two types of exercises that you can carry out to ensure that your company is ready for any disaster; these are structured walkthroughs and tabletop exercises. Let's look at both of these:
    - **Tabletop exercise**: A tabletop exercise is paper-based, where all parties meet around a table and discuss how they would deal with a disaster scenario.
    - **Structured walkthrough**: A structured walkthrough is where a mock disaster is enacted physically with all parties involved (similar to a fire drill).

- **After-action reports**: Once a company has suffered a disaster, the management of the company needs to review all of the information so that they can reduce the impact or prevent the disaster from re-occurring—this is known as lessons learned.
- **Failover**: Failover can be measured in two different ways. You may set up servers in a cluster, where the passive server will take over when the active server fails. Another method of failover is where the company has two or more different sites, so that when one site fails, the other site takes over and keeps the business functioning.
- **Alternate processing sites**: There are two main alternate processing sites that you could use following a disaster. You could use a mobile site or you could use a cloud provider to provide the infrastructure that you need.
- **Alternate business practices**: You may adopt an alternate business practice to ensure that you can keep the business going, or you may need to purchase services from another company.

Exam tip

If we don't hold a post-incident meeting, then we will not prevent the incident from re-occurring. This vital stage of learning these lessons, funnily enough, is known as lessons learned.

Review Questions

1. What type of BIOS needs to be implemented if we want an operating system to be able to securely boot?
2. When a Windows 10 OS securely boots, what checks does it carry out relating to drivers?
3. What type of trust model is being used if we use FDE?
4. If my laptop is going to use FDE, what type of chip do I need to have installed on the motherboard?
5. Why would you need to vet your supply chain?
6. Where does EMI come from and how can it affect your computer systems?
7. What is the difference between EMI and an EMP?
8. What can a company install to reduce the threat of an EMP?
9. What is the purpose of a kiosk?
10. Describe a trusted OS.

11. Name two mobile device operating systems.

12. When we receive a new IT system or IoT device, what is the first step we need to carry out?

13. Why would you disable unnecessary ports and services?

14. What is the purpose of using STIG?

15. How can I protect an external storage device against data theft?

16. What should I do to reduce the attack surface on a digital camera?

17. What is the best way to test a bespoke application before moving it into production?

18. What are the four stages when designing a new application?

19. What is an example of access violation?

20. If I purchase a new X509 certificate and it does not work, what two actions should I carry out?

21. How can I tell whether someone is stealing data using steganography?

22. What can we do to prevent someone stealing PII or sensitive data?

23. What is the most common authentication method that can be incorrectly configured?

24. How can we prevent someone from stealing a laptop or a tablet?

25. If a remote user is accessing the company's network externally and decides not to use a VPN, what are they guilty of?

26. What information should I not post on social media platforms, such as Twitter or Facebook?

27. What are two symptoms that someone is downloading unauthorized software?

28. Give an example of license compliance violation.

29. What is the fastest site for quick disaster recovery?

30. If my company is a multinational corporation, can I store New York data in London, in case the New York site falls over?

31. If my hot site is over 200 miles away, what should I consider to make recovery much faster?

32. What is a theory-based or paper-based disaster recovery exercise called?

33. What is the purpose of an after-action report?

34. What is the cheapest but slowest site to get back up and running during disaster recovery?

35. What is the difference between Geotracking and geotagging?

Answers and Explanations

1. You would implement the **Unified Extensible Firmware Interface (UEFI)**, as it is more secure and has the ability to securely boot an OS.
2. When a Windows 10 OS securely boots, it checks that all of the drivers are digitally signed.
3. A hardware root of trust is used by FDE.
4. FDE needs a TPM chip on the motherboard or a portable HSM.
5. You need to vet people working for companies in your supply chain and also ensure that can sufficiently supply goods and services.
6. EMI coming from motors, fluorescent lights, and radio frequencies affects a system's performance and could prevent IT systems from working properly.
7. EMI interferes with IT systems, but an EMP destroys them.
8. A company installs a UPS or surge protector to reduce the threat of EMPs.
9. A kiosk is a computer in a reception area or foyer that needs to be tied down so that only information about the building is available.
10. A trusted OS is a secure system, normally used by the military, that has multiple layers of security as it is used to access classified data. It is tied down tightly and changes to the OS are controlled.
11. Apple's iOS is an OS for Apple's mobile devices, such as the iPhone and the iPad, and Android is used by other mobile telephones, such as those produced by Samsung.
12. The first step to take when we receive a new IT system or IoT device is changing the default administrator username and password.
13. You disable unnecessary ports and services to harden the OS and reduce the attack surface.
14. A **Security Technical Implementation Guides (STIG)** is used by the military to ensure that operating systems are tied down tightly.
15. You should use FDE to protect an external storage device against data theft.
16. You should remove the memory card to reduce the attack surface on a digital camera.
17. You should use sandboxing to test a bespoke application before moving it into production.

18. The four stages when designing a new application are developing, testing, staging, and production.

19. Access violation is where a user is accesses data that they should not be able to see.

20. You would first of all check that the certificate is valid and then check whether it has been added to the Trusted Root Certification Authorities folder.

21. A file would be larger and an image would be lighter in color.

22. We can use DLP to prevent someone stealing PII or sensitive data.

23. The most common authentication method that can be incorrectly configured is a password.

24. We can use cable locks to prevent someone from stealing a laptop or a tablet.

25. They are guilty of policy violation.

26. Company information should never be posted on social media.

27. Your internet bandwidth has increased and your local disk space has been reduced.

28. This is where you steal the license to an application and then install it on your desktop without consent or install more application than purchased licences.

29. The fastest disaster recovery site is the hot site.

30. No, data can only be stored regionally; you would need a backup site in the USA.

31. You should consider moving your hot site to the cloud.

32. A tabletop exercise is a theory-based or paper-based disaster recovery exercise.

33. An after-action report looks at how an incident happened and what measures to put in place to prevent re-occurrence; it is sometimes known as lessons learned.

34. The cheapest disaster recovery site is the cold site; it is the slowest to get back up and running as it has power and water and nothing else.

35. Geotracking can tell you the location of a mobile device and geotagging puts the location and time of capture on a picture.

12
Mock Exam 1

1. What type of attack is a Padding Oracle On Downgrading Legacy Encryption attack? Choose two options from the following list:

    A. IV attack

    B. Replay attack

    C. Man-in-the-middle attack

    D. TLS 1.0 with electronic code book

    E. SSL 3.0 with chain block cipher

2. You are the security administrator for the British secret service. What type of access method will you use for secret and top-secret data?

    A. You will use DAC, with the owner of the data giving the access

    B. You will use DAC, with the custodian of the data giving access

    C. You will use DAC, with the security administrator giving access

    D. You will use MAC, with the security administrator giving access

3. Your company wants to encrypt DNS traffic by using DNSSEC. Once you have signed the zone, what records are created for each host?

    A. CNAME

    B. AAAA

    C. RRSIG

    D. MX

    E. PTR

4. You are a security administrator. A user called Ben is having a discussion with one of his colleagues. They have four choices for two-factor authentication. They have asked for your advice as to which of the following is a two-factor authentication method. Select the best answer:

    A. Smart card

    B. Password and PIN

    C. Passphrase and username

    D. Retina and fingerprint scan

5. Two separate CAs need to work together on a joint venture. What can they implement so that certificates can be used for cross certification?

    A. Bridge trust model

    B. Certificate pinning

    C. Certificate stapling

    D. Wildcard certificates

6. John goes to a sports website and gets the following error:

   `THIS WEBSITE CANNOT BE TRUSTED.`

   What two actions does the website administrator need to take to resolve this error?

   A. Ask the key escrow to store their private key

   B. Ensure that the website uses a valid SAN certificate

   C. Update the root certificate in the client computer Trusted Root Certificate Authorities Store

   D. Verify that the certificate on the server has not expired

7. A security administrator discovers that an attacker used a compromised host as a platform for launching attacks deeper in a company's network. What terminology best describes the use of the compromised host?

   A. Brute force

   B. Active reconnaissance

   C. Pivoting

   D. Passing point

8. Mary is managing the company's wireless network, which uses WPA2-PSK. What kind of encryption is most likely to be used?

   A. SHA-1

   B. AES

   C. MD5

   D. DES

9. Who is responsible for setting permissions when using a **Mandatory Access Control (MAC)** model?

   A. Owner

   B. Manager

   C. Administrator

   D. User

10. Company A is due to upgrade all of its IT systems, and has been investigating the possibility of moving to the cloud, as there is no capital expenditure because the CSP provides the hardware. Company A would still like to control the IT systems in the cloud. Which cloud model would best serve company A's needs?

    A. **Software as a Service (SaaS)**

    B. **Infrastructure as a Service (IaaS)**

    C. **Monitoring as a Service (MaaS)**

    D. **Platform as a Service (PaaS)**

11. You are the security administrator and the IT director has tasked you with collecting the volatile memory on Server 1, as it is currently experiencing a cyberattack. Which of the following are the two best forms of volatile memory to collect?

    A. Secure boot

    B. Swap/page file

    C. USB flash drive

    D. ROM

    E. RAM

12. Bill and Ben, the flowerpot men are going to encrypt data using asymmetric encryption, which uses public and private keys. What is the first step they need to take?

    A. Exchange public keys

    B. Exchange private keys

    C. Exchange digital signatures

    D. Exchange telephone numbers

13. At what stage in the SDLC are computer systems no longer supported by the original vendor?

    A. Sandboxing

    B. End-of-life systems

    C. Resource exhaustion

    D. System sprawl

14. Company A has just developed a bespoke system for booking airline tickets. What is it called if a freelance coding specialist tests it for security flaws?

    A. Code review

    B. Static code review

    C. Regression testing

    D. Dynamic code review

15. You are the security administrator for a company that has just replaced two file servers. Which of the following is the best solution for disposing of the hard drives that are used to store top-secret data?

    A. Hashing

    B. Degaussing

    C. Low-level formatting

    D. Shredding

16. You are the security administrator for an airline company whose systems suffered a loss of availability last month. Which of the following attacks would most likely affect the availability of your IT systems?

    A. Spear phishing

    B. Replay

    C. **Man-in-the-middle (MITM)**

    C. DoS

17. You are a network administrator setting up an L2TP/IPSec VPN tunnel, as your company needs to move a large amount of encrypted data between a branch office and the head office. Why is Diffie Hellman used for an IKE phase before the data is forwarded via symmetric encryption?

    A. It is a symmetric encryption technique that protects keys

    B. It is a hashing technique that protects keys

    C It is an ephemeral technique that protects keys

    D. It is an asymmetric technique that protects keys by setting up a secure channel

18. You are a lecturer at a college and you need to deliver a session on salting passwords. What are the two main reasons you would salt passwords?

    A. To prevent brute force attacks

    B. To make access to the password slower

    C. To prevent duplicate passwords being stored

    D. To stop simple passwords from being used

19. Which of the following methods of authentication are known as two-factor authentication?

    A. PIN and passphrase

    B. Mastercard and PIN

    C. Username and password

    D. Retina and facial recognition

20. During a forensic investigation, the judge decrees that any data that is investigated should remain in its original form of integrity. Which of the following are used for the integrity of data? Choose two:

    A. MD5

    B. AES

    C. SHA 1

    D. DES

21. Company A has suffered a DDoS attack, and the company has decided that their RPO should be set at four hours. The directors are holding a board meeting to discuss the progress that is being made. During the meeting, the IT manager mentions the RTO, and the CEO looks confused. How can you explain the meaning of the RTO to the CEO?

    A. Acceptable downtime

    B. Return to operational state

    C. Measure of reliability

    D. Average time to repair

22. The following is a list of different controls. Which of these are physical security controls?

    A. Change management

    B. Antivirus software

    C. Cable locks

    D. Firewall rules

    F. Iris scanner

23. The security team has identified an unknown vulnerability and isolated it. What technique is the best for investigating and testing it?

    A. Steganography

    B. Fuzzing

    C. Sandboxing

    D. Containerization

24. What is it called when a user has exploited an IT system so that they have obtained access to all files on the file server?

    A. Remote exploit

    B. Zero-day exploit

    C. Privilege escalation

    D. Pivoting

25. You are the security administrator for your company, and the IT manager has asked you to brief him on XML authentication methods. Which of the following should you tell him uses XML-based authentication? Select all that apply:

    A. TOTP

    B. Federation services

    C. Smart card

D. SSO

E. SOAP

F. SAML

26. There is a group of certificates in a folder, and you need to identify which certificate uses the **Privacy Enhanced Mail** (**PEM**) format. Which of the following is the best choice to make?

    A. PFX

    B. CER

    C. BASE 64

    D. P12

27. Three different companies want to develop an application where they will share the cost of developing resources and future running costs. Which cloud model best describes this?

    A. Public cloud

    B. SaaS

    C. Private cloud

    D. PaaS

    E. IaaS

    F. Community cloud

28. What type of keys does a key escrow manage?

    A. Public

    B. Session

    C. Shared

    D. Private

29. Which of the following is an email-based attack on all members of the sales team?

   A. Phishing

   B. Vishing

   C. Spear phishing

   D. Pharming

30. An attacker tried to target a high-level executive, but has to leave a voicemail as he did not answer the telephone. What was the intended attack and what attack will eventually be used? Select all that apply from the following list:

   A. Whaling

   B. Vishing

   C. Phishing

   D. Spear phishing

31. An auditor has been investigating the theft of money from a charity, and they have discovered that the finance assistant has been embezzling money, as he was the only person who dealt with finances, receiving donations and paying all of the bills. Which of the following is the best option that the auditor should recommend to reduce the risk of this happening again?

   A. Hashing

   B. Job rotation

   C. Separation of duties

   D. Mandatory vacations

   E. Encryption

32. You are a security administrator and you have moved departments. You are now working with the certificate authority and training Mary, who is a new intern. Mary has asked you what the certificate **Object Identifier** (**OID**) consists of. What should you tell her?

    A. Certificate-signing request

    B. Certificate pinning

    C. Certificate stapling

    D. Certificate serial number

33. You are the operational manager for a multinational corporation, and you are writing a policy in which you mention the RPO. Which of the following is the CLOSEST definition of an RPO?

    A. Acceptable downtime

    B. Return to operational state

    C. A measure of system reliability

    D. Average time to repair

34. You are carrying out annual training for your company and need to put a PowerPoint slide together on the symptoms of a backdoor virus. Which three points should you include in the slide? Each provides part of the explanation of a backdoor virus:

    A. Programs will not open at all, even though you are clicking many times

    B. You must click on several items

    C. They can be included in an email attachment

    D. Files open quicker than before

    E. Your system can only get infected through a link on a web page

35. You are a security administrator and need to set up a new wireless access point so that it is not backward compatible with legacy systems, as these may be vulnerable to attack, and it must be the strongest encryption that you can use. Which is the best solution to meet your needs?

    A. WPA2 PSK

    B. WPA TKIP

    C. WPA2 TKIP

    D. WPA2 CCMP

36. Which of the following commands can be used to create a buffer overflow? Choose all that apply:

    A. `var char`

    B. `strcpy`

    C. `var data`

    D. `strcat`

37. James has raised a ticket with the IT help desk. He has been tampering with the settings on his computer and he can no longer access the internet. The help desk technicians have checked the configuration on his desktop and the settings are the same as everyone else's. Suddenly, three other people have also reported that they cannot connect to the internet. Which network device should be checked first?

    A. Switch

    B. Router

    C. Hub

    D. Repeater

38. Which of the following is a secure wireless protocol that uses TLS?

    A. NTLM

    B. PAP

    C. EAP

    D. AES

39. You are the security administrator for a multinational corporation, and the development team has asked your advice on how to prevent SQL-injection, integer-overflow, and buffer-overflow attacks. Which of the following should you advise them to use?

    A. Input validation

    B. A host-based firewall with advanced security

    C. Strcpy

    D. Hashing

40. Your company is opening up a new data center in Galway, Ireland. A server farm, has been installed there and now a construction company has come in to put a six-foot mantrap in the entrance. What are the two main reasons for this mantrap being installed?

    A. To prevent theft

    B. To prevent tailgating

    C. To prevent unauthorized personnel gaining access to the data center

    D. To allow faster access to the facility

41. Which of the following devices can prevent unauthorized access to a network and prevent attacks from unknown sources?

    A. Router

    B. Load balancer

    C. Web security gateway

    D. UTM

42. **Internet of Things (IoT)** is a concept that has recently taken off. Can you identify which of the following devices fall under this category? Select all that apply:

    A. ATM

    B. Banking system

    C. Smart TV

    D. Refrigerator

    E. Router

    F. Wearable technology

43. Which feature of DNS will help balance a load without needing to install a network load balancer, or, when coupled with a load balancer, makes it more dynamic?

    A. DNS CNAME

    B. DNSSEC

    C. DNS round robin

    D. DNS SRV records

44. What is the benefit of certificate pinning?

    A. It prevents a certificate-signing request from a non-administrator

    B. It is used by a web server, and it bypasses the CRL for faster authentication

    C. It stops people from spoofing, issuing certificates, or compromising your CA

    D. It is used for cross certification between two separate root CAs

45. An auditor has just finished a risk assessment of the company, and he has recommended that we need to mitigate some of our risks. Which of the following are examples of risk mitigation?

    A. Turning off host-based firewalls on laptops

    B. Installing antivirus software on a new laptop

C. Insuring your car against fire and theft

D. Outsourcing your IT to another company

E. Deciding not to jump into the Grand Canyon

46. A security engineer wants to implement a site-to-site VPN that will require SSL certificates for mutual authentication. Which of the following will you choose?

A. L2TP/IPSec

B. SSL VPN

C. PPTP VPN

D. IKEv2 VPN

47. You are the Active Directory administrator and you have been training new interns on the *Kerberos ticket-granting ticket session*. One of the interns has asked about the relationship between a service ticket and session ticket used by Kerberos authentication. Which of the following is the best description for this?

A. The user exchanges their service ticket with the server's session ticket for mutual authentication and single sign-on

B. The service key is unencrypted and is matched with the value in the session ticket

C. The user shows the server his session ticket; and the server sends him a service ticket

D. The user shows the server his service ticket; and the server sends him a session ticket to keep

48. Your company has a guest wireless network that can be used by visitors during the day, sales staff during the evening, and customer-service staff at lunchtime.

They set up a captive portal that fulfills the following criteria:

- Guests do not need to authenticate
- Sales staff do not need to insert any credentials
- Customer-service staff must use the highest level of encryption

How will you set up your captive portal? Select three answers, each answer provides part of the solution:

A. WEP 40 bit key

B. WPA2 TKIP

C. WPA-TKIP

D. Open-system authentication

E. WPA2 CCMP

F. WPS

49. You are a security administrator, and the IT team has been using RSA for the encryption of all its data, but has found that it is very slow. Which of the following should the security administrator recommend to improve the speed of the encryption?

A. Asymmetric encryption using DES

B. Asymmetric encryption using Diffie-Hellman

C. Symmetric encryption

D. Running a vulnerability scan to find a better solution

50. Robert, who is an intern, has been assigned to the security team. A user has called him to ask who signs the X509 certificates. Which one of the following should Robert give as an answer?

A. CRL

B. Key escrow

C. CSR

D. CA

You can find the answers under Assessment at the rear of the book.

13
Mock Exam 2

1. You are the security administrator for a large multinational corporation, and you have used a black box penetration tester to find vulnerabilities in your company and exploit them as far you can. During the penetration test, it was found that there were some vulnerabilities in your Windows 10 desktop operating system. There were no vulnerabilities in any of your Linux or Unix systems. Which of the following reasons best describes why the penetration tester was successful with the Windows 10 machines, but not with the Linux or Unix machines?

   A. Linux and Unix are more secure than Windows 10

   B. The penetration tester did not attempt to exploit the Linux/Unix machines

   C. The Linux and Unix operating systems never have any vulnerabilities

   D. The operating systems' attack vectors are very different

2. You are a security administrator and you wish to implement an encrypted method of authentication for your wireless network. Which of the following protocols is the most secure for your wireless network?

   A. PAP

   B. WPA2-PSK

   C. EAP-TLS

   D. PEAP

3. You are designing the network topology for a new company that is rapidly expanding from a one-premises company with 20 users to a medium-sized company with 300 users. The company tells you that it was subjected to a DDoS attack last year that took the company down for over a day. In your network design, they don't want to implement a DMZ; therefore, traffic will be coming directly from the internet. How do you propose to best mitigate against future DDoS attacks? Select two answers from the following list; each is part of the solution:

A. Install a stateless firewall at the edge of your network to prevent incoming traffic

B. Install a stateful firewall at the edge of your network to prevent incoming traffic

C. Install a NIDS on your network as an additional layer of protection

D. Install a NIPS on your network as an additional layer of protection

E. Install an inline NIPS on your network as an additional layer of protection

4. You work on the cyber security team of a large multinational corporation, and you have been alerted to an attack on the web server inside your DMZ that is used for selling your products on the internet. You can see by running `netstat` that you have an unknown active connection. What should be the first step you take when investigating this incident?

A. Isolate the web server by disconnecting it from the network to prevent further damage

B. Disconnect all external active connections to ensure that any attack is stopped

C. Run a packet sniffer to capture the network traffic to identify the attacker

D. Take a screenshot of the damage done to the website and report the incident to the police

5. I need to purchase a certificate that I can install on five mail servers. Which one should I purchase?

    A. PEM certificate

    B. Wildcard certificate

    C. **Subject Alternative Name (SAN)** certificate

    D. Root certificate

6. You are the manager of a large IT company and it is your duty to authorize the administrative controls. Which of the following are actions that you would normally authorize? Select all that apply:

    A. Collecting an ID badge

    B. Creating an IT security policy

    C. Purchasing a cable lock

    D. Creating a new firewall rule

7. You are the operational manager for a financial company that has just suffered a disaster. Which of the following sites will you choose to be fully operational in the smallest amount of time?

    A. Cold site

    B. Warm site

    C. Hot site

    D. Campus site

8. The serious crimes agency has just taken control of a laptop belonging to a well-known criminal that they have been trying to track down for the last 20 years. They want to ensure that everything is done by the book and no errors are made. What is the first step in their forensic investigation, prior to starting the chain of custody?

   A. Making a system image of the laptop

   B. Placing it in a polythene bag and sealing it

   C. Hashing the data so that data integrity is assured

   D. Asking for proof of ownership of the laptop

9. If an attacker is looking for information about the software versions that you use on your network, which of the following tools could he/she use? Select all that apply:

   A. Protocol analyzer

   B. Port scanning

   C. Network mapper

   D. Baseline analyzer

10. Footage of people relaxing in their homes started appearing on the internet without the knowledge of the people being filmed. The people being filmed were warned by relatives and coworkers, resulting in an enquiry being launched by the police. Initial evidence reported a similarity in that they had all recently purchased IoT devices, such as health monitors, baby monitors, smart TVs, and refrigerators. Which of the following best describes why the attacks were successful?

    A. The devices' default configurations had not been changed

    B. Their houses had been broken into and hidden cameras were installed

    C. Their victims' wireless networks were broadcasting beyond the boundaries of their homes

    D. The manufacturers of the devices installed hidden devices allowing them to film

11. You are the network administrator for an IT training company that has over 20 training rooms that are all networked together in their Miami office. Your corporate admin team could not access the internet last week as they were getting their IP settings from one of the training room's DHCP servers. The training manger has asked you to separate the corporate admin machines into their own network with a different IP range from the training rooms. What is the most secure way of implementing this? Select the best option from the following:

    A. Create a VLAN on the switch and put the corporate admin team in the VLAN

    B. Install a router in the LAN and place the corporate admin team in the new subnet

    C. Create a NAT from the firewall and put the corporate machines in that network

    D. Install a proxy server

12. Your organization has many different ways of connecting to your network, ranging from VPN and RAS to 802.1x authentication switches. You need to implement a centrally managed authentication system that will log periods of access. Select the two most suitable methods of authentication:

    A. PAP

    B. TACACS+

    C. NTLM

    D. RADIUS

13. From a security perspective, what is the major benefit of using imaging technology, such as Microsoft WDS server or Symantec Ghost, to image desktop computers and laptops that are being rolled out?

    A. It provides a consistent baseline for all new machines

    B. It ensures that all machines are patched

    C. It reduces the number of vulnerabilities

    D. It allows a non-technical person to roll out the images

14. A company that is allowing people to access their internet application wants the people who log into the application to use an account managed by someone else. An example of this is using their Facebook account with a technology called Open ID Connect. Which of the following protocols is this based on? Select the best choice:

    A. Kerberos

    B. SAML

    C. OAuth 2.0

    D. Federation services

15. You are the security administrator for a medium-sized company that needs to enforce a much stricter password policy via group policy. The aims of this policy are to do the following:
    - Prevent using the same password within 12 password changes.
    - Ensure that they cannot change the password more than once a day.
    - Prevent weak passwords or simple passwords, such as `123456` or `password`, from being used.

    Select the options that you will need to fulfill all of these goals:

    A. Enforce password history

    B. Minimum password length

    C. Passwords must meet complexity requirements

    D. Minimum password age

    E. Maximum password length

16. You provide a service for people who have recently fulfilled their contract with their mobile phone provider to unlock their phone and then install third-party applications on it. They will then no longer be tied to using the mobile phone vendor's app store. Which of the following techniques will you use to achieve this? Select all that apply:

    A. Tethering

    B. Sideloading

C. Slipstreaming

D. Jailbreaking or rooting

E. Degaussing

17. You are the security administrator of a multinational company that has recently prevented brute force attacks by using account lockout settings with a low value using group policy. The CEO of the company has now dictated that the company will no longer use account lockout settings as he read an article about it and got the wrong impression. Facing this dilemma, how can you ensure that you can make it more difficult for brute force to be successful?

    A. Obfuscation

    B. PBKDF2

    C. XOR

    D. bcrypt

18. You want to join a wireless network by using a password. Which of the following wireless features would be most appropriate to achieve this objective?

    A. WPA2-Enterprise

    B. WPA2-TKIP

    C. WPS

    D. WPA2-PSK

    E. WPA2-CCMP

19. What is the one main purpose of a **Network Intrusion Detection System (NIDS)**? Select the MOST appropriate option:

    A. Identifies vulnerabilities

    B. Identifies new network hosts

    C. Identifies viruses

    D. Identifies new web servers

20. A web server was the victim of an integer overflow attack. How could this be prevented in the future?

    A. Install a proxy server

    B. Install an SQL injection

    C. Input validation on forms

    D. Install a web application firewall

21. You have recently set up a new virtual network with over 1,000 guest machines. One of the hosts is running out of resources, such as memory and disk space. Which of the following best describes what is happening?

    A. Virtual machine escape

    B. End of system lifespan

    C. System sprawl

    D. Poor setup

22. You are the system administrator for a multinational company that wants to implement two-factor authentication. At present, you are using facial recognition as the method of access. Which of the following would allow you to obtain two-factor authentication? Select all that apply:

    A. Palm reader

    B. Signature verification

    C. Thumb scanner

    D. Gait

    E. Iris scanner

23. The security auditor has just visited your company and is recommending change management to reduce the risks from the unknown vulnerabilities of any new software introduced into the company. What will the auditor recommend to reduce the risk when you first evaluate the software? Select the best two practices to adopt from the following list:

    A. Jailbreaking

    B. Sandboxing

    C. Bluesnarfing

    D. Chroot jail

    E. Fuzzing

24. You are the security administrator for a multinational corporation. You recently detected and thwarted an attack on your network when someone hacked into your network and took full control of one of the hosts. What type of attack best describes the attack you stopped?

    A. Man-in-the-middle attack

    B. Replay attack

    C. Packet filtering

    D. Remote exploit

25. You are the security administrator for a multinational corporation and who recently carried out a security audit. Following the audit, you told the server administrators to disable NTLM on all servers. Which of the following types of attack best describes why you have taken this action?

    A. It will improve the server's performance

    B. To prevent a man-in-the-middle attack

    C. To prevent a pass-the-hash attack

    D. To prevent a poodle attack

26. The political adviser to the Prime Minister of the United Kingdom has returned from the two months of summer break that all staff are entitled to. He has applied for an immediate transfer to another department, stating that his health is bad and the job was far too intense. When his replacement arrives, he finds that, during the summer recess, the political adviser has shredded all documents relating to a political inquiry that has involved his cousin. The police are immediately called in and say that they cannot prosecute the political adviser due to lack of evidence. What precautions could the Houses of Parliament security team take to prevent further events such as this happening in the future?

    A. Create a change-management document to ensure that the receptionists are more vigilant to people coming in out of hours

    B. Enforce time-of-day restrictions so that nobody can access the IT systems during summer breaks

    C. Enforce separation of duties to ensure that any document that is destroyed has been witnessed by a second person

    D. Enforce mandatory vacations to prevent him coming in during the recess

27. You work in the forensics team of a very large multinational corporation, where an attack has happened across three different sites in two different countries. You have been collecting the following log files from these locations:
    - Firewall logs

    - NIPS logs

    - NIDS logs

    What is the first action that you need to take when collating these logs?

    A. Apply time normalization to these logs

    B. Copy them into a worm drive so that they cannot be tampered with

    C. Sort out the sequence of events by site

    D. Raise chain of custody documentation for these logs

28. You are an Active Directory administrator and have been having problems with the time synchronization that is used by the Kerberos authentication protocols. Consequently, you have now contacted a third party to provide your time synchronization. They use Stratum **network time protocol** (**NTP**) servers. What is the most secure method of setting up a Stratum server for time synchronization?

    A. The servers should connect to an internal Stratum 1 NTP server

    B. The servers should connect to an internal Stratum 2 NTP server

    C. The servers should connect to an internal Stratum 0 NTP server

    D. The servers should connect to an external Stratum 0 NTP server

29. You are the network administrator for a company that runs an Active Directory domain environment where the system administrator is failing to keep you updated when new hosts are added to the network. You now decide that you will use your networking tools for the following tasks:
    - Identifying new hosts

    - Operating system versions

    - Services that are running

    Which of the following network-based tools provide the information that you require? Select the tools that you are most likely to use:

    A. Protocol scanner

    B. Microsoft baseline analyzer

    C. Nmap

    D. Penetration testing

30. You are working for the serious crimes unit of the United Nations and have been given a laptop to investigate. You need to ensure that the evidence you are investigating has not been tampered with during your investigation. How are you going to prove this to the court when it is time to present your findings? Which of the following techniques will you adopt to best prove this? Select all that apply:

    A. MD5

    B. 3DES

    C. SHA1

    D. Blowfish

31. You are the security administrator for a multinational corporation that has an Active Directory domain. What type of attack uses HTML tags with JavaScript inserted between the `<script>` and `</script>` tags?

    A. Cross-site scripting

    B. Man-in-the-middle

    C. Cross-site forgery attack

    D. SQL injection

32. You are a system administrator working for a multinational company that has a Windows domain and is using an active passive model. Which of the following are the BEST reasons why your company would have adopted this model?

    A. It provides vendor diversity

    B. It provides much faster disaster recovery

    C. It is the best model to use for symmetric encryption

    D. It provides availability of your IT systems

33. You are the system administrator for an Active Directory domain and deal with authentication on a daily basis. Which of the following do you use as an authentication method by entering a `PIN` instead of a password?

    A. Smart card

    B. Kerberos

    C. WPS

    D. TOTP

34. You are the security administrator for a large multinational corporation and you have a meeting with the CEO about the security posture of the company. He wants you to ensure that the following are carried out effectively:

    • Firewall logs are stored securely so that nobody can tamper with them
    • Elevation of privileges attack

    Which of the following is the best solution to implement? Select all that apply:

    A. Robocopy firewall logs to a worm drive

    B. Robocopy firewall logs to a RAID 5 volume

    C. Implement usage auditing and reviews

    D. Carry out permission audits and review every seven days

35. You are the security administrator for a multinational company, and you know that one of your X509 certificates, used in at least 300 desktop machines, has been compromised. What action are you going to take to protect the company, using the least amount of administrative effort?

    A. Email the people involved and ask them to delete the X509 from their desktop immediately

    B. Carry out certificate pinning to prevent the CA from being compromised

    C. Revoke the root CA X509 so it is added to the CRL

    D. Revoke the X509 so it is added to the CRL

36. You need to install a new wireless access point that should be as secure as possible while also being backward compatible with legacy wireless systems. Which of the following do you use?

    A. WPA2 PSK

    B. WPA

    C. WPA2 CCMP

    D. WPA2 TKIP

37. You are the capacity planning administrator for a large multinational corporation, and find that Server 1 is running out of disk space and, when you monitor its network card, you see that it is at 100% utilization. Which of the following reasons best describes what is happening?

    A. There are hardware errors on the server

    B. Unauthorized software is being downloaded

    C. Event logs are getting full and slowing down the system

    D. The disks that were selected were too small

38. You are the security administrator and someone has just tried to attack your web server, which is protected by a web application firewall. When you look into the log files of the web application firewall, two of the rows of the log file have the following two entries:

    ```
    var data = "<blackbeard> ++ </../etc/passwd>"
    Select* from customers where 1=1
    ```

    Which of the following attacks are most likely to be have been attempted? Select all that apply:

    A. Integer overflow

    B. SQL injection

    C. JavaScript

    D. Buffer overflow

39. Data has been classified as internal data and external data. The company recently added two new classifications of data: legal and financial. What would be the benefit of these new classifications? Select the best solution for the new data classifications:

    A. You need a minimum of three classifications for it to be effective

    B. Better data classification

    C. Quicker indexing

    D. Faster searching

40. You are the security administrator for a multinational corporation based in Miami, and your company has recently suffered a replay attack. After lessons learned, you have decided to use a protocol that uses time stamps and USN to prevent replay attacks. Which of the following protocols is being implemented here? Select the best answer:

    A. Federation services

    B. EAP-TLS

    C. Kerberos

    D. RADIUS federation

41. Which of the following threat actors would be the most likely to steal a company's research and development data?

    A. Organized crime

    B. Competitor

    C. Script kiddie

    D. Nation state

42. You are a security administrator for a large multinational corporation based in the United Kingdom. You have just attended an annual seminar about the various types of password attacks. You have already disabled NTLM on all of the servers to prevent pass-the-hash attacks. Which of the following statements involves storing passwords as a hash value?

    A. A collision attack—the hash value and the data match

    B. A collision attack—the hash values match

    C. A rainbow-table attack performs a search of simple passwords

    D. A rainbow-table attack performs a search of precomputed hashes

43. You are the new IT director of a small, family-owned business that is rapidly expanding. You have submitted your annual budget for the IT team and the owners of the company want to know why you have asked for funds for vendor diversity. They have asked you to provide two good reasons as to why they should grant you the funds. Which of the following are the most suitable reasons why you wish to implement vendor diversity?

    A. Reliability

    B. Regulatory compliance

    C. It is a best practice in your industry

    D. Resilience

44. You are the network administrator for a large multinational corporation, and you have captured packets that show that the traffic between the company's network devices is in clear text. Which of the following protocols could be used to secure the traffic between the company's network devices? Select all that apply:

    A. SNMP V 3

    B. SNMP

    C. SCP

    D. SFTP

45. You are the auditor of a large multinational corporation and the SIEM server has been finding vulnerabilities on a server. Manual inspection proves that it has been fully hardened and has no vulnerabilities. What are the two main reasons why the SIEM server is producing this output?

    A. There was a zero-day virus

    B. False negatives

    C. False positives

    D. The wrong filter was used to audit

46. You are a forensic investigator who has been called out to deal with a virus attack. You collect the information from the network card and volatile memory. After gathering, documenting, and securing the evidence of a virus attack, what is the best method to prevent further losses to the company?

    A. Send a copy of the virus to the lab for analysis

    B. Mitigate the attack and get the system back up and running

    C. Initiate a chain of custody

    D. Initiate business-impact analysis

47. You are the purchasing manager for a very large multinational company, and you are looking at the company's policy of dealing with the insurance of laptops. Last year, the company lost a record number of laptops. Your company is losing 10 laptops per month and the monthly insurance cost is $10,000. Which of the following laptop purchases would prevent you from purchasing insurance?

    A. A budget laptop at $1,300 each

    B. A budget laptop at $1,200 each

    C. A budget laptop at $1,000 each

    D. A budget laptop at $1,001 each

48. Your company has suffered a system-sprawl attack, and you need to be able to identify what has caused the attack, and what the symptoms of the attack are. Which of the following attacks could cause system sprawl and what would be a tell-tale sign of it? Select the best two answers; each is a part of the solution:

    A. SQL injection

    B. DoS attack

    C. CPU at 100% utilization

    D. Buffer overflow

49. Which of the following is a measure of reliability?

    A. MTTR

    B. MTBF

    C. MTTF

    D. RPO

50. Which of the following are the characteristics of a third party to third party authentication protocol that uses XML-based authentication? Select the best three answers:

    A. **Single sign on (SSO)**

    B. Kerberos

    C. SAML

    D. Federation services

 You can find the answers in Assessment at the rear of the book.

Preparing for the CompTIA Security+ 501 Exam

This guide is to help students pass the Security+ exam the first time round. More resources, such as flashcards, virtual machines, and PowerPoint slides are available at www.securityplus.training.

The CompTIA Security+ 501 exam is a very tricky exam and the only way to pass it is by having a solid knowledge base and good analytical thinking.

The exam consists of 83 questions, lasts for 90 minutes, and the pass mark is 750/900, which equates to 83.33%. I think you can get maybe 12-13 questions wrong, but nobody knows how the exam is scored as scores in the 750s are even, yet scores of 760, 770, and 780 seem to be odd and don't increase in the same increments.

The exam starts with simulations that are graphics, where you will drag and drop the answers, usually with four or five different sections. I believe that you get partial points for dragging in a correct answer. To get a look and feel of what a simulation looks like, Google **Security+ 401 exam simulations** under images and many will appear. This will give you an idea of what to expect, but these simulations will be very different, as 501 is a different exam.

This book is designed with open questions at the end of each chapter, since you need to know the material thoroughly to obtain certification. If we had used multiple choice all of the way through and you were good at guessing, you may have a false impression of your knowledge base. I will give you tips for the exam, followed by additional exam preparation material, including drag-and-drop practical exercises to help you tackle simulation type of questions, followed by some useful Linux commands.

Tips on Taking the Exam

When taking the exam, you need to read the questions thoroughly and look at their grammar, especially if you are a native English speaker, as we tend to scan, and your answer must meet the objective of the question. Adopt a subtractive method by first of all ruling out the answers that are wrong and then selecting the correct answer; the hardest way to tackle this exam is to immediately pick an answer.

As previously mentioned, the exam starts with simulations. If you are finding a question tricky, go to the top right-hand corner and there will be a button saying something like **Flag for review**, but do NOT attempt to answer that particular question. Do this with any question you find difficult, no matter how large or small it is. When you have finished the final question, you will automatically be taken to the review screen. Don't waste time working out a difficult question; mark it up, bank your points, and then give yourself a chance when you are less pressured.

The review screen is larger than the display screen, therefore go to the top of the left-hand column and work your way down that column, then move onto the middle column, and the right-hand column.

If you have not answered the review question, there will be a string in red saying something like **You need to answer this question**, making them very easy to spot. If you have answered the question, the review question will be a different shade of blue than the questions that haven't been answered; this can be tricky if you are color blind. When it asks you if you are finished with the review, scroll up to the top, where you should see 0/83 questions. If it says 2/83, then this means that you have not answered two questions. If you cannot answer a question, give it your best shot since there is no penalty for entering a wrong answer; you never know, you may guess correctly.

When you finish the exam, you will be taken to a few screens where you answer questions based on your profile. However, when it thanks you, and you click on **Next**, that is the heart-attack moment, as your score will appear on the screen. In the middle of the screen, you will see a Security+ logo—look directly below it and look for the word **Congratulations**—this is all you need to see. Anything else is a bonus.

Exam Preparation

An exam preparation guide with a checklist, drag-and-drop questions, and Linux commands is given here. Follow the checklist to ensure that you are as best prepared as you can be:

Security +—Checklist Ensure you hit the mark before testing	
Task to complete	**Date completed**
Read `Chapter 1`, *Understanding Security Fundamentals*, and score 100% on review questions	
Read `Chapter 2`, *Conducting Risk Analysis*, and score 100% on review questions	

Read Chapter 3, *Implementing Security Policies and Procedures*, and score 100% on review questions	
Read Chapter 4, *Delving into Identity and Access Management*, and score 100% on review questions	
Read Chapter 5, *Understanding Network Components*, and score 100% on review questions	
Read Chapter 6, *Understanding Cloud Models and Virtualization*, and score 100% on review questions	
Read Chapter 7, *Managing Hosts and Applications Deployment*, and score 100% on review questions	
Read Chapter 8, *Protecting Against Attacks and Vulnerabilities*, and score 100% on review questions	
Read Chapter 9, *Implementing Public Key Infrastructure*, and score 100% on review questions	
Read Chapter 10, *Responding to Security Incidents*, and score 100% on review questions	
Read Chapter 11, *Managing Business Continuity*, and score 100% on review questions	
Score 100% on mock exam 1	
Score 100% on mock exam 2	
Score 100% on drag and drop—attacks	
Score 100% on drag and drop—certificates	
Score 100% on drag and drop—ports/protocols	
Score 100% on drag and drop—authentication	
Score 100% on drag and drop—general	
Read and understand Linux commands	
Read all exam tips in the book	

Practical 1—Drag and Drop—Attacks

Please place the answers against their description:

Session hijacking—familiarity—whaling—DDoS—smurf—pharming—phishing—zero-day virus—tailgating—virus—replay attack—vishing—spear phishing—worm—man-in-the-middle—social engineering, urgency—XSS—ransomware—remote access Trojan—logic bomb—christmas tree attack—pass-the-hash—bluejacking

Practical 1—drag and drop—attacks Put the correct answer against each item	
Targets the CEO only	
A directed IP broadcast to the border router	
Holding the door open for someone else	
An attack using port 5000	
An interception attack in real time	
An interception attack—one-day delay	
Stealing someone's cookie	
Leaving a voicemail for the CEO	
Letting a fireman into your server room	
Redirected to a fraudulent website	
An email to a group of people to get bank details	
An email to one person to get bank details	
Letting someone you know access a secure area	
Forcing someone to pay to recover their data	
Sending login details back to an attacker	
An attack using port 445	
Triggered by an event or action	
Set the PSH, Fin, and URG to 1	
An attack using port 1900	
An attack that NTLM is vulnerable to	
A host flooded by multiple SYN flood attacks	
An attack using HTML tags and JavaScript	
Taking control of someone's phone	
An attack for which there is no fix	

Practical 2—Drag and Drop—Certificates

Please place the answers against their description:

SAN—HSM—exchange keys—Wildcard—CSR—Bridge Trust
Model—CRL—pinning—OCSP—PGP—Base64 format—Diffie-Hellman—P12—public
CA—OID—key escrow—P7B—certificate template—`.pfx`—the faster it is but less
secure—`.cer`—CA—architect—stapling

Practical 2—drag and drop—certificates Put the correct answer against each item	
The CA used for b2b	
A certificate used on multiple servers with one domain	
Private key file extension	
Is my certificate valid?	
First part of encryption	
Public key file format	
A certificate used on servers in multiple domains	
Who signs the X509 certificates?	
Create new keys	
CRL is going slow, so we implement what?	
Private key format	
Prevent CA compromise	
X509 serial number	
Stores private keys	
PKI to PKI trust	
PEM	
Creates a secure tunnel	
Stores the keys for the key escrow	
Public key file format	
They build the CA and/or intermediary	
Web server bypassing CRL to go to OCSP	
Where is the X509 issuance policy held?	
What uses a web of trust?	
The smaller the key...	

Practical 3—Drag and Drop—Ports/Protocols

Please place the answers against their description:

636—21—443—389—UDP 161—22—5060 -53—989/990—5000—3389—UDP
162—1900—22—443 137-139—993—445—23 -110—142—80—25—995

Practical 3—drag and drop—ports/protocols Put the correct answer against each item	
Lightweight Directory Access Protocol (LDAP)	
Domain Naming System (DNS)	
Remote Desktop Protocol (RDP)	
Simple network management protocol	
Secure copy protocol	
Lightweight Directory Access Protocol Secure (LDAPS)	
File transfer protocol—passive	
FTPS	
Simple network management protocol—secure	
Secure shell	
Telnet	
IMAP 4	
POP 3 secure	
Simple Mail Transfer Protocol (SMTP)	
SIP	
Worm	
IMAP 4 secure	
Virus	
Ransomware	
NETBIOS	
TLS	
HTTP	
POP 3	
HTTPS	

Practical 4—Drag and Drop—Authentication Factors

Please place the answers against their description:

Palm reader—federation services—PIN—Gait—PSK—password—London—WPS—fingerprint—natural signature—smart card—birth date—Kerberos—token—retina—swipe—Iris—federation services

Practical 4—drag and drop—authentication factors—answers Put the correct answer against each item	
Somewhere you are	
Third-party to third-party authentication	
SAML—XML-based authentication	
Something you are	
Something you are	
Something you are	
Something you are	
Something you know	
Something you know	
Something you know	
Something you do	
Something you do	
Something you do	
Prevents replay attacks	
Wireless router password	
Wireless—no password	
Something you have	
Something you have	

Practical 5—Drag and Drop—General

Please place the answers against their description:

Stored procedure—SSO—disable account, reset password—screen locks—symmetric encryption—cable locks—2—office—standard naming convention—geotracking—protocol analyzer—banner grabbing—proximity card—on-boarding—3—group policy—input validation—double—single—strong passwords—cable locks—office—passwords—RFID—2—4

Practical 5—drag and drop—general—answers	
Put the correct answer against each item	
Captures a command on a network	
Where you keep a safe	
Authentication—provides most errors	
Web server information	
Identity type of computer in a report	
Prevents SQL injection	
Prevents SQL injection	
RAID 0—minimum disks	
Where you keep keys	
Configures multiple settings on computers	
RAID 6—parity	
Policy used for BYOD commencing	
Kerberos authentication	
Prevents laptops being stolen	
Authentication for an office	
RAID 5—minimum disks	
Encrypts large amounts of data	
RAID 5—parity	
Finds a mobile device	
A person leaves—what do you do with the account?	
Prevents a device from being stolen from a ship	
Makes mobile devices secure	
RAID 1—number of disks	2
Prevents tablets from being stolen	
Makes mobile devices secure	
RAID 6—minimum disks	

Drag and Drop—Answers

Practical 1—drag and drop—attacks—answer Put the correct answer against each item	
Target the CEO only	Whaling
Directed IP broadcast to the border router	Smurf
Holding the door open for someone else	Tailgating
Attack using port 5000	Worm
Interception attack in real time	Man-in-the-Middle
Interception attack—one-day delay	Replay attack
Stealing someone's cookie	Session Hijacking
Leaving a voicemail for the CEO	Vishing
Letting a fireman into your server room	Social Engineering—Urgency
Redirected to a fraudulent website	Pharming
An email to a group of people to get bank details	Spear Phishing
An email to one person to get bank details	Phishing
Letting someone you know access a secure area	Familiarity
Forcing someone to pay to recover their data	Ransomware
Sending login details back to an attacker	Remote Access Trojan
An attack using port 445	Ransomware
Triggered by an event or action	Logic Bomb
Set the PSH, Fin, and URG to 1	Christmas Tree Attack
An attack using port 1900	Virus
An attack that NTLM is vulnerable to	Pass-the-Hash
A host flooded by multiple SYN flood attacks	DDoS
An attack using HTML tags and JavaScript	XSS
Taking control of someone's phone	Bluejacking
An attack for which there is no fix	Zero-day virus

Practical 2—drag and drop—certificates—answers	
Put the correct answer against each item	
The CA used for b2b	Public CA
A certificate used on multiple servers with one domain	Wildcard
Private key file extension	`.pfx`
Is my certificate valid?	CRL
First part of encryption	Exchange keys
Public key file format	`.cer`
A certificate used on servers in multiple domains	SAN
Who signs the X509 certificates	CA
Create new keys	CSR
CRL going slow, implement what?	OCSP
Private key format	P12
Prevent CA compromise	Pinning
X509 serial number	OID
Stores private keys	Key escrow
PKI to PKI trust	Bridge Trust Model
PEM	Base 64 format
Creates a secure tunnel	Diffie—Hellman
Stores the keys for the key escrow	HSM
Public key file format	P7B
They build the CA and/or intermediary	Architect
Web server bypassing CRL to go to OCSP	Stapling
Where is the X509 issuance policy held?	Certificate Template
What uses a web of trust?	PGP
The smaller the key...	The faster but less secure the encryption

Practical 3—drag and drop—ports/protocols—answers	
Put the correct answer against each item	
Lightweight Directory Access Protocol (LDAP)	389
Domain Naming System (DNS)	53
Remote Desktop Protocol (**RDP**)	3389
Simple network management protocol	UDP 161
Secure copy protocol	22
Lightweight Directory Access Protocol Secure (LDAPS)	636
File transfer protocol—passive	21
FTPS	989/990
Simple network management protocol— secure	UDP 162
Secure shell	22
Telnet	23
IMAP 4	142
POP 3 secure	995
Simple Mail Transfer Protocol (SMTP)	25
SIP	5061
Worm	5000
IMAP 4 secure	993
Virus	1900
Ransomware	445
NETBIOS	137-139
TLS	443
HTTP	80
POP 3	110
HTTPS	443

Practical 4—drag and drop—authentication factors—answers	
Put the correct answer against each item	
Somewhere you are	London
Third-party to third-party authentication	Federation services
SAML—XML-based authentication	Federation services
Something you are	Palm reader
Something you are	Retina
Something you are	Iris
Something you know	Password
Something you know	PIN
Something you know	Birth Date
Something you do	Swipe
Something you do	Natural signature
Something you do	Gait
Prevents replay attacks	Kerberos
Wireless router password	PSK
Wireless—no password	WPS
Something you have	Token
Something you have	Smart Card

Practical 5—drag and drop—general—answers	
Put the correct answer against each item	
Captures the command on a network	Protocol analyzer
Where you keep a safe	Office
Authentication—provides most errors	Passwords
Web server information	Banner grabbing
Identity type of computer in a report	Standard naming convention
Prevent SQL injection	Input validation
Prevent SQL injection	Stored procedure
RAID 0—minimum disks	2
Where you keep keys	Office
Configures multiple settings on computers	Group policy
RAID 6— parity	Double
Policy used for BYOD commencing	Onboarding
Kerberos authentication	SSO
Prevent laptops from being stolen	Cable locks
Authentication for an office	Proximity card
RAID 5—minimum disks	3
Encrypts large amounts of data	Symmetric encryption
RAID 5—parity	Single
Finds a mobile device	Geolocation
A person leaves—what do you do with the account?	Disable account, reset password
Prevents a device from being stolen from a ship	RFID
Makes mobile devices secure	Strong passwords
RAID 1—number of disks	2
Prevents tablets being stolen	Cable locks
Makes mobile devices secure	Screen locks
RAID 6—minimum disks	4

Linux Information

Although Linux is not mentioned in the exam syllabus, the Security+ exam is vendor neutral and the following commands may help you determine what is being asked:

- **Admin accounts**: Root top level
- sudo: Admin
- su: Lower admin
- Kill : Stops applications
- Ls : List
- Grep : Search
- Pwd : Parent Working Directory
- Chmod : Changes permissions
- Mkdir: Make directory
- SetFACL : Used to set permissions on a given file
- Ifconfig: Equivalent of ipconfig
- IpTables: Firewall rules
- Chroot: Change root directory
- **Root directories**: /bin, /boot, /dev, /etc, /home, /mnt, /sbin, and /usr

Acronyms

Triple Digital Encryption Standard (3DES)

Authentication, Authorization, and Accounting (AAA)

Attribute-Based Access Control (ABAC)

Access Control List (ACL)

Advanced Encryption Standard (AES)

Authentication Header (AH)

Annualized Loss Expectancy (ALE)

Access Point (AP)

Application Programming Interface (API)

Advanced Persistent Threat (APT)

Annualized Rate of Occurrence (ARO)

Address Resolution Protocol (ARP)

Acceptable Use Policy (AUP)

Asset Value (AV)

Business Continuity Planning (BCP)

Business Impact Analysis (BIA)

Business Partners Agreement (BPA)

Bring Your Own Device (BYOD)

Certificate Authority (CA)

Common Access Card (CAC)

Cloud Access Security Broker (CASB)

Cipher Block Chaining (CBC)

Counter-Mode/CBC-Mac Protocol (CCMP)

Closed-circuit Television (CCTV)

Certificate (CER)

Cross-over Error Rate (CER)

Challenge Handshake Authentication Protocol (CHAP)

Chief Information Officer (CIO)

Computer Incident Response Team (CIRT)

Content Management System (CMS)

Continuity of Operations Plan (COOP)

Corporate Owned, Personally Enabled (COPE)

Contingency Planning (CP)

Certificate Revocation List (CRL)

Computer Security Incident Response Team (CSIRT)

Chief Security Officer (CSO)

Cloud Service Provider (CSP)

Certificate Signing Request (CSR)

Cross-Site Request Forgery (CSRF)

Chief Technology Officer (CTO)

Choose Your Own Device (CYOD)

Discretionary Access Control (DAC)

Distributed Denial of Service (DDoS)

Data Execution Prevention (DEP)

Distinguished Encoding Rules (DER)

Digital Encryption Standard (DES)

Dynamic Host Configuration Protocol (DHCP)

Diffie—Hellman (DH)

Diffie—Hellman Ephemeral (DHE)

Dynamic Link Library (DLL)

Data Loss Prevention (DLP)

Demilitarized Zone (DMZ)

Domain Name Service (Server) (DNS)

Denial of Service (DoS)

Disaster Recovery Plan (DRP)

Extensible Authentication Protocol (EAP)

Electronic Code Book (ECB)

Elliptic Curve Cryptography (ECC)

Elliptic Curve Diffie—Hellman Ephemeral (ECDHE)

Encrypted File System (EFS)

Electromagnetic Interference (EMI)

Electro-Magnetic Pulse (EMP)

Encapsulated Security Payload (ESP)

End User License Agreement (EULA)

File System Access Control List (FACL)

False Acceptance Rate (FAR)

Full Disk Encryption (FDE)

False Rejection Rate (FRR)

File Transfer Protocol (FTP)

Secured File Transfer Protocol (FTPS)

Galois Counter Mode (GCM)

Gnu Privacy Guard (GPG)

Group Policy Object (GPO)

Global Positioning System (GPS)

High Availability (HA)

Hard Disk Drive (HDD)

Host-based Intrusion Detection System (HIDS)

Host-based Intrusion Prevention System (HIPS)

Hashed Message Authentication Code (HMAC)

HMAC-based One-Time Password (HOTP)

Hardware Security Module (HSM)

Infrastructure-as-a-Service (IaaS)

Internet Control Message Protocol (ICMP)

Intrusion Detection System (IDS)

Institute of Electrical and Electronic Engineers (IEEE)

Internet Information System (IIS)

Internet Key Exchange (IKE)

Instant Messaging (IM)

Internet Message Access Protocol v4 (IMAP4)

Internet of Things (IoT)

Internet Protocol (IP)

Internet Protocol Security (IPSec)

Incident Response (IR)

Incident Response Plan (IRP)

Interconnection Security Agreement (ISA)

Internet Service Provider (ISP)

Information Systems Security Officer (ISSO)

Initialization Vector (IV)

Layer 2 Tunneling Protocol (L2TP)

Local Area Network (LAN)

Lightweight Directory Access Protocol (LDAP)

Lightweight Extensible Authentication Protocol (LEAP)

Monitoring-as-a-Service (MaaS)

Mandatory Access Control (MAC)

Media Access Control (MAC)

Master Boot Record (MBR)

Message Digest 5 (MD5)

Mobile Device Management (MDM)

Multi-Factor Authentication (MFA)

Multi-Function Device (MFD)

Multipurpose Internet Mail Exchange (MIME)

Man-in-the-Middle (MITM)

Multimedia Message Service (MMS)

Memorandum of Agreement (MOA)

Memorandum of Understanding (MOU)

Microsoft Challenge Handshake Authentication Protocol (MSCHAP)

Mean Time Between Failures (MTBF)

Mean Time to Failure (MTTF)

Mean Time to Recover or Mean Time to Repair (MTTR)

Network Access Control (NAC)

Network Address Translation (NAT)

Non-Disclosure Agreement (NDA)

Near Field Communication (NFC)

Network-based Intrusion Detection System (NIDS)

Network-based Intrusion Prevention System (NIPS)

New Technology File System (NTFS)

New Technology LAN Manager (NTLM)

Network Time Protocol (NTP)

Open Authorization (OAUTH)

Online Certificate Status Protocol (OCSP)

Object Identifier (OID)

Operating System (OS)

Peer to Peer (P2P)

Platform as a Service (PaaS)

Password Authentication Protocol (PAP)

Port Address Translation (PAT)

Password-based Key Derivation Function 2 (PBKDF2)

Protected Extensible Authentication Protocol (PEAP)

Privacy-enhanced Electronic Mail (PEM)

Perfect Forward Secrecy (PFS)

Personal Exchange Format (PFX)

Pretty Good Privacy (PGP)

Personal Health Information (PHI)

Personally Identifiable Information (PII)

Personal Identity Verification (PIV)

Public Key Infrastructure (PKI)

Padding Oracle on Downgrade Legacy Encryption (POODLE)

Post Office Protocol (POP)

Pre-Shared Key (PSK)

Recovery Agent (RA)

Registration Authority (RA)

Remote Authentication Dial-in User Server (RADIUS)

Redundant Array of Inexpensive Disks (RAID)

Remote Access Server (RAS)

Remote Access Trojan (RAT)

Role-based Access Control (RBAC)

Rule-based Access Control (RBAC)

Rivest Cipher version 4 (RC4)

Remote Desktop Protocol (RDP)

Representational State Transfer (REST)

Radio Frequency Identifier (RFID)

RACE Integrity Primitives Evaluation Message Digest (RIPEMD)

Return on Investment (ROI)

Risk Management Framework (RMF)

Recovery Point Objective (RPO)

Rivest, Shamir, and Adleman (RSA)

Recovery Time Objective (RTO)

Real-Time Operating System (RTOS)

Real-time Transport Protocol (RTP)

Secure/Multipurpose Internet Mail Extensions (S/MIME)

Software-as-a-Service (SaaS)

Security Assertions Markup Language (SAML)

Storage Area Network (SAN)

Subject Alternative Name (SAN)

System Control and Data Acquisition (SCADA)

Security Content Automation Protocol (SCAP)

Simple Certificate Enrollment Protocol (SCEP)

Secure Copy (SCP)

Small Computer System Interface (SCSI)

Software Development Kit (SDK)

Self-Encrypting Drive (SED)

Structured Exception Handler (SEH)

Secured File Transfer Protocol (SFTP)

Secure Hashing Algorithm (SHA)

Security Information and Event Management (SIEM)

Subscriber Identity Module (SIM)

Session Initiation Protocol (SIP)

Session Initiation Protocol Secure (SIPS)

Service Level Agreement (SLA)

Single Loss Expectancy (SLE)

Server Message Block (SMB)

Short Message Service (SMS)

Simple Mail Transfer Protocol (SMTP)

Simple Mail Transfer Protocol Secure (SMTPS)

Simple Network Management Protocol (SNMP)

System on Chip (SoC)

Sender Policy Framework (SPF)

Spam over Internet Messaging (SPIM)

Single Point of Failure (SPoF)

Structured Query Language (SQL)

Secure Real-Time Protocol (SRTP)

Solid State Drive (SSD)

Secure Shell (SSH)

Service Set Identifier (SSID)

Secure Sockets Layer (SSL)

Single Sign-on (SSO)

Terminal Access Controller Access Control System Plus (TACACS+)

Transmission Control Protocol/Internet Protocol (TCP/IP)

Ticket Granting Ticket (TGT)

Temporal Key Integrity Protocol (TKIP)

Transport Layer Security (TLS)

Time-based One-Time Password (TOTP)

Trusted Platform Module (TPM)

User Acceptance Testing (UAT)

Unmanned Aerial Vehicle (UAV)

User Datagram Protocol (UDP)

Unified Extensible Firmware Interface (UEFI)

Uniform Resource Identifier (URI)

Universal Resource Locator (URL)

Universal Serial Bus (USB)

OTG USB On The Go (USB OTG)

Unified Threat Management (UTM)

Unshielded Twisted Pair (UTP)

Virtual Desktop Environment (VDE)

Virtual Desktop Infrastructure (VDI)

Virtual Local Area Network (VLAN)

Virtual Machine (VM)

Voice Over IP (VoIP)

Virtual Private Network (VPN)

Video Teleconferencing (VTC)

Web Application Firewall (WAF)

Wireless Access Point (WAP)

Wired Equivalent Privacy (WEP)

Wireless Intrusion Prevention System (WIPS)

Write Once Read Many (WORM)

Wi-Fi Protected Access (WPA)

Wi-Fi Protected Access 2 (WPA2)

Wi-Fi Protected Setup (WPS)

Exclusive Or (XOR)

Cross-Site Request Forgery (XSRF)

Cross-Site Scripting (XSS)

Assessment

Mock Exam 1

1. What type of attack is a padding oracle on downgraded legacy encryption attack? Choose two from the following list:

   A. IV attack

   B. Replay attack

   C. Man-in-the-middle attack

   D. TLS 1.0 with electronic code book

   E. SSL 3.0 with chain block cipher

   Answer: C and E

   Concept: A Poodle attack is a man-in-the-middle attack that exploits a downgraded browser using SSL 3.0 with CBC.

2. You are the security administrator for the British Secret Service. What type of access method will you use for secret and top-secret data?

   A. DAC, with the owner of the data giving access

   B. DAC, with the custodian of the data giving access

   C. DAC, with the security administrator giving access

   D. MAC, with the security administrator giving access

   Answer: D

   Concept: MAC is used as the access method for classified data and the security administrator is responsible for giving users access to the data once the person has been vetted and access is justified.

3. Your company wants to encrypt the DNS traffic by using DNSSEC. Once you have signed the zone, what records are created for each host?

    A. CNAME

    B. AAAA

    C. RRSIG

    D. MX

    E. PTR

    Answer: C

    Concept: DNSSEC creates DNSKEY and RRSIG records.

    Wrong answers:

    A. CNAME is an alias

    B. AAAA is a host record for IP version 6

    D. An MX record is for a mail server

    E. PTR records are created in the reverse lookup zone

4. You are a security administrator and a user called Ben is having a discussion with one of his colleagues. They have four choices for two-factor authentication. They have asked for your advice on which of the following involves two-factor authentication. Select the best answer:

    A. Smart card

    B. Password and PIN

    C. Passphrase and username

    D. Retina and fingerprint scan

Answer: A

Concept: Two-factor authentication entails using two different groups of something you have, something you know, something you are, or somewhere you are. A smart card is something you have, but needs a PIN, which is something you know.

Wrong answers:

B. Both are something you know

C. Both are something you know

D. Both are something you are

5. Two separate CAs need to work together on a joint venture; what can they implement so that certificates can be used for cross-certification?

A. Bridge trust model

B. Certificate pinning

C. Certificate stapling

D. Wildcard certificates

Answer: A

Concept: A bridge trust model is used where two root CAs are used to set up cross-certification.

Wrong answers:

B. Pinning prevents someone hacking the CA and issuing fraudulent certificates

C. Stapling is used by a web server that bypasses the CRL and use the OCSP for faster validation

D. Wildcard certificates can be used by multiple servers in the same domain

6. John goes to a sports website and gets the following error:

   `THIS WEBSITE CANNOT BE TRUSTED.`

   What two actions does the website administrator need to take to resolve this error?

   A. Ask the key escrow to store his private key

   B. Ensure that the website uses a valid SAN certificate

   C. Update the root certificate into the client computer's trusted root certificate authorities store

   D. Verify whether the certificate on the server has expired

   Answer: C and D

   Concept: A certificate needs to be valid and trusted by the computer.

   Wrong answers:

   A. The key escrow only stores private keys

   B. A SAN certificate can be used across multiple domains

7. A security administrator discovers that an attacker used a compromised host as a platform for launching attacks deeper into a company's network. What terminology best describes the use of the compromised host?

   A. Brute force

   B. Active reconnaissance

   C. Pivoting

   D. Passing point

   Answer: C

   Concept: Pivoting involves using a weak host to launch an attack further into the network.

Wrong answers:

    A. Brute force is a password attack

    B. Active reconnaissance is a penetration attack method

    D. Passing point does not exist; it just sounds good—a red herring

8. Mary is managing the company's wireless network, which will use WPA2-PSK. What encryption is most likely to be used?

    A. SHA-1

    B. AES

    C. MD5

    D. DES

Answer: B

Concept: The encryption that WPA2 is most likely to use is AES.

Wrong answers:

    A. SHA-1 is used for hashing

    C. MD5 is also used for hashing

    D. DES is not used by wireless technology

9. Who is responsible for setting permissions when using a **Mandatory Access Control (MAC)** model?

    A. The owner

    B. The manager

    C. The administrator

    D. The user

Answer: C

Concept: MAC gives access to data based on the file classification (for example, top secret); the security administrator sets permissions.

Wrong answers:

A. Owners can give access using the DAC model, but once a classified document is written, it has no owner, and it is controlled centrally

B. Managers cannot grant any permissions to data

D. A user cannot grant access to any data

10. Company A is due to upgrade all of its IT systems and has been investigating moving to the cloud as there is no capital expenditure, since the CSP provides the hardware. Company A would still like to control the IT systems in the cloud. Which cloud model would best serve Company A's needs?

    A. **Software as a Service (SaaS)**

    B. **Infrastructure as a Service (IaaS)**

    C. **Monitoring as a Service (MaaS)**

    D. **Platform as a Service (PaaS)**

    Answer: B

    Concept: IaaS provides the bare metal hardware. Then you need to install the software, configure it, and patch it.

    Wrong answers:

    A. SaaS is where you lease a bespoke software package that is accessed through a web browser

    C. MaaS is where someone monitors your network or applications for you

    D. PaaS is a development platform in the cloud

11. You are a security administrator, and the IT director has tasked you with collecting the volatile memory on Server 1 as it is currently under a cyber attack. Which of the following are the two best forms of volatile memory to collect?

    A. Secure boot

    B. Swap/page file

    C. USB flash drive

D. ROM

E. RAM

Answers: B and E

Concept: Always collect the volatile evidence before stopping a cyber attack in order to detect the source. Volatile memory evaporates if the power is switched off. RAM is volatile and the swap/page file is where applications run when RAM is full.

Wrong answers:

A. Secure boot checks that all drivers are signed on boot up

C. USB flash drives are non-volatile

D. ROM is non-volatile

12. Bill and Ben, the flowerpot men, are now going to encrypt data using asymmetric encryption, which uses public and private keys. What is the first step they need to take?

A. Exchange public keys

B. Exchange private keys

C. Exchange digital signatures

D. Exchange telephone numbers

Answer: A

Concept: The first stage in any encryption is key exchange, where you send your public key to someone else.

Wrong answers:

B. You should never give your private key away

C. You digitally sign the document and email using your private key to provide non-repudiation and integrity; they are never exchanged

D. Exchanging telephone numbers is just a red herring

13. At what stage of the SDLC are computer systems no longer supported by the original vendor?

    A. Sandboxing

    B. End-of-life systems

    C. Resource exhaustion

    D. System sprawl

    Answer: B

    Concept: End-of-life systems are no longer operational or supported by the vendor.

    Wrong answers:

    A. Sandboxing is the isolation of an application for testing, patching, or isolation, as it is dangerous

    C. Resource exhaustion is where a system has run out of resources

    D. System sprawl is where a system is overutilizing resources and is heading toward resource exhaustion

14. Company A has just developed a bespoke system for booking airline tickets. What is it called if a freelance coding specialist tests it for security flaws?

    A. Code review

    B. Static code review

    C. Regression testing

    D. Dynamic code review

    Answer: C

    Concept: Regression testing is part of program development, and in larger companies is done by code-testing specialists.

Wrong answers:

A. Code review is carried out on a regular basis to identify dead code

B. Static code review is done when the code is not being used

D. Dynamic code review is done when the code is running

15. You are the security administrator for a company that has just replaced two file servers. Which of the following is the best solution for disposing of hard drives that used to store top secret data?

A. Hashing

B. Degaussing

C. Low-level formatting

D. Shredding

Answer: D

Concept: You can shred a whole hard drive down until it looks like powder—let someone try to put that back together again.

Wrong answers:

A. Hashing does not destroy data; it merely says where integrity is intact

B. Degaussing should dispose of the data, but the better solution would be to totally destroy the hard drive itself

C. Low-level formatting replaces the tracks and sectors, but is not as effective as shredding

16. You are the security administrator for an airline company whose systems suffered a loss of availability last month. Which of the following attacks would most likely affect the availability of your IT systems?

A. Spear phishing

B. Replay

C. MITM

D. DoS

Answer: D

Concept: DDoS and DoS attack the availability of IT systems, as they both aim to take them down.

Wrong answers:

A. Spear phishing is an email scam targeted at a group of people

B. Replay is an MITM attack that replays messages between two entities at a later date

C. MITM intercepts conversations between two entities, making them believe that they are talking to each other when they are actually talking to the attacker

17. You are a network administrator setting up a L2TP/IPSec VPN tunnel, as your company needs to move a large amount of encrypted data between the branch office and the head office. Why is Diffie-Hellman used for the IKE phase before the data is forwarded via symmetric encryption?

   A. It is a symmetric encryption technique that protects keys

   B. It is a hashing technique that protects keys

   C It is an ephemeral technique that protect keys

   D. It is an asymmetric technique that protects keys, but sets up a secure channel

Answer: D

Concept: Diffie-Hellman is asymmetric and has both a private and public key pair. Its role is not encryption but the creation of a secure tunnel for symmetric data to flow through and protect the only key from being stolen.

Wrong answers:

> A. Diffie-Hellman has two keys, while symmetric encryption has only one key
>
> B. Hashing provides integrity of data, but you can still read it, so it doesn't actually protect it
>
> C. Ephemeral techniques use short-lived, one-session-only keys

18. You are a lecturer at a college and you need to deliver a session on salting passwords. What are the two main reasons you would salt passwords?

    A. To prevent brute-force attacks

    B. To make access to the password slower

    C. To prevent duplicate passwords from being stored

    D. To stop simple passwords from being used

    Answer: A and C

    Concept: Salting passwords adds a random number to the password, making it longer in order to prevent brute-force attacks. This will prevent duplicate passwords, as each salt is different, and therefore each password will be unique as each will have a unique salt.

    Wrong answers:

    > B. This is probably true, but is not a main reason. We don't salt for speed—we salt to protect the password
    >
    > D. Salting cannot prevent someone from using `12345678` as their password; that would be password complexity

19. Which of the following methods of authentication is known as two-factor authentication?

    A. PIN and passphrase

    B. Mastercard and PIN

    C. Username and password

    D. Retina and facial recognition

Answer: B

Concept: Two-factor authentication involves using two separate instances of something you have, something you know, something you are, or somewhere you are. A card is something you have and a PIN is something you know.

Wrong answers:

A. Both are something you know

C. Both are something you know

D. Both are something you are

20. During a forensic investigation, the judge has decreed that any data that is investigated should remain in its original form of integrity. Which of the following is used for the integrity of data? Choose two:

A. MD5

B. AES

C. SHA 1

D. DES

Answer: A and C

Concept: Hashing is used to provide integrity of data; MD5 and SHA1 are two forms of hashing.

Wrong answers:

B. AES is used for encryption

D. DES is used for encryption

21. Company A has suffered a DDoS attack, and the company has decided that their RPO should be set at four hours. The directors are holding a board meeting to discuss the progress that is being made. During this meeting, the IT manager has mentioned the **RTO**, and the CEO looks confused. How can you explain the meaning of the RTO to the CEO?

    A. Acceptable downtime

    B. Return to operational state

    C. Measure of reliability

    D. Average time to repair

    Answer: B

    Concept: The RTO means that the system updates are running. This can also be known as the return to operational state.

    Wrong answers:

    A. Acceptable downtime is another way of saying recovery point objective

    C. A measure of reliability would be the **Mean Time Between Failures (MTBF)**

    D. Average time to repair is the same as the MTTR

22. The following is a list of different controls. Which of these are physical security controls?

    A. Change management

    B. Antivirus software

    C. Cable locks

    D. Firewall rule

    F. Iris scanner

Answers: C and F

Concept: You can touch physical security controls; therefore, cable locks are physical and the iris scanner is a physical device for biometric authentication.

Wrong answers:

A. Change management is an administrative control

B. Antivirus is a technical control

D. Firewall rules are technical controls

23. The security team has identified an unknown vulnerability and isolated it. What technique is best for investigating and testing it?

A. Steganography

B. Fuzzing

C. Sandboxing

D. Containerization

Answer: C

Concept: Sandboxing is where we put an application in an isolated virtual machine to test patches, or maybe just because the application is too dangerous to run on our network.

Wrong answers:

A. Steganography involves hiding a file, image, audio file, or video file inside another file, image, audio file, or video file

B. Fuzzing is a technique for inserting random data inside an application to test for vulnerabilities

D. Containerization is where data is isolated in a mobile phone to separate business data from personal data, such as pictures of family and friends

24. What is it called when a user has exploited an IT system so that they have obtained access to all files on the file server?

    A. Remote exploit

    B. Zero-day exploit

    C. Privilege escalation

    D. Pivoting

    Answer: C

    Concept: Privilege escalation is where a normal user has obtained admin rights to access resources they should not normally be allowed to access.

    Wrong answers:

    A. A remote exploit scans a network for vulnerabilities and then attacks it

    B. A zero-day exploit is where an exploit has just been discovered (on day zero), but there is not going to be a patch for it for maybe another 2-3 days

    D. Pivoting involves accessing a machine inside a network from which you can launch a second attack

25. You are the security administrator for your company, and the IT manager has asked you to brief them on XML authentication methods. Which of the following should you tell them uses XML-based authentication? Select all that apply:

    A. TOTP

    B. Federation services

    C. Smart card

    D. SSO

    E. SOAP

    F. SAML

Answer: A, B, and F

Concept: SAML is an XML-based types of authentication used in federation services; TOTP is also XML-based.

Wrong answers:

C. A smart card uses X509 and a PIN for authentication

D. SSO means you sign in once and then gain access to all resources without putting your credentials in again

E. SOAP messages are used in SAML

26. There are a group of certificates in a folder and you need to identify which certificate uses the **Privacy-Enhanced Mail (PEM)** format. Which of the following is the best choice to make?

A. PFX

B. CER

C. Base64

D. P12

Answer: C

Concept: PEM uses Base64 format.

Wrong answers:

A. This is a private certificate

B. This is a public certificate

D. This is a private certificate

27. Three different companies want to develop an application where they will share the cost of developing resources and future running costs. Which cloud model best describes this?

A. Public cloud

B. SaaS

C. Private cloud

D. PaaS

E. IaaS

F. Community cloud

Answer: F

Concept: Community clouds involve companies from the same industry developing their own cloud that they can then share resources on.

Wrong answers:

A. A public cloud is multitenant, and the tenants never share resources

B. SaaS is where a bespoke application is leased by different people

C. A private cloud is single tenant. They don't share with anyone

D. PaaS refers to a development platform, such as Azure

E. IaaS refers to leasing hardware

28. What type of key does a key escrow manage?

A. Public

B. Session

C. Shared

D. Private

Answer: D

Concept: The key escrow stores private keys for third parties.

Wrong answers:

A. The public key is used for encryption; it is always given away, but never stored

B. The session key is used for communication between two hosts

C. The shared key is used for symmetric encryption

29. Which of the following is an email-based attack on all members of the sales team?

    A. Phishing

    B. Vishing

    C. Spear phishing

    D. Pharming

    Answer: C

    Concept: Spear phishing is an attack on a group of users.

    Exam tip: Whereas the plural of spear phishing is spear phishing, the singular can be phishing.

    Wrong answers:

        A. Phishing is an email attack against one person

        B. A vishing attack is launched by using a telephone or leaving a voicemail

        D. A pharming attack involves redirecting

30. An attacker tries to target a high-level executive, but has to leave a voicemail as he did not answer the telephone. What was the intended attack, and what attack was eventually used? Select all that apply:

    A. Whaling

    B. Vishing

    C. Phishing

    D. Spear phishing

    Answer: B

    Concept: Vishing involves targeting a victim using a telephone or leaving a telephone message.

Wrong answers:

A. This is not whaling, as the medium of attack was a telephone—don't be tricked

C and D. Phishing and spear phishing are email attacks

31. The auditor has been investigating money being stolen from a charity, and they have discovered that the finance assistant has been embezzling money, as he was the only person who dealt with finance, receiving donations and paying all of the bills. Which of the following is the best option that the auditor should recommend to reduce the risk of this happening again?

    A. Hashing

    B. Job rotation

    C. Separation of duties

    D. Mandatory vacations

    E. Encryption

    Answer: C

    Concept: Separation of duties prevents one person from authorizing the whole transaction, and also prevents fraud. The CA signs the X509 certificates.

    Wrong answers:

    A. Hashing ensures that data has not been tampered with, thus providing integrity

    B. Job rotation prevents fraud; however, a charity may only have one person working in finance

    D. Mandatory vacations prevent fraud, but require someone else who can deal with finance work

    E. Encrypting data protects data, but has nothing to do with financial transactions

32. You are a security administrator and you have now moved departments. You are now working with the certificate authority and training Mary, who is a new intern. Mary has asked you what the certificate **Object Identifier** (**OID**) consists of. What should you tell her?

    A. Certificate signing request

    B. Certificate pinning

    C. Certificate stapling

    D. Certificate serial number

    Answer: D

    Concept: The OID identifies the X509 itself. It is similar to a serial number; each X509 has a different OID.

    Wrong answers:

    A. A CSR is a request for a new certificate

    B. Pinning prevents the compromise of the CA and the issuing of certificates

    C. Stapling is where a web server goes directly to the OCSP for faster authentication, bypassing the CRL

33. You are the operational manager for a multinational corporation and you are writing a policy in which you mention the RPO. Which of the following is the CLOSEST definition to a RPO?

    A. Acceptable downtime

    B. Return to operational state

    C. A measure of the system reliability

    D. Average time to repair

    Answer: A

    Concept: The RPO is the amount of downtime your system can have without having access to its data.

Wrong answers:

B. The return to operational state is the RTO

C. The mean time between failures is a measure of the system's reliability

D. The mean time to repair is the average time to repair

34. You are carrying out annual training for your company and need to put a PowerPoint slide together for the symptoms of a backdoor virus. Which three points will you include in the slide? Each provides part of the explanation of a backdoor virus:

A. Programs will not open at all, even though you click many times

B. You must click on several items

C. Can be included in an email attachment

D. Files open quicker than before

E. You can only get infected through a link on a web page

Answers: A, B, and C

Concept: Backdoor viruses can come in through email. They cannot install themselves; this is done by the users unwittingly installing a program. Once installed, the virus may prevent your programs from running.

35. You are a security administrator and need to set up a new wireless access point so that it is not backward compatible with legacy systems, as these may be vulnerable to attack, and it must be the strongest encryption that you can use. Which is the BEST solution that meets your needs?

A. WPA2 PSK

B. WPA TKIP

C. WPA2 TKIP

D. WPA2 CCMP

Answer: D

Concept: WPA2 CCMP uses AES, which is the strongest wireless encryption and is not backward compatible.

Wrong answers:

A. WPA2 PSK is for home users, where the wireless router password is used to connect to the wireless network

B. WPA TKIP is backward compatible

C. WPA2 TKIP is the strongest backward compatible

36. Which of the following commands can be used to create a buffer-overflow? Choose all that apply:

    A. `var char`

    B. `strcpy`

    C. `var data`

    D. `strcat`

    Answers: B and D

    Concept: `strcpy` and `strcat` are used to copy and concatenate strings to a char array, and both can cause buffer-overflow, depending on the number of characters allowed.

    Wrong answers:

    A. `var char` sets the variable length of characters

    C. `var data` sets the data type to be used in Java

37. James has raised a ticket with the IT help desk. He had been tampering with the settings on his computer and he can no longer access the internet. The help desk technicians have checked the configuration on his desktop and the settings are the same as everyone else's. Suddenly, three other people have also reported that they also cannot connect to the internet. Which network device should be checked first?

    A. Switch

B. Router

C. Hub

D. Repeater

Answer: B

Concept: A router gives you access to the internet; on a computer, it is known as the default gateway.

Wrong answers:

A. A switch joins resources on an internal network

C. A hub is an internal device that is slower than a switch, as it broadcasts traffic

D. A repeater is a device that extends cables beyond their length

38. Which of the following is a secure wireless protocol that uses TLS?

A. NTLM

B. PAP

C. EAP

D. AES

Answer: C

Concept: EAP-TLS is used for wireless encryption.

Wrong answers:

A. NTLM is a legacy Windows protocol

B. PAP stores passwords in clear text

D. AES involves symmetric encryption and is commonly used with L2TP/IPSec

39. You are the security administrator for a multinational corporation, and the development team have asked for your advice on how to prevent SQL-injection, integer-overflow, and buffer-overflow attacks. Which of the following should you advise them to use?

    A. Input validation

    B. A host-based firewall with advanced security

    C. `strcpy`

    D. Hashing

    Answer: A

    Concept: Input validation controls the format and characters of data input and will prevent SQL-injection, buffer-overflow, and integer-overflow attacks.

    Wrong answers:

    B. A host-based firewall protects a desktop or laptop from attack

    C. `strcpy` can cause buffer overflow if the string of data is larger than the maximum number of characters used in a data field

    D. Hashing only confirms data integrity; it has no control over the input used

40. Your company is opening up a new data center in Galway, Ireland. A server farm has been installed there and now a construction company have come in to put a six-foot mantrap in the entrance. What are the two main reasons why this mantrap has been installed?

    A. To prevent theft

    B. To prevent tailgating

    C. To prevent unauthorized personnel gaining access to the data center

    D. To allow faster access to the facility

    Answer: B and C

    Concept: A mantrap provides a safe and controlled environment in the data center as it allows you to control access.

Wrong answers:

> A. Although this will be prevented, it is not the main reason; a mantrap's main purpose is to stop or control people
>
> D. A mantrap will slow access to the data center

41. Which of the following devices can prevent unauthorized access to the network and prevent attacks from unknown sources?

    A. Router

    B. Load balancer

    C. Web security gateway

    D. UTM

    Answer: D

    Concept: A UTM is a firewall that can prevent unauthorized network access. It can also perform URL filtering, content filtering, and malware inspection.

    Wrong answers:

    > A. A router can prevent access to the network based on the port, protocol, or IP address
    >
    > B. A load balancer controls the volume of web traffic coming into your web server
    >
    > C. A web security gateway prevents attacks on web servers

42. **Internet of Things** (**IoT**) is a concept that has recently taken off. Can you identify which of the following devices fall under this category? Select all that apply:

    A. ATM

    B. Banking system

    C. Smart TV

    D. Refrigerator

    E. Router

    F. Wearable technology

Answer: A, C, D, and F

Concept: IoT involves small devices such as household appliances, wearable technology, and ATMs.

Wrong answers:

B. A banking system is not a small device; it is an IT system

E. A router is used to route packets and join networks together

43. Which feature of DNS will help balance a load without needing to install a network load balancer, or, when coupled with a load balancer, makes it more dynamic?

A. DNS CNAME

B. DNSSEC

C. DNS round robin

D. DNS SRV records

Answer: C

Concept: A DNS round robin is a redundancy used by DNS to ensure that a server is always available, even when it suffers from hardware failure. If you have three records for a web server, it will go from the first to the second to the third record and rotate back to the first again.

Wrong answers:

A. A CNAME is an alias; a shortened name for a host with an extremely long hostname

B. DNSSEC creates RRSIG records as it encrypts DNS traffic with TLS

D. SRV records help you find services such as domain controllers or global catalog servers

44. What is the benefit of certificate pinning?

A. It prevents a certificate signing request from a non-administrator

B. It is used by a web server, and it bypasses the CRL for faster authentication

C. It stops people from spoofing, issuing certificates, or compromising your CA

D. It is used for cross certification between two separate root CAs

Answer: C

Concept: Certificate pinning prevents people from compromising your CA and issuing fraudulent certificates.

Wrong answers:

    A. A non-administrator can submit a CSR to obtain a new certificate

    B. This is known as certificate stapling

    D. This is known as a bridge trust model or a trust model

45. An auditor has just finished a risk assessment of the company, and he has recommended that we need to mitigate some of our risks. Which of the following are examples of risk mitigation?

    A. Turning off host-based firewalls on laptops

    B. Installing antivirus software on a new laptop

    C. Insuring your car against fire and theft

    D. Outsourcing your IT to another company

    E. Deciding not to jump into the Grand Canyon

Answer: B

Concept: Risk mitigation involves reducing the risk of an attack or event. These are basically technical controls.

Wrong answers:

    A. This increases the risk, as it leaves your laptop vulnerable to attack

    C. This is risk transference

    D. This also is risk transference

    E. This is risk avoidance, as it is deemed too risky

46. A security engineer wants to implement a site-to-site VPN that will require SSL certificates for mutual authentication. Which of the following will you choose?

    A. L2TP/IPSec

    B. SSL VPN

    C. PPTP VPN

    D. IKEv2 VPN

    Answer: B

    Concept: SSL VPN is legacy that uses SSL certificates. SSL has been replaced by TLS as it is more secure.

47. You are the Active Directory administrator and you have been training new interns on the Kerberos ticket granting session. One of the interns has asked about the relationship between a service ticket and session ticket used by Kerberos authentication. Which of the following is the best description?

    A. The user exchanges their service ticket with the server's session ticket for mutual authentication and single sign on

    B. The service key is unencrypted and is matched with the value in the session ticket

    C. The user shows the server their session ticket and the server sends him a service ticket

    D. The user shows the server their service ticket and the server sends him a session ticket to keep

    Answer: A

    Concept: Kerberos uses tickets for authentication, mutual authentication, and **Single Sign On (SSO)**. Service and session tickets are exchanged for mutual authentication. The service ticket is encrypted.

48. Your company has a guest wireless network that can be used by visitors during the day, the sales staff in the evening, and the customer service staff at lunchtime.

They set up a captive portal that fulfills the following criteria:

- Guests do not need to authenticate
- Sales staff do not need to insert any credentials
- Customer service staff must use the highest level of encryption

How will you set up your captive portal? Select three answers; each answer provides part of the solution:

A. WEP 40-bit key

B. WPA2 TKIP

C. WPA-TKIP

D. Open-system authentication

E. WPA2 CCMP

F. WPS

Answer: D, E, and F

Concept: We use open-system authentication for the guest network as it requires no authentication. WPS is used for sales staff as they just need to push a button. Customer-services staff use WPA2 CCMP as it uses AES and is the highest level of WPA.

Wrong answers:

A. WEP should not be used as it is too weak

B. WPA2 TKIP is used for backward compatibility, and is not as strong as WPA2 CCMP

C. A weaker version of B

49. You are a security administrator, and the IT team has been using RSA for the encryption of all of their data, but has found that it is very slow. Which of the following should the security administrator recommend to improve the speed of encryption?

A. Asymmetric encryption using DES

B. Asymmetric encryption using Diffie-Helman

C. Symmetric encryption

D. Running a vulnerability scan to find a better solution

Answer: C

Concept: Symmetric data is used to encrypt large amounts of data.

Wrong answers:

A. Totally wrong as DES is not asymmetric

B. Diffie-Hellman does not encrypt; it only creates a secure channel

D. Vulnerability scans are for missing patches, not encryption

50. Robert, who is an intern, has been assigned to the security team. A user has called him to ask who signs the X509 certificates. Which one of the following should Robert give as an answer?

A. CRL

B. Key escrow

C. CSR

D. CA

Answer: D

Concept: The CA signs the X509 certificates.

Wrong answers:

A. The CRL checks the certificate validity

B. The key escrow stores private keys for third parties

C. The CSR is the process of requesting a new certificate

Mock Exam 2

1. You are the security administrator for a large multinational corporation, and you have used a black box penetration tester to find vulnerabilities in your company and exploit them as far you can. During the penetration test, it was found that there were some vulnerabilities in your Windows 10 desktop operating system. There were no vulnerabilities in any of your Linux or Unix systems. Which of the following best describes why the penetration tester was successful with the Windows 10 machines, but not with the Linux or Unix machines?

   A. Linux and Unix are more secure than Windows 10

   B. The penetration tester did not attempt to exploit the Linux/Unix machines

   C. The Linux and Unix operating systems never have any vulnerabilities

   D. The operating systems' attack vectors are very different

   Answer: D

   Concept: Different operating systems have different structures, so the attack vectors and the paths taken to attack them are different.

   Wrong answers:

   A. Not a proven fact—red herring

   B. The penetration tests did attempt the exploit—that is why they had negative results

   C. All operating systems suffer from vulnerabilities at one time or another

2. You are a security administrator and you wish to implement an encrypted method of authentication for your wireless network. Which of the following protocols is the most secure for your wireless network?

   A. PAP

   B. WPA2-PSK

   C. EAP-TLS

   D. PEAP

Answer: C

Concept: EAP-TLS is a secure wireless authentication protocol, as it uses certificates. It is the most secure EAP standard.

Wrong answers:

A. PAP shows the passwords in clear text and is used by VPN, not wireless networks

B. WPA2-PSK uses a wireless router password; therefore, it is not secure

D. PEAP encrypts EAP packets for secure wireless authentication, but it is not as secure as EAP-TLS

3. You are designing the network topology for a new company that is rapidly expanding from a one-premises company with 20 users to a medium-sized company with 300 users. The company tells you that it was subject to a DDoS attack last year that took the company down for over a day. In your network design, they don't want to implement a DMZ; therefore, the traffic will be coming directly from the internet. How do you propose to best mitigate against future DDoS attacks? Select two answers from the following list; each forms part of the solution:

A. Install a stateless firewall on the edge of your network to prevent incoming traffic

B. Install a stateful firewall on the edge of your network to prevent incoming traffic

C. Install an NIDS in your network as an additional layer of protection

D. Install an NIPS in your network as an additional layer of protection

E. Install an inline NIPS in your network as an additional layer of protection

Answer: B and E

Concept: A stateful firewall on the edge of your network can prevent a DDoS attack as it inspects the traffic, including the verbs. An inline NIPS will ensure that all network traffic coming from the firewall will go through it and be inspected thoroughly.

Wrong answers:

> A. A stateless firewall is a basic firewall that will prevent unauthorized access, but does not really inspect the traffic thoroughly.

> C. An NIDS cannot be an additional layer of protection, as it just detects changes in traffic patterns and cannot prevent attacks

> D. Although installing an NIPS behind the firewall is a good idea, the inline NIPS is a much better solution, as all of the traffic passes through it

4. You work on the cyber security team of a large multinational corporation, and you have been alerted to an attack on the web server inside your DMZ that is used for selling your products on the internet. You can see by running `netstat` that you have an unknown active connection. What should be the first step you take when investigating this incident?

> A. Isolate the web server by disconnecting it from the network to prevent further damage

> B. Disconnect all external active connections to ensure that the attack is stopped

> C. Run a packet sniffer to capture the network traffic and identify the attacker

> D. Take a screenshot of the damage done to the website and reporting it to the police

Answer: C

Concept: The first stage in any attack is to capture the volatile evidence. In this incident you would capture the network traffic to identify the source of the attack.

Wrong answers:

> A. Disconnecting the attack will prevent further damage, but will not identify the attacker and prevent it from happening again

> B. Again, this option will not identify the attacker, but may instead stop legitimate customers

D. A screenshot may not show the real damage being done, and will not identify the attacker

5. I need to purchase a certificate that I can install on five mail servers. Which one should I purchase?

A. PEM certificate

B. Wildcard certificate

C. Subject Alternate Name (SAN) certificate

D. Root certificate

Answer: B

Concept: A wildcard certificate can be used on multiple servers in the same domain.

Wrong answers:

A. PEM is a base64 format

C. A SAN certificate can be used in servers in different domains

D. A root certificate can only be used by a CA

6. You are the manager of a large IT company, and it is your duty to authorize administrative controls. Which of the following are actions that you would normally authorize? Select all that apply:

A. Collecting an ID badge

B. Creating an IT security policy

C. Purchasing a cable lock

D. Creating a new firewall rule

Answer: A and B

Concept: Writing policies, filling out forms, and anything to do with applying for ID badges are administrative controls.

Wrong answers:

C. A cable lock is a physical control

D. A firewall rule is a technical control to mitigate risk

7. You are the operational manager for a financial company that has just suffered a disaster. Which of the following sites will you choose to be fully operational in the least amount of time?

A. Cold site

B. Warm site

C. Hot site

D. Campus site

Answer: C

Concept: The hot site should be up and running with data less than one hour old.

Wrong answers:

A. The cold site is the hardest site to get up and running, as it only has power and water.

B. A warm site has non-critical data, and the data is about a day old.

D. This is a red herring, and has nothing to do with disaster recovery.

8. The serious crimes agency has just taken control of a laptop belonging to a well-known criminal that they have been trying to track down for the last 20 years. They want to ensure that everything is done by the book and no errors are made. What is the first step in their forensic investigation, prior to starting the chain of custody?

A. Making a system image of the laptop

B. Placing the laptop in a polythene bag and sealing it

C. Hashing the data so that data integrity is assured

D. Asking for proof of ownership of the laptop

Answer: A

Concept: The first step is to create a system image; or, if it is a hard drive, create a forensic copy.

Wrong answers:

B. This is the second step

C. This is one of the steps when we start to investigate the contents of the laptop

D. This is not relevant

9. If an attacker is looking for information about the software versions that you use on your network, which of the following tools could they use? Select all that apply:

A. Protocol analyzer

B. Port scanner

C. Network mapper

D. Baseline analyzer

Answer: A and C

Concept: A **Network mapper** (**Nmap**) can identify new hosts on the network, identify what services are running, and identify what operating systems are installed. A **protocol analyzer** can tell what operating systems run on network hosts. This is sometimes called a packet sniffer.

Wrong answers:

B. A port scanner only tells you which ports are open

D. A baseline analyzer is a vulnerability scanner, and tells you about missing patches

10. Footage of people relaxing in their homes started appearing on the internet without the knowledge of the people being filmed. The people being filmed were warned by relatives and coworkers, resulting in an inquiry being launched by the police. Initial evidence reported that the victims had recently purchased IoT devices, such as health monitors, baby monitors, smart TVs, and refrigerators. Which of the following best describes why the attacks were successful?

    A. The devices' default configurations had not been changed

    B. The victims' houses had been broken into and hidden cameras were installed

    C. The victims' wireless networks were broadcasting beyond the boundaries of their homes

    D. The manufacturers of the devices installed hidden devices to allow them to film

    Answer: A

    Concept: IoT home-based automated devices should have the default configurations of the username and password changed.

    Wrong answers:

    B. This would be very unlikely for so many people

    C. This may be a possibility, but is unlikely to be the main reason

    D. This would not happen, or the manufacturer would lose their market share

11. You are the network administrator for an IT training company that has over 20 training rooms that are all networked together in their Miami office. Your corporate admin team could not access the internet last week as they were getting their IP settings from one of the training room's DHCP servers. The training manager has asked you to separate the corporate admin machines into their own network with a different IP range from the training rooms. What is the most secure way of implementing this? Select the best option from the following list:

    A. Create a VLAN on the switch and put the corporate admin team in the VLAN

B. Install a router in the LAN and place the corporate admin team in the new subnet

C. Create a NAT from the firewall and put the corporate machines in that network

D. Install a proxy server

Answer: C

Concept: A NAT hides the internal network from external resources and will separate the training machines from the corporate admin machines.

Wrong answers:

A. Putting a VLAN on the switch will segment the two networks, but it's not the best option

B. Installing a router creates a subnet and would also segment the two entities, but this is not the best option either

D. A proxy caches web pages and also filters traffic to and from the internet

12. Your organization has many different ways of connecting to your network, ranging from VPN and RAS to 802.1x authentication switches. You need to implement a centrally managed authentication system that will allow for long periods of access. Select the two most suitable methods of authentication:

A. PAP

B. TACACS+

C. NTLM

D. RADIUS

Answer: B and D

Concept: AAA servers are used for centralized authentication as they provide authentication, authorization, and accounting, where they can record all log-ins and log-outs in a database.

Wrong answers:

> A. PAP is a weak authentication system where passwords are shown in clear text

> C. NTLM is a weak authentication protocol that is susceptible to pass-the-hash attacks

13. From a security perspective, what is the major benefit of using imaging technologies such as Microsoft WDS or Symantec Ghost to image desktops and laptops that are being rolled out?

    A. It provides a consistent baseline for all new machines

    B. It ensures that all machines are patched

    C. It reduces the number of vulnerabilities

    D. It allows a non-technical person to roll out the images

    Answer: A

    Concept: When you build an image, all of the applications will have the same settings and updates and therefore will be consistent. A baseline consists of the applications that are installed at the current time.

    Wrong answers:

    > B. Updates come out almost every week, so you will still need to patch an image, especially if it was taken a month or two ago

    > C. Vulnerabilities are discovered on a frequent basis, therefore this is not true

    > D. The fact is true, but from a security point of view it could pose a risk

14. A company that is allowing people to access their internet application wants the people who log into the application to use an account managed by someone else. An example of this is a user accessing their Facebook account with a technology called Open ID Connect. Which of the following protocols is this based on? Select the best choice:

    A. Kerberos

    B. SAML

C. OAuth 2.0

D. Federation services

Answer: C

Concept: OAuth 2.0 is the industry-standard protocol for authorization. It is used by Open ID Connect, where people can be authenticated using their Facebook or Google account.

Wrong answers:

A. Kerberos is used only in Microsoft Active Directory

B. SAML is an XML-based authentication used in federation services

D. Federation services is third-party-to-third-party authentication that uses SAML, an XML-based authentication protocol

15. You are the security administrator for a medium-sized company that needs to enforce a much stricter password policy via Group Policy. The aims of this policy are to do the following:

    - Prevent using the same password within 12 password changes
    - Ensure that they cannot change the password more than once a day
    - Prevent weak passwords or simple passwords, such as 123456 or password, from being used

   Select the following options that you will need to use to fulfill all of these goals:

   A. Enforce password history

   B. Minimum password length

   C. Passwords must meet complexity requirements

   D. Minimum password age

   E. Maximum password length

Answers: A and C

Concept: The password history is the number of passwords that you need to remember before you can reuse them. Password complexity requires users to use three of the four following characters in the password: lowercase, uppercase, numbers, and special characters not used in programming. A minimum password age set to 1 means that you can change the password only once a day, preventing password rotation until you get back to the original password.

Wrong answers:

B. Password length was a requirement, but the longer the password length, the longer it will take a brute force attack to crack

E. In a Group Policy, there is no option for maximum password length

16. You provide a service for people who have recently fulfilled their contract with their mobile phone provider to unlock their phone and then install third-party applications on it. They will then no longer be tied to using the mobile phone vendor's app store. Which of the following techniques will you use to achieve this? Select all that apply:

A. Tethering

B. Sideloading

C. Slipstreaming

D. Jailbreaking or rooting

E. Degaussing

Answers: B and D

Concept: Sideloading involves loading third-party applications onto an unlocked mobile phone. Jailbreaking (iOS), or rooting (Android), is where the phone has been unlocked, removing the vendor's restrictions on the mobile phone.

Wrong answers:

A. Tethering involves connecting your phone to a laptop to give the laptop internet access

C. Slipstreaming is a technique for installing drivers into an `.iso` file

E. Degaussing involves passing a charge over a hard drive to erase data

17. You are the security administrator of a multinational company that has recently prevented brute-force attacks by using account lockout settings with a low value using Group Policy. The CEO of the company has now dictated that the company will no longer use account lockout settings as he read an article about it and got the wrong impression. Facing this dilemma, how can you ensure that you can make it more difficult for brute force to be successful?

A. Obfuscation

B. PBKDF2

C. XOR

D. bcrypt

Answer: B and D

Concept: PBKDF2 and bcrypt are key-stretching algorithms that insert random characters into password hashes, making them longer so that brute-force attacks need more processing and computation resources to crack them.

Wrong answers:

A. Obfuscation makes code obscure so that if someone steals your code, they cannot make sense of it

C. XOR (express OR) can be used to encrypt binary numbers

18. You want to join a wireless network using a password. Which of the following wireless features would be most appropriate to achieve this objective?

A. WPA2-Enterprise

B. WPA2-TKIP

C. WPS

D. WPA2-PSK

E. WPA2-CCMP

Answer: D

Concept: PSK uses the WAP password to join the network.

Wrong answers:

A. WPA2-Enterprise uses 802.1x with RADIUS for authentication

B. WPA2-TKIP is backward compatible with legacy devices

C. WPS pushes a button to access the network

E. WPA2-CCMP is the strongest encryption, as it uses AES

19. What is the main purpose of a **Network Intrusion Detection System (NIDS)**? Select the MOST appropriate option:

A. Identifying vulnerabilities

B. Identifying new network hosts

C. Identifying viruses

D. Identifying new web servers

Answer: B

Concept: NIDS identifies changes to the network and the network traffic.

Wrong answers:

A. This is the job of a vulnerability scanner

C. This is the job of a virus scanner

D. Web servers are not based in the LAN; normally, they are based in the DMZ

20. A web server was the victim of an integer-overflow attack. How could this be prevented in the future?

    A. Install a proxy server

    B. Install SQL injection

    C. Input validation on forms

    D. Install a web application firewall

    Answer: C

    Concept: Input validation prevents buffer-overflow attacks, integer-overflow attacks, and SQL injection by restricting the input to a certain format.

    Wrong answers:

       A. A proxy server is used for web page caching and URL and content filtering

       B. SQL injection is a form of attack where the phrase *1 = 1* is used in a script

       D. A web application firewall is used to protect web servers and their applications

21. You have recently set up a new virtual network with over 1,000 guest machines. One of the hosts is running out of resources, such as memory and disk space. Which of the following best describes what is happening?

    A. Virtual machine escape

    B. End of system lifespan

    C. System sprawl

    D. Poor setup

    Answer: C

    Concept: System sprawl over-utilizes resources. This means that the system has started to run out of resources.

Wrong answers:

    A. Virtual machine escape is where an attacker uses a virtual machine so that they can attack the host

    B. This is where a vendor no longer supports an application

    D. This is where the configuration is not set properly

22. You are the system administrator for a multinational company that wants to implement two-factor authentication. At present, you are using facial recognition as the method of access. Which of the following would allow you to achieve two-factor authentication? Select all that apply:

    A. Palm reader

    B. Signature verification

    C. Thumb scanner

    D. Gait

    E. Iris scanner

Answer: B and D

Concept: Facial recognition is something you are for authentication. B and D are both something you do—you have a unique signature and your gait is how you walk.

Wrong answers:

    A, C, and E all come under the *something you are* category.

23. The security auditor has just visited your company and is recommending change management to reduce the risk from the unknown vulnerabilities of any new software introduced into the company. What will the auditor recommend for reducing the risk when you first evaluate the software? Select the best practices to adopt from the following list:

    A. Jailbreaking

    B. Sandboxing

    C. Bluesnarfing

D. Chroot jail

E. Fuzzing

Answer: B and D

Concept: Sandboxing and chroot jail allow you to isolate an application inside a virtual guest machine.

A. This is the removal of the restriction that apple set on an iOS device

C. This is stealing contacts from a mobile device

E. This is putting random characters into an application

24. You are the security administrator for a multinational corporation. You recently detected and thwarted an attack on your network when someone hacked into your network and took full control of one of the hosts. What type of attack best describes the attack you stopped?

A. Man-in-the-middle attack

B. Replay attack

C. Packet filtering

D. Remote exploit

Answer: D

Concept: An exploit looks for vulnerabilities in a system; a remote exploit is someone coming from outside your network.

Wrong answers:

A. A man-in-the-middle attack is an interception attack where messages are changed in real time as they pass between two hosts

B. A replay attack is a man-in-the-middle attack where the messages are replayed at a later date

C. Packet filtering is used by a firewall to stop certain protocols from accessing your network

25. You are the security administrator for a multinational corporation recently carried out a security audit. Following the audit, you told the server administrators to disable NTLM on all servers. Which of the following best describes why you have taken this action?

    A. It will improve the server's performance

    B. It will prevent a man-in-the-middle attack

    C. It will prevent a pass-the-hash attack

    D. It will prevent a Poodle attack

    Answer: C

    Concept: Disabling NTLM will prevent pass-the-hash attacks.

    Wrong answers:

    A. This is a red herring; it has nothing to do with performance

    B. A man-in-the-middle attack is an interception attack

    D. A Poodle attack is a man-in-the-middle attack that targets downgrade browsers—SSL3.0 CBC

26. The political adviser to the prime minister of the United Kingdom has returned from the two month of summer break that all staff are entitled to. He applied for an immediate transfer to another department, stating that his health is bad and the job was far too intense. When his replacement arrives, they find that during the summer recess, the political adviser shredded all documents relating to a political inquiry that involved their cousin. The police are immediately called in and say that they cannot prosecute the political adviser because of a lack of evidence. What precautions could the Houses of Parliament security team take to prevent further events such as this happening in the future?

    A. Create a change-management document to ensure that the receptionists are more vigilant about people coming in out of hours

    B. Enforce time-of-day restrictions so that nobody can access the IT systems during summer breaks

C. Enforce separation of duties to ensure that any document that is destroyed has been witnessed by a second person.

D. Enforce mandatory vacations to prevent staff coming in during the recess.

Answer: B

Concept: Time-of-day restrictions would have prevented someone accessing the system during the holidays.

Wrong answers:

A. If the staff of the House of Commons are on holiday, then there will be no receptionists present

C. Separation of duties cannot be enforced during a shutdown period

D. Mandatory vacations cannot be enforced when nobody is working

27. You work in the forensics team of a very large multinational corporation where an attack has happened across three different sites in two different countries. You have been collecting the following log files from these locations:
    - Firewall logs
    - NIPS logs
    - NIDS logs

    What is the first action that you need to take when collating these logs?

    A. Apply time normalization to these logs.

    B. Copy them into a worm drive so that they cannot be tampered with.

    C. Sort out the sequence of events by site.

    D. Raise chain of custody documentation for these logs.

    Answer: A

    Concept: When collating forensic evidence, it needs to be put in a time sequence. In this case, we use time normalization to put it all in order. If we collect physical evidence from different computers, we use the record time offset to put the data and events in time sequence by using the regional time on the machine.

Wrong answers:

> B. Copying into a worm drive will prevent deletion, but not the analysis of data.
>
> C. This could be a first step, but it will not collate the information properly.
>
> D. A chain of custody would be needed once you hand the evidence to someone else, but it is too early at this time for this. A chain of custody records who has handled the evidence.

28. You are an Active Directory administrator and have been having problems with time synchronization regarding the Kerberos authentication protocols. Consequently, you have now contacted a third party to provide your time synchronization. They use Stratum **Network Time Protocol** (**NTP**) servers. What is the most secure method of setting up a Stratum server for time synchronization?

> A. Having the servers connect to an internal Stratum 1 NTP server
>
> B. Having the servers connect to an internal Stratum 2 NTP server
>
> C. Having the servers connect to an internal Stratum 0 NTP server
>
> D. Having the servers connect to an external Stratum 0 NTP server

Answer: A

Concept: The time server must be internal. The Stratum 1 NTP server connects to the Stratum 0 NTP server, which is the ultimate time source. However, if there is no internal Stratum 1 NTP server, then we will use an internal Stratum 0 NTP server.

Wrong answers:

> B. A Stratum 2 server can only connect to a Stratum 1 time server
>
> C. Only use an internal Stratum 0 server when an internal Stratum 1 server is not available
>
> D. The connection to the time server should come from the internal network

29. You are the network administrator for a company that runs an Active Directory domain environment where the system administrator is failing to keep you updated when new hosts are added to the network. You now decide that you will use your networking tools to do the following:

    - Identify new hosts
    - Identify operating system versions
    - Identify services that are running

    Which of the following network-based tools provide the information that you require? Select the tools that you are most likely to use:

    A. Protocol scanner

    B. Microsoft baseline analyzer

    C. Nmap

    D. Penetration testing

    Answers: A and C

    Concept: Protocol scanners and network mappers can identify new hosts, operating system versions, and services that are running. An NIDS can detect new hosts.

    Wrong answers:

    B. The Microsoft baseline analyzer is a vulnerability scanner

    D. A penetration tester is trying to break into your network

30. You are working for the serious crimes unit of the United Nations and have been given a laptop to investigate. You need to ensure that the evidence you are investigating has not been tampered with during your investigation. How are you going to prove this to the court when it is time to present your findings? Which of the following techniques will you adopt to best prove this? Select all that apply:

    A. MD5

    B. 3DES

C. SHA1

D. Blowfish

Answer: A and C

Concept: Hashing proves data integrity, and SHA1 and MD5 are both hashing algorithms.

Explanation: When data is collected as part of a chain of custody, all data is hashed by SHA1, MD5, or HMAC. HMAC prior to looking through the data. When you finish the investigation you will run the hash a second time, if the hash matches then the data integrity is confirmed.

Wrong answers:

B and D are both used with encryption, not hashing.

31. You are the security administrator for a multinational corporation that has an Active Directory domain. What type of attack uses HTML tags with JavaScript inserted between the `<script>` and `</script>` tags?

    A. Cross-site scripting

    B. Man-in-the-middle

    C. Cross-site forgery attack

    D. SQL injection

    Answer: A

    Concept: **Cross-Site Scripting (XSS)** uses HTML tags with JavaScript. JavaScript can be identified by using the word `var` for variable—for example, `varchar` or `var data`.

32. You are a system administrator working for a multinational company that has a windows domain and is using an active-passive model. Which of the following are the BEST reasons why your company would have adopted this model?

    A. It provides vendor diversity

    B. It provides much faster disaster recovery

C. It is the best model to use for symmetric encryption

D. It provides availability of your IT systems

Answers: B and D

Concept: Clustering provides availability, and it has a quick failover to the passive host should the active host fail.

Explanation: We would use an active-passive or active-active setup in the failover cluster so that if one node failed, the passive or second server would be up and running within seconds; users would not even be aware of this. This provides both faster disaster recovery and 99.999% availability, otherwise known as the five nines.

Wrong answers:

A. The cluster would come from the same vendor

C. Clustering is about availability—nothing to do with encryption

33. You are the system administrator for an Active Directory domain and deal with authentication on a daily basis. Which of the following do you use as an authentication method by entering a PIN instead of a password?

A. Smart card

B. Kerberos

C. WPS

D. TOTP

Answer: A

Concept: A smart card uses a PIN.

Wrong answers:

B. Kerberos can be accessed by entering a username and password

C. WPS is accessed by pushing a button to connect to a wireless network

D. TOTP uses a secret key or code

34. You are the security administrator for a large multinational corporation and you have a meeting with the CEO about the security posture of the company. He wants you to ensure the following are carried out effectively:

    - The firewall logs are stored securely so that nobody can tamper with them.
    - Prevent elevation-of-privilege attacks.

    Which of the following are the best solutions to implement? Select all that apply:

    A. Robocopy firewall logs to a worm drive

    B. Robocopy firewall logs to a RAID 5 volume

    C. Implement usage auditing and reviews

    D. Carry out permission audits and reviews every seven days

    Answer: A and D

    Concept: Storing files on a worm drive prevents deletion. Continuous audits of permissions will help track escalations of privilege.

    Wrong answers:

    B. Storing data on a RAID volume is a solution for redundancy, but not the deletion of data

    C. Account reviews may be quarterly, and so are not the best option

35. You are the security administrator for a multinational company, and you know that one of your X509 certificates, used in at least 300 desktop machines, has been compromised. What action are you going to take to protect the company, using the least amount of administrative effort?

    A. Email the people involved and ask them to delete the X509 from their desktop immediately

    B. Carry out certificate pinning to prevent the CA from being compromised

    C. Revoke the root CA X509 so it is added to the CRL

    D. Revoke the X509 so it is added to the CRL

Answer: D

Concept: Once a certificate has been compromised, it should immediately be revoked so it is added to the CRL.

Wrong answers:

> B. Certificate pinning cannot be set up after an event; it is set up to protect the CA against being compromised. This was only a low-level X509 that was compromised.
>
> C. There is no reason to revoke the root CA certificate as the certificate authority has not been compromised.

36. You need to install a new wireless access point that should be as secure as possible while also being backward compatible with legacy wireless systems. Which of the following would help you in this?

    A. WPA2 PSK

    B. WPA

    C. WPA2 CCMP

    D. WPA2 TKIP

    Answer: D

    Concept: WPA2 is the most secure and TKIP is backward compatible.

    Wrong answers:

    > A. WPA2 is used to connect to the wireless access point using a password
    >
    > B. Although WPA is backward compatible, it is not strong
    >
    > C. Although WPA2 CCMP is the most secure, it is not backward compatible

37. You are the capacity planning administrator for a large multinational corporation, and find that Server 1 is running out of disk space. When you monitor its network card, it is at 100% utilization. Which of the following reasons best describes what is happening?

    A. There are hardware errors on the server

    B. Unauthorized software is being downloaded

    C. Event logs are getting full and slowing down the system

    D. The disks that were selected were too small

    Answer: B

    Concept: Unauthorized software takes up disk space and causes high network utilization.

    Wrong answers:

    A. If there were hardware errors, no download would have happened, and there would not be a decrease in disk space

    C. The event logs are text files and will not use up too much space

    D. This is not a good choice as the disks that are purchased would be of a reasonable size

38. You are the security administrator and someone has just tried to attack your web server, which is protected by a web application firewall. When you look into the log files of the web application firewall, two of the rows of the log file have the following two entries:

    ```
    var data = "<blackbeard> ++ </../etc/passwd>"
    Select* from customers where 1=1
    ```

    Which of the following attacks are most likely to be have been attempted? Select all that apply:

    A. Integer overflow

    B. SQL injection

    C. JavaScript

    D. Buffer overflow

Answers: B and C

Concept: An SQL injection attack uses the phrase `1` `=` `1`. JavaScript is commonly used in XSS attacks and uses the `var` variable, so if you see `var`, it is most likely to be JavaScript.

Wrong answers:

A. Integer overflow is where larger numbers are used than should be used, normally with multiplication.

C. Buffer overflow is where more characters are used than should be. The `strcat` and `strcpy` are applications that cause buffer overflow.

39. Data has previously only been classified as internal data and external data. The company recently added two new classifications: legal and financial. What would be the benefit of these new classifications? Select the best solution for the new data classifications:

A. You need a minimum of three classifications for it to be effective

B. Better data classification

C. Quicker indexing

D. Faster searching

Answer: B

Concept: The more data classifications there are, the easier to classify it will be.

Wrong answers:

A. Data classification has no minimum values

C. Indexing will be slower for more classifications

D. Faster searching is done by reducing the amount of data

40. You are the security administrator for a multinational corporation based in Miami, and your company has recently suffered a replay attack. After lessons learned, you have decided to use a protocol that uses time stamps and USN to prevent replay attacks. Which of the following protocols is being implemented here? Select the best answer:

    A. Federation services

    B. EAP-TLS

    C. Kerberos

    D. RADIUS federation

    Answer: C

    Concept: Kerberos issues tickets for authentication, and each change has a different **Updated Sequence Number** (**USN**) and time stamps.

    Wrong answers:

    A. Federation services use SAML, an XML-based authentication protocol

    B. EAP-TLS uses certificates and is used for wireless authentication

    D. The RADIUS federation is a federation that uses wireless as its method of access

41. Which of the following threat actors would be the most likely to steal a company's R&D data?

    A. Organized criminals

    B. A competitor

    C. A script kiddie

    D. A nation state

Answer: B

Concept: The R&D department creates a lot of company's trade secrets; therefore, a competitor would steal them to beat you to the marketplace.

Wrong answers:

> A. Organized crime is most likely to target financial transactions rather than R&D data
>
> C. A script kiddie reuses someone else's scripts
>
> D. A nation state is more interested in attacking foreign governments than R&D data

42. You are a security administrator for a large multinational corporation based in the United Kingdom. You have just attended an annual seminar about the various types of password attacks. You have already disabled NTLM on all of the servers to prevent pass-the-hash attacks. Which of the following statements involves storing passwords as a hash value?

    A. A collision attack, the hash value, and the data match

    B. A collision attack, the hash values match

    C. A rainbow-table attack performs a search of simple passwords

    D. A rainbow-table attack performs a search of precomputed hashes

Answer: B and D

Concept: A rainbow table is a list of precomputed hashes. A collision attack is where two hashes match.

Wrong answers:

> A. When a hash is created, it takes the data inside a file and turns it into a hexadecimal hash value—they don't match
>
> C. This is false; look at the explanation of the concept

43. You are the new IT Director of a small, family-owned business that is rapidly expanding. You have submitted your annual budget for the IT team and the owners of the company want to know what you have asked for funds for vendor diversity. They have asked you to provide two good reasons why they should grant you the funds. Which of the following are the most suitable reasons why you wish to implement vendor diversity?

     A. Reliability

     B. Regulatory compliance

     C. It is a best practice in the industry

     D. Resilience

     Answer: A and D

     Concept: Vendor diversity involves getting a service from two different providers at the same time. Vendor diversity provides reliability and resilience. For example, if broadband from one provider fails, then the second provider's broadband should still be up and running.

     Wrong answers:

     B. There are no regulations that say you must get services from two suppliers

     C. It is not an industry best practice, though it may well be advisable

44. You are the network administrator for a large multinational corporation, and you have captured packets that show that the traffic between the company's network devices is in clear text. Which of the following protocols could be used to secure the traffic between the company's network devices? Select all that apply:

     A. SNMP V 3

     B. SNMP

     C. SCP

     D. SFTP

Answer: A

Concept: Traffic between network devices uses a simple network transport protocol; the secure version is SMTPv3.

Wrong answers:

B. SNMP is not secure

C. SCP copies files securely

D. SFTP secures downloaded traffic from FTP sites

45. You are the auditor of a large multinational corporation and the SIEM server has been finding vulnerabilities on a server. Manual inspection proves that it has been fully hardened and has no vulnerabilities. What are the two main reasons why the SIEM server is producing this output?

    A. There was a zero-day virus

    B. False negatives

    C. False positives

    D. The wrong filter was used to audit

    Answer: C and D

    Concept: If we are using the wrong configuration for the SIEM server, we will get poor monitoring, resulting in false positives.

    Wrong answers:

    A. A zero-day virus would not have been detected in the first place

    B. False negatives allow attacks to happen, but are not detected

46. You are a forensic investigator who has been called out to deal with a virus attack. You collect the information from the network card and volatile memory. After gathering, documenting, and securing the evidence of a virus attack, what is the best method for preventing further losses to the company?

    A. Send a copy of the virus to the lab for analysis

    B. Mitigate the attack and get the system back up and running

C. Initiate a chain of custody

D. Initiate business-impact analysis

Answer: B

Concept: Collecting the volatile evidence, mitigating the attack, removing the virus, and getting the system back up and running is the best thing to do.

Wrong answers:

A. This does not get you back up and running

C. A chain of custody records who has handled the evidence and does not get you back up and running

D. BIA only tells you the losses that you have incurred and does not generate any income.

47. You are the purchasing manager for a very large multinational company, and you are looking at the company's policy that deals with the insurance of laptops. Last year, the company lost a record number of laptops. Your company is losing 10 laptops per month and the monthly insurance cost is $10,000. Which of the following laptop purchases would prevent you from purchasing insurance?

    A. Budget laptops at $1,300 each

    B. Budget laptops at $1,200 each

    C. Budget laptops at $1,000 each

    D. Budget laptops at $1,001 each

    Answer: C

    Concept:

    SLE = ALE/ARO

    ALE = 12 x 10,000 = $120,000

    ARO = 12 X 10 = 120 laptops a year

    Single loss expectancy = $120,000/120 = $1000

Explanation: The cost of losing the laptops is *$120,000*, the same as purchasing the insurance. You should not take out the insurance in the hope that next year you may lose fewer laptops, as a record number of laptops has already been lost.

Wrong answers:

A, B, and D would cost more than the insurance; therefore, in these cases, you would do better to take out the insurance.

48. Your company has suffered a system-sprawl attack, and you need to be able to identify what has caused the attack and what the symptoms of the attack are. Which of the following attacks could cause system sprawl and what would be a tell-tale sign of it? Select the best two answers; each is a part of the solution:

    A. SQL injection

    B. DoS attack

    C. CPU at 100% utilization

    D. Buffer overflow

    Answer: B and C

    Concept: System sprawl is when your resources are running out, for example, if your CPU was at 100% utilization. When your system is running like this, it could also suffer from DoS, which makes resources unavailable with too many SYN flood attacks.

    Wrong answers:

    A. An SQL injection attack involves placing the phrase *1 = 1* into a transact SQL script

    D. A buffer-overflow attack involves putting more data into a field than it was programmed to handle

49. Which of the following is a measure of reliability?

    A. MTTR

    B. MTBF

C. MTTF

D. RPO

Answer: B

Concept: **Mean Time Between Failures (MTBF)** is the measure of the number of failures. If I purchased a car and it broke down every day for the next week, I would take it back, as it would be unreliable.

Wrong answers:

A. MTTR is the mean time to repair. If I break down at 1 pm and it is repaired by 2 pm, the MTTR is 1 hour.

C. MTTF is the mean time to failure; this is the lifespan of a piece of equipment.

D. RPO is the recovery point objective. It is the amount of time a company can be without its data, meaning the acceptable downtime.

50. Which of the following are the characteristics of a third-party-to-third-party authentication protocol that uses XML-based authentication? Select the three best answers:

A. **Single Sign-On (SSO)**

B. Kerberos

C. SAML

D. Federation services

Answers: A, C, and D

Concept: Federation services is a third-party-to-third-party authentication method that uses SAML, an XML-based method for authentication. It also provides SSO. This means that you only log in once in order to get access to resources.

Wrong answer:

B. Kerberos uses a *ticket granting ticker* = *t* and only works on a Microsoft Active Directory domain.

Other Books You May Enjoy

If you enjoyed this book, you may be interested in these other books by Packt:

Python Penetration Testing Cookbook
Rejah Rehim

ISBN: 978-1-78439-977-1

- Learn to configure Python in different environment setups.
- Find an IP address from a web page using BeautifulSoup and Scrapy
- Discover different types of packet sniffing script to sniff network packets
- Master layer-2 and TCP/ IP attacks
- Master techniques for exploit development for Windows and Linux
- Incorporate various network- and packet-sniffing techniques using Raw sockets and Scrapy

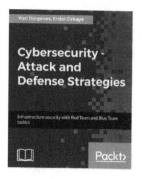

Cybersecurity – Attack and Defense Strategies

Yuri Diogenes, Erdal Ozkaya

ISBN: 978-1-78847-529-7

- Learn the importance of having a solid foundation for your security posture
- Understand the attack strategy using cyber security kill chain
- Learn how to enhance your defense strategy by improving your security policies, hardening your network, implementing active sensors, and leveraging threat intelligence
- Learn how to perform an incident investigation
- Get an in-depth understanding of the recovery process
- Understand continuous security monitoring and how to implement a vulnerability management strategy
- Learn how to perform log analysis to identify suspicious activities

Leave a review - let other readers know what you think

Please share your thoughts on this book with others by leaving a review on the site that you bought it from. If you purchased the book from Amazon, please leave us an honest review on this book's Amazon page. This is vital so that other potential readers can see and use your unbiased opinion to make purchasing decisions, we can understand what our customers think about our products, and our authors can see your feedback on the title that they have worked with Packt to create. It will only take a few minutes of your time, but is valuable to other potential customers, our authors, and Packt. Thank you!

Index

type 2 hypervisor 192

I